W9-ADB-934

J.M.Synge

Collected Works II

PROSE

J. M. SYNGE: COLLECTED WORKS

General Editor: ROBIN SKELTON

PROSE

J. M. SYNGE

COLLECTED WORKS

Volume II

PROSE

EDITED BY

ALAN PRICE

1982

COLIN SMYTHE

GERRARDS CROSS, BUCKS

THE CATHOLIC UNIVERSITY OF AMERICA PRESS

WASHINGTON, D.C.

This edition published in 1982
by Colin Smythe Limited, Gerrards Cross,
Buckinghamshire

British Library Cataloguing in Publication Data

Synge, John Millington
The collected works of J. M. Synge
Vol. 2: Prose
I. Price, Alan, *b.1921*
822'.9'12 PR5530

ISBN 0-86140-135-2
ISBN 0-86140-059-3 Pbk.

First published in North America in 1982
by The Catholic University of America Press, Washington, D.C.

ISBN 0-8132-0565-4
ISBN 0-8132-0564-6 Pbk.
Library of Congress Catalog Card No. 82-70363

Printed in Great Britain
Set by Oxford University Press
Printed from copy supplied, and bound by
Billing & Sons Ltd., Worcester and London

CONTENTS

ILLUSTRATIONS

The thirty-five drawings are all by Jack B. Yeats

ILLUSTRATIONS

These drawings first appeared as follows: twelve drawings, those on pp. 46, 55, 78, 81, 90, 101, 109, 119, 123, 131, 146, and 155, in the 1907 edition of *The Aran Islands*; eight drawings, those on pp. 205, 222, 227, 243, 273, 285, 311, and 335, in the 1911 Library edition of *In Wicklow, West Kerry and Connemara*; the remaining fifteen, on pp. 289, 293, 297, 300, 301, 303, 313, 319, 331, and 342, in the *Manchester Guardian*, to accompany twelve articles by Synge, from 10 June to 26 July 1905.

We are indebted to Miss Anne Yeats for permission to reproduce these drawings.

A memorial letter by Jack B. Yeats, published in the *Evening Sun* (New York) of 20 July 1909, is printed as an Appendix.

INTRODUCTION

DURING the past fifty years J. M. Synge has been recognized as an important dramatist and as a key figure in the Anglo-Irish literary renaissance, but much of his work has been unavailable.

The lack of his prose works has probably been felt most. It has been possible to buy a copy of *The Aran Islands*, but many other pieces, though here and there referred to and regarded as significant by critics of Synge, have been difficult to find. The American Random House edition, *The Complete Works of John M. Synge* (1935), apart from other omissions, does not include six of the seven Wicklow essays printed in the 1910 edition of *The Works of John M. Synge*. The Vintage Books paperback, V-53, *The Aran Islands and Other Writings*, edited with an introduction and notes by Robert Tracy (New York, September 1962), contains nearly all Synge's prose then believed to be in print, but it does not contain any copyright material, and it repeats several small textual errors present in the Random House edition. Now, however, in this Oxford volume are assembled all Synge's prose writings of any merit or interest. Over half of it consists of a reprint of *The Aran Islands* and *In Wicklow, West Kerry and Connemara*, checked against and supplemented from Synge's own manuscripts and proofs. About a quarter consists of articles not previously collected outside America, and the rest is work never published before. Thus, for the first time, the prose of Synge can be seen as a whole.

All the material here published for the first time has been edited from the mass of material, in varying degrees of coherence or legibility and often in several versions, that Synge left to the beneficiaries and trustees of his estate. Synge had put much work into these unpublished writings, and for some time before his death he was concerned about them. Before undergoing an operation on 4 May 1908 for Hodgkin's disease which brought about his death ten months later he wrote:

Dear Yeats,

This is only to go to you if anything should go wrong with me under the operation or after it.

I am a little bothered about my 'papers'. I have a certain amount of verse that I think would be worth preserving, possibly also the I and III acts of Deirdre, and then I have a lot of Kerry and Wicklow articles that would go together into a book; the other early stuff I wrote, I have kept as a sort of curiosity but I am anxious that it should *not* get into print.

I wonder could you get someone—say MacKenna who is now in Dublin—to go through them for you and do whatever you and Lady Gregory think desirable. It is rather a hard thing to ask you, but I do not want my good things destroyed, or my bad things printed rashly—especially a morbid thing about a mad fiddler in Paris, which I hate. Do what you can. Good Luck.

J. M. Synge[1]

This was not, however, Synge's settled and final view. Before and after this date he made plans for publishing and in the autumn of 1908, while preparing for the Cuala Press a collection of poems and translations, he included some that he had previously spoken of slightingly. In Notebook 16 in a draft of a preface, quoted in the Oxford edition of the *Poems*, pp. xiii–xiv, he said:

In publishing the following verses and sketches I am doing what I have sometimes decided it would be better to leave undone. They were written from five to eight years ago and, as is obvious enough, in Paris among all the influences of the so-called decadent and symbolist schools. Still I think as a man has no right to kill one of his children if it is diseased or insane, so a man who has made the gradual and conscious expression of his personality in literature the aim of his life, has no right to suppress himself any carefully considered work which seemed good enough when it was written suppression if it is deserved will come rapidly enough from the same causes that suppress the unworthy members of a man's family. To burn what one has written without giving at least one chance of existence is a sort of intellectual suicide against which ones instinct crys out, and if as in the present the piece were written some years ago, we the chances always are that the writer himself is no longer suited to judge what he has written. At the moment of creation the balance of the critical and creative impulses which works in the forming of any artistic production is the essential artistic element of the writers temperament. . . . To let his critical judgement of thirty five overthrow his creative impulse of twenty five is a quite different thing, and one which is only, if ever, quite justifiable in the case of work which appears to the maturer mind whole bad from a technical point of view. That is not so in my present judgement of what is now printed. . . .

[1] A copy of this letter is in Item 99. The 'morbid thing' is *Étude Morbide*: see p. 25.

Yeats himself, fastidious, who had unsuccessfully opposed the inclusion of certain poems and essays in *The Works of John M. Synge* (Maunsel, 1910), nevertheless stated, on a fairly large brown envelope in Item 50, that the 'Letter to the Gaelic League' and 'a number of fragments seemingly of a biographical nature very curious and dreamy and impressionistic, though marked by Synge as rubbish, should be published'.

The writings here published for the first time are referred to by the numbers assigned to them by Dr. Ann Saddlemyer in her list of the material held by the Synge Estate, and by some brief description such as 'Notebook', 'Box-file', 'Clip-binder', or 'Item'—an envelope containing sundry pieces of writing. Use has also been made of the invaluable Life of Synge by his nephew, Edward M. Stephens, consisting of 3,287 quarto pages of typescript, well over a million words. It is referred to as the Stephens Typescript.

Part One, The Man Himself, consists mainly of previously unpublished material. In my Introduction to *The Autobiography of J. M. Synge* (Dublin: The Dolmen Press, 1965) I wrote:

> . . . Synge made several attempts at writing autobiography. It is not certain why he did not bring them together into a finished whole and seek publication. Maybe they did not reach the high standard he required; maybe they were too self-revealing—he did not wish *Vita Vecchia* or *Étude Morbide* to appear during his life-time, even though the autobiographical elements in them were veiled. Still, fortunately, the drafts of autobiography remain among his unpublished writings . . . in the possession of the Synge Estate. The material from which the *Autobiography* is constructed is taken from a note-book (No. 15) written between 1896 and 1898, sheets (No. 21) written about 1898, and typewritten sheets of revisions, made probably in 1907, of a small part of the preceding material (No. 52). The numbers in red in the margins indicate which of these sources is being used. This material was left by Synge in an unfinished state, and the sundry drafts and revisions, in varying degrees of coherence or legibility, hardly have meaning as they stand alone. Hence they have been edited, punctuation and spelling have been supplied or corrected, and occasionally a word or two has been provided, in square brackets, to maintain sense and continuity.

For this volume of the Collected Prose I have felt it best to present a simplified version, reproducing the interlinked passages exactly as they appear in the drafts and without conflating varying versions of the same phrase or sentence. 'Under Ether' was published in the *Works* of 1910, some poems from 'Vita Vecchia' were published in the Oxford *Collected Works: Vol. I, Poems*, in 1962, and parts of the other items appeared in the Greene and Stephens biography. But most of it is here edited for the first time.

Part Two, *The Aran Islands*, was published jointly by Elkin Mathews of London and Maunsel & Co., Ltd., of Dublin in 1907. It contained twelve drawings by Jack B. Yeats. Some copies exist with the date 1906; the reason for this is not known. A large-paper numbered edition of 150 copies (with the Yeats drawings coloured by hand), signed by author and artist, was published simultaneously. Noteworthy reprintings of *The Aran Islands* are:

1910 as Volume Three of *The Works of John M. Synge* (with no drawings but with a photograph of Synge by Chancellor as frontispiece), Maunsel, Dublin;

1911 Library edition (with the twelve drawings by Jack B. Yeats), Maunsel, Dublin. An impression of this was printed in 1912 with a cancel title-page bearing the imprint of George Allen & Unwin Ltd.;

1911 Single volume (with drawings by Jack B. Yeats), Luce, Boston;

1912 Pocket edition in two volumes, Maunsel, Dublin. Reprinted by Maunsel & Roberts, Ltd., Dublin, and George Allen & Unwin, Ltd., London, in 1921;

1921 French edition, translated by Leon Bazalgette, Rieder, Paris;

1926 German edition, Tauchnitz, Leipzig;

1935 In the one-volume *The Complete Works of John M. Synge*, Random House, New York;

1941 Selections from *The Aran Islands* in Everyman's Library, No. 968, *Plays, Poems and Prose*, Dent, London;

1962 in *Four Plays and The Aran Islands*, edited and introduced by Robin Skelton, The World's Classics, No. 585, Oxford University Press, London.

The text presented in this Oxford *Prose* volume is that of the 1907 edition, with additions from the unpublished material. Further particulars can be found in the footnotes.

Part Three: Volume Four of *The Works of John M. Synge* was published by Maunsel & Co., Ltd., Dublin, in 1910. It was entitled *In Wicklow, In West Kerry, In the Congested Districts and Under Ether*. The frontispiece was a drawing of Synge by James Paterson. The Library edition of 1911 by Maunsel entitled *In Wicklow, West Kerry and Connemara* was identical, except that 'Under Ether' and the Paterson drawing were omitted, the third section was re-named 'In Connemara', and eight drawings by Jack B. Yeats (who had previously made fifteen other drawings to accompany the *Manchester Guardian* articles, which were collected to form the 'In Connemara' section) were included. The 1911 edition was printed from the same plates as the 1910 edition. Parts only of this 1911 Library edition have been issued since, except for the Vintage paperback, V-53. They are:

1912 *In Wicklow and West Kerry*, pocket edition, Maunsel, Dublin. Reprinted in 1921 by Maunsel & Roberts, Ltd., Dublin and George Allen & Unwin, Ltd., London;

1935 *The Complete Works of John M. Synge*, Random House, New York, provides the West Kerry and Connemara sections and 'Under Ether' but only two of the Wicklow essays.

The text presented in this Oxford *Prose* volume is that of the 1911 Library edition, with certain additions to five essays and two extra essays. Further particulars can be found in the footnotes.

In Wicklow, West Kerry and Connemara consists of articles by Synge, collected after his death. The 'In Wicklow' section was made up of four articles from the *Manchester Guardian*, two articles from *The Shanachie*, and a previously unpublished article. The 'West Kerry' section was made up of three articles from *The Shanachie*. The 'Connemara' section was made up of twelve articles from the *Manchester Guardian*. The compilation of this book led to a quarrel between W. B. Yeats and George Roberts, a director of Maunsel & Co. Synge had told Yeats (see p. x here) that he had 'a lot of Kerry and Wicklow articles that would go together into a book'. Yeats approved of this. Roberts, however, wished to reprint also the twelve *Manchester Guardian* articles about Connemara. Yeats disagreed, declaring that they were inferior to the rest of Synge's published work and that to reprint them would harm his friend's reputation: it should be Synge's fortune, Yeats said, to 'escape the commercial hand', and to leave behind him 'nothing but distinguished work, as perfect as a beautiful statue'. Roberts's case was that the authority Synge gave to Yeats to decide on what was to be published referred only to unpublished material, that Synge had often spoken of reprinting the *Manchester Guardian* articles, and that in the agreement made between Maunsel and Synge's executors it was stated that the *Manchester Guardian* articles were to be included in the collected edition. Yeats, interpreting Synge's directions differently, said that his authority extended to all Synge's writings not previously published in book form, that Roberts had surreptitiously inserted the clause about the *Manchester Guardian* articles into the agreement, and that he had gone ahead with printing them while pretending to be considering with Yeats whether or not they should be included. Edward Synge, J. M. Synge's brother, was involved as an executor. While wishing to pacify Yeats, he realized that Maunsel had a legal right to reprint the articles. He was relieved when a scrap of paper in Synge's hand turned up, indicating that Synge had envisaged the reprinting of parts at least of the Connemara articles. This scrap of paper (now in Item 102—see p. 283) is torn and creased, about $5\frac{1}{2} \times 2\frac{1}{2}$ in. in size, and bears the following words written in thick blue pencil: 'Wicklow articles 1. People of the Glens 2. Vagrants of Wicklow 3. The Oppression of the Hills 4. At the Fair 5. and In a Landlord's Garden can be published with what is permanent in Connemara articles in *Manchester Guardian* and the three articles on Kerry which have been in *Shanachie*. J. M. S. See Maunsel and Co.' All twelve *Manchester Guardian* Connemara articles were then published in Volume Four of the *Works* of 1910, with the following note, based on a suggestion by Edward Synge: 'the author intended to revise [the articles] before reprinting, but his preoccupation with his dramatic work, and eventually his illness, prevented him from doing so . . . although only the hastily written records of a journey through the West of Ireland, they contain many characteristic passages which it is felt those interested in Synge's work will wish to have in this permanent form.' The Introduction which Yeats had written for this collected edition was, of course, withdrawn by Yeats and published separately as *J. M. Synge and the Ireland of his Time* (Cuala Press, Dundrum, 1911).

Part Four, About Literature, is made up of hitherto uncollected or unpublished pieces dealing with the nature and evaluation of literature. Most of this section consists of articles and reviews which appeared in periodicals in Ireland, France, and England between 1899 and 1906.

The process of establishing a valid and definitive text out of the diverse mass of work, published and unpublished, that a writer may leave is rarely straightforward. The difficulties of dealing with Synge's material are described by Professor Robin Skelton in the Introduction to his edition of the *Poems* (pp. xiv, xxiv, xxv, xxvii):

> Synge's handwriting (not to mention spelling and punctuation) was always erratic . . . difficulties frequently occur in reading Synge's manuscripts, and it is a difficulty of which Synge himself was well aware. In the same notebook as the draft preface [to the *Poems*] there is a note: 'I'm a good scholar at reading but a blotting kind of writer when you give me a pen—J. M. S.' It is appropriate that the reading 'blotting' must be considered conjectural. . . . Synge's manuscripts are not easy to edit. . . . Synge's method of composition . . . was to rewrite continually. A poem is likely to begin in a notebook draft, continue through several typescript versions, be amended by several notebook jottings, and end up again in three or four typescripts, none of the different versions having been dated. . . . The notebooks, admittedly, do contain some dated material, but these dates are not always as helpful as they might appear, as Synge was quite as likely to scribble a poem of 1902 in a notebook containing material of 1897 as he was to transcribe an early poem into a later notebook. To add to this confusion, Synge's handwriting after about 1898 did not alter sufficiently for it to be of much help in determining dates of composition. . . . It is not possible to use [the various files of unpublished work] with any real reliance upon [their] headings, as even the most cursory examination of the material reveals that, over the years, manuscripts have become misplaced, and the contents of the files altered.

Accordingly, editorial activity is necessary, especially in regard to the unpublished prose, which is greater in bulk, in a more rudimentary condition, and no less difficult to decipher than the unpublished poems or plays. The facsimile (between pp. 40–41) shows two fairly representative pages. The inaccuracies or obscurities in Synge's spelling, punctuation, or syntax, and the unsystematic deployment of his words on the page, result from the fact that he was drafting or revising his material and probably writing quickly. He had no unusual theories about spelling or punctuation. Comparisons of work published in his lifetime with the drafts of it show that he tidied it up for publication. This is what has been done for the present edition. Where necessary, punctuation and spelling have been corrected, some selection and construction carried out (see p. 37 and the facsimile, between pp. 40–41, for an example), and an occasional word or two (shown in square brackets) provided to maintain sense and continuity. The dots (. . .) are used to separate passages from different parts of a given source. Particulars are given in the footnotes.

In making this edition I have been helped by a number of people in various ways. I acknowledge my indebtedness and offer my thanks to them, and especially to Mrs. Lily M. Stephens for her hospitality and for access to her late husband's papers and typescript biography of his uncle; to her and Professor John L. Synge, representing the trustees and beneficiaries of the Synge estate, for kindly making available all relevant material; to Professor Robin Skelton for useful advice; to Miss Elizabeth Coxhead for encouraging suggestions; to the National City Bank, Ltd., Dublin, and its staff, especially Mr. Giblin, for readily making the Synge material available and giving me facilities to work there; to the editorial staff of the Oxford University Press; and to my wife.

ALAN PRICE

The Queen's University of Belfast
1965

PART ONE

THE MAN HIMSELF

AUTOBIOGRAPHY[1]

(21)EVERY life is a symphony, and the translation of this life into music, and from music back to literature or sculpture or painting is the real effort of the artist. The emotions which pass through us have neither end nor beginning—are a part of the sequence of existence—and as the laws of the world are in harmony it is this almost cosmic element in the person which gives great art, as that of Michelangelo or Beethoven, the dignity of nature.

I do not think biography—even autobiography—can give this revelation. But while the thoughts and deeds of a lifetime are impersonal and concrete—might have been done by anyone—art is the expression of the essential or abstract beauty of the person. . . . If by the study of an adult who is before his time we can preconstruct the tendency of life and if—as I believe—we find in childhood perfect traces of the savage, the expression of a personality will reveal evolution from before history to beyond the science of our epoque. . . .

For three days a south wind has been blowing over Paris. (52)I have put syringa and white lilac in green vases round my room and left my windows open so that I can hear the crowds passing under them. This contact of perfume and sound recalls my childhood with peculiar surety.

(15)The first moment that I remember I was sitting upon my nurse's knee while she arranged my clothes. I do not think I can have been more than two years old. Then I remember walking in under some shelves in the corner of my nursery and looking up at them with a vague curiosity how long it would take my head to reach them.

My promotion to knickerbockers and a severe cough or croup came about the time that I began to remember coherently. If I

[1] The Autobiography has been constructed from these sources: Notebook 15, written 1896–8; Item 21, manuscript sheets, written about 1898; Item 52, typewritten sheets of revisions, made probably in 1907, of a small part of the material in Notebook 15 and Item 21. The superior figures in round brackets indicate which of these sources is being used, and precede the passage from that source. The dots (. . .) are used to separate passages from different parts of a given source. The editor's version of the *Autobiography*, including a number of conjectural passages not printed here, was first published by the Dolmen Press, Dublin, in 1965.

could know the dates of my nurses I could trace the whole course of my opening memory, but they are lost. I remember old Maria, Liz, squatty Kate, Agnes, a handsome girl that I admired who was soon sent away, a girl who cried in the evenings when I was in bed, and red-haired Sarah who still starts up [in my mind] when people talk of red hair. In all I remember eight or nine nurses, and as I was rid of them when I was eight years old my memory goes back a good way.

My childhood was a long series of coughs and colds, with plenty of amusement in the intervals and summer visits to the sea-side which were delightful. I have a vivid recollection of being caught in a heavy shower in the ladies' bathing place and bundled into a bathing-box that was not empty! Little boys are rightly considered inoffensive but some of them who have unusual memories grow up with souvenirs that illustrate a celebrated line in Dante.

I was painfully timid, and while still very young the idea of Hell took a fearful hold on me. One night I thought I was irretrievably damned and cried myself to sleep in vain yet terrified efforts to form a conception of eternal pain. In the morning I renewed my lamentations and my mother was sent for. She comforted me with the assurance that the Holy Ghost was convicting me of sin and thus preparing me for ultimate salvation. This was a new idea, and I rather approved. Later in the day while I was playing in the drawing-room I overheard my mother telling my aunt about my experience. While I gave no sign of attention I was inwardly flattered that I had caused this excitement and that the Holy Ghost should single me out so distinctively. I must have been quite young as my mother would not have talked about me in my presence for she was always judicious—except perhaps in her portrayal of Hell.

Religion remained a difficulty and occasioned terror to me for many years, though I do not think the brand I was brought up on was peculiarly Calvinistic. When I went to church I remember wondering whether it might not all be a fraud got together to aid the bringing-up of children which I believed to be arduous. Later in my early teens I think I had moments of great fervour and thought myself saved, but never for long at a time. [Still] the well-meant but extraordinary cruelty of introducing the idea of Hell into the imagination of a nervous child has probably caused more misery than many customs that the same people send missionaries to eradicate.[1]

Before I went to school I used to go out to walk every day with my maid or my relations. Even at this time I was a worshipper of nature. I remember that I would not allow my nurses to sit down on the seats by the [River] Dodder because they were [man-]made. If they wished to sit down they had to find a low branch of a tree or a bit of rock or bank. I do not seem to have lacked a certain authority for they all obeyed. My brother also had this idea about 'made' things, perhaps he gave it to me. (21)I had a very strong feeling for the colour of locality which I expressed in syllables of no meaning, but my elders checked me for talking gibberish when I was heard practising them.

(15)[My brother and I] had several elaborate games which were not, I think, usual. There was a legendary character we called 'Squirelly' who was a sort of folk-lore creation. We would spend hours inventing adventures for him to pass through. (21) I was a sort of poet with the frank imagination by which folk lore is created. I imagined myself half human monsters that went through series of supernatural adventures of which I kept a record. . . . I do not think this legendary instinct was suggested by fairy tales. We knew Grimm's alone, and our myths had no relation with the domestic instincts of the Germans. (15)Then we had a number of 'Men'—spools with red flannel belts sewed round them—who lived a most complicated life with war and commerce between our opposite settlements. I sometimes gained in the war but at the commerce I was rarely successful.

I was then about seven, and soon afterwards I made an attempt at literary composition, a poem intended to be a satire on an aunt who had slightly offended me. I remember walking into the drawing-room and telling the company that I had 'invented' a poem. I was proud of the achievement and wanted to read it aloud, but got very nervous in the middle and had to give it up. This was the first time I remember feeling nervous, apart from direct fear.

(21)I studied the arabs of the streets. . . . I remember coming out of St. Patrick's, Sunday after Sunday, strained almost to torture by the music, and walking out through the slums of Harold's Cross as the lamps were being lit. Hordes of wild children used to

[1] The preceding four paragraphs, 'My promotion . . . eradicate', are a conflation of two versions on opposite pages in Notebook 15.

play round the cathedral of St. Patrick and I remember there was something appalling—a proximity of emotions as conflicting as the perversions of the Black Mass—in coming out suddenly from the white harmonies of the Passion according to St. Matthew among this blasphemy of childhood. The boys and girls were always in groups by themselves, for the utterly wild boy seems to regard a woman with the instinct of barbarians. I often stood for hours in a shadow to watch their manoeuvres and extraordinarily passionate quarrels. . . .

If we find in Bach an agreeable vibration of some portion of the brain and in the study of these children the vibration of another portion a little inferior—the attitude of science—we loose in the music our transcendent admiration, and in the slums the ecstasy of pity and with it the thin relish of delightful sympathy with the wildness of evil which all feel but few acknowledge even to themselves. The man who feels most exquisitely the joy of contact with what is perfect in art and nature is the man who from the width and power of his thought hides the greatest number of Satanic or barbarous sympathies. His opposite is the narrow churchman or reformer who knows no ecstasy and is shocked chiefly by the material discomforts of earth or Hell. . . .

Although I had the usual affection for my near relations I began while still very young to live in my imagination in enchanted premises that had high walls with glass upon the top where I sat and drank ginger-beer in a sort of perpetual summer with one companion, usually some small school-fellow I hardly knew. One day the course of my class put me for a moment beside my temporary god, and before I could find a fit term of adulation he whispered an obscene banality which shattered my illusions.

Soon afterwards—when I was about ten—my real affections and imagination acted together in a friendship with a girl of my own age (15) who was our neighbour. . . . We had a large establishment of pets—rabbits, pigeons, guinea pigs, canaries, dogs—which we looked after together. I was now going to school, but I had many holidays from ill health—six months about this time especially which were recommended on account of continual head-aches that I suffered from which gave us a great deal of time to wander about among the fields near our houses. We were left in complete liberty and never abused it. . . . She was, I think, a very pleasant-featured child and must have had an excellent character as for years I do not remember a single quarrel—with brothers, of course, I had plenty, sometimes of considerable violence. She was handy with her pencil and on wet days we used to draw animals from Vere Foster's copy books with great assiduity. . . .

About this same time an aunt of mine died in our own house. My mother asked me the day after if I was not sorry. I answered with some hesitation—at this time I was truthful to an almost morbid degree—that I feared not. My mother was much shocked and began telling me little things about my aunt till I wept copiously. In reality the death impressed with a sort of awe and wonder, but although I was fond of my aunt [it] did not grieve me—I suppose I did not realize what death meant. The days when the house was darkened—it was August—I spent in some woods near Rathfarnham with my little friend. They were wonderfully delightful, though I hardly remember what we did or talked of. (21) The sense of death seems to have been only strong enough to evoke the full luxury of the woods. I had never been so happy. It is a feeling like this makes all primitive people inclined to merry making at a funeral.

We were always primitive. (15)We both understood all the facts of life and spoke of them without much hesitation but a certain propriety that was decidedly wholesome. (21)We talked of sexual matters with an indifferent and sometimes amused frankness that was identical with the attitude of folk-tales. We were both superstitious, and if we had been allowed . . . we would have evolved a pantheistic scheme like that of all barbarians. . . . I never spoke of religion with my companion, although we were both well-versed in Christianity. The monotheistic doctrines seem foreign to the real genius of childhood in spite of the rather maudlin appeal Christianity makes to little children. . . .

As I grew older I became more interested in definite life, and I used to hide in bushes to watch with amorous fellowship the mere movements of the birds. People said I had an interesting taste for natural history and gave me books. (15)[My girl friend] took fire at my enthusiasm and we devoted a great deal of our spare time to observation and reading books on ornithology. Further we clubbed our resources and bought a ten-shilling telescope, which led to trouble afterwards. This period was probably the happiest of my life. It was admirable in every way.

The following summer, however, I had a horrible awakening. Our two families joined in a large country house in June where some Indian[1] cousins of mine were coming to spend the later months with us. This June was absolutely delightful. I had my friend now under the same roof, and we were inseparable. In the day-time we played tennis or watched the birds . . . and we wandered arm in arm about among the odours of the old-fashioned garden till it was quite dark watching the bats and moths. I loved her with a curious affection that I cannot pretend to analyse and (21)I told her, with more virile authority than I since possess, that she was to be my wife. She was not displeased. (15)My cousins arrived, a small boy and a girl of my own age. My friend threw [me] over completely, apparently without a shadow of regret, and became the bosom friend of her new companion, my accursed cousin. I was stunned with horror. I complained to no-one, but I fretted myself ill in lonely corners whistling 'Down in Alabama', the only love-song I knew. My mother knew what was in my mind, and contrived occasionally to get me a walk with my old comrade but our old friendship was at an end, for the time at any rate. Thus I learned very young the weakness of the false gods we are obliged to worship.

The following winter I do not recollect very clearly. I had a tutor, and a dog, and devoted myself to birds and Euclid with a good deal of success. When the spring returned I began a collection of birds' eggs, in finding which I was remarkably fortunate, far more so than my cousin or brother who sometimes [searched] with me. I kept careful notes of all that I thought interesting, with the intention of publishing a book on birds when old enough. I used to rise at six in the morning and slip out to a quiet corner in the woods or fields near our house and watch for birds building. In this way I found water ouzels and other nests by the Dodder that no ordinary search could have revealed. My friend was still absorbed by her new companion yet we were again on good terms. I remember telling—or intending to tell her—that each egg I found gave three distinct moments of rapture: the finding of the nest, the insertion of [the] egg successfully blown in my collection, and, lastly, the greatest, exhibiting it to her. I still believed that she was a naturalist, though her interest in birds—at least in wild birds—had been only a development of her friendship for

[1] The cousins in fact came from South America.

myself. The following summer my cousins went abroad. My affection was again [freely accepted.] Now, however, it took a different shade, it was less a steady liking than a curious form of being in love. I used to kiss the chair she had sat on and kiss the little notes she sometimes sent me till I blotted the ink. Formerly we had always walked arm in arm but now we never touched each other even to shake hands. I had moved into long trousers, begun to read Scott and felt myself a man.

I was now at school again, but ill continually. This ill health led to a curious resolution which has explained in some measure all my subsequent evolution. Without knowing, or, as far as I can remember, hearing anything about doctrines of heredity I surmised that unhealthy parents should have unhealthy children—my rabbit breeding may have put the idea into my head. Therefore, I said, I am unhealthy, and if I marry I will have unhealthy children. But I will never create beings to suffer as I am suffering, so I will never marry. I do not know how old I was when I came to this decision, but I was between thirteen and fifteen and it caused me horrible misery.

The following spring I had measles and gave up school finally. When I recovered I began to collect moths and butterflies and other insects, a pursuit which kept me engrossed for several years. It gave me a great fondness for the eerie and night and encouraged a lonely temperament which was beginning to take possession of me. My girl friend was now absent a good deal so that our childish intimacy was no longer possible. I had realized too that though we were excellent companions we knew each other too well and were both eager for more exciting flirtations.

In my sixteenth year everything changed. I took to the violin and the study of literature with wild excitement and lost almost completely my interest in natural science although the beauty of nature influenced me more than ever. I had a tutor three times a week, for the rest I was alone. I began taking very long walks among the Dublin mountains, of which I soon knew every turn and crevice. (52)Natural history did [much] for me. . . . To wander as I did for years through the dawn of night with every nerve stiff and strained with expectation gives one a singular acquaintance with the essences of the world. The obscure noises of the owls and rabbits, the heavy scent of the hemlock and the flowers of the elder, the silent flight of the moths I was in search of gave me a passionate and receptive mood like that of early [man]. (21)The hunter, poacher and painter are the only men who know nature. The poet too often lets his intellect draw the curtain of connected thought between him and the glory that is round him. (52)The forces which rid me of theological mysticism reinforced my innate feeling for the profound mysteries of life. I had even psychical adventures which throw perhaps an interesting light on some of the data of folklore.

One evening when I was collecting on the brow of a long valley in County Wicklow wreaths of white mist began to rise from the narrow bogs beside the river. Before it was quite dark I looked round the edge of the field and saw two immense luminous eyes looking at me from the base of the valley. I dropped my net and caught hold of a gate in front of me. Behind the eyes there rose a black sinister forehead. I was fascinated. For a moment the eyes seemed to consume my personality, then the whole valley became filled with a pageant of movement and colour, and the opposite hillside covered itself with ancient doorways and spires and high turrets. I did not know where or when I was existing. At last someone spoke in the lane behind me—it was a man going home—and I came back to myself. The night had become quite dark and the eyes were no longer visible, yet I recognized in a moment what had caused the apparition—two clearings in a wood lined with white mist divided again by a few trees which formed the eye-balls. For many days afterwards I could not look on these fields even in daylight without terror. (21)It would not be easy to find a better instance of the origin of local superstitions, which have their origin not in some trivial accident of colour but in the fearful and genuine hypnotic influence such things possess upon the prepared personality.

(15)Before I abandoned science it rendered me an important service. When I was about fourteen I obtained a book of Darwin's. It opened in my hands at a passage where he asks how can we explain the similarity between a man's hand and a bird's or bat's wings except by evolution. I flung the book aside and rushed out into the open air—it was summer and we were in the country—the sky seemed to have lost its blue and the grass its green. I lay down and writhed in an agony of doubt. (21)My studies showed me the force of what I read, [and] the more I put it from me the more it rushed back with new instances and power. (15)Till then

I had never doubted and never conceived that a sane and wise man or boy could doubt. I had of course heard of atheists but as vague monsters that I was unable to realize. (21)It seemed that I was become in a moment the playfellow of Judas. Incest and parricide were but a consequence of the idea that possessed me. (15)My memory does not record how I returned home nor how long my misery lasted. I know only that I got the book out of the house as soon as possible and kept it out of sight, saying to myself logically enough that I was not yet sufficiently advanced in science to weigh his arguments, so I would do better to reserve his work for future study. In a few weeks or days I regained my composure, but this was the beginning.[1] Soon afterwards I turned my attention to works of Christian evidence, reading them at first with pleasure, soon with doubt, and at last in some cases with derision.

My study of insects had given me a scientific attitude—probably a crude one—which did not and could not interpret life and nature as I heard it interpreted from the pulpit. By the time I was sixteen or seventeen I had renounced Christianity after a good deal of wobbling, although I do not think I avowed my decision quite so soon. I felt a sort of shame in being thought an infidel, a term which I have always used as a reproach. For a while I denied everything, then I took to reading Carlyle, [Leslie] Stephen and Matthew Arnold, and made myself a sort of incredulous belief that illuminated nature and lent an object to life without hampering the intellect. This story is easily told, but it was a terrible experience. By it I laid a chasm between my present and my past and between myself and my kindred and friends. Till I was twenty-three I never met or at least knew a man or woman who shared my opinions. Compared with the people about me, compared with the Fellows of Trinity, I seemed a presumptuous boy yet I felt that the views which I had arrived at after sincere efforts to find what was true represented, in spite of my immediate surroundings, the real opinion of the world.

[1] The impression remained. Edward Stephens says that in November 1902 he went to the Museum in Dublin and told Synge of the natural history section and the room where Irish birds were arranged. Suddenly Synge 'became intensely interested. With a strange abruptness he asked me whether we had seen in a case near the door the skeleton of a man's hand, a monkey's paw, and a bat's wing. I hesitated as I tried to remember the case. Without waiting for me to answer he went on with the same intensity: "You wouldn't have seen it. It was the most interesting thing in the room. Of course you didn't notice it." I felt the strain in his manner, but he did not explain himself further.' Stephens Typescript, p. 1495.

Sometimes I was absorbed by the ideas that beset men at this period and thought myself a low miscreant because I had a tendency which was really natural and healthy. Often, however, I worked myself into a sort of mystical ecstasy with music and the works of Carlyle and Wordsworth which usually ended by throwing me back into all manner of forebodings. I began to write verses and compose. I wished to be at once Shakespeare, Beethoven and Darwin; my ambition was boundless and amounted to a real torture in my life. I would go down on my knees at times with my music paper on a chair before me and cry to God for a melody. I lay awake whole nights planning poems or struggling with geometrical problems—which I was now studying for my entrance to Trinity—creeping downstairs at daybreak for a piece of bread or if it was fine slipping out to watch the sun-rise, and then going back to bed for a couple of hours' sleep. When I was fiddling I mourned over the books I wished to read; when I was reading I yearned for all manner of adventures. Vulgar sensuality did not attract me but I was haunted by dreams of the [21]verdant liberty that seemed to reign in pagan forests of the south. Often I threw my books or music aside [15]and darted off on my bicycle among the loneliest hollows of the hills in vain hopes of an adventure.

[21]In my childhood the presence of furze bushes and rocks and flooded streams and strange mountain fogs and sunshine gave me a strange sense of enchantment and delight but I think when I [rested] on a mountain I sat quite as gladly looking on the face of a boulder as at the finest view of glen and river. My wish was that nature should be untouched by man, whether the view was beautiful or not did not interest me. A wood near Rathfarnham represented my idea of bliss until someone told me it was a piece of artificially arranged planting on an artificial hillock. I hated the neighbourhood from that day. This feeling has never entirely left me, and I remember fifteen years later after a long afternoon in a French forest that I enquired in the evening with real anxiety whether or not this forest was a mere recent plantation. It was the same with the people who were round me. There is no doubt that I was sensible to beauty but I distinguished only forces that attracted or repelled me. I remember when I was very young, watching a lady in the pew before me [in church] and wishing vaguely to stroke her cheek, but I did not know for years that she was considered singularly beautiful. About puberty when the boy

begins to look out with an uneasy awakened gaze that lingers because it is not satisfied, I saw in one hour that both nature and women were alive with indescribable radiance—with beauty. Even when the animal feelings were at their height a beautiful woman seemed an always intangible glory. All earth [was] transfigured in a moment. I became a pilgrim to the sun and used to arrange my excursions to reach a certain corner where there was [a] fine outlook of hill and sky half an hour before twilight. . . .

I think the consciousness of beauty is awakened in persons as in peoples by a prolonged unsatisfied desire. . . . Perhaps the modern feeling for the beauty of nature as a particular quality—an expression of divine ecstasy rather than a mere decoration of the world—arose when men began to look on everything about them with the unsatisfied longing which has its proper analogue in puberty. . . . The feeling of primitive people is still everywhere the feeling of the child; an adoration that has never learned or wished to admire its divinity. This feeling everyone will recognize in Wordsworth's *Ode*, though he does not seem perhaps to give it its truest interpretation.

(15)When I realized that the life about could not give me any real satisfaction my desire for study came on me again. I ran through history, chemistry, physics, botany, Hebrew, Irish, Latin, Greek, something of French and German and made a really serious study of the history and theory of music. English literature also I read with much care though I was painfully conscious of my uncertain judgement and formed my opinions reluctantly for fear a blunder might lower me in my proper estimation. I believe I never allowed myself to like a book that was not famous, though there were many famous books, such as Tennyson's poems, that I did not care for. The Irish ballad poetry of 'The Spirit of the Nation' school engrossed me for a while and made [me] commit my most serious literary error; I thought it excellent for a considerable time and then repented bitterly.

Soon after I had relinquished the Kingdom of God I began to take a real interest in the kingdom of Ireland. My politics went round from a vigorous and unreasoning loyalty to a temperate Nationalism. Everything Irish became sacred . . . and had a charm that was neither quite human nor divine, rather perhaps as if I had fallen in love with a goddess, although I had still sense enough not to personify Erin in the patriotic verse I now sought to fabricate.

Patriotism gratifies Man's need for adoration and has therefore a peculiar power upon the imaginative sceptic, as we see in France at the present time.

About this time I entered Trinity, but did not gain much after the first emotion had gone over. All my time was given to the violin and vague private reading, and the work for my examinations received just enough attention to attain the pass standard. I joined an amateur orchestra, which gave me unusual pleasure. [21]The collective passion produced by a band working together with one will and ideal is unlike any other exaltation. . . . We played the *Jupiter Symphony* of Mozart. It was in an academy and a Jewess was playing at the desk before me. No other emotion that I have received was quite so puissant or complete. A slight and altogether subconscious avidity of sex wound and wreathed itself in the extraordinary beauty of the movement, not unlike the sexual element that exists in all really fervent ecstasies of faith. . . . I found the mysterious mansion I had dreamed, [and] I played with morbid assiduity. I remember particularly the long blue days of a June that I spent looking out over the four strings of my violin into the filling leaves and white erect florescence of a chestnut and a wilderness of plants beneath it that crushed and strangled each other in a green and silent frenzy of expression. . . . One is lost in a blind tempest [of music] that wails round one with always beautiful passion, the identity is merged in a . . . symmetrical joy, cathedrals build themselves about one with the waves of purple storm, yet one remains sane and a man. [52]Then there were the slow movements which perhaps fulfil more exactly the peculiar mission of harmony. This sigh of beautiful relief which comes as an explanation rather than as a mere cessation of an excitement near to pain is perhaps the greatest utterance of man. [It resembles] [21]the assuagement of morning and spring which follows feverish nights and desolate winters, and the assuagement of autumn and evening which follows the passions of summer and sultry days, the first depending on the cessation of pain, the other on the cessation of indulgence. [52]A cycle of experience is the only definite unity, and when all has been passed through, and every joy and pain has been resolved in one passion of relief, the only rest that can follow is in the dissolution of the person.

[21]This extraordinary instinct of music which leads to such ecstasy, [15]the suave balm that draws out intricate characteristics

from places not open to the world [helped me] to realize that all emotions depend upon and answer the abstractions of ideal form and that humanity as God is but the first step toward a full comprehension of this art. For the hypersensitive organization the musical excitement is perhaps too powerful, too nearly a physical intoxication, but it is not surprising that when I found in the orchestra the world of magical beauty I dreamed of, I threw aside all reasonable counsel and declared myself a professional musician.[1]

[1] This was probably when Synge was 21. In July 1893 he went to Germany to study music.

VITA VECCHIA[1]

A YOUNG girl of the Roman Catholic Church spent nine weeks in the house where I lodged when I was studying music in Germany. Two days before she moved on to Venice I promised to play for her on the violin. The following night I dreamed that I did so, and that when I began a crowd of people rushed into the room with such noise and disturbance that I stopped playing and threw down my fiddle on the floor with the horror of nightmare.

The next morning I played for her as she wished, and as I was in the middle of an old love song I had chosen, a number of children ran into the room and began to make fun of my performance. I was playing from memory. I began to lose notes, and in the end I broke down utterly.

[1] *Vita Vecchia* was written between 1895 and 1897 and partly revised later, probably in 1907. Several versions of it exist, in Clip-binder 22, in Clip-binder 51, and in Item 52. *Vita Vecchia*, in so far as it is a whole, consists of fourteen poems connected by prose narrative. It is the 'whole' version, taken from Item 52, that is here printed. Synge revised eight of these poems and kept them separate from the rest. These eight poems and two others were published in the Oxford edition of the *Poems*, and they are reprinted here. The four poems (marked with an asterisk) here published for the first time are taken from Item 52.

Étude Morbide (the 'morbid thing about a mad fiddler in Paris' which Synge once hated) was written about 1899 and partly revised probably in 1907. Several versions of it exist in Notebook 15, in Clip-binder 22, in Item 50, in Clip-binder 51, and in Item 52. The version here published is based on Item 52, collated with Clip-binder 51, and with additions from Notebook 15.

Vita Vecchia and *Étude Morbide* continue Synge's account of his life, though in a veiled and subjective form. In Clip-binder 22 he says: 'The story is not one that I would care to narrate in all particulars.' The two pieces present his interior difficulties and growth, his spiritual and artistic condition and strivings, and his feelings about the women who were important to him during the years when he lived a good deal on the Continent. The 'young girl of the Roman Catholic Church' is called Scherma in Clip-binder 22; this was Synge's name for Cherry Matheson, and she may be linked with this 'friend' to whom he 'was desolately faithful', particularly as her religious beliefs (Evangelical Protestant) probably stood in the way of her acceptance of Synge's offers of marriage. The 'second person', the one who breaks off an engagement, is called the Chouska in Clip-binder 22, and thus figures in both *Vita Vecchia* and *Étude Morbide*; she may be linked with Hope Rea, a writer on art, in whom it seems Synge confided after Cherry Matheson had rejected him. The third woman who 'answered' the writer's dream seems to appear again in *Étude Morbide* as the Celliniani, the name of a girl Synge met in a pensione in Florence, but whether she or Cherry Matheson or both or neither was a model for this character it is impossible to decide. In any case speculation is probably vain. Although a characteristic mingling of the main tensions in Synge—arising from women, religion, art, and nature—makes up *Vita Vecchia* and *Étude Morbide*, they are both the expression of dreams and ideas, longings and discoveries, rather than a record of actual lives or material events. At the beginning of the version in Clip-binder 22 are these words: 'This is a story I have inscribed in verses called *Vita Vecchia*, which is a series of dreams to my later life as told in the study [*Étude Morbide*] I am now trying to finish.'

A year later my thoughts were turning continually to the same person, and I dreamed that I was sitting beside her as her accepted lover in a gathering of people. Then a sad deserted woman passed near us and I stood up and followed her. In the morning I wrote these lines:—

By my light and only love
Long I lived in glee
Marked her musing deep delight
Murmur love for me

A footfall faint arose
Timid touched the way
Of one that many loved
In days passed away.

I faltered, found my feet
Bound me to her side
We wandered years and years
Till she drooped and died.[1]

I learned afterwards that this second person that I dreamed of was engaged to be married two days later at the other end of the world.

In a few months I came back into the neighbourhood of my friend, and I lived in a house where I could see her window at the other side of the street when I was practising. I made many simple poems the days that I saw her:—

I have seen her brows and head,
Trimmed around with angel-thread,
Bending o'er the lines she read.

I have seen her pearly eyes
Peering round her, quaintly wise,
Seeking souls to sympathise.

I have seen her finger white,
Round those leaves to linger light,
Happy leaves though crumpled quite.*

[1] Where poems occur in the narrative or footnotes, I have taken the text from the Oxford *Poems* volume unless otherwise stated in the footnote.

She was a devout Christian in her heart, and was always busy doing good among the poor. One day I heard people in the street talking of her great beauty, and goodness, and I made these lines:—

Sweet seemeth it when people praise,
  What fair I deem,
When many turn on one to gaze,
  That I esteem.
So find I joy when many meet
  Where thou art known,
For eulogies my yearning greet
  Of thee alone.*

Even at this time I began to mock my proper exaltation, although I was still full of wonder and delight that after my desolate youth a person of such beauty should be ready to regard me.

I continued my way to the south, and in a little time I was in Rome wandering in the streets. One day I went into a church, where they were celebrating a High Mass for the princes that had been killed in the Abyssinian war. I saw a woman kneeling by a pillar who was like my friend. I made these lines:—

I heard low music wail
Woe wanton, wed to fear,
Heard chords to cleave and quail
Quelled by terror sheer.

I saw a women bend,
Bowed in saintly prayer,
Where shadow round did wend,
Won by face so fair,

Like yours that kneeling form,
Far under mine that woe,
Our sorrow's rage and storm,
Stern gods had died to know.

I dreamed afterwards, when I went in out of the moonlight, that I was walking in the street before her house, and that she came into the window, and closed the curtains when she saw me, without any salutation. This is the end of the poem I made in the morning:—

I saw thee start and quake,
When we in face did meet,
I saw dead passion wake,
One thrill of yearning sweet.

Then came a change, a wave,
Of bitterness, disdain,
That through my grassy grave
Will rack my haunted brain.[1]

The same week the second person[2] I had dreamed of broke off her engagement in peculiar circumstances. She came to Italy, and I learned to know her in Venice, with another woman[3] who also answered my dream.

Then my friend to whom I was still desolately faithful,[4] wrote to tell me that her confessor had made her believe that it would be a sin to marry a man who was not a Christian.[5]

After many months I find these lines in my note-book:—

I curse my bearing, childhood, youth
I curse the sea, sun, mountains, moon,
I curse my learning, search for truth,
I curse the dawning, night, and noon.

Cold, joyless I will live, though clean,
Nor, by my marriage, mould to earth
Young lives to see what I have seen,
To curse—as I have cursed—their birth.[6]

One night I went back to the town where she lodged, and went to look upon her door. As I passed she came into her window, and

[1] The version in Clip-binder 22 has at this stage: 'At this time I began a long poem in blank verse about a nun who was set free from her bondage by the influence of the statues in the Vatican and met and married a person who represented myself.'

[2] That is, the Chouska of *Étude Morbide*, who there also, significantly, on a strong intuition, sought out the writer: see entry of 15 September, p. 33 here.

[3] That is, apparently, the Celliniani of *Étude Morbide*. Clip-binder 22 says: 'I was in Florence/Venice and fell in with a woman who has suggested with other things my subsequent creation I call the Celliniani although neither her circumstances nor our relations had any similarity with the figure in my study. She corresponded in some sense to the woman of my first dream, and the Chouska came to Florence also on the same day as I did although we did not meet till nearly a year later at the other end of Europe.'

[4] Scherma (probably Cherry Matheson).

[5] A version in Clip-binder 22 says here: 'I remember staggering from my bed before dawn and lighting a candle to see if [my] hair had turned grey in the night. I thought of suicide—I was still young—but preserved my life for a crusade against the crude force [of] Christianity.'

[6] This poem is in the repunctuated version presented in the Oxford *Poems* volume, p. 14. There is a version in Notebook 25, headed 'My lady left me and I said'.

looked down on me with no sign of recognition. I went back to Ireland into the heart of the hills.[1]

I fled from all the wilderness of cities,
And nature's choristers my art saluted,
Chanting aloud to me their tunes and ditties
And to my silent songs like joys imputed;

But when they heard me singing in my sorrow,
My broken voice that spoke a bosom breaking,
They fled afar and cried I Hell did borrow
As through their notes my notes fell discord waking.

I [had] a strange feeling as I [returned] among the hills I worshipped in my childhood. . . . I [rested] by low beds of the streams where there [was] nothing but heather and granite and blue sky, with a brown current near me, and the tumult of the bees. . . . The autumn [was beginning and I sensed] the dismay that is blended for many of us with all that is [lovely and] puissant on the earth. . . .

I wrote in a nook by a river:

Wind and stream and leaves and lake,
    Still sweeter make
    The songs they wake
A thrill my throes would prisoner take.

Birds and flies and fish that glide,
    Why would ye hide
    Or slip aside
From one who loves your lonely pride?* . . .

[I stood] on the side of [a hill] watching the stars and the moon and listening to the crying of the snipe. . . . [An] earth breath came up across the bogs, carrying essences of heath, and obscure plants and the ferment of the soil . . . In a little while the same moon will rise and there will be wonderful perfumes and darkness and silver and gold lights in the pathways of Wicklow, and I will be [lying] under the clay. . . . I am [haunted] by the briefness

[1] The latest version of *Vita Vecchia* ceases abruptly here. To it are attached various typewritten sheets, in no particular order. Parts of these apparently continue the story, and the rest of *Vita Vecchia* here printed has been constructed from them (checked against Item 51 and an earlier version on smaller sheets in Item 52).

of my world. It brings me at times a passionate thirst for the fulfilment of every passive or active capacity of my person. It seems a crime that I should go home and sleep in trite sheets while heaven and earth slip away from me for ever. . . .

[Later] I thought I was better and returned to Paris.[1] I wrote [this] little verse:—

Wet winds and rain are in the street,
  Where I must pass alone,
Where no one wayfarer I meet
  That I have loved or known.

'Tis winter in my heart, the air
  Is wailing, bitter cold,
While I am wailing with despair,
  As I have wailed of old.

At this time also I wrote this sonnet:

Through ways I went where waned a lurid light,
While round about lewd women wan did glide,
Yet no hard hand I sought to soothe my side
But will-less went, held from the earth my sight:
Then saw among the clouds one woman white
Star-like descend; when I her aim descried
My temples reeled, I staggered, scarlet dyed,
Then sightless stood, heard weeping swift indite.

'From Heaven have I seen thee, wherefore here?
'I loved thee, named thee noble, praised thee pure,
'How canst thow to defilement turn thee near,
'How loathsome lust, thus tolerate, endure?'

I moaned, 'Sad, innocent, I torture flee,
'Him wouldst thou blame, joy-exiled, damned by thee?'[2]

[1] A version in Clip-binder 22 has at this stage: 'What I did or rather thought then is written in *The Valley of the Shadow* [an early title for *Étude Morbide*] where I have made a prolonged study of a part of my condition.'

[2] This is the early, unrevised, version which is printed beneath the later revised version in the Oxford *Poems* volume on page 17. The third line printed here is one written in manuscript over the original typescript of that early version. The original line read:

Yet none to my lone weeping I allied.

The later, fully revised, version adopted as the standard text in the *Poems* is one of only ten lines, and is based upon the last ten lines of the text presented here.

At last I met her in the street:

> Again, again, I sinful see
>   Thy face, as men who weep
> Doomed by eternal Hell's decree
>   Might meet their Christ in sleep.

I find two short poems at the end of my note-book:

> Five fives this year my years
> Half life I live to dread,
> Yet judged by weight of tears
> Now were I calmed, were dead.
>
> Not craven crushed in heart
> Loves longing love decayed
> I living learn my part
> In sternness steeped arrayed
>
> Yet bliss our credence new
> That sleeping soothes the strife,
> Annihilation due
> To pall the pang of life.[1]

And again:

> Thrice cruel fell my fate,
> Did I, death tortured, see,
> A God, inhuman, great,
> Sit weaving woes for me.
>
> So hung as Hell the world,
> Death's light with venom stung,
> Toward God high taunts I hurled,
> With cursing parched my tongue.

[At last:]

A Dream

> Mid rush, rose, lavender, luxuriant piled,
> Low melodies I marked a soul to sing
> That passed the woodland, singing, warmly wild
> Through lilies lulled, late bees from harvesting,
> And still sad songs intoning touched in me
> A quivering of passions pale with ecstasy.

[1] This follows the longer, earlier, version printed as a footnote in the *Poems*, p. 19.

Toward banking violets in dreaming rest,
A woman from the shadow passed to sight
And I beheld drowse on her drooping breast
A babe that breathed with bliss of bland delight
Till both a dual joy self-solaced seemed
As some calm incarnation soul of seraph dreamed.

Then I awoke.—The morn was cold and keen,
I viewed the grey-faced, straggling Paris street
Where fouler sight in life hath sorrow seen
Than starved disease in bitter rains and sleet? . . . *

A week ago the lilacs flowered in the Luxembourg, but it rained yesterday and there is nothing left but a mass of withered petals. Do flowers mourn like women for their briefness? In the Luxembourg I see also girls from eighteen to twenty in the blossom of their beauty, and women with a few babies who are withered.

Are men durable by contrast? A young man cannot express; a man who has passed thirty is not able to experience. We go out among the woods and mountains and kiss the lips of girls in wild efforts to remember. We are less fortunate than women. The frailest suckling is robust beside the offspring we have borne in travail darker than a woman's, and all our honour and glory is in the shadow of a dream. . . .

Nature is cruel to living things. Rubies and crystals that do not feel are beautiful for ever, but flowers and women and artists fulfil their swift task of propagation and pass in a day. . . .[1]

This person that I am now will not be next year, and the child that I was twenty years ago has perished and left no trace but the scars upon my body and my mind. If I should beget a child who resembles me he would be a more real survival of my childhood than I am. His body would have passed out of my body as directly, in a certain sense, as my present body has passed out of the body of my childhood. He would have fair hair and skin as I had, not the dark hair and sallow skin that I have. . . .

[I remembered] spring in Ireland. . . . Soft grey days came first with quiet clouds, and the woods grew purple with sap, while a few birches that stood out before them like candle-sticks with wrought silver stems covered themselves with a mist of red. Then

[1] The paragraph beginning 'Nature is cruel' is taken from Item 18. The passage beginning 'This person that I am now' and the rest of *Vita Vecchia* are taken from Item 52.

the hazels came out and hung the woods with straight ear-rings of gold, till one morning after rain spectres of pale green and yellow and pink began to look out between the trees. Then everything stood waiting for a moment till warmth came in the beginning of May, and the whole country broke out into wonderful glory—infinitely timid greens and yellows and whites, and birds singing everywhere, and strange odours creeping up into my room.

I used to lie in the evening while my nurse sat in her white veil by the window with the twilight on the hills behind her and read out old books from my uncle's library.

We do wrong to seek a foundation for ecstasy in philosophy or the hidden things of the spirit—if there is spirit—for when life is at its simplest, with nothing beyond or before it, the mystery is greater than we can endure. Every leaf and flower [and] insect is full of deeper wonder than any sign the cabbalists have invented. . . . We must live like the birds that have been singing or will soon be singing over the way. They are shot and maimed and tortured, yet they go on singing—I mean those that are left—and what does the earth care or what do we care for the units? The world is an orchestra where every living thing plays one entry and then gives his place to another. We must be careful to play all the notes; it is for that we are created. If we play well we are not exorbitantly wretched.

ÉTUDE MORBIDE

OR 'AN IMAGINARY PORTRAIT'[1]

May 3. This evening the Celliniani destroyed a print from Leonardo that hung over my bed. She says there are some things so full of beauty that they fill her with unendurable excitement. We are not good companions.

[1] This was written about 1899 and partly revised, probably in 1907. It is the 'morbid thing about a mad fiddler which Synge once hated. See letter to Yeats on pp. ix–x. The text here is based on Item 52, collated with Clip-binder 51, and with additions from Notebook 15. The version on thin paper in Item 52 is used here. An earlier and rejected version (written 1897–8) in Notebook 15 helps to show the circumstances before the study begins:

'In the early summer's evening one wanders with peculiar delight among the Boulevards of Paris. The damp odour of the well-watered pavements grows pleasant in association with the first greenness of the trees. One such evening in May a young man was seated at a café in the Boulevard Saint Michel smoking nervously and drinking a bock with calculated slowness. The fingers of his left hand moved continually with almost serpentine progression that showed the long apprenticeship they had served upon a violin or cello. Like all who live alone in Paris he had the habit of passing some of his evening in the cafés as a relief from the dead loneliness of his chamber. Presently he called for writing materials and taking some papers which he afterwards pinned together as a diary he wrote the record of his week. . . . "I have mastered the Spohr Concerto. Tomorrow I try Paganini. This evening I will rest as I am haunted in nightmares by a woman's face." . . . He folded up his paper but as he rose to move away his eyes were caught by a woman who stood by the terrace and looked in at him with [a] strange expression. She was not clothed like the women of the streets, and in her face there was a surprising joy without trace of provocation. He went out and joined her and they went down the boulevard with her arm in his. Till that night he had never made advances or casual acquaintance on the ways but in this woman he saw the presence that had filled his dreams and he had not force to quit her. They passed the Seine and [moved on] till they came where the world of Paris was leaving the Comédie-Française, and stopped for a moment to watch the faces coming out. A lady from the crowd turned at the door of her carriage and looked at them with some intentness, and to his heated brain she appeared also a version of his dream. He turned and wandered along to his dwelling [with the woman he had met outside the café]. . . . Henceforth his life was changed. His companion took up and lived with him permanently, and for a while at least revived and pleased him by her sympathy and friendship and a vague beauty . . . and southern grace.

'Soon a letter came from a new pupil [who turned out to be] the lady of the Théâtre Français, named Chouska, Russian by birth but in part American by education. For a while she chilled him by her coldly accurate expression but as he knew her more completely a hidden charm enraptured him, and he lived as in a fairy land with the two ladies of [his] dream. He wrote in his journal about this woman: "Her technique is underdeveloped but she has verve and talent and may do a great deal if she [perseveres.] I hope she will be satisfied with my teaching, but I doubt my power as a professor. She is a perfect physical type. The finer organism of women seems to be able to preserve the intensity and delicacy of perception necessary for an artist with perfect physical health in a way that is rare with men. I have had presentiments and dreams before but never anything like this. I hope it may end without calamity." '

May 6. A letter from a new pupil—a Mademoiselle Chouska; I have never known such a week.[1] First there was my engagement to play at Lemerre's concert in the autumn, then this extraordinary Celliniani, and now a new pupil who will keep us through the summer.

May 7. It is a queer business. I have written to explain. . . .

'Chère Mademoiselle

For three nights before my engagement for the autumn I dreamed of a woman who led me into strange adventures that I cannot recollect. When Lemerre's letter came I went out on the Boulevards to walk off my excitement, and as I was coming out of a café I found the woman I had dreamed of watching me from the corner of the terrace. An hour later you drove past us as we were passing under the arches of the Louvre, and I saw that you were also a version of my dream. I am telling you these things to explain my embarrassment when I found that you were the pupil who had written to me, and also my relation with the woman you saw me with. . . .'

May 14. Second lesson with the Chouska. I keep comparing her with the Celliniani. The first is like an oak or fir tree, the other some vague growth of the sea. We were at Meudon last night. At first she seemed like an intruder, then she changed and showed a strange instinct for colour and sound. We are a queer pair.

May 17. The heat is intense, and my nerves are a trouble, yet I must practise.

May 19. A Sunday of delicious rain. I walked all the morning in the Luxembourg to feel the green smell of the leaves, and then went to the Louvre where the Celliniani came to meet me from St. Germain des Prés. I looked a long time at the Joconde and the Victoire, for they remind me of my two friends—the Celliniani has something of Mona Lisa and the Chouska when moved by music is like the statue. I seem to love two parts of one ideal, rather than two separate women. I do not know how it will end, but for the moment I am finding new power of expression in this strange attachment.

[1] The words 'a Mademoiselle Chouska; I have never known such a week', are added, for the sake of clarity, from the version on smaller, thicker sheets in Item 52.

June 12. The personality tends to assimilate itself with the ideal that is formed of it by love; hence in the fullest friendship my ideal of my friend goes about with her ideal of myself, and a man with two friends of different tendencies is developed in opposite ways neither of which is really his own. Perhaps this is the reason why a man who does not know love is usually narrow.

My dreams which came true were less strange than this truth which is like a dream. It is midnight. The Celliniani had a terrible nightmare last night. I fear her nervousness is increasing. I am far from well.

June 18. The Chouska has gone away for the rest of the summer, and has left a blank behind her, though the Celliniani is jubilant. It is so sultry that I can only practise in the evening, and sometimes my exaltation grows so strong in the twilight I seem to lose all hold on my existence, and to know nothing but the passion of sound and the shadowy Celliniani who sits and listens by the window.

I wish there was some hall where recognised musicians might play when they liked for people that came and went as in the churches. If I could slip down now, and beginning softly to myself,[1] wake out gradually to my full power! In a vulgar concert I am not likely to succeed. I depend too much on my surroundings.

The Celliniani thinks no one ever played as I do. I am her religion, yet I doubt if this musical excitement is good for her, she is sometimes hysterical and we both sleep badly.

Sept. 25. The concert is in a month. I am playing well—better I think than many who succeed,—but my nervousness is appalling. Would to Heaven the thing were over, the heat and agitation are killing us!

Oct. 24. I have written to the Chouska to try and distract my thoughts. . . .

'My concert is tomorrow and I am terribly unwell. I have been trying all the week to draw off my attention to natural science or pictures or anything that used to interest me, but it is no use. . . . I have given up everything for music, and tomorrow I am going to fail utterly. I must go to the rehearsal. . . .'

[1] The phrase 'and beginning softly to myself' is added from the version on smaller, thicker paper in Item 52. E. M Stephens also added it in the version he had typed out.

Later. When we reached the hall night had fallen and the rehearsal was going on. I stood for a while with the Celliniani at the dark end of the hall and listened to the orchestra playing Beethoven's 'Marche Funèbre'. The vague shadows of the hall gave me courage and I had an absolute success. Lemerre was delighted. Everybody congratulated me. But tomorrow?—I shall not sleep tonight.

Oct. 25. The concert is this afternoon. I am trembling like a leaf. Everything is going round. I am bent double with pain. Failure is certain, yet I must play. The poor Celliniani is in terrible distress to see my degradation,—it is nothing less. Whatever happens I am bound to her for ever. Her goodness could not be surpassed. . . .

Nov. 1.[1] I have the same name and features as last week. I am not the same man. The Celliniani is still in the mad-house.

Nov. 15. I have forced myself to write to the Chouska:—

. . . 'We reached the hall. The people in the artists' room talked and laughed with me and gave me wine. It was no use. My face was grey when I saw it in the glass, and I spilt the wine on the carpet. I saw them whispering about me: it made me worse. I do not remember how I came on the platform. When I reached the difficult phrases I woke a little and felt a sort of hope, but my fingers were trembling and I missed everything. I heard the gallery hissing: it got worse. I thought I ought to give up, but was uncertain. . . . Then someone cried out most terribly: it was the Celliniani. They had to take her away. Her hysteria has been increasing through the summer, and this shock upset her altogether.'

Nov. 20. They say·I must give up music and be cheerful. The damned fools.

Nov. 29. The snow is beginning. I am trying to read,—philosophy science, anything. Sometimes I follow easily, sometimes I cannot get rid of the concert, and the Celliniani, and the dread that I may follow her.

Nov. 30. A man is mad who believes that he has a disease which he is really without. Suppose he believes himself insane. Is he mad? If so his conviction is well founded and he is so far sane. Is he sane?

[1] The version on smaller, thicker paper in Item 52 is used from here onwards.

Then he believes delusively that he [is] mad: therefore he is mad. Are these the uses of adversity?

Dec. 1. I have been reading Herbert Spencer and my creed is now very simple. Humanity has evolved from the conditions of the world, and will return to the nothing it has come from. Each separate life is but a ripple on the waves,—a blade of grass on the roadside. For those who fail, there is no hope. They are like the dead leaves in autumn, blown here and there before their final dissolution. In my useless agony I am only hurtful to my fellows. Why should I endure it? It is not now:—'To sleep: perchance to dream: ay; there 's the rub,' but to sleep eternally and completely; to be free from the present and the past and from forebodings which are still more frightful. The dread of imprisonment is enough to deter any ruffian from the crime he desires, and shall I go forward to wake up by and by in the four walls of a madhouse, caged and barred like a dangerous animal and without hope of release?

Dec. 10. Every day some new morbid idea strikes through my brain like the thrust of a poisoned dagger. How long can it continue? I have no delusion, no definite mania, yet I watch myself day and night with appalling apprehension.

Dec. 12. I caught my face in the glass today as I sat at my table; I had the terrified look I have sometimes seen in trapped animals. Even when other matters enter my mind I keep a hold on my torture, as a man with the bag of jewels in his pocket feels again and again to know of its security. My nervousness is increasing. My brain by some horrible decadence is grown a register for appalling things, and my almost preternatural destiny throws such things continually about me. In the newspapers I read of men who have gone mad and slain their kindred; in reviews I find analysis of nerve decay; if I go among the streets I fall in with wretched beings on the brink of total alienation. Today I am not able to read, I dare not play, I have no one to visit, and I sit here turning over my anguish with half triumphant ecstasy of pain. I love music, it is barred from me; I was ambitious, I am thrust aside, I have loved this strange woman with immeasurable passion, and my love for her has crushed us. I know the lives of men who were supremely miserable, yet their grief seems nothing to my own. In this community of madness, this delirium of two souls begotten and wrought by a more than human exaltation, the earth seems to have invented a new torture, to have added a new ingenious instrument to the rack-chamber of life. I feel a lack in my scepticism which leaves no name for malediction, and envy Job who had his choice to curse God and die.

Dec. 24. Is it I—I—who am cowering here on the brink of insanity? To-night when I had made my supper and sat down alone and very cold, my gorge rose in revolt at my own misery, and I almost did the deed I am approaching. I am not able to endure it. Cursed be God.

'Bonum nobis est quod aliquando habemus aliquas gravitates et contrarietates, quia saepe hominem ad cor revocant quatenus se in exilio esse cognoscat, nec spem suam in alia re mundi ponat.'

This monk seems never wholly in the wrong and I ask myself as I read over this passage what it may signify in the language of the day. It may be that the misery which makes the individual unit an instrument of immeasurable torture, forces a man from his own limits to regain a sympathy with the world. 'O veritas Dei, fac me unum tecum in caritate perpetua.' The unyielding quiet of this book has rescued yet appalled me. Am I so utterly debased—I who have known the country and the hills—that I yield up my life to the first stroke of destiny? If I am anything I am equal to the saints. I will endure as they endured.

Jan. 2. Chère mademoiselle Chouska,

'I have found one of your books, this [is] how it happened. . . . When I had read the letter I rushed from the house. I avoided crowded streets where the people shunned yet dogged me. I reached the quai Voltaire, and kicked an old book under my feet. It was a copy of the *Imitation of Christ* with your name on the fly-leaf. All thought of suicide seemed to leave me in an instant, and I walked home up the Bd. St. Michel, wondering how the book had fallen on the quay. Then I read it till daylight and grew as quiet as a child. "Post hiemem sequitur aestas; post noctem redit dies; et post tempestatem magna serenitas."[1] For a week I have nurtured myself in a more than saintly exaltation. I am forming from my own spirit a divine and beautiful existence and I am

[1] The whole of this Latin sentence and the words 'on the quay' at the end of the previous sentence but one are added, for the sake of clarity, from an earlier version in Clip-binder 51.

as much an artist in my peculiar precincts as Beethoven or Wagner.' . . .

Jan. 4. I am trying to co-ordinate the inner life of this monk and my own inner life as a musician. It seems as I read him that his joy in its essence was identical with my own. As all thirst is quenched by liquid, so perhaps the inner longing of the personality is only assuaged by an ecstasy which is as multiform as the varieties of liquid, and exists as essentially in prayer as in the sound of the violin. Even in the preparatory discipline there is much that is similar in the saint's life and in the artist's. We have the same joy of progress, the same joy in infinitely exact manipulation, (the saint with his daily actions, the artist with his materials) the same joy of creation, for the saints and I suppose the Stoics create their own powerful yet exquisite personality.

Jan. 6. I am distraught again and miserably nervous. Have I power to redeem my brain by one desperate resolution, or am I doomed to madness with my eyes on a possible release?

'Think nothing great,' says Marcus Aurelius (I am reading the Stoics also) 'but to act as nature leads thee, and to suffer as the all-nature may decree.'

'God, use me as it may please Thee,' says Epictetus, 'I refuse nothing that Thou mayst send me, and will defend Thy justice before all men.'

In the *Imitation*:—'Fili, non potes perfectam possidere libertatem nisi totaliter abnegas temet ipsum. Demitte omnia et invenies omnia.'

I realised today that the nearly miraculous power of the saint lies in his system of daily self-suggestion which he calls prayer and meditation. I will try something similar.

Jan. 10. I have never been so happy. Beyond my readings of the saints and philosophers which I turn to three times a day, to suggest my will with power, I take some beautiful thing every morning and regard it till my admiration ends in a moment of passionate ecstasy. This is my equivalent for the adoration of the saints.

Feb. 2. The Celliniani is dead. I have just come from her funeral. In the face of death what are all my plans of adoration?

Feb. 22. All living things demand their share of joy, and I see no permanent joy apart from the creation or touching of beautiful forms or ideas. This is the immortal fragment of religion. As art may decorate what is useful or exist for its own beauty in itself, so an action done with a beautiful motive is decorated and joyful, and for souls that are barred from the joy of activity there is still the quiescent ecstasy of resignation.

Feb. 28. I question sometimes whether this religious ecstasy I live in is not a morbid growth,—a glad infatuation I have wrought to heal the sad one. I try to persuade myself that my personality is also my universe, and that the difficulties in my system only enhance its perfection by the joy I gain as I surmount them. Yet I feel at times that I am a fool.

March 11. A magnificent spring day. In thus moulding myself upon the model of the saints am I gaining the glory of a marble statue, or only the contortion of mosaics? Is my personality worth the effort I spend upon it? Could any sculptor work with real ecstasy if he had only decayed wood for his material?

April 3. The Chouska writes that she cannot return to Paris till the autumn. I am almost glad. I seem to have passed whole epochs in the limits of my own delight. How will this appear when I show it to another? She says also that she has made a profound study of mysticism, and recommends me to read Spinoza as a change from the saints.

April 6. I have found another flaw in my spiritual system. A great part of my happiness has lain in the evergrowing perfection of my personality. I opened Spinoza the other day and found this great definition:—'Laetitia est hominis transitio a minore ad majorem perfectionem.' It follows that as we approach perfection our progress is likely to become less rapid and therefore less joyful; and at perfection joy must cease. Is this the Eastern doctrine of Nirvana? For the moment I am perfect, my will is strong, moral, altruistic. What remains to seek for? Yet joy is an element of perfection and if my joy is lost I am fallen and must recommence. It is the old symbol—the serpent with its tail in its mouth.[1]

May 5. I am in the country at last—near the end of Finisterre. Since I came here my daily readings of the saints and Stoics have lost

[1] The version in Clip-binder 51 ends abruptly here as several pages have been torn out.

their interest, and I live simply and naturally as the peasants do. This ordeal I have passed through has left me without a trace of apprehension. My system saved me, yet when I look back on it now, it seems a childish escapade. I have my fiddle here and I make the peasants dance in the evenings. My skin shivers while I play to see that in spite of the agony of the world there are still men and women joyous enough to leap and skip with exultation.

May 7. Yesterday I was out fishing with some of the fishermen, and as I walked home to the village, sunburnt, hungry and healthy, with my old coat on my arm, I could not find any connection between my present self and the self of last winter's diary.

May 20. I am hearing many ghost-stories. Since I have come back to nature my rather crude materialism has begun to dissatisfy me. Nature is miraculous and my own dreams were something extra-human.

September 15. Paris again. It has given a certain tremor to my nerves, to come back to these places that recall the Celliniani and my own despair. The Chouska is here again and talks a great deal of her spiritualistic studies. She says the ordeal I have passed through and what she is pleased to call the bravery with which I overcame it, form a direct initiation to the spiritual power that is needful for the mystic. It appears that she came to Paris the day before I saw her in the street, under the impulse of a strong intuition, and now she believes that the work intended for her was to make my acquaintance and to insert the keystone in the arch I have constructed.

Sept. 23. She is a wonderful woman, and, I think, has grown more like the Celliniani since she has given herself up so exclusively to the study of these mysterious tenets. Yesterday she came dressed in the pale green material the Celliniani wore at the concert. We are indeed such stuff as dreams are made of. At first I loved, as it were, one ideal woman divided between my two friends, now I find two women in the one.

I am reading her books, and assenting with provisional delight to complex theories of the world. If four or five scientists are agreed on any subject which they alone have studied the opposite opinion of the rest of the world is of no value. In this sense the great mystics are surely worth more attention than they are usually given. The Chouska is urging me to write for my occupation as I dare not return to music.

Nov. 1. I am yielding up my imagination to the marvellous. These things cannot be understood without an intimate if cautious sympathy, and I long to lift the veil and to see with my own inward sight the pretended symbols of the soul. In this mood I seem to gain the width and dignity my efforts of the spring lacked so utterly.

Nov. 11. Yesterday when the Chouska was here the concierge's child came up to me with a letter. As she was running away she fell over my violin case and hurt her knees. The Chouska picked her up and as we consoled her a new idea came between us—if we love?

Nov. 15. I have passed the threshold and seen the face of the unseen. I have moved amid a myriad Egyptian forms, have called in defiance to the reptile godheads of the East, bidding them place their foreheads upon mine that knew no apprehension.

I have seen symphonies of colour that moved with musical recurrence round centres I could not understand: I have passed the solitude of seas and felt with cold hands the tropical profusion in their caverns of undulating gloom and then all these things rolled themselves in a vortex and left a single lily in their wake.

Nov. 16. My hands bound upon my now imperial forehead I count the glories I have known. But what is to follow?

Nov. 20. Symbols of things beyond my comprehension cloud through the waving of the inward light. Strange stars shine upon me with prophetic rays. Purple feathers float in my hands, and choral symphonies wind themselves about me. Two divine children haunt the twilight of my sleep. Are they souls that would create their lives in my passion for the Chouska?

Nov. 23. I am sick of the ascetic twaddle of the saints. I will not deny my masculine existence nor rise, if I can rise, by facile abnegation. I despise the hermit and the monk and pity only the adulterer and the drunkard. There is one world of souls and no flesh and no devil.

Dec. 10.[1] A letter from the Chouska:—

'We dream and marriage would wake us. Do not talk of it. I leave your love not as a thing that I renounce, but cling rather to the heaven I know. I have learned in Paris that I am not destined to achieve distinction in my art; you tell me that your poetry is of no value. But be sure that we at least have failed because we feel the inexpressible. Art is but expression. Without any pride or self delusion we can look upon the writers and sculptors around us "with a sad disdain". Mon ami, we have walked with God; do not envy the frail glory of your comrades.' . . .

Feb. 22. I have answered at last:—

'For us marriage would be a mere copy of the world, and I see that in this you are wiser than I am. . . .

'I have come out among the hills to write music again if I am able. . . . All art that is not conceived by a soul in harmony with some mood of the earth is without value, and unless we are able to produce a myth more beautiful than nature—holding in itself a spiritual grace beyond and through the earthly—it is better to be silent. . . . When I am here I do not think without a shudder of the books of Baudelaire or Huysmans. Among heather I experience things that are divine, yet I know not how I should express them. Music is the finest art, for it alone can express directly what is not utterable, but I am not fitted to be a composer. To-day I burned many sonnets written in Paris with an ecstasy of pride, for they were but a playing with words and I blushed to bear them before the solemnity of God. . . . There is little poetry that I can read here, except the songs of the peasants and some of Wordsworth and Dante.' . . .

[Another letter from the Chouska:—]

'. . . Your letter shows that my instinct did not lead me erroneously. Is it not better that two souls who have loved in each other the quiet that surpasses love should retain their solitary mood . . . and not descend to common oblivion. Simple human life has health and dignity, yet no one would put a bride bed in the Sainte Chapelle, and my room and yours are not commoner than Christ's. Mon ami, our love is religion. When all mankind

[1] The version in Notebook 15 is used from here to the end. The elucidation of this difficult passage in Notebook 15 has been helped by a torn and creased typewritten fragment, at the top of which Synge has scrawled 'concluding page', in Item 52, and by a draft in Clip-binder 22.

are religious humanity will cease for the task of flesh will be accomplished. This mood of it may be more than saintly isolation is one fit to be arrayed in art, yet what form is undefiled? When I think of Paris my marble dreams shrink from incarnation. In art as in love tranquillity is heaven.'

[I reply to her:—]

'Do not exceed, nor lose all life in exaltation. If you renounce all offspring from your body do not likewise with your soul. You have elected a life [of] saint-like meditation, yet heed the actions of the soul . . . and the things that spring from it. Forget Paris and the world and shape your clay without fear or hesitation. I turn daily further from the poetry which is but a shaping of jewels and seek a tone as long and calm as night upon the hills. Yet stories in verse are [pointless] now, sincere drama has the weight [of] earthly passion, description is vain, and lyrical poetry is but a substitute for the singing voice or violin. Literature is not alive. I will be silent.'

[Final words from the Chouska:—]

'. . . The earth is beautiful, and I live as I write in a mist of abstract meditations, though the children teach me that I am a woman.

'You will not follow my advice even as I have not followed yours. In the end we will dream away our existences, happier than in the world.'[1]

[1] A rejected draft (written about 1899) in Notebook 15 is relevant here:

'Epilogue

Dear M.

'Our lives are allegorical. We have lived through a cycle of existence. You who lived in spiritual art were as the soul; I was at first the intellect and the Celliniani was the beautiful but instinctive vegetative life. The last act is over and the curtain is down. We have suffered, enjoyed and learned. We must go on to learn more not together but separately. You will understand. Our currents may cross again and unite us more closely: but they are broken.

Chouska'

[ON A TRAIN TO PARIS][1]

ONE night when I was travelling from London I found myself in a compartment with eight ballet girls for the last stage of our journey from Dieppe to Paris. Our crossing had been the wildest of the season, and the boisterous gaiety of my companions contrasted curiously with their crumpled clothes and their drawn, handsome faces. For a while they sang songs and talked eagerly about Paris and their journey. Then one by one they leaned over on each other and went to sleep. Some had laid aside their hats and thrown loose shawls over their heads; others had retained their hats but allowed them to work down gradually with their unfolding hair upon their ears. The whole party, swaying in two lines of sorrow, gave the impression of feminine weakness and disorder which produces a potent yet human influence on a man with a conscience. What were these weak and tired girls that they should be compelled nightly to exhibit the strained nudity of their limbs to amuse the dregs of masculine cupidity? Opposite from myself, one who lay back in the corner with a wisp of hair pushed out beneath the shawl she held tightly round her small half-childish face recalled with grotesque yet irresistible irony a picture of Little Red Riding Hood and the Wolf that I had delighted in, in one of my first picture books. Her face was still radiant, even in fatigue, with the imperial grace and purity of childhood, although she was probably seventeen or eighteen.

The strong coffee I had taken on leaving the boat kept me awake. The sun was rising on the fresh and tranquil fields, and I looked out every few moments into the wonderful purity of the September morning, then back again to the gallery of sleeping girls. Is life a stage and all the men and women merely players, or an arena where men and women and children are captives to be torn with beasts and gladiators who appear only to destroy and be destroyed?

[1] From Notebook 15, probably written about 1897. Two versions, neither quite complete, exist on opposite pages in Notebook 15. Both versions seem to have been drafted hurriedly and are scrawled across the pages in almost illegible handwriting much altered and crossed-out, as the photograph (between pp. 40–41) indicates. Only a conflation of them would make sense, and this is here provided. Titles given in square brackets are not Synge's own.

After a while I grew so bitter in my strange and solitary watch that I sprang up and cried out to them that we were nearing Paris. They roused themselves with stiff and dreary expectation. I could have kissed and comforted them each in turn despite the rouge and sea salt that lay upon their lips. In a few moments their traditional gaiety reasserted itself. They threw aside their shawls and hats and began to do their hair with combs and looking-glasses, plying me with questions about Paris life and theatres, throwing in at times a remark of naïve yet frank obscenity.

Morituri te salutamus! The pity I felt changed gradually to admiration as I warmed myself with their high spirits and good humour.[1]

[1] A passage (probably written in 1896) in Notebook 15 and seeming to combine impressions in Dublin and Paris has a similar mood.

'The lower paths and laneways of a city, the dark doorposts venerable in unrecorded antiquity, the swarms of children growing up in gradual defilement, the lewd-tongued girls and low contaminated men . . . yield an impulse to our jaded senses akin to what is won from the poems or pictures of a madman, rousing admiration and abhorrence with pity it is not possible to gauge.

'More than any other thing I yearn to acquaint myself with the true personalities of these women—these bastard daughters of the Enduring Life—and perpetually I wander among them reading in their faces and their transient gesticulation the mysterious record of their divinity. I have seen the young hands of girls straying lewdly on their comrades, I have seen the crude animal propensities known still always to exist in men and women laid forth with plain indifference, yet these things stir not within me the instinctive blame pure men profess to cherish, for no action is more lawless than a thought, no thought than the dark mood from whence it may arise; and this mood, straying forever as unwarded winds mid strange effluvias horrible to name, what caution were capable to reach?'

UNDER ETHER[1]

Personal Experiences During an Operation

THE operation was fixed for Saturday; so at ten o'clock on Friday evening I found myself at the door of the private hospital where I was to lodge. I was received in the office by Nurse Smith. . . . Nurse Smith gave me her parting directions—I was to be in bed before midnight, when a night nurse would come round to bandage my neck—and went off to other duties. The door closed behind her and I was alone. For a while I roved through my room, peering into cupboards and presses, half dreading to unearth the débris of mutilated victims. Then I sank into a chair, and drew out the last volume I had been studying. It was Spinoza's ethics, and I found my excited thoughts refused the lead of the great pantheist, and I abandoned myself again to incoherent reverie till eleven and a half struck heavily on the clock before my door. Then I unpacked the few necessaries I had brought with me and arranged them in drawers with which the room abounded, and went to bed in a few moments.

Next morning I found the operation was not to take place till mid-day, so I had long to wait. However I found a fellow patient in the drawing-room, and the morning passed languidly in conversation.[2]

At half-past eleven I slipped down to get a look at the preparations in my own room. They were worth seeing. In the window stood a long stretcher, some four feet high and two wide, rigged out as a bed but looking ghastly enough. Every available table was covered with enamelled hardware, showing many fantastic shapes whose use I was yet to learn. Strange bottles stood in groups

[1] First published in Volume Four of the *Works* of 1910. In December 1897 Synge underwent an operation in Dublin for the removal of swollen glands in his neck; this was perhaps the first sign of the disease which eventually killed him. The essay was written shortly after this operation. In September 1907 Synge underwent a similar operation on his neck. Edward Stephens says: 'Synge told me that as he was coming out of the anaesthetic the first thing he shouted out was "Damn the bloody Anglo-Saxon language that a man can't swear in without being vulgar." ' Greene and Stephens, *J. M. Synge* (The Macmillan Company, New York, 1959), p. 277.

[2] This sentence appears, with a line through it, in Synge's typescript in Box File C, but it was not included in Volume Four of the *Works* of 1910.

beside articles I had never seen, even in the windows of surgical outfitters. My room looked south, and the low winter sun threw in an almost dazzling illumination at the large panes from which all blinds had been removed. While I was taking an inventory of what was to be seen a nurse came in, and was horrified to find me on the scene of action. Patients, as I afterwards learned, are banished till the last moment to avoid needless anxiety.

The doctors were now announced, and I was hurried upstairs to give them a moment to make ready their own instruments. In a few minutes Nurse Smith came and brought me down. Three doctors were awaiting me, and I was followed by Nurse Smith and two younger nurses. I was irritated by the solemnity of the whole party. When I tried jokes on my own account they met them with sickly smiles, as an attempt to cloak a timidity I did not feel. In a moment the surgeon directed me to mount the scaffold. At other times one would feel an embarrassment in divesting oneself to a single smock in the presence of three young women, but it seemed as natural in the circumstances as walking bareheaded in a church. I mounted the operating table, warning them as I did so that they would have no slight task to retain me on my plank bed. The moment my head touched the pillow one of the doctors bent over me to test my heart. An instant later he placed something over my mouth and nose directing me to breathe with usual regularity. He was standing behind my head, so I saw only his face stooping above me. I clasped my hands over my breast, and decided to allow my fingers some motion to let off the inevitable excitement. The only anxiety I remember to have felt was lest I should become unruly as the ether gained on me, and disgrace my stoic resolution.

For what seemed an eternity no change came. Suddenly the light grew brighter, and a rigidity tingled through my limbs. It was not pleasant, and I felt my fingers flying in a rhythm of fearful velocity. Even this was not enough; my toes—always agile as a monkey's—joined in the dance. I wondered how long I could retain self-control in presence of such awful discomfort. A change passed across me, and my fingers locked with sudden stiffness. Speech was gone. Volition was gone. I was a dead weight; a subject on a board; toy of other wills. It was agony. My eyes rolled swiftly from one side to the other, seeing now with phantasmal and horrible distortion. A break came, and I forgot one moment where I was. I passed again into sense; my mouth was uncovered; no one seemed at hand. Horrible noises were in my ears. The ceiling, which now shone with terrible distinctness, seemed bending over the nurses; and the nurses, some without heads, some with two, were floating in the air. Voices were behind me. Fifty suggestions flashed through my brain; had the ether apparatus broken? Did they think me insensible? Would I have to lie feeling all with treble intensity, unable to speak or move? I raised myself on my elbows and asked with sudden effort:

'What has happened?'

Two doctors were at my side in an instant. They assured me that I was doing excellently, and begged me to lie still for my further dose of ether.

Now I was told to draw long breaths, and I drew eagerly and angrily, resolved to put myself, at any cost, out of pain.

I felt what seemed currents of blue vapour curling to my utmost extremities. Suddenly I was in a chaos of excitement, talking loudly and incoherently. Clouds of luminous mist were swirling round me, through which heads broke only at intervals. I felt I was talking of a lady I had known years before, and sudden terror seized me that I should spread forth all the secrets of my life. I could not be silent, The name was on my lips. With wild horror I screamed:

'Oh, no, I won't!'

'No, I won't!'

'No I won't!'

'Oh, no, I won't!'

'No, I won't!'

'No, I won't!'

using the sullen rhythm that forms in one's head during a railway journey. This did not suffice; I changed to a shrieking imprecation. Another blast of ether rolled through my veins. My hands broke from my control and waved in the luminous clouds. I saw them, and in an instant one hand went out before the other, my fingers spread and one thumb approached my nose after the manner of a street arab. At the same moment the clouds rolled aside, and I saw the doctor bending over me. He called to the surgeon:

'Batby, look!'

The words reached me and I echoed:

'Batby, look, amn't I funny?'

They laughed aloud.

'Now you're laughing,' I cried: 'Ha, ha, ha!' Mimicking with a frantic crescendo. Then their mirth infuriated me.

'I'm an initiated mystic,' I yelled with fury; 'I could rend the groundwork of your souls.'

Not wishing to exasperate me they grew serious. 'Ha, ha, ha!' I roared in ironical triumph, 'now you're serious. Now you know what you have to deal with.'

The clouds rolled over me again, now heavy, now opaque. Something thrilled in my neck. Were they beginning? The memory of control was obliterated; I yelled, I writhed with appalling agony. Another paroxysm of frenzy, and my life seemed to go out in one spiral yell to the unknown.

The next period I remember but vaguely. I seemed to traverse whole epochs of desolation and bliss. All secrets were open before me, and simple as the universe to its God. Now and then something recalled my physical life, and I smiled at what seemed a moment of sickly infancy. At other times I felt I might return to earth, and laughed aloud to think what a god I should be among men. For there could be no more terror in my life. I was a light, a joy.

These earthly recollections were few and faint, for the rest I was in raptures I have no power to translate. At last clouds came over me again. My joy seemed slipping from my grasp, and at times I touched the memory of the operation as one gropes for a forgotten dream. I heard noises and grew conscious of weight. The weight took shape; it was my body lying motionless in a bed. The clouds broke, and I saw a gaselier over my head. I realized with intense horror that my visions were fleeing away, leaving scarcely a trace. I groaned in misery.

'Oh, if I could only remember! If I could only remember—remember.'

I was sick, and people were attending me.

I groaned still: 'Oh, if I could only remember.'

The clouds rolled further away; I recognised one of the nurses, and called out to her with sudden incongruity:

'By Jove, there's Nurse Smith!'

She heard me, and bending over me she said: 'Are you coming to? It was very satisfactory.' 'What was satisfactory?' I asked, still dwelling on my dreams.

'The operation,' she replied.

'D——— the operation,' I groaned. 'If I could only remember, I'd write books upon books; I'd teach all earth of delight.'

Every moment the recollection of my dreams was going off from me, being replaced by drunken exhilaration.

I was still suffering a good deal from nausea, but was so impressed with my wit that my drunken vanity left no room for low spirits. At this stage I began to regain power over my body; I remember moving each limb in succession, calling out in delight as I did so:

'There goes one leg. There's the other. There's one hand. There's the other.'

Then I tried to raise my head but failed, and apostrophised it in language too racy to repeat.

Presently the nurses left me for their dinner, putting a hand-bell in easy reach.

The nausea returned and I rang lustily. My hand was still weak, and the bell slipped from my hold, tumbling nearly into my mouth. When the nurses ran in I cried out in mock anger:

'Why the devil do you leave a fellow alone like that, I've been sick into the bell!'

This was my last joke, and for the rest of the afternoon and evening I lay quiet enough.

The next day I felt unenterprising enough but in no pain or uneasiness. My weakness made it most natural and agreeable of all things to lie still and be talked to. The room I occupied opened from a hall, so a pleasant stir outside kept me gently alert. The doctors looked in during the forenoon, and now that the ordeal was over, threw aside their gravity, and were as jovial as one could desire.

When they left me I looked vaguely through some books that were brought to me, and here became aware of my own collapse, for all allusion to sadness or affairs of the heart sent up a dew into my eyes. That afternoon my friends were admitted to see me, and my weakness came still more to the front. From five o'clock deep drowsiness came over me, and I lay as in lethargy with the lights carefully lowered. A faint jingle of tram-bells sounded far away, and the voices of Sunday travellers sometimes broke into my room. I took notice of every familiar occurrence as if it were something I had come back to from a distant country. The impression was very strong on me that I had died the preceding day and come to life again, and this impression has never changed.

PART TWO

THE ARAN ISLANDS

AN ISLAND MAN

THE ARAN ISLANDS[1]

INTRODUCTION

THE geography of the Aran Islands is very simple, yet it may need a word to itself. There are three islands: Aranmor, the north island, about nine miles long; Inishmaan, the middle island, about three miles and a half across, and nearly round in form; and the south island, Inishere—in Irish, east island,—like the middle island but slightly smaller. They lie about thirty miles from Galway, up the centre of the bay, but they are not far from the cliffs of County Clare, on the south, or the corner of Connemara on the north.

Kilronan, the principal village on Aranmor, has been so much changed by the fishing industry, developed there by the Congested Districts Board, that it has now very little to distinguish it from any fishing village on the west coast of Ireland. The other islands are more primitive, but even on them many changes are being made, that it was not worth while to deal with in the text.

In the pages that follow I have given a direct account of my life on the islands, and of what I met with among them, inventing nothing, and changing nothing that is essential. As far as possible, however, I have disguised the identity of the people I speak of, by making changes in their names, and in the letters I quote, and by altering some local and family relationships. I have had nothing to say about them that was not wholly in their favour, but I have made this disguise to keep them from ever feeling that a too direct

[1] *The Aran Islands* was first published jointly by Elkin Mathews, London, and Maunsel, Dublin, in April 1907. The text here printed is that of the 1907 edition, with additions from the unpublished material. In the course of an unpublished letter dated 2 August 1907 to James Patterson in Edinburgh, Synge said; 'It is a great relief that *The Aran Islands* is thought well of after all. It was refused by publishers often in London for three or four years so that I had begun to think it was a failure. I hope to do a book on Wicklow peasant life, more or less of the same kind, in the next year or two, and perhaps another on the Kerry Islands.' In unpublished letters to Spencer Brodney on 10 and 12 December 1907, Synge says: 'I look on *The Aran Islands* as my first serious piece of work—it was written before any of my plays. In writing out the talk of the people and their stories in this book, and in a certain number of articles on the Wicklow peasantry which I have not yet collected, I learned to write the peasant dialect and dialogue which I use in my plays. . . . *The Aran Islands* throws a good deal of light on my plays.'

Synge stayed on the Aran Islands for several weeks each summer or autumn from 1898 to 1902. The book is based on the first four of his five annual visits.

use had been made of their kindness, and friendship, for which I am more grateful than it is easy to say.[1]

[1] In Synge's final typescript in Box-file G is this passage: 'In arranging my chapters I have, of course, used a good deal of freedom, bringing kindred things together and keeping jarring things apart. The general plan of the book is, it will be seen at once, largely borrowed from Pierre Loti, who has, I think, treated this sort of subject more adequately than any other writer of the present day.' This last sentence, 'The general plan . . . day', has a line through it. His view of Loti changed: see pp. 102–3 here. Synge soon caught the atmosphere of the islands in a sentence in Notebook 19 (written in 1898), which he did not print: 'I have been sitting all the morning over the great turf fire in the kitchen where an old man had been brought to tell me stories while the family drew round on their stools and the daughter of the house in her wonderful red garments span her wheel at my side.'

PART I

I AM in Aranmor, sitting over a turf fire, listening to a murmur of Gaelic that is rising from a little public-house under my room.[1]

The steamer which comes to Aran sails according to the tide, and it was six o'clock this morning when we left the quay of Galway in a dense shroud of mist.

A low line of shore was visible at first on the right between the movement of the waves and fog, but when we came further it was lost sight of, and nothing could be seen but the mist curling in the rigging, and a small circle of foam.

There were few passengers; a couple of men going out with young pigs tied loosely in sacking, three or four young girls who sat in the cabin with their heads completely twisted in their shawls, and a builder, on his way to repair the pier at Kilronan, who walked up and down and talked with me.

In about three hours Aran came in sight. A dreary rock appeared at first sloping up from the sea into the fog; then as we drew nearer, a coastguard station and the village.

A little later I was wandering out along the one good roadway of the island, looking over low walls on either side into small flat fields of naked rock. I have seen nothing so desolate. Grey floods of water were sweeping everywhere upon the limestone, making at times a wild torrent of the road, which twined continually over low hills and cavities in the rock or passed between a few small fields of potatoes or grass hidden away in corners that had shelter. Whenever the cloud lifted I could see the edge of the sea below me on the right, and the naked ridge of the island above me on the other side. Occasionally I passed a lonely chapel or schoolhouse, or a line of stone pillars with crosses above them and inscriptions asking a prayer for the soul of the person they commemorated.

I met few people; but here and there a band of tall girls passed

[1] This section, from the opening words of Part I, 'I am in Aranmor' (p. 49) to 'beyond the bay' (p. 53) was originally published as an article, 'An Impression of Aran', in the *Manchester Guardian* on 24 January 1905. The name Killeany and the passages (here in brackets) on p. 51, from 'When he went away' to 'foot upon the mainland' and on p. 52, from 'After a while' to 'my riches to continue' were not in the article, but were in the 1907 edition.

me on their way to Kilronan, and called out to me with humorous wonder, speaking English with a slight foreign intonation that differed a good deal from the brogue of Galway. The rain and cold seemed to have no influence on their vitality, and as they hurried past me with eager laughter and great talking in Gaelic, they left the wet masses of rock more desolate than before.

A little after midday when I was coming back one old half-blind man spoke to me in Gaelic, but, in general, I was surprised at the abundance and fluency of the foreign tongue.

In the afternoon the rain continued, so I sat here in the inn looking out through the mist at a few men who were unlading hookers that had come in with turf from Connemara, and at the long-legged pigs that were playing in the surf. As the fishermen came in and out of the public-house underneath my room, I could hear through the broken panes that a number of them still used the Gaelic, though it seems to be falling out of use among the younger people of this village.

The old woman of the house had promised to get me a teacher of the language, and after a while I heard a shuffling on the stairs, and the old dark man I had spoken to in the morning groped his way into the room.

I brought him over to the fire, and we talked for many hours. He told me that he had known Petrie and Sir William Wilde, and many living antiquarians, and had taught Irish to Dr. Finck, and Dr. Pedersen, and given stories to Mr. Curtin of America. A little after middle age he had fallen over a cliff, and since then he had had little eyesight, and a trembling of his hands and head.

As we talked he sat huddled together over the fire, shaking and blind, yet his face was indescribably pliant, lighting up with an ecstasy of humour when he told me of anything that had a point of wit or malice, and growing sombre and desolate again when he spoke of religion or the fairies.

He had great confidence in his own powers and talent, and in the superiority of his stories over all other stories in the world. When we were speaking of Mr. Curtin, he told me that this gentleman had brought out a volume of his Aran stories in America, and made five hundred pounds by the sale of them.

'And what do you think he did then?' he continued; 'he wrote a book of his own stories after making that lot of money with mine.

And he brought them out, and the divil a halfpenny did he get for them. Would you believe that?'

Afterwards he told me how one of his children had been taken by the fairies.

One day a neighbour was passing, and she said, when she saw it on the road, 'That's a fine child.'

Its mother tried to say 'God bless it,' but something choked the words in her throat.

A while later they found a wound on its neck, and for three nights the house was filled with noises.

'I never wear a shirt at night,' he said, 'but I got up out of bed, all naked as I was, when I heard the noises in the house, and lighted a light, but there was nothing in it.'

Then a dummy came and made signs of hammering nails in a coffin.

The next day the seed potatoes were full of blood, and the child told his mother that he was going to America.

That night it died, and 'Believe me,' said the old man, 'the fairies were in it.'

(When he went away, a little bare-footed girl was sent up with turf and the bellows to make a fire that would last for the evening.

She was shy, yet eager to talk, and told me that she had good spoken Irish, and was learning to read it in the school, and that she had been twice to Galway, though there are many grown women in the place who have never set a foot upon the mainland.)

The rain has cleared off, and I have had my first real introduction to the island and its people.

I went out through Killeany—the poorest village in Aranmor—to a long neck of sandhill that runs out into the sea towards the south-west. As I lay there on the grass the clouds lifted from the Connemara mountains and, for a moment, the green undulating foreground, backed in the distance by a mass of hills, reminded me of the country near Rome. Then the dun top-sail of a hooker swept above the edge of the sandhill and revealed the presence of the sea.

As I moved on a boy and a man came down from the next village to talk to me, and I found that here, at least, English was imperfectly understood. When I asked them if there were any trees in the island they held a hurried consultation in Gaelic, and then the man asked if 'tree' meant the same thing as 'bush', for if so there were a few in sheltered hollows to the east.

They walked on with me to the sound which separates this island from Inishmaan—the middle island of the group—and showed me the roll from the Atlantic running up between two walls of cliff.

They told me that several men had stayed on Inishmaan to learn Irish, and the boy pointed out a line of hovels where they had lodged running like a belt of straw round the middle of the island. The place looked hardly fit for habitation. There was no green to be seen, and no sign of the people except these beehive-like roofs, and the outline of a Dun that stood out above them against the edge of the sky.

(After a while my companions went away and two other boys came and walked at my heels, till I turned and made them talk to me. They spoke at first of their poverty, and then one of them said—

'I dare say you do have to pay ten shillings a week in the hotel?'

'More,' I answered.

'Twelve?'

'More.'

'Fifteen?'

'More still.'

Then he drew back and did not question me any further, either thinking that I had lied to check his curiosity, or too awed by my riches to continue.)

Repassing Killeany I was joined by a man who had spent twenty years in America, where he had lost his health and then returned, so long ago that he had forgotten English and could hardly make me understand him. He seemed hopeless, dirty, and asthmatic, and after going with me for a few hundred yards he stopped and asked for coppers. I had none left, so I gave him a fill of tobacco, and he went back to his hovel.

When he was gone, two little girls took their place behind me and I drew them in turn into conversation.

They spoke with a delicate exotic intonation that was full of charm, and told me with a sort of chant how they guide 'ladies and gintlemins' in the summer to all that is worth seeing in their neighbourhood, and sell them pampooties and maidenhair ferns, which are common among the rocks.

We were now in Kilronan, and as we parted they showed me holes in their own pampooties, or cowskin sandals, and asked me the price of new ones. I told them that my purse was empty, and then with a few quaint words of blessing they turned away from me and went down to the pier.

All this walk back had been extraordinarily fine. The intense insular clearness one sees only in Ireland, and after rain, was throwing out every ripple in the sea and sky, and every crevice in the hills beyond the bay.

This evening an old man came to see me, and said he had known a relative of mine who passed some time on this island forty-three years ago.[1]

'I was standing under the pier-wall mending nets,' he said, 'when you came off the steamer, and I said to myself in that moment, if there is a man of the name of Synge left walking the world, it is that man yonder will be he.'

He went on to complain in curiously simple yet dignified language of the changes that have taken place here since he left the island to go to sea before the end of his childhood.

'I have come back,' he said, 'to live in a bit of a house with my sister. The island is not the same at all to what it was. It is little good I can get from the people who are in it now, and anything I have to give them they don't care to have.'

From what I hear this man seems to have shut himself up in a world of individual conceits and theories, and to live aloof at his trade of net-mending, regarded by the other islanders with respect and half-ironical sympathy.

A little later when I went down to the kitchen I found two men from Inishmaan who had been benighted on the island. They seemed a simpler and perhaps a more interesting type than the people here, and talked with careful English about the history of the Duns, and the Book of Ballymote, and the Book of Kells, and other ancient MSS., with the names of which they seemed familiar.

In spite of the charm of my teacher, the old blind man I met the day of my arrival, I have decided to move on to Inishmaan, where Gaelic is more generally used, and the life is perhaps the most primitive that is left in Europe.

[1] Synge's uncle, the Reverend Alexander Synge, had been a missionary on the islands. See the account in Greene and Stephens, *J. M. Synge*, pp. 75–76.

I spent all this last day with my blind guide, looking at the antiquities that abound in the west or north-west of the island.

As we set out I noticed among the groups of girls who smiled at our fellowship—old Mourteen says we are like the cuckoo with its pipit—a beautiful oval face with the singularly spiritual expression that is so marked in one type of the West Ireland women. Later in the day, as the old man talked continually of the fairies and the women they have taken, it seemed that there was a possible link between the wild mythology that is accepted on the islands and the strange beauty of the women.[1]

At midday we rested near the ruins of a house, and two beautiful boys came up and sat near us. Old Mourteen asked them why the house was in ruins, and who had lived in it.

'A rich farmer built it a while since,' they said, 'but after two years he was driven away by the fairy host.'

The boys came on with us some distance to the north to visit one of the ancient beehive dwellings that is still in perfect preservation. When we crawled in on our hands and knees, and stood up in the

[1] Synge commented upon the Aran women further, as is shown by these passages brought together from various parts of Notebook 19:

'The coming out of the steamer from Galway is marked by much movement on the pier. I recall Petrie's words that the clothing of the Irish peasant . . . has rich positive tints with nothing gaudy. The peasants have a further intuition for picturesque arrangement and each group is in perfect pose for my camera. I have noticed many beautiful girls whose long luxuriant lashes lend a shade to wistful eyes. They are amused to watch while I work my camera and observe keenly on whom I happen to light. What a joy has been [lost] by the condition of our poor [on the mainland] whose grey miserable life has struck all colour from their clothes. Rich women give colour yet suggest rather butterflies . . . or the tawdry rags tied by children to the May bush than the fruit of natural growth. I looked lately through a batch of photos taken in the islands, where the collector had planted his friends among the ruins and marred their beauty. A peasant if conspicuously clothed lends a life to his surroundings. I have never seen a finer raiment than on these islands. The dull red of the petticoats especially if surmounted by a deep blue shawl is more quietly fair than any peasant costume I have met in Europe. . . . What has guided the women of grey-brown western Ireland to clothe them in red? The island without this simple red relief would be a nightmare fit to drive one to murder in order to gloat a while on the fresh red flow of blood. . . . The tints of the men are less marked yet their flannel shirts and the piquant colour and [shape] of their tam-o-shanters and pampooties . . . harmonize with the limestone and the blue-grey . . . All the unoccupied women have thrown their shawls or petticoats over their heads and come down to sit in beautiful groups along the sea-wall and watch what goes on. Excitement is added by the arrival of the Indian meal sent as relief, and the Irish runs round me faster than I can understand. . . . I am so much a stranger I cannot dare under the attention I excite to gaze as I would wish at a beautiful oval face that looks from a brown shawl near me. . . . [Later] as I wandered with Martin Conneelly my blind guide . . . I saw suddenly the beautiful girl I had noticed on the pier, and her face came with me all day among the rocks. She is madonna-like, yet has a rapt majesty as far from easy exaltation as from the maternal comeliness of Raphael's later style. . . . The expression of her eyes is so overwhelmingly beautiful that I remember no single quality of her colour.'

THE PIER

gloom of the interior, old Mourteen took a freak of earthy humour and began telling what he would have done if he could have come in there when he was a young man and a young girl along with him.

Then he sat down in the middle of the floor and began to recite old Irish poetry, with an exquisite purity of intonation that brought tears to my eyes though I understood but little of the meaning.

On our way home he gave me the Catholic theory of the fairies.

When Lucifer saw himself in the glass he thought himself equal with God. Then the Lord threw him out of Heaven, and all the angels that belonged to him. While He was 'chucking them out,' an archangel asked Him to spare some of them, and those that were falling are in the air still, and have power to wreck ships, and to work evil in the world.

From this he wandered off into tedious matters of theology, and repeated many long prayers and sermons in Irish that he had heard from the priests.

A little further on we came to a slated house, and I asked him who was living in it.

'A kind of schoolmistress,' he said; then his old face puckered with a gleam of pagan malice.

'Ah, master,' he said, 'wouldn't it be fine to be in there, and to be kissing her?'

A couple of miles from this village we turned aside to look at an old ruined church of the Ceathair Aluinn (The Four Beautiful Persons), and a holy well near it that is famous for cures of blindness and epilepsy.

As we sat near the well a very old man came up from a cottage near the road, and told me how it had become famous.

'A woman of Sligo had a son who was born blind, and one night she dreamed that she saw an island with a blessed well in it that could cure her son. She told her dream in the morning, and an old man said it was of Aran she was after dreaming.

'She brought her son down by the coast of Galway, and came out in a curagh, and landed below where you see a bit of a cove.

'She walked up then to the house of my father—God rest his soul—and she told them what she was looking for.

'My father said that there was a well like what she had dreamed of, and that he would send a boy along with her to show her the way.

'"There 's no need, at all," said she; "haven't I seen it all in my dream?"

'Then she went out with the child and walked up to this well, and she kneeled down and began saying her prayers. Then she put her hand out for the water, and put it on his eyes, and the moment it touched him he called out: "O mother, look at the pretty flowers!"'

After that Mourteen described the feats of poteen drinking and fighting that he did in his youth, and went on to talk of Diarmid, who was the strongest man after Samson, and of one of the beds of Diarmid and Grainne, which is on the east of the island. He says that Diarmid was killed by the druids, who put a burning shirt on him,—a fragment of mythology that may connect Diarmid with the legend of Hercules, if it is not due to the 'learning' in some hedge-school master's ballad.

Then we talked about Inishmaan.

'You'll have an old man to talk with you over there,' he said, 'and tell you stories of the fairies, but he's walking about with two sticks under him this ten year. Did ever you hear what it is goes on four legs when it is young, and on two legs after that, and on three legs when it does be old?'

I gave him the answer.

'Ah, master,' he said, 'you're a cute one, and the blessing of God be on you. Well, I'm on three legs this minute, but the old man beyond is back on four; I don't know if I'm better than the way he is; he's got his sight and I'm only an old dark man.'

I am settled at last on Inishmaan in a small cottage with a continual drone of Gaelic coming from the kitchen that opens into my room.

Early this morning the man of the house came over for me with a four-oared curagh—that is, a curagh with four rowers and four oars on either side, as each man uses two—and we set off a little before noon.

It gave me a moment of exquisite satisfaction to find myself moving away from civilisation in this rude canvas canoe of a model that has served primitive races since men first went on the sea.

We had to stop for a moment at a hulk that is anchored in the bay, to make some arrangements for the fish-curing of the middle island, and my crew called out as soon as we were within earshot that they had a man with them who had been in France a month from this day.

When we started again, a small sail was run up in the bow, and we set off across the sound with a leaping oscillation that had no resemblance to the heavy movement of a boat.

The sail is only used as an aid, so the men continued to row after it had gone up, and as they occupied the four cross seats I lay on the canvas at the stern and the frame of slender laths, which bent and quivered as the waves passed under them.

When we set off it was a brilliant morning of April, and the green, glittering waves seemed to toss the canoe among themselves, yet as we drew nearer this island a sudden thunderstorm broke out behind the rocks we were approaching, and lent a momentary tumult to this still vein of the Atlantic.

We landed at a small pier, from which a rude track leads up to the village between small fields and bare sheets of rock like those in Aranmor. The youngest son of my boatman, a boy of about seventeen, who is to be my teacher and guide, was waiting for me at the pier and guided me to his house, while the men settled the curagh and followed slowly with my baggage.

My room is at one end of the cottage, with a boarded floor and ceiling, and two windows opposite each other. Then there is the kitchen with earth floor and open rafters, and two doors opposite each other opening into the open air, but no windows. Beyond it there are two small rooms of half the width of the kitchen with one window apiece.

The kitchen itself, where I will spend most of my time, is full of beauty and distinction. The red dresses of the women who cluster round the fire on their stools give a glow of almost Eastern richness, and the walls have been toned by the turf-smoke to a soft brown that blends with the grey earth-colour of the floor. Many sorts of fishing-tackle, and the nets and oil-skins of the men, are hung upon the walls or among the open rafters; and right overhead, under the thatch, there is a whole cowskin from which they make pampooties.

Every article on these islands has an almost personal character, which gives this simple life, where all art is unknown, something of the artistic beauty of mediæval life. The curaghs and spinning-wheels, the tiny wooden barrels that are still much used in the place of earthenware, the home-made cradles, churns, and baskets, are all full of individuality, and being made from materials that are common here, yet to some extent peculiar to the island, they seem to exist as a natural link between the people and the world that is about them.

The simplicity and unity of the dress increases in another way the local air of beauty. The women wear red petticoats and jackets of the island wool stained with madder, to which they usually add a plaid shawl twisted round their chests and tied at the back. When it rains they throw another petticoat over their heads with the waistband round their faces, or, if they are young, they use a heavy shawl like those worn in Galway. Occasionally other wraps are worn, and during the thunderstorm I arrived in I saw several girls with men's waistcoats buttoned round their bodies. Their skirts do not come much below the knee and show their powerful legs in the heavy indigo stockings with which they are all provided.

The men wear three colours: the natural wool, indigo, and a grey flannel that is woven of alternate threads of indigo and the natural wool. In Aranmor many of the younger men have adopted the usual fisherman's jersey, but I have only seen one on this island.

As flannel is cheap—the women spin the yarn from the wool of their own sheep, and it is then woven by a weaver in Kilronan for fourpence a yard—the men seem to wear an indefinite number of waistcoats and woollen drawers one over the other. They are usually surprised at the lightness of my own dress, and one old man I spoke to for a minute on the pier, when I came ashore, asked me if I was not cold with 'my little clothes.'

As I sat in the kitchen to dry the spray from my coat, several men who had seen me walking up came in to talk to me, usually murmuring on the threshold, 'The blessing of God on this place,' or some similar words.

The courtesy of the old woman of the house is singularly attractive, and though I could not understand much of what she said—she has no English—I could see with how much grace she motioned each visitor to a chair, or stool, according to his age, and said a few words to him till he drifted into our English conversation.

For the moment my own arrival is the chief subject of interest, and the men who come in are eager to talk to me.

Some of them express themselves more correctly than the ordinary peasant, others use the Gaelic idioms continually and substitute 'he' or 'she' for 'it', as the neuter pronoun is not found in modern Irish.

A few of the men have a curiously full vocabulary, others know only the commonest words in English, and are driven to ingenious devices to express their meaning. Of all the subjects we can talk of war seems their favourite, and the conflict between America and Spain is causing a great deal of excitement. Nearly all the families have relations who have had to cross the Atlantic, and all eat the flour and bacon that is brought from the United States, so they have a vague fear that 'if anything happened to America,' their own island would cease to be habitable.

Foreign languages are another favourite topic, and as these men are bilingual they have a fair notion of what it means to speak and think in many different idioms. Most of the strangers they see on the islands are philological students, and the people have been led to conclude that linguistic studies, particularly Gaelic studies, are the chief occupation of the outside world.

'I have seen Frenchmen, and Danes, and Germans,' said one man, 'and there does be a power of Irish books along with them, and they reading them better than ourselves. Believe me there are few rich men now in the world who are not studying the Gaelic.'

They sometimes ask me the French for simple phrases, and when they have listened to the intonation for a moment, most of them are able to reproduce it with admirable precision.

When I was going out this morning to walk round the island with Michael, the boy who is teaching me Irish, I met an old man making his way down to the cottage. He was dressed in miserable black clothes which seemed to have come from the mainland, and was so bent with rheumatism that, at a little distance, he looked more like a spider than a human being.

Michael told me it was Pat Dirane,[1] the story-teller old Mourteen had spoken of on the other island. I wished to turn back, as he appeared to be on his way to visit me, but Michael would not hear of it.

[1] Apparently his actual name. As he died in 1899 Synge probably felt no need to disguise his identity. See pp. 47–48.

'He will be sitting by the fire when we come in,' he said; 'let you not be afraid, there will be time enough to be talking to him by and by.'

He was right. As I came down into the kitchen some hours later old Pat was still in the chimney-corner, blinking with the turf smoke.

He spoke English with remarkable aptness and fluency, due, I believe, to the months he spent in the English provinces working at the harvest when he was a young man.

After a few formal compliments he told me how he had been crippled by an attack of the 'old hin' (i.e. the influenza), and had been complaining ever since in addition to his rheumatism.

While the old woman was cooking my dinner he asked me if I liked stories, and offered to tell one in English, though he added, it would be much better if I could follow the Gaelic. Then he began:—

There were two farmers in County Clare. One had a son, and the other, a fine rich man, had a daughter.

The young man was wishing to marry the girl, and his father told him to try and get her if he thought well, though a power of gold would be wanting to get the like of her.

'I will try,' said the young man.

He put all his gold into a bag. Then he went over to the other farm, and threw in the gold in front of him.

'Is that all gold?' said the father of the girl.

'All gold,' said O'Conor (the young man's name was O'Conor).

'It will not weigh down my daughter,' said the father.

'We'll see that,' said O'Conor.

Then they put them in the scales, the daughter in one side and the gold in the other. The girl went down against the ground, so O'Conor took his bag and went out on the road.

As he was going along he came to where there was a little man, and he standing with his back against the wall.

'Where are you going with the bag?' said the little man.

'Going home,' said O'Conor.

'Is it gold you might be wanting?' said the man.

'It is surely,' said O'Conor.

'I'll give you what you are wanting,' said the man, 'and we can bargain in this way—you'll pay me back in a year the gold I give you, or you'll pay me with five pounds cut off your own flesh.'

That bargain was made between them. The man gave a bag of gold to O'Conor, and he went back with it, and was married to the young woman.

They were rich people, and he built her a grand castle on the cliffs of Clare, with a window that looked out straightly over the wild ocean.

One day when he went up with his wife to look out over the wild ocean, he saw a ship coming in on the rocks, and no sails on her at all. She was wrecked on the rocks, and it was tea that was in her, and fine silk.

O'Conor and his wife went down to look at the wreck, and when the lady O'Conor saw the silk she said she wished a dress of it.

They got the silk from the sailors, and when the Captain came up to get the money for it, O'Conor asked him to come again and take his dinner with them. They had a grand dinner, and they drank after it, and the Captain was tipsy. While they were still drinking a letter came to O'Conor, and it was in the letter that a friend of his was dead, and that he would have to go away on a long journey. As he was getting ready the Captain came to him.

'Are you fond of your wife?' said the Captain.

'I am fond of her,' said O'Conor.

'Will you make me a bet of twenty guineas no man comes near her while you'll be away on the journey?' said the Captain.

'I will bet it,' said O'Conor; and he went away.

There was an old hag who sold small things on the road near the castle, and the lady O'Conor allowed her to sleep up in her room in a big box. The Captain went down on the road to the old hag.

'For how much will you let me sleep one night in your box?' said the Captain.

'For no money at all would I do such a thing,' said the hag.

'For ten guineas?' said the Captain.

'Not for ten guineas,' said the hag.

'For twelve guineas?' said the Captain.

'Not for twelve guineas,' said the hag.

'For fifteen guineas,' said the Captain.

'For fifteen I will do it,' said the hag.

Then she took him up and hid him in the box. When night came the lady O'Conor walked up into her room, and the Captain watched her through a hole that was in the box. He saw her take off her two rings and put them on a kind of board that was over her head like a chimney-piece, and take off her clothes, except her shift, and go up into her bed.

As soon as she was asleep the Captain came out of his box, and he had some means of making a light, for he lit the candle. He went over to the bed where she was sleeping without disturbing her at all, or doing any bad thing, and he took the two rings off the board, and blew out the light, and went down again into the box.

He paused for a moment, and a deep sigh of relief rose from the men and women who had crowded in while the story was going on, till the kitchen was filled with people.

As the Captain was coming out of his box the girls, who had appeared to know no English, stopped their spinning and held their breath with expectation.

The old man went on—

When O'Conor came back the Captain met him, and told him that he had been a night in his wife's room, and gave him the two rings.

O'Conor gave him the twenty guineas of the bet. Then he went up into the castle, and he took his wife up to look out of the window over the wild ocean. While she was looking he pushed her from behind, and she fell down over the cliff into the sea.

An old woman was on the shore, and she saw her falling. She went down then to the surf and pulled her out all wet and in great disorder, and she took the wet clothes off of her, and put on some old rags belonging to herself.

When O'Conor had pushed his wife from the window he went away into the land.

After a while the lady O'Conor went out searching for him, and when she had gone here and there a long time in the country, she heard that he was reaping in a field with sixty men.

She came to the field and she wanted to go in, but the gate-man would not open the gate for her. Then the owner came by, and she told him her story. He brought her in, and her husband was there, reaping, but he never gave any sign of knowing her. She showed him to the owner, and he made the man come out and go with his wife.

Then the lady O'Conor took him out on the road where there were horses, and they rode away.

When they came to the place where O'Conor had met the little man, he was there on the road before them.

'Have you my gold on you?' said the man.

'I have not,' said O'Conor.

'Then you'll pay me the flesh off your body,' said the man.

They went into a house, and a knife was brought, and a clean white cloth was put on the table, and O'Conor was put upon the cloth.

Then the little man was going to strike the lancet into him, when says lady O'Conor—

'Have you bargained for five pounds of flesh?'

'For five pounds of flesh,' said the man.

'Have you bargained for any drop of his blood?' said lady O'Conor.

'For no blood,' said the man.

'Cut out the flesh,' said lady O'Conor, 'but if you spill one drop of his blood I'll put that through you.' And she put a pistol to his head.

The little man went away and they saw no more of him.

When they got home to their castle they made a great supper, and they invited the Captain and the old hag, and the old woman that had pulled the lady O'Conor out of the sea.

After they had eaten well the lady O'Conor began, and she said they would all tell their stories. Then she told how she had been saved from the sea, and how she had found her husband.

Then the old woman told her story, the way she had found the lady O'Conor wet, and in great disorder, and had brought her in and put on her some old rags of her own.

The lady O'Conor asked the Captain for his story, but he said they would get no story from him. Then she took her pistol out of her pocket, and she put it on the edge of the table, and she said that any one that would not tell his story would get a bullet into him.

Then the Captain told the way he had got into the box, and come over to her bed without touching her at all, and had taken away the rings.

Then the lady O'Conor took the pistol and shot the hag through the body, and they threw her over the cliff into the sea.

That is my story.

It gave me a strange feeling of wonder to hear this illiterate native of a wet rock in the Atlantic telling a story that is so full of European associations.

The incident of the faithful wife takes us beyond Cymbeline to the sunshine on the Arno, and the gay company who went out from Florence to tell narratives of love. It takes us again to the low vineyards of Würzburg on the Main, where the same tale was told in the middle ages, of the 'Two Merchants and the Faithful Wife of Ruprecht von Würzburg.'

The other portion dealing with the pound of flesh, has a still wider distribution, reaching from Persia and Egypt to the *Gesta Romanorum*, and the *Pecorone* of Ser Giovanni, a Florentine notary.

The present union of the two tales has already been found among the Gaels, and there is a somewhat similar version in Campbell's *Popular Tales of the Western Highlands*.[1]

Michael walks so fast when I am out with him that I cannot pick my steps, and the sharp-edged fossils which abound in the limestone have cut my shoes to pieces.

The family held a consultation on them last night, and in the end it was decided to make me a pair of pampooties, which I have been wearing to-day among the rocks.

They consist simply of a piece of raw cowskin, with the hair outside, laced over the toe and round the heel with two ends of fishing-line that work round and are tied above the instep.

In the evening, when they are taken off, they are placed in a basin of water, as the rough hide cuts the foot and stocking if it is allowed to harden. For the same reason the people often step into the surf during the day, so that their feet are continually moist.

At first I threw my weight upon my heels, as one does naturally in a boot, and was a good deal bruised, but after a few hours I learned the natural walk of man, and could follow my guide in any portion of the island.

In one district below the cliffs, towards the north, one goes for

[1] This story was originally published as 'A Story from Inishmaan' in *The New Ireland Review*, November 1898. Synge revised it for his book. The original story ended with this passage: 'It is hard to assert at what date such stories as these reached the west. There is little doubt that our heroic tales which show so often their kinship with Grecian myths, date from the pre-ethnic period of the Aryans, and it is easy to believe that some purely secular narratives share their antiquity. Further, a comparison of all the versions will show that we have here one of the rudest and therefore, it may be, most ancient settings of the material.'

nearly a mile jumping from one rock to another without a single ordinary step; and here I realised that toes have a natural use, for I found myself jumping towards any tiny crevice in the rock before me, and clinging with an eager grip in which all the muscles of my feet ached from their exertion.

The absence of the heavy boot of Europe has preserved to these people the agile walk of the wild animal, while the general simplicity of their lives has given them many other points of physical perfection. Their way of life has never been acted on by anything much more artificial than the nests and burrows of the creatures that live round them, and they seem in a certain sense to approach more nearly to the finer types of our aristocracies—who are bred artificially to a natural ideal—than to the labourer or citizen, as the wild horse resembles the thoroughbred rather than the hack or cart-horse. Tribes of the same natural development are, perhaps, frequent in half-civilised countries, but here a touch of the refinement of old societies is blended, with singular effect, among the qualities of the wild animal.

While I am walking with Michael some one often comes to me to ask the time of day. Few of the people, however, are sufficiently used to modern time to understand in more than a vague way the convention of the hours, and when I tell them what o'clock it is by my watch they are not satisfied, and ask how long is left them before the twilight.

The general knowledge of time on the island depends, curiously enough, on the direction of the wind. Nearly all the cottages are built, like this one, with two doors opposite each other, the more sheltered of which lies open all day to give light to the interior. If the wind is northerly the south door is opened, and the shadow of the door-post moving across the kitchen floor indicates the hour; as soon, however, as the wind changes to the south the other door is opened, and the people, who never think of putting up a primitive dial, are at a loss.

This system of doorways has another curious result. It usually happens that all the doors on one side of the village pathway are lying open with women sitting about on the thresholds, while on the other side the doors are shut and there is no sign of life. The moment the wind changes everything is reversed, and sometimes when I come back to the village after an hour's walk there seems to have been a general flight from one side of the way to the other.

In my own cottage the change of the doors alters the whole tone of the kitchen, turning it from a brilliantly-lighted room looking out on a yard and laneway to a sombre cell with a superb view of the sea.

When the wind is from the north the old woman manages my meals with fair regularity, but on the other days she often makes my tea at three o'clock instead of six. If I refuse it she puts it down to simmer for three hours in the turf, and then brings it in at six o'clock full of anxiety to know if it is warm enough.

The old man is suggesting that I should send him a clock when I go away. He'd like to have something from me in the house, he says, the way they wouldn't forget me, and wouldn't a clock be as handy as another thing, and they'd be thinking on me whenever they'd look on its face.

The general ignorance of any precise hours in the day makes it impossible for the people to have regular meals.

They seem to eat together in the evening, and sometimes in the morning, a little after dawn, before they scatter for their work, but during the day they simply drink a cup of tea and eat a piece of bread, or some potatoes, whenever they are hungry.

For men who live in the open air they eat strangely little. Often when Michael has been out weeding potatoes for eight or nine hours without food, he comes in and eats a few slices of home-made bread, and then he is ready to go out with me and wander for hours about the island.

They use no animal food except a little bacon and salt fish. The old woman says she would be very ill if she ate fresh meat.

Some years ago, before tea, sugar, and flour had come into general use, salt fish was much more the staple article of diet than at present, and, I am told, skin diseases were very common, though they are now rare on the islands.

No one who has not lived for weeks among these grey clouds and seas can realise the joy with which the eye rests on the red dresses of the women, especially when a number of them are to be found together, as happened early this morning.

I heard that the young cattle were to be shipped for a fair on the mainland, which is to take place in a few days, and I went down on the pier, a little after dawn, to watch them.

The bay was shrouded in the greys of coming rain, yet the thinness of the cloud threw a silvery light on the sea, and an unusual depth of blue to the mountains of Connemara.

As I was going across the sandhills one dun-sailed hooker glided slowly out to begin her voyage, and another beat up to the pier. Troops of red cattle, driven mostly by the women, were coming up from several directions, forming, with the green of the long tract of grass that separates the sea from the rocks, a new unity of colour.

The pier itself was crowded with bullocks and a great number of the people. I noticed one extraordinary girl in the throng who seemed to exert an authority on all who came near her. Her curiously formed nostrils and narrow chin gave her a witch-like expression, yet the beauty of her hair and skin made her singularly attractive.[1]

When the empty hooker was made fast its deck was still many feet below the level of the pier, so the animals were slung down by a rope from the mast-head, with much struggling and confusion. Some of them made wild efforts to escape, nearly carrying their owners with them into the sea, but they were handled with wonderful dexterity, and there was no mishap.

When the open hold was filled with young cattle, packed as tightly as they could stand, the owners with their wives or sisters, who go with them to prevent extravagance in Galway, jumped down on the deck, and the voyage was begun. Immediately afterwards a rickety old hooker beat up with turf from Connemara, and while she was unlading all the men sat along the edge of the pier and made remarks upon the rottenness of her timber till the owners grew wild with rage.

The tide was now too low for more boats to come to the pier, so a move was made to a strip of sand towards the south-east, where the rest of the cattle were shipped through the surf. Here the hooker was anchored about eighty yards from the shore, and a curagh was rowed round to tow out the animals. Each bullock was caught in its turn and girded with a sling of rope by which it could be hoisted on board. Another rope was fastened to the horns and passed out to a man in the stern of the curagh. Then the animal was forced down through the surf and out of its depth

[1] In Notebook 19 Synge says she was like 'the conventional figure of Becky Sharp', and adds, 'she must have before her a very terrible old age'.

before it had time to struggle. Once fairly swimming, it was towed out to the hooker and dragged on board in a half-drowned condition.

The freedom of the sand seemed to give a stronger spirit of revolt, and some of the animals were only caught after a dangerous struggle. The first attempt was not always successful, and I saw one three-year-old lift two men with his horns, and drag another fifty yards along the sand by his tail before he was subdued.

While this work was going on a crowd of girls and women collected on the edge of the cliff and kept shouting down a confused babble of satire and praise.

When I came back to the cottage I found that among the women who had gone to the mainland was a daughter of the old woman's, and that her baby of about nine months had been left in the care of its grandmother.

As I came in she was busy getting ready my dinner, and old Pat Dirane, who usually comes at this hour, was rocking the cradle. It is made of clumsy wicker-work, with two pieces of rough wood fastened underneath to serve as rockers, and all the time I am in my room I can hear it bumping on the floor with extraordinary violence. When the baby is awake it sprawls on the floor, and the old woman sings it a variety of inarticulate lullabies that have much musical charm.

Another daughter, who lives at home, has gone to the fair also, so the old woman has both the baby and myself to take care of as well as a crowd of chickens that live in a hole beside the fire. Often when I want tea, or when the old woman goes for water, I have to take my own turn at rocking the cradle.

One of the largest Duns, or pagan forts, on the islands, is within a stone's-throw of my cottage, and I often stroll up there after a dinner of eggs or salt pork, to smoke drowsily on the stones. The neighbours know my habit, and not infrequently some one wanders up to ask what news there is in the last paper I have received, or to make inquiries about the American war. If no one comes I prop my book open with stones touched by the Fir-bolgs, and sleep for hours in the delicious warmth of the sun. The last few days I have almost lived on the round walls, for, by some miscalculation, our turf has come to an end, and the fires are kept up with dried cow-dung—a common fuel on the island—the smoke from which filters through into my room and lies in blue layers above my table and bed.

Fortunately the weather is fine, and I can spend my days in the sunshine. When I look round from the top of these walls I can see the sea on nearly every side, stretching away to distant ranges of mountains on the north and south. Underneath me to the east there is the one inhabited district of the island, where I can see red figures moving about the cottages, sending up an occasional fragment of conversation or of the old island melodies.

The baby is teething, and has been crying for several days. Since his mother went to the fair they have been feeding him with cow's milk, often slightly sour, and giving him, I think, more than he requires.

This morning, however, he seemed so unwell they sent out to look for a foster-mother in the village, and before long a young woman, who lives a little way to the east, came in and restored him his natural food.

A few hours later, when I came into the kitchen to talk to old Pat, another woman performed the same kindly office, this time a person with a curiously whimsical expression.

Pat told me a story of an unfaithful wife, which I will give further down, and then broke into a moral dispute with the visitor, which caused immense delight to some young men who had come down to listen to the story. Unfortunately it was carried on so rapidly in Gaelic that I lost most of the points.

This old man talks usually in a mournful tone about his ill-health, and his death, which he feels to be approaching, yet he has occasional touches of humour that remind me of old Mourteen on the north island. To-day a grotesque twopenny doll was lying on the floor near the old woman. He picked it up and examined it as if comparing it with her. Then he held it up: 'Is it you is after bringing that thing into the world,' he said, 'woman of the house?'

Here is his story:—

One day I was travelling on foot from Galway to Dublin, and the darkness came on me and I ten miles from the town I was wanting to pass the night in. Then a hard rain began to fall and I was tired walking, so when I saw a sort of house with no roof on it up against the road, I got in the way the walls would give me shelter.

As I was looking round I saw a light in some trees two perches off, and thinking any sort of a house would be better than where I was, I got over a wall and went up to the house to look in at the window.

I saw a dead man laid on a table, and candles lighted, and a woman watching him. I was frightened when I saw him, but it was raining hard, and I said to myself, if he was dead he couldn't hurt me. Then I knocked on the door and the woman came and opened it.

'Good evening, ma'am,' says I.

'Good evening kindly, stranger,' says she. 'Come in out of the rain.'

Then she took me in and told me her husband was after dying on her, and she was watching him that night.

'But it's thirsty you'll be, stranger,' says she. 'Come into the parlour.'

Then she took me into the parlour—and it was a fine clean house—and she put a cup, with a saucer under it, on the table before me with fine sugar and bread.

When I'd had a cup of tea I went back into the kitchen where the dead man was lying, and she gave me a fine new pipe off the table with a drop of spirits.

'Stranger,' says she, 'would you be afeard to be alone with himself?'

'Not a bit in the world, ma'am,' says I; 'he that's dead can do no hurt.'

Then she said she wanted to go over and tell the neighbours the way her husband was after dying on her, and she went out and locked the door behind her.

I smoked one pipe, and I leaned out and took another off the table. I was smoking it with my hand on the back of my chair—the way you are yourself this minute, God bless you—and I looking on the dead man, when he opened his eyes as wide as myself and looked at me.

'Don't be afeard, stranger,' said the dead man; 'I'm not dead at all in the world. Come here and help me up and I'll tell you all about it.'

Well, I went up and took the sheet off of him, and I saw that he had a fine clean shirt on his body, and fine flannel drawers.

He sat up then, and says he—

'I've got a bad wife, stranger, and I let on to be dead the way I'd catch her goings on.'

Then he got two fine sticks he had to keep down his wife, and he put them at each side of his body, and he laid himself out again as if he was dead.

In half an hour his wife came back and a young man along with her. Well, she gave him his tea, and she told him he was tired, and he would do right to go and lie down in the bedroom.

The young man went in and the woman sat down to watch by the dead man. A while after she got up and 'Stranger,' says she, 'I'm going in to get the candle out of the room; I'm thinking the young man will be asleep by this time.' She went into the bedroom, but the divil a bit of her came back.

Then the dead man got up, and he took one stick, and he gave the other to myself. We went in and we saw them lying together with her head on his arm.

The dead man hit him a blow with the stick so that the blood out of him leapt up and hit the gallery.

That is my story.

In stories of this kind he always speaks in the first person, with minute details to show that he was actually present at the scenes that are described.

At the beginning of this story he gave me a long account of what had made him be on his way to Dublin on that occasion, and told me about all the rich people he was going to see in the finest streets of the city.

A week of sweeping fogs has passed over and given me a strange sense of exile and desolation. I walk round the island nearly every day, yet I can see nothing anywhere but a mass of wet rock, a strip of surf, and then a tumult of waves.

The slaty limestone has grown black with the water that is dripping on it, and wherever I turn there is the same grey obsession twining and wreathing itself among the narrow fields, and the same wail from the wind that shrieks and whistles in the loose rubble of the walls.

At first the people do not give much attention to the wilderness that is round them, but after a few days their voices sink in the kitchen, and their endless talk of pigs and cattle falls to the whisper of men who are telling stories in a haunted house.

The rain continues; but this evening a number of young men were in the kitchen mending nets, and the bottle of poteen was drawn from its hiding-place.

One cannot think of these people drinking wine on the summit of this crumbling precipice, but their grey poteen, which brings a shock of joy to the blood, seems predestined to keep sanity in men who live forgotten in these worlds of mist.

I sat in the kitchen part of the evening to feel the gaiety that was rising, and when I came into my own room after dark, one of the sons came in every time the bottle made its round, to pour me out my share.

It has cleared, and the sun is shining with a luminous warmth that makes the whole island glisten with the splendour of a gem, and fills the sea and sky with a radiance of blue light.

I have come out to lie on the rocks where I have the black edge of the north island in front of me, Galway Bay, too blue almost to look at, on my right, the Atlantic on my left, a perpendicular cliff under my ankles, and over me innumerable gulls that chase each other in a white cirrus of wings.

A nest of hooded crows is somewhere near me, and one of the old birds is trying to drive me away by letting itself fall like a stone every few moments, from about forty yards above me to within reach of my hand.

Gannets are passing up and down above the sound, swooping at times after a mackerel, and further off I can see the whole fleet of hookers coming out from Kilronan for a night's fishing in the deep water to the west.

As I lie here hour after hour, I seem to enter into the wild pastimes of the cliff, and to become a companion of the cormorants and crows.

Many of the birds display themselves before me with the vanity of barbarians, forming in strange evolutions as long as I am in sight, and returning to their ledge of rock when I am gone. Some are wonderfully expert, and cut graceful figures for an inconceivable time without a flap of their wings, growing so absorbed in their own dexterity that they often collide with one another in their flight, an incident always followed by a wild outburst of abuse. Their language is easier than Gaelic, and I seem to understand the greater part of their cries, though I am not able to answer. There is one plaintive note which they take up in the middle of their usual babble with extraordinary effect, and pass on from one to another along the cliff with a sort of an inarticulate wail, as if they remembered for an instant the horror of the mist.

On the low sheets of rock to the east I can see a number of red and grey figures hurrying about their work. The continual passing in this island between the misery of last night and the splendour of to-day, seems to create an affinity between the moods of these people and the moods of varying rapture and dismay that are frequent in artists, and in certain forms of alienation. Yet it is only in the intonation of a few sentences or some old fragment of melody that I catch the real spirit of the island, for in general the men sit together and talk with endless iteration of the tides and fish, and of the price of kelp in Connemara.

After Mass this morning an old woman was buried. She lived in the cottage next mine, and more than once before noon I heard a faint echo of the keen. I did not go to the wake for fear my presence might jar upon the mourners, but all last evening I could hear the strokes of a hammer in the yard, where, in the middle of a little crowd of idlers, the next of kin laboured slowly at the coffin. To-day, before the hour for the funeral, poteen was served to a number of men who stood about upon the road, and a portion was brought to me in my room. Then the coffin was carried out sewn loosely in sailcloth, and held near the ground by three cross-poles lashed upon the top. As we moved down to the low eastern portion of the island, nearly all the men, and all the oldest women, wearing petticoats over their heads, came out and joined in the procession.

While the grave was being opened the women sat down among the flat tombstones, bordered with a pale fringe of early bracken, and began the wild keen, or crying for the dead. Each old woman, as she took her turn in the leading recitative, seemed possessed for the moment with a profound ecstasy of grief, swaying to and fro, and bending her forehead to the stone before her, while she called out to the dead with a perpetually recurring chant of sobs.

All round the graveyard other wrinkled women, looking out from under the deep red petticoats that cloaked them, rocked themselves with the same rhythm, and intoned the inarticulate chant that is sustained by all as an accompaniment.

The morning had been beautifully fine, but as they lowered the coffin into the grave, thunder rumbled overhead and hailstones hissed among the bracken.

In Inishmaan one is forced to believe in a sympathy between man and nature, and at this moment when the thunder sounded a death-peal of extraordinary grandeur above the voices of the women, I could see the faces near me stiff and drawn with emotion.[1]

When the coffin was in the grave, and the thunder had rolled away across the hills of Clare, the keen broke out again more passionately than before.

This grief of the keen is no personal complaint for the death of one woman over eighty years, but seems to contain the whole passionate rage that lurks somewhere in every native of the island. In this cry of pain the inner consciousness of the people seems to lay itself bare for an instant, and to reveal the mood of beings who feel their isolation in the face of a universe that wars on them with winds and seas. They are usually silent, but in the presence of death all outward show of indifference or patience is forgotten, and they shriek with pitiable despair before the horror of the fate to which they all are doomed.

Before they covered the coffin an old man kneeled down by the grave and repeated a simple prayer for the dead.[2]

There was an irony in these words of atonement and Catholic belief spoken by voices that were still hoarse with the cries of pagan desperation.

A little beyond the grave I saw a line of old women who had recited in the keen sitting in the shadow of a wall beside the roofless shell of the church. They were still sobbing and shaken with grief, yet they were beginning to talk again of the daily trifles that veil from them the terror of the world.

When we had all come out of the graveyard, and two men had rebuilt the hole in the wall through which the coffin had been carried in, we walked back to the village, talking of anything, and joking of anything, as if merely coming from the boat-slip, or the pier.

[1] Synge adds in Notebook 17 (written in 1899): 'I cannot say it too often, the supreme interest of the island lies in the strange concord that exists between the people and the impersonal limited but powerful impulses of the nature that is round them.'

[2] A passage in Notebook 19 gives more details: 'The priest had held service the day before over the dead and had now been recalled to Aranmore so when at last the grave was complete an old grey-haired man knelt simply on a stone and repeated a prayer whose wording I was not able to understand.'

One man told me of the poteen drinking that takes place at some funerals.

'A while since,' he said 'there were two men fell down in the graveyard while the drink was on them. The sea was rough that day, the way no one could go to bring the doctor, and one of the men never woke again and found death that night.'

The other day the men of this house made a new field. There was a slight bank of earth under the wall of the yard, and another in the corner of the cabbage garden. The old man and his eldest son dug out the clay, with the care of men working in a gold-mine, and Michael packed it in panniers—there are no wheeled vehicles on this island—for transport to a flat rock in a sheltered corner of their holding, where it was mixed with sand and seaweed and spread out in a layer upon the stone.

Most of the potato-growing of the island is carried on in fields of this sort—for which the people pay a considerable rent—and if the season is at all dry, their hope of a fair crop is nearly always disappointed.

It is now nine days since rain has fallen, and the people are filled with anxiety, although the sun has not yet been hot enough to do harm.

The drought is also causing a scarcity of water. There are a few springs on this side of the island, but they come only from a little distance, and in hot weather are not to be relied on. The supply for this house is carried up in a water-barrel by one of the women. If it is drawn off at once it is not very nauseous, but if it has lain, as it often does, for some hours in the barrel, the smell, colour, and taste are unendurable. The water for washing is also coming short, and as I walk round the edges of the sea, I often come on a girl with her petticoats tucked up round her, standing in a pool left by the tide and washing her flannels among the sea-anemones and crabs. Their red bodices and white tapering legs make them as beautiful as tropical sea-birds, as they stand in a frame of seaweeds against the brink of the Atlantic. Michael, however, is a little uneasy when they are in sight, and I cannot pause to watch them. This habit of using the sea water for washing causes a good deal of rheumatism on the island, for the salt lies in the clothes and keeps them continually moist.

The people have taken advantage of this dry moment to begin

the burning of the kelp, and all the islands are lying in a volume of grey smoke. There will not be a very large quantity this year, as the people are discouraged by the uncertainty of the market, and do not care to undertake the task of manufacture without a certainty of profit.

The work needed to form a ton of kelp is considerable. The seaweed is collected from the rocks after the storms of autumn and winter, dried on fine days, and then made up into a rick, where it is left till the beginning of June.

It is then burnt in low kilns on the shore, an affair that takes from twelve to twenty-four hours of continuous hard work, though I understand the people here do not manage well and spoil a portion of what they produce by burning it more than is required.

The kiln holds about two tons of molten kelp, and when full it is loosely covered with stones, and left to cool. In a few days the substance is as hard as the limestone, and has to be broken with crowbars before it can be placed in curaghs for transport to Kilronan, where it is tested to determine the amount of iodine it contains, and paid for accordingly. In former years good kelp would bring seven pounds a ton, now four pounds are not always reached.

In Aran even manufacture is of interest. The low flame-edged kiln, sending out dense clouds of creamy smoke, with a band of red and grey clothed workers moving in the haze, and usually some petticoated boys and women who come down with drink, forms a scene with as much variety and colour as any picture from the East.

The men feel in a certain sense the distinction of their island, and show me their work with pride. One of them said to me yesterday, 'I'm thinking you never saw the like of this work before this day?'

'That is true,' I answered, 'I never did.'

'Bedad, then,' he said, 'isn't it a great wonder that you've seen France, and Germany, and the Holy Father, and never seen a man making kelp till you come to Inishmaan.'

All the horses from this island are put out on grass among the hills of Connemara from June to the end of September, as there is no grazing here during the summer.

KELP-MAKING

Their shipping and transport is even more difficult than that of the horned cattle. Most of them are wild Connemara ponies, and their great strength and timidity make them hard to handle on the narrow pier, while in the hooker itself it is not easy to get them safely on their feet in the small space that is available. They are dealt with in the same way as for the bullocks I have spoken of already, but the excitement becomes much more intense, and the storm of Gaelic that rises the moment a horse is shoved from the pier, till it is safely in its place, is indescribable. Twenty boys and men howl and scream with agitation, cursing and exhorting, without knowing, most of the time, what they are saying.

Apart, however, from this primitive babble, the dexterity and power of the men are displayed to more advantage than in anything I have seen hitherto. I noticed particularly the owner of a hooker from the north island that was loaded this morning. He seemed able to hold up a horse by his single weight when it was swinging from the masthead, and preserved a humorous calm even in moments of the wildest excitement. Sometimes a large mare would come down sideways on the backs of the other horses, and kick there till the hold seemed to be filled with a mass of struggling centaurs, for the men themselves often leap down to try and save the foals from injury. The backs of the horses put in first are often a good deal cut by the shoes of the others that arrive on top of them, but otherwise they do not seem to be much the worse, and as they are not on their way to a fair, it is not of much consequence in what condition they come to land.

There is only one bit and saddle in the island, which are used by the priest, who rides from the chapel to the pier when he has held the service on Sunday.

The islanders themselves ride with a simple halter and a stick, yet sometimes travel, at least in the larger island, at a desperate gallop. As the horses usually have panniers, the rider sits sideways over the withers, and if the panniers are empty they go at full speed in this position without anything to hold to.

More than once in Aranmor I met a party going out west with empty panniers from Kilronan. Long before they came in sight I could hear a clatter of hoofs, and then a whirl of horses would come round a corner at full gallop with their heads out, utterly indifferent to the slender halter that is their only check. They generally travel in single file with a few yards between them, and as there is no traffic there is little fear of an accident.

Sometimes a woman and a man ride together, but in this case the man sits in the usual position, and the woman sits sideways behind him, and holds him round the waist.

Old Pat Dirane continues to come up every day to talk to me, and at times I turn the conversation to his experiences of the fairies.

He has seen a good many of them, he says, in different parts of the island, especially in the sandy districts north of the slip. They are about a yard high with caps like the 'peelers' pulled down over their faces. On one occasion he saw them playing ball in the evening just above the slip, and he says I must avoid that place in the morning or after nightfall for fear they might do me mischief.

He has seen two women who were 'away' with them, one a young married woman, the other a girl. The woman was standing by a wall, at a spot he described to me with great care, looking out towards the north.

Another night he heard a voice crying out in Irish, 'A mháthair tá mé marbh' ('O mother, I'm killed'), and in the morning there was blood on the wall of his house, and a child in a house not far off was dead.

Yesterday he took me aside, and said he would tell me a secret he had never yet told to any person in the world.

'Take a sharp needle,' he said, 'and stick it in under the collar of your coat, and not one of them will be able to have power on you.'

Iron is a common talisman with barbarians, but in this case the idea of exquisite sharpness was probably present also, and, perhaps, some feeling for the sanctity of the instrument of toil, a folk-belief that is common in Brittany.

The fairies are more numerous in Mayo than in any other county, though they are fond of certain districts in Galway, where the following story is said to have taken place.

'A farmer was in great distress as his crops had failed, and his cow had died on him. One night he told his wife to make him a fine new sack for flour before the next morning; and when it was finished he started off with it before the dawn.

'At that time there was a gentleman who had been taken by the fairies, and made an officer among them, and it was often people

AN ISLAND HORSEMAN

would see him and her riding on a white horse at dawn and in the evening.

'The poor man went down to the place where they used to see the officer, and when he came by on his horse, he asked the loan of two hundred and a half of flour, for he was in great want.

'The officer called the fairies out of a hole in the rocks where they stored their wheat, and told them to give the poor man what he was asking. Then he told him to come back and pay him in a year, and rode away.

'When the poor man got home he wrote down the day on a piece of paper, and that day year he came back and paid the officer.'

When he had ended his story the old man told me that the fairies have a tenth of all the produce of the country and make stores of it in the rocks.

It is a Holy Day, and I have come up to sit on the Dun while the people are at Mass.

A strange tranquillity has come over the island this morning, as happens sometimes on Sunday, filling the two circles of sea and sky with the quiet of a church.

The one landscape that is here lends itself with singular power to this suggestion of grey luminous cloud. There is no wind, and no definite light. Aranmor seems to sleep upon a mirror, and the hills of Connemara look so near that I am troubled by the width of the bay that lies before them, touched this morning with individual expression one sees sometimes in a lake.

On these rocks, where there is no growth of vegetable or animal life, all the seasons are the same, and this June[1] day is so full of autumn that I listen unconsciously for the rustle of dead leaves.

The first group of men are coming out of the chapel, followed by a crowd of women, who divide at the gate and troop off in different directions, while the men linger on the road to gossip.

The silence is broken; I can hear far off, as if over water, a faint murmur of Gaelic.

In the afternoon the sun came out and I was rowed over for a visit to Kilronan.

As my men were bringing round the curagh to take me off a headland near the pier, they struck a sunken rock, and came ashore

[1] Synge's first visit lasted from 10 May to 25 June 1898.

shipping a quantity of water. They plugged the hole with a piece of sacking torn from a bag of potatoes they were taking over for the priest, and we set off with nothing but a piece of torn canvas between us and the Atlantic.

Every few hundred yards one of the rowers had to stop and bail, but the hole did not increase.

When we were about half way across the sound we met a curagh coming towards us with its sail set. After some shouting in Gaelic, I learned that they had a packet of letters and tobacco for myself. We sidled up as near as was possible with the roll, and my goods were thrown to me wet with spray.

After my weeks in Inishmaan, Kilronan seemed an imposing centre of activity. The half-civilised fishermen of the larger island are inclined to despise the simplicity of the life here, and some of them who were standing about when I landed asked me how at all I passed my time with no decent fishing to be looking at.

I turned in for a moment to talk to the old couple in the hotel, and then moved on to pay some other visits in the village.

Later in the evening I walked out along the northern road, where I met many of the natives of the outlying villages, who had come down to Kilronan for the Holy Day, and were now wandering home in scattered groups.

The women and girls, when they had no men with them, usually tried to make fun with me.

'Is it tired you are, stranger?' said one girl. I was walking very slowly, to pass the time before my return to the east.

'Bedad, it is not, little girl,' I answered in Gaelic, 'it is lonely I am.'

'Here is my little sister, stranger, who will give you her arm.'

And so it went on. Quiet as these women are on ordinary occasions, when two or three of them are gathered together in their holiday petticoats and shawls, they are as wild and capricious as the women who live in towns.

About seven o'clock I got back to Kilronan, and beat up my crew from the public-houses near the bay. With their usual carelessness they had not seen to the leak in the curagh, nor to an oar that was losing the brace that holds it to the toll-pin, and we moved off across the sound at an absurd pace with a deepening pool at our feet.

A superb evening light was lying over the island, which made me rejoice at our delay. Looking back there was a golden haze behind the sharp edges of the rock, and a long wake from the sun, which was making jewels of the bubbling left by the oars.

The men had had their share of porter and were unusually voluble, pointing out things to me that I had already seen, and stopping now and then to make me notice the oily smell of mackerel that was rising from the waves.

They told me that an evicting party is coming to the island to-morrow morning, and gave me a long account of what they make and spend in the year, and of their trouble with the rent.

'The rent is hard enough for a poor man,' said one of them, 'but this time we didn't pay, and they're after serving processes on every one of us. A man will have to pay his rent now, and a power of money with it for the process, and I'm thinking the agent will have money enough out of them processes to pay for his servant-girl and his man all the year.'

I asked afterwards who the island belonged to.

'Bedad,' they said, 'we've always heard it belonged to Miss ——, and she is dead.'

When the sun passed like a lozenge of gold flame into the sea the cold became intense. Then the men began to talk among themselves, and losing the thread, I lay half in a dream looking at the pale oily sea about us, and the low cliffs of the island sloping up past the village with its wreath of smoke to the outline of Dun Conor.

Old Pat was in the house when I arrived, and he told a long story after supper:—

There was once a widow living among the woods, and her only son living along with her. He went out every morning through the trees to get sticks, and one day as he was lying on the ground he saw a swarm of flies flying over what the cow leaves behind her. He took up his sickle and hit one blow at them, and hit that hard he left no single one of them living.

That evening he said to his mother that it was time he was going out into the world to seek his fortune, for he was able to destroy a whole swarm of flies at one blow, and he asked her to make him three cakes the way he might take them with him in the morning.

He started the next day a while after the dawn, with his three cakes in his wallet, and he ate one of them near ten o'clock.

He got hungry again by midday and ate the second, and when night was coming on him he ate the third. After that he met a man on the road who asked him where he was going.

'I'm looking for some place where I can work for my living,' said the young man.

'Come with me,' said the other man, 'and sleep to-night in the barn, and I'll give you work to-morrow to see what you're able for.'

The next morning the farmer brought him out and showed him his cows and told him to take them out to graze on the hills, and to keep good watch that no one should come near them to milk them. The young man drove out the cows into the fields, and when the heat of the day came on he lay down on his back and looked up into the sky. A while after he saw a black spot in the north-west, and it grew larger and nearer till he saw a great giant coming towards him.

He got up on to his feet and he caught the giant round the legs with his two arms, and he drove him down into the hard ground above his ankles, the way he was not able to free himself. Then the giant told him to do him no hurt, and gave him his magic rod, and told him to strike on the rock, and he would find his beautiful black horse, and his sword, and his fine suit.

The young man struck the rock and it opened before him, and he found the beautiful black horse, and the giant's sword and the suit lying before him. He took out the sword alone, and he struck one blow with it and struck off the giant's head. Then he put back the sword into the rock, and went out again to his cattle, till it was time to drive them home to the farmer.

When they came to milk the cows they found a power of milk in them, and the farmer asked the young man if he had seen nothing out on the hills, for the other cow-boys had been bringing home the cows with no drop of milk in them. And the young man said he had seen nothing.

The next day he went out again with the cows. He lay down on his back in the heat of the day, and after a while he saw a black spot in the north-west, and it grew larger and nearer, till he saw it was a great giant coming to attack him.

'You killed my brother,' said the giant; 'come here, till I make a garter of your body.'

The young man went to him and caught him by the legs and drove him down into the hard ground up to his ankles.

Then he hit the rod against the rock, and took out the sword and struck off the giant's head.

That evening the farmer found twice as much milk in the cows as the evening before, and he asked the young man if he had seen anything. The young man said that he had seen nothing.

The third day the third giant came to him and said, 'You have killed my two brothers; come here, till I make a garter of your body.'

And he did with this giant as he had done with the other two, and that evening there was so much milk in the cows it was dropping out of their udders on the pathway.

The next day the farmer called him and told him he might leave the cows in the stalls that day, for there was a great curiosity to be seen, namely, a beautiful king's daughter that was to be eaten by a great fish, if there was no one in it that could save her. But the young man said such a sight was all one to him, and he went out with the cows on to the hills. When he came to the rocks he hit them with his rod and brought out the suit and put it on him, and brought out the sword and strapped it on his side, like an officer, and he got on the black horse and rode faster than the wind till he came to where the beautiful king's daughter was sitting on the shore in a golden chair, waiting for the great fish.

When the great fish came in on the sea, bigger than a whale, with two wings on the back of it, the young man went down into the surf and struck at it with his sword and cut off one of its wings. All the sea turned red with the bleeding out of it, till it swam away and left the young man on the shore.

Then he turned his horse and rode faster than the wind till he came to the rocks, and he took the suit off him and put it back in the rocks, with the giant's sword and the black horse, and drove the cows down to the farm.

The man came out before him and said he had missed the greatest wonder ever was seen, and that a noble person was after coming down with a fine suit on him and cutting off one of the wings from the great fish.

'And there'll be the same necessity on her for two mornings more,' said the farmer, 'and you'd do right to come and look on it.'

But the young man said he would not come.

The next morning he went out with his cows, and he took the sword and the suit and the black horse out of the rock, and he rode faster than the wind till he came where the king's daughter was sitting on the shore. When the people saw him coming there was great wonder on them to know if it was the same man they had seen the day before. The king's daughter called out to him to come and kneel before her, and when he kneeled down she took her scissors and cut off a lock of hair from the back of his head and hid it in her clothes.

Then the great worm came in from the sea, and he went down into the surf and cut the other wing off from it. All the sea turned red with the bleeding out of it, till it swam away and left them.

That evening the farmer came out before him and told him of the great wonder he had missed, and asked him would he go the next day and look on it. The young man said he would not go.

The third day he came again on the black horse to where the king's daughter was sitting on a golden chair waiting for the great worm. When it came in from the sea the young man went down before it, and every time it opened its mouth to eat him, he struck into his mouth, till his sword went out through its neck, and it rolled back and died.

Then he rode off faster than the wind, and he put the suit and the sword and the black horse into the rock, and drove home the cows.

The farmer was there before him, and he told him that there was to be a great marriage feast held for three days, and on the third day the king's daughter would be married to the man that killed the great worm, if they were able to find him.

A great feast was held, and men of great strength came and said it was themselves were after killing the great worm.

But on the third day the young man put on the suit, and strapped the sword to his side like an officer, and got on the black horse and rode faster than the wind, till he came to the palace.

The king's daughter saw him, and she brought him in and made him kneel down before her. Then she looked at the back of his head and she saw the place where she had cut off the lock with her own hand. She led him in to the king, and they were married, and the young man was given all the estate.

That is my story.

Two recent attempts to carry out evictions on the island came to nothing, for each time a sudden storm rose, by, it is said, the power of a native witch, when the steamer was approaching, and made it impossible to land.

This morning, however, broke beneath a clear sky of June, and when I came into the open air the sea and rocks were shining with wonderful brilliancy. Groups of men, dressed in their holiday clothes, were standing about, talking with anger and fear, yet showing a lurking satisfaction at the thought of the dramatic pageant that was to break the silence of the seas.

About half-past nine the steamer came in sight, on the narrow line of sea-horizon that is seen in the centre of the bay, and immediately a last effort was made to hide the cows and sheep of the families that were most in debt.

Till this year no one on the island would consent to act as bailiff, so that it was impossible to identify the cattle of the defaulters. Now, however, a man of the name of Patrick has sold his honour, and the effort of concealment is practically futile.

This falling away from the ancient loyalty of the island has caused intense indignation, and early yesterday morning, while I was dreaming on the Dun, this letter was nailed on the doorpost of the chapel:—

'Patrick, the devil, a revolver is waiting for you. If you are missed with the first shot, there will be five more that will hit you.

'Any man that will talk with you, or work with you, or drink a pint of porter in your shop, will be done with the same way as yourself.'

As the steamer drew near I moved down with the men to watch the arrival, though no one went further than about a mile from the shore.

Two curaghs from Kilronan with a man who was to give help in identifying the cottages, the doctor, and the relieving officer, were drifting with the tide, unwilling to come to land without the support of the larger party. When the anchor had been thrown it gave me a strange throb of pain to see the boats being lowered, and the sunshine gleaming on the rifles and helmets of the constabulary who crowded into them.

Once on shore the men were formed in close marching order, a word was given, and the heavy rhythm of their boots came up over the rocks. We were collected in two straggling bands on either side of the roadway, and a few moments later the body of magnificent armed men passed close to us, followed by a low rabble, who had been brought to act as drivers for the sheriff.

After my weeks spent among primitive men this glimpse of the newer types of humanity was not reassuring. Yet these mechanical police, with the commonplace agents and sheriffs, and the rabble they had hired, represented aptly enough the civilisation for which the homes of the island were to be desecrated.

A stop was made at one of the first cottages in the village, and the day's work began. Here, however, and at the next cottage, a compromise was made, as some relatives came up at the last moment and lent the money that was needed to gain a respite.

In another case a girl was ill in the house, so the doctor interposed, and the people were allowed to remain after a merely formal eviction. About midday, however, a house was reached where there was no pretext for mercy, and no money could be procured. At a sign from the sheriff the work of carrying out the beds and utensils was begun in the middle of a crowd of natives who looked on in absolute silence, broken only by the wild imprecations of the woman of the house. She belonged to one of the most primitive families on the island, and she shook with uncontrollable fury as she saw the strange armed men who spoke a language she could not understand driving her from the hearth she had brooded on for thirty years. For these people the outrage to the hearth is the supreme catastrophe. They live here in a world of grey, where there are wild rains and mists every week in the year, and their warm chimney corners, filled with children and young girls, grow into the consciousness of each family in a way it is not easy to understand in more civilised places.

The outrage to a tomb in China probably gives no greater shock to the Chinese than the outrage to a hearth in Inishmaan gives to the people.

When the few trifles had been carried out, and the door blocked with stones, the old woman sat down by the threshold and covered her head with her shawl.

Five or six other women who lived close by sat down in a circle round her, with mute sympathy. Then the crowd moved on with the police to another cottage where the same scene was to take place, and left the group of desolate women sitting by the hovel.

THE EVICTIONS

There were still no clouds in the sky, and the heat was intense. The police when not in motion lay sweating and gasping under the walls with their tunics unbuttoned. They were not attractive, and I kept comparing them with the islandmen, who walked up and down as cool and fresh-looking as the sea-gulls.

When the last eviction had been carried out a division was made: half the party went off with the bailiff to search the inner plain of the island for the cattle that had been hidden in the morning, the other half remained on the village road to guard some pigs that had already been taken possession of.

After a while two of these pigs escaped from the drivers and began a wild race up and down the narrow road. The people shrieked and howled to increase their terror, and at last some of them became so excited that the police thought it time to interfere. They drew up in a double line opposite the mouth of a blind laneway where the animals had been shut up. A moment later the shrieking began again in the west and the two pigs came in sight, rushing down the middle of the road with the drivers behind them.

They reached the line of the police. There was a slight scuffle, and then the pigs continued their mad rush to the east, leaving three policemen lying in the dust.

The satisfaction of the people was immense. They shrieked and hugged each other with delight, and it is likely that they will hand down these animals for generations in the tradition of the island.

Two hours later the other party returned, driving three lean cows before them, and a start was made for the slip. At the public-house the policemen were given a drink while the dense crowd that was following waited in the lane. The island bull happened to be in a field close by, and he became wildly excited at the sight of the cows and of the strangely-dressed men. Two young islanders sidled up to me in a moment or two as I was resting on a wall, and one of them whispered in my ear—

'Do you think they could take fines of us if we let out the bull on them?'

In face of the crowd of women and children, I could only say it was probable, and they slunk off.

At the slip there was a good deal of bargaining, which ended in all the cattle being given back to their owners. It was plainly of no use to take them away, as they were worth nothing.

When the last policeman had embarked, an old woman came forward from the crowd and, mounting on a rock near the slip, began a fierce rhapsody in Gaelic, pointing at the bailiff and waving her withered arms with extraordinary rage.

'This man is my own son,' she said; 'it is I that oguht to know him. He is the first ruffian in the whole big world.'

Then she gave an account of his life, coloured with a vindictive fury I cannot reproduce. As she went on the excitement became so intense I thought the man would be stoned before he could get back to his cottage.

On these islands the women live only for their children, and it is hard to estimate the power of the impulse that made this old woman stand out and curse her son.

In the fury of her speech I seem to look again into the strangely reticent temperament of the islanders, and to feel the passionate spirit that expresses itself, at odd moments only, with magnificent words and gestures.

Old Pat has told me a story of the goose that lays the golden eggs, which he calls the Phœnix:—

A poor widow had three sons and a daughter. One day when her sons were out looking for sticks in the wood they saw a fine speckled bird flying in the trees. The next day they saw it again, and the eldest son told his brothers to go and get sticks by themselves, for he was going after the bird.

He went after it, and brought it in with him when he came home in the evening. They put it in an old hencoop, and they gave it some of the meal they had for themselves;—I don't know if it ate the meal, but they divided what they had themselves; they could do no more.

That night it laid a fine spotted egg in the basket. The next night it laid another.

At that time its name was on the papers and many had heard of the bird that laid the golden eggs, for the eggs were of gold, and there's no lie in it.

When the boys went down to the shop the next day to buy a stone of meal, the shopman asked if he could buy the bird of them. Well, it was arranged in this way. The shopman would marry the boys' sister—a poor simple girl without a stitch of good clothes—and get the bird with her.

Some time after that one of the boys sold an egg of the bird to a gentleman that was in the country. The gentleman asked him if he had the bird still. He said that the man who had married his sister was after getting it.

'Well,' said the gentleman, 'the man who eats the heart of that bird will find a purse of gold beneath him every morning, and the man who eats its liver will be king of Ireland.'

The boy went out—he was a simple poor fellow—and told the shopman.

Then the shopman brought in the bird and killed it, and he ate the heart himself and he gave the liver to his wife.

When the boy saw that there was great anger on him, and he went back and told the gentleman.

'Do what I'm telling you,' said the gentleman. 'Go down now and tell the shopman and his wife to come up here to play a game of cards with me, for it's lonesome I am this evening.'

When the boy was gone he mixed a vomit and poured the lot of it into a few naggins of whisky, and he put a strong cloth on the table under the cards.

The man came up with his wife and they began to play.

The shopman won the first game and the gentleman made them drink a sup of the whisky.

They played again and the shopman won the second game. Then the gentleman made him drink a sup more of the whisky.

As they were playing the third game the shopman and his wife got sick on the cloth, and the boy picked it up and carried it into the yard, for the gentleman had let him know what he was to do. Then he found the heart of the bird and he ate it, and the next morning when he turned in his bed there was a purse of gold under him.

That is my story.

When the steamer is expected I rarely fail to visit the boat-slip, as the men usually collect when she is in the offing, and lie arguing among their curaghs till she has made her visit to the south island, and is seen coming towards us.

This morning I had a long talk with an old man who was rejoicing over the improvement he has seen here during the last ten or fifteen years.

Till recently there was no communication with the mainland except by hookers, which were usually slow, and could only make the voyage in tolerably fine weather, so that if an islander went to a fair it was often three weeks before he could return. Now, however, the steamer comes here twice in the week, and the voyage is made in three or four hours.

The pier on this island is also a novelty, and is much thought of, as it enables the hookers that still carry turf and cattle to discharge and take their cargoes directly from the shore. The water round it, however, is only deep enough for a hooker when the tide is nearly full, and will never float the steamer, so passengers must still come to land in curaghs. The boat-slip at the corner next the south island is extremely useful in calm weather, but it is exposed to a heavy roll from the south, and is so narrow that the curaghs run some danger of missing it in the tumult of the surf.

In bad weather four men will often stand for nearly an hour at the top of the slip with a curagh in their hands, watching a point of rock towards the south where they can see the strength of the waves that are coming in.

The instant a break is seen they swoop down to the surf, launch their curagh, and pull out to sea with incredible speed. Coming to land is attended with the same difficulty, and, if their moment is badly chosen, they are likely to be washed sideways and swamped among the rocks.

This continual danger, which can only be escaped by extraordinary personal dexterity, has had considerable influence on the local character, as the waves have made it impossible for clumsy, foolhardy, or timid men to live on these islands.

When the steamer is within a mile of the slip, the curaghs are put out and range themselves—there are usually from four to a dozen—in two lines at some distance from the shore.

The moment she comes in among them there is a short but desperate struggle for good places at her side. The men are lolling on their oars talking with the dreamy tone which comes with the rocking of the waves. The steamer lies to, and in an instant their faces become distorted with passion, while the oars bend and quiver with the strain. For one minute they seem utterly indifferent to their own safety and that of their friends and brothers. Then the sequence is decided, and they begin to talk again with the dreamy tone that is habitual to them, while they make fast and clamber up into the steamer.

While the curaghs are out I am left with a few women and very old men who cannot row. One of these old men, whom I often talk with, has some fame as a bone-setter, and is said to have done remarkable cures, both here and on the mainland. Stories are told of how he has been taken off by the quality in their carriages through the hills of Connemara, to treat their sons and daughters, and come home with his pockets full of money.

Another old man, the oldest on the island, is fond of telling me anecdotes—not folk-tales—of things that have happened here in his lifetime.

He often tells me about a Connaught man who killed his father with the blow of a spade when he was in passion, and then fled to this island and threw himself on the mercy of some of the natives with whom he was said to be related. They hid him in a hole—which the old man has shown me—and kept him safe for weeks, though the police came and searched for him, and he could hear their boots grinding on the stones over his head. In spite of a reward which was offered, the island was incorruptible, and after much trouble the man was safely shipped to America.

This impulse to protect the criminal is universal in the west. It seems partly due to the association between justice and the hated English jurisdiction, but more directly to the primitive feeling of these people, who are never criminals yet always capable of crime, that a man will not do wrong unless he is under the influence of a passion which is as irresponsible as a storm on the sea. If a man has killed his father, and is already sick and broken with remorse, they can see no reason why he should be dragged away and killed by the law.

Such a man, they say, will be quiet all the rest of his life, and if you suggest that punishment is needed as an example, they ask, 'Would any one kill his father if he was able to help it?'

Some time ago, before the introduction of police, all the people of the islands were as innocent as the people here remain to this day. I have heard that at that time the ruling proprietor and magistrate of the north island used to give any man who had done wrong a letter to a jailer in Galway, and send him off by himself to serve a term of imprisonment.

As there was no steamer, the ill-doer was given a passage in some chance hooker to the nearest point on the mainland. Then he walked for many miles along a desolate shore till he reached the town. When his time had been put through, he crawled back along the same route, feeble and emaciated, and had often to wait many weeks before he could regain the island. Such at least is the story.

It seems absurd to apply the same laws to these people and to the criminal classes of a city. The most intelligent man on Inishmaan has often spoken to me of his contempt of the law, and of the increase of crime the police have brought to Aranmor. On this island, he says, if men have a little difference, or a little fight, their friends take care it does not go too far, and in a little time it is forgotten. In Kilronan there is a band of men paid to make out cases for themselves; the moment a blow is struck they come down and arrest the man who gave it. The other man he quarrelled with has to give evidence against him; whole families come down to the court and swear against each other till they become bitter enemies. If there is a conviction the man who is convicted never forgives. He waits his time, and before the year is out there is a cross summons, which the other man in turn never forgives. The feud continues to grow, till a dispute about the colour of a man's hair may end in a murder, after a year's forcing by the law. The mere fact that it is impossible to get reliable evidence in the island—not because the people are dishonest, but because they think the claim of kinship more sacred than the claims of abstract truth—turns the whole system of sworn evidence into a demoralising farce, and it is easy to believe that law dealings on this false basis must lead to every sort of injustice.

While I am discussing these questions with the old men the curaghs begin to come in with cargoes of salt, and flour, and porter.

To-day a stir was made by the return of a native who had spent five years in New York. He came on shore with half a dozen people who had been shopping on the mainland, and walked up and down on the slip in his neat suit, looking strangely foreign to his birthplace, while his old mother of eighty-five ran about on the slippery seaweed, half crazy with delight, telling every one the news.

When the curaghs were in their places the men crowded round him to bid him welcome. He shook hands with them readily enough, but with no smile of recognition.

He is said to be dying.

Yesterday—a Sunday—three young men rowed me over to Inisheer, the south island of the group.

The stern of the curagh was occupied, so I was put in the bow with my head on a level with the gunnel. A considerable sea was running in the sound, and when we came out from the shelter of this island, the curagh rolled and vaulted in a way not easy to describe.

At one moment, as we went down into the furrow, green waves curled and arched themselves above me; then in an instant I was flung up into the air and could look down on the heads of the rowers, as if we were sitting on a ladder, or out across a forest of white crests to the black cliff of Inishmaan.

The men seemed excited and uneasy, and I thought for a moment that we were likely to be swamped. In a little while, however, I realised the capacity of the curagh to raise its head among the waves, and the motion became strangely exhilarating. Even, I thought, if we were dropped into the blue chasm of the waves, this death, with the fresh sea saltness in one's teeth, would be better than most deaths one is likely to meet.

When we reached the other island, it was raining heavily, so that we could not see anything of the antiquities or people.

For the greater part of the afternoon we sat on the tops of empty barrels in the public-house, talking of the destiny of Gaelic. We were admitted as travellers, and the shutters of the shop were closed behind us, letting in only a glimmer of grey light, and the tumult of the storm. Towards evening it cleared a little and we came home in a calmer sea, but with a dead head-wind that gave the rowers all they could do to make the passage.[1]

[1] A passage in Notebook 19 is interesting:

'A heavy roll from the Atlantic is today on the north west of the island and the surf line is of wonderful splendour. I am used to it and look now backwards to the morning a few weeks ago when I looked out first unexpectedly over the higher cliffs of Aranmore, and stopped trembling with delight. A so sudden gust beautiful is a danger. It is well arranged that for the most part we do not realize the beauty of a new wonderful experience till it has grown familiar and so safe to us. If a man could be supposed to come with a fully educated perception of music, yet quite ignorant of it and hear for the first time let us say Lamoureux's Orchestra in a late symphony of Beethoven I doubt his brain would ever recover from the shock. If a man could come with a full power of appreciation and stand for the first time before a woman—a woman perhaps who was very beautiful—what would he suffer? If a man grew up knowing nothing of death or decay and found suddenly a grey corpse in his path what would [he] suffer? Some such emotion was in me the day I looked first on these rising magnificent waves towering in dazzling white and green before the cliff; if I had not seen waves before I would have likely lost my sense. It would be an interesting if cruel experiment to bring some sensitive nature from the central portion of Ireland—who had never seen the sea—to carry him blindfold

On calm days I often go out fishing with Michael. When we reach the space above the slip where the curaghs are propped, bottom upwards, on the limestone, he lifts the prow of the one we are going to embark in, and I slip underneath and set the centre of the foremost seat upon my neck. Then he crawls under the stern and stands up with the last seat upon his shoulders. We start for the sea. The long prow bends before me so that I see nothing but a few yards of shingle at my feet. A quivering pain runs from the top of my spine to the sharp stones that seem to pass through my pampooties, and grate upon my ankles. We stagger and groan beneath the weight; but at last our feet reach the slip, and we run down with a half-trot like the pace of barefooted children.

A yard from the sea we stop and lower the curagh to the right. It must be brought down gently—a difficult task for our strained and aching muscles—and sometimes as the gunnel reaches the slip I lose my balance and roll in among the seats.

Yesterday we went out in the curagh that had been damaged on the day of my visit to Kilronan, and as we were putting in the oars the freshly-tarred patch stuck to the slip which was heated with the sunshine. We carried up water in the bailer—the 'cupeen', a shallow wooden vessel like a soup-plate—and with infinite pains we got free and rowed away. In a few moments, however, I found the water spouting up at my feet.

The patch had been misplaced, and this time we had no sacking. Michael borrowed my pocket scissors, and with admirable rapidity cut a square of flannel from the tail of his shirt and squeezed it into the hole, making it fast with a splint which he hacked from one of the oars.

During our excitement the tide had carried us to the brink of the rocks, and I admired again the dexterity with which he got his oars into the water and turned us out as we were mounting on a wave that would have hurled us to destruction.

With the injury to our curagh we did not go far from the shore. After a while I took a long spell at the oars, and gained a certain dexterity, though they are not easy to manage. The handles overlap by about six inches—in order to gain leverage, as the curagh is

to Aran on a calm day and keeping [him] in confinement till a great storm arose lead him on the cliff and take away the cloth from his eyes. I am not able to imagine any shock more great.'

narrow—and at first it is almost impossible to avoid striking the upper oar against one's knuckles. The oars are rough and square, except at the ends, so one cannot do so with impunity. Again, a curagh with two light people in it floats on the water like a nutshell, and the slightest inequality in the stroke throws the prow round at least a right angle from its course. In the first half-hour I found myself more than once moving towards the point I had come from, greatly to Michael's satisfaction.

This morning we were out again near the pier on the north side of the island. As we paddled slowly with the tide, trolling for pollock, several curaghs, weighed to the gunnel with kelp, passed us on their way to Kilronan.

An old woman, rolled in red petticoats, was sitting on a ledge of rock that runs into the sea at the point where the curaghs were passing from the south, hailing them in quavering Gaelic, and asking for a passage to Kilronan.

The first one that came round without a cargo turned in from some distance and took her away.

The morning had none of the supernatural beauty that comes over the island so often in rainy weather, so we basked in the vague enjoyment of the sunshine, looking down at the wild luxuriance of the vegetation beneath the sea, which contrasts strangely with the nakedness above it.

Some dreams I have had in this cottage seem to give strength to the opinion that there is a psychic memory attached to certain neighbourhoods.

Last night, after walking in a dream among buildings with strangely intense light on them, I heard a faint rhythm of music beginning far away on some stringed instrument.

It came closer to me, gradually increasing in quickness and volume with an irresistibly definite progression. When it was quite near the sound began to move in my nerves and blood, and to urge me to dance with them.

I knew that if I yielded I would be carried away to some moment of terrible agony, so I struggled to remain quiet, holding my knees together with my hands.

The music increased continually, sounding like the strings of harps, tuned to a forgotten scale, and having a resonance as searching as the strings of the 'cello.

Then the luring excitement became more powerful than my will, and my limbs moved in spite of me.

In a moment I was swept away in a whirlwind of notes. My breath and my thoughts and every impulse of my body, became a form of the dance, till I could not distinguish between the instruments and the rhythm and my own person or consciousness.

For a while it seemed an excitement that was filled with joy, then it grew into an ecstasy where all existence was lost in a vortex of movement. I could not think there had ever been a life beyond the whirling of the dance.

Then with a shock the ecstasy turned to an agony and rage. I struggled to free myself, but seemed only to increase the passion of the steps I moved to. When I shrieked I could only echo the notes of the rhythm.

At last with a moment of uncontrollable frenzy I broke back to consciousness and awoke.

I dragged myself trembling to the window of the cottage and looked out. The moon was glittering across the bay, and there was no sound anywhere on the island.[1]

I am leaving in two days, and old Pat Dirane has bidden me good-bye. He met me in the village this morning and took me into 'his little tint,' a miserable hovel where he spends the night.

I sat for a long time on his threshold, while he leaned on a stool behind me, near his bed, and told me the last story I shall have from him—a rude anecdote not worth recording. Then he told me with careful emphasis how he had wandered when he was a young man, and lived in a fine college, teaching Irish to the young priests!

They say on the island that he can tell as many lies as four men: perhaps the stories he has learned have strengthened his imagination.

When I stood up in the doorway to give him God's blessing, he leaned over on the straw that forms his bed, and shed tears. Then he turned to me again, lifting up one trembling hand, with the mitten worn to a hole on the palm, from the rubbing of his crutch.

[1] This passage, beginning on page 99, 'Some dreams I have had', to 'on the island', was originally published as 'A Dream on Inishmaan' in *The Green Sheaf*, No. 2, 1903 (Elkin Mathews, London), and reprinted in *The Gael*, March 1904 (New York).

THE MAN WHO TOLD THE STORIES

'I'll not see you again,' he said, with tears trickling on his face, 'and you're a kindly man. When you come back next year I won't be in it. I won't live beyond the winter. But listen now to what I'm telling you; let you put insurance on me in the city of Dublin, and its five hundred pounds you'll get on my burial.'

This evening, my last in the island, is also the evening of the 'Pattern'—a festival something like 'Pardons' of Brittany.

I waited specially to see it, but a piper who was expected did not come, and there was no amusement. A few friends and relations came over from the other island and stood about the public-house in their best clothes, but without music dancing was impossible.

I believe on some occasions when the piper is present there is a fine day of dancing and excitement, but the Galway piper is getting old, and is not easily induced to undertake the voyage.

Last night, St. John's Eve, the fires were lighted and boys ran about with pieces of the burning turf, though I could not find out if the idea of lighting the house fires from the bonfire is still found on the island.

I have come out of an hotel full of tourists and commercial travellers, to stroll along the edge of Galway bay, and look out in the direction of the islands. The sort of yearning I feel towards those lonely rocks is indescribably acute.[1] This town, that is usually

[1] Synge says on typescript page 86 in Box-file G: 'The charm I have found among these people is not easy to describe. Their minds have been coloured by endless suggestions from the sea and sky, and seem to form a unity in which all kinds of emotion match one another like the leaves or petals of a flower. When this atmosphere of humanity is felt in the place where it has been evolved, one's whole being seems to be surrounded by a scheme of exquisitely arranged sensations that have no analogue except in some services of religion or in certain projects of art we owe to Wagner and Mallarmé.' And also at the end of his first visit he records in Notebook 19:

'A wet day with a close circumference of wet stones and fog showing only at my window and inside white wash, red petticoats, turf smoke, my long pipe and Maeterlinck. I take stock slowly of my knowledge gained in Inishmaan. I cannot yet judge these strange primitive natures closely enough to divine them. I feel only what they are. I read *Grania* before I came here and enjoyed it, but the real Aran spirit is not there. The [islanders] are pure and spiritual, yet have all the healthy animal blood of a peasant and delight in broad jests and deeds. The young men are simple and friendly, never speaking however to strangers till they are addressed, the old men are chatty, cheerful and inquisitive. The girls are inclined to deride me when there are a handful together; singly they are at first shy or pretend to it but show exquisite bright frankness when the ice is once crushed away. Older women are full of good fellowship but have mostly little English and my Gaelic does not carry me beyond a few comments on the weather and the island. To write a real novel of the island life one would require to pass several years among the people, but Miss Lawless does not appear to have lived here. Indeed it would be hardly possible perhaps for a lady [to stay] longer than a few days. Compare the peasants of

so full of wild human interest, seems in my present mood a tawdry medley of all that is crudest in modern life. The nullity of the rich and the squalor of the poor give me the same pang of wondering disgust; yet the islands are fading already and I can hardly realise that the smell of the seaweed and the drone of the Atlantic are still moving round them.

One of my island friends has written to me:—

DEAR JOHN SYNGE,—I am for a long time expecting a letter from you and I think you are forgetting this island altogether.

Mr. —— died a long time ago on the big island and his boat was on anchor in the harbour and the wind blew her to Black Head and broke her up after his death.

Tell me are you learning Irish since you went. We have a branch of the Gaelic League here now and the people is going on well with the Irish and reading.

I will write the next letter in Irish to you. Tell me will you come to see us next year and if you will you'll write a letter before you. All your loving friends is well in health.—*Mise do chara go buan.*

Another boy I sent some baits to has written to me also, beginning his letter in Irish and ending it in English:—

DEAR JOHN,—I got your letter four days ago, and there was pride and joy on me because it was written in Irish, and a fine, good, pleasant letter it was. The baits you sent are very good, but

Grania with those of Fiona Macleod who I feel sure has a real deep knowledge. Take the passage in *Grania* where the heroine makes up the fire of kelp before she goes home to her rest as an example [of] how superficially travellers speak. The kelp-fire lasts at most twenty-four hours and is tended all the time by some half dozen who pile on the weed continually. Such at least is now the custom, and I am told none other could exist. Miss Lawless if she has erred has not done so as deeply as Pierre Loti in his *Pêcheur d'Islande*. . . . "You cannot make a pet book of a book everybody reads," nor I add a pet place of a place every one visits or would learn to love if they did visit. Shelley's grave, Le Vialli dei colli, le Salle de Venus de Milo, Killarney, the Mosque, Westminster, Le Moulin Rouge have all their own peculiar beauty, interest or instruction yet one grows not easily *in love* with them. With this limestone Inishmaan however I am in love, and hear with galling jealousy of the various priests and scholars who have lived here before me. They have grown to me as the former lover of one's mistress, horrible existences haunting with dreamed kisses the lips she presses to your own. The thought that this island will gradually yield to the ruthlessness of "progress" is as the certainty that decaying age is moving always nearer the cheeks it is your ecstasy to kiss. How much of Ireland was formerly like this and how much of Ireland is today Anglicized and civilized and brutalized. . . . Am I not leaving in Inishmaan spiritual treasure unexplored whose presence is as a great magnet to my soul? In this ocean alone is [there] not every symbol of the cosmos?'

I lost two of them and half of my line. A big fish came and caught the bait, and the line was bad and half of the line and the baits went away. My sister has come back from America, but I'm thinking it won't be long till she goes away again, for it is lonesome and poor she finds the island now.—I am your friend. . . .

Write soon and let you write in Irish, if you don't I won't look on it.

PART II

THE evening before I returned to the west I wrote to Michael—who had left the islands to earn his living on the mainland—to tell him that I would call at the house where he lodged the next morning, which was a Sunday.

A young girl with fine western features, and little English, came out when I knocked at the door. She seemed to have heard all about me, and was so filled with the importance of her message that she could hardly speak it intelligibly.

'She got your letter,' she said, confusing the pronouns, as is often done in the west, 'she is gone to Mass, and she'll be in the square after that. Let your honour go now and sit in the square and Michael will find you.'

As I was returning up the main street I met Michael wandering down to meet me, as he had got tired of waiting.

He seemed to have grown a powerful man since I had seen him, and was now dressed in the heavy brown flannels of the Connaught labourer. After a little talk we turned back together and went out on the sandhills above the town. Meeting him here a little beyond the threshold of my hotel I was singularly struck with the refinement of his nature, which has hardly been influenced by his new life, and the townsmen and sailors he has met with.

'I do often come outside the town on Sunday,' he said while we were talking, 'for what is there to do in a town in the middle of all the people when you are not at your work?'

A little later another Irish-speaking labourer—a friend of Michael's—joined us, and we lay for hours talking and arguing on the grass. The day was unbearably sultry, and the sand and the sea near us were crowded with half-naked women, but neither of the young men seemed to be aware of their presence. Before we went back to the town a man came out to ring a young horse on the sand close to where we were lying, and then the interest of my companions was intense.

Late in the evening I met Michael again, and we wandered round the bay, which was still filled with bathing women, until it was quite dark. I shall not see him again before my return from the islands, as he is busy to-morrow, and on Tuesday I go out with the steamer.

I returned to the middle island this morning, in the steamer to Kilronan, and on here in a curagh that had gone over with salt fish. As I came up from the slip the doorways in the village filled with women and children, and several came down on the roadway to shake hands and bid me a thousand welcomes.

Old Pat Dirane is dead, and several of my friends have gone to America; that is all the news they have to give me after an absence of many months.

When I arrived at the cottage I was welcomed by the old people, and great excitement was made by some little presents I had bought them—a pair of folding scissors for the old woman, a strop for her husband, and some other trifles.

Then the youngest son, Columb, who is still at home, went into the inner room and brought out the alarm clock I sent them last year when I went away.

'I am very fond of this clock,' he said, patting it on the back; 'it will ring for me any morning when I want to go out fishing. Bedad, there are no two cocks on the island that would be equal to it.'

I had some photographs to show them that I took here last year, and while I was sitting on a little stool near the door of the kitchen, showing them to the family, a beautiful young woman I had spoken to a few times last year slipped in, and after a wonderfully simple and cordial speech of welcome, she sat down on the floor beside me to look on also.

The complete absence of shyness or self-consciousness in most of these people gives them a peculiar charm, and when this young and beautiful woman leaned across my knees to look nearer at some photograph that pleased her, I felt more than ever the strange simplicity of the island life.

Last year when I came here everything was new, and the people were a little strange with me, but now I am familiar with them and their way of life, so that their qualities strike me more forcibly than before.

When my photographs of this island had been examined with immense delight, and every person in them had been identified—even those who only showed a hand or a leg—I brought out some

I had taken in County Wicklow. Most of them were fragments, showing fairs in Rathdrum or Aughrim, men cutting turf on the hills, or other scenes of inland life, yet they gave the greatest delight to these people who are wearied of the sea.

This year I see a darker side of life in the islands. The sun seldom shines, and day after day a cold south-western wind blows over the cliffs, bringing up showers of hail and dense masses of cloud.

The sons who are at home stay out fishing whenever it is tolerably calm, from about three in the morning till after nightfall, yet they earn little, as fish are not plentiful.

The old man fishes also with a long rod and ground-bait, but as a rule has even smaller success.

When the weather breaks completely, fishing is abandoned, and they both go down and dig potatoes in the rain. The women sometimes help them, but their usual work is to look after the calves and do their spinning in the house.

There is a vague depression over the family this year, because of the two sons who have gone away, Michael to the mainland, and another son, who was working in Kilronan last year, to the United States.

A letter came yesterday from Michael to his mother. It was written in English, as he is the only one of the family who can read or write in Irish, and I heard it being slowly spelled out and translated as I sat in my room. A little later the old woman brought it in for me to read.

He told her first about his work, and the wages he is getting. Then he said that one night he had been walking in the town, and had looked up among the streets, and thought to himself what a grand night it would be on the Sandy Head of this island—not, he added, that he was feeling lonely or sad. At the end he gave an account, with the dramatic emphasis of the folk-tale, of how he had met me on the Sunday morning, and, 'believe me,' he said, 'it was the fine talk we had for two hours or three.' He told them also of a knife I had given him that was so fine, no one on the island 'had ever seen the like of her.'

Another day a letter came from the son who is in America, to say that he had had a slight accident to one of his arms, but was well again, and that he was leaving New York and going a few hundred miles up the country.

All the evening afterwards the old woman sat on her stool at the corner of the fire with her shawl over her head, keening piteously to herself. America appeared far away, yet she seems to have felt that, after all, it was only the other edge of the Atlantic, and now when she hears them talking of railroads and inland cities where there is no sea, things she cannot understand, it comes home to her that her son is gone for ever. She often tells me how she used to sit on the wall behind the house last year and watch the hooker he worked in coming out of Kilronan and beating up the sound, and what company it used to be to her the time they'd all be out.

The maternal feeling is so powerful on these islands that it gives a life of torment to the women. Their sons grow up to be banished as soon as they are of age, or to live here in continual danger on the sea; their daughters go away also, or are worn out in their youth with bearing children that grow up to harass them in their own turn a little later.

There has been a storm for the last twenty-four hours, and I have been wandering on the cliffs till my hair is stiff with salt. Immense masses of spray were flying up from the base of the cliff, and were caught at times by the wind and whirled away to fall at some distance from the shore. When one of these happened to fall on me, I had to crouch down for an instant, wrapped and blinded by a white hail of foam.

The waves were so enormous that when I saw one more than usually large coming towards me, I turned instinctively to hide myself, as one blinks when struck upon the eyes.

After a few hours the mind grows bewildered with the endless change and struggle of the sea, and an utter despondency replaces the first moment of exhilaration.

At the south-west corner of the island I came upon a number of people gathering the seaweed that is now thick on the rocks. It was raked from the surf by the men, and then carried up to the brow of the cliff by a party of young girls.

In addition to their ordinary clothing these girls wore a raw sheepskin on their shoulders, to catch the oozing sea-water, and they looked strangely wild and seal-like with the salt caked upon their lips and wreaths of seaweed in their hair.

For the rest of my walk I saw no living thing but one flock of curlews, and a few pipits hiding among the stones.

CARRYING SEAWEED FOR KELP

About the sunset the clouds broke and the storm turned to a hurricane. Bars of purple cloud stretched across the sound where immense waves were rolling from the west, wreathed with snowy phantasies of spray. Then there was the bay full of green delirium, and the Twelve Pins touched with mauve and scarlet in the east.

The suggestion from this world of inarticulate power was immense, and now at midnight, when the wind is abating, I am still trembling and flushed with exultation.

I have been walking through the wet lanes in my pampooties in spite of the rain, and I have brought on a feverish cold.

The wind is terrific. If anything serious should happen to me I might die here and be nailed in my box, and shoved down into a wet crevice in the graveyard before any one could know it on the mainland.[1]

Two days ago a curagh passed from the south island—they can go out when we are weatherbound because of a sheltered cove in their island—it was thought in search of the Doctor. It became too rough afterwards to make the return journey, and it was only this morning we saw them repassing towards the south-east in a terrible sea.

[1] Synge records in Notebook 17 (written in 1899):

'I have talked with no one through another day of rain and tempest, and now in the evening have drifted away among memories I still hold and cherish from my years of roving in the world. Sometimes I sit upon a couch that stands at the end of a balcony grown over with wild vines where birds are singing in the acacias and the Rhine is running within a stone's throw but I look only at a girl who sits with her work a little way from my feet and hear her quaint and childish complaining of the small things that [happened] during the months I spent in another part of Germany. Again I [picture] a river, the Arno, at the same season of a later year. I am kneeling [on] the floor of an attic listening to an Italian that is singing love songs in the street. Beside me a girl is kneeling also and talking Italian with only seldom a turn that shows her Polish origin. A sod of turf falls in the grate and another frantic burst of the hurricane shakes the island underneath me. I turn on the other side in my chair and dream of things still further off. I am in a cathedral far down the nave in the obscure tranquillity of the unlit evening ceremonials far before us voices are intoning a litany, and a form kneeling at my side is sending prayers to Heaven that have hampered my career. Then the raging winds chant a cadence to my inner powers and I am playing with my whole adolescent excitement in an orchestra of men and women. On the desk before me is spread out the *Eroica* score of Beethoven but I know it almost entirely by heart and my eyes are turning without ceasing to a desk near the front of the platform where a Jewish woman is playing also with the rarest talent and precision. A cry from the baby, and I wake to a winter's night upon this bare rock in the Atlantic. Have I not reason to join my wailing with the winds, who have behind me the summer where I lived and had no flowers and the autumn with the red leaves of the forest and never gathered any store for the winter that is freezing at my feet? I have wandered only some few thousand miles yet I am already beyond the dwelling place of man.'

A four-oared curagh with two men in her besides the rowers—probably the Priest and the Doctor—went first, followed by the three-oared curagh from the south island, which ran more danger. Often when they go for the Doctor in weather like this, they bring the Priest also, as they do not know if it will be possible to go for him if he is needed later.

As a rule there is little illness, and the women often manage their confinements among themselves without any trained assistance. In most cases all goes well, but at times a curagh is sent off in desperate haste for the Priest and the Doctor when it is too late.

The baby that spent some days here last year is now established in the house; I suppose the old woman has adopted him to console herself for the loss of her own sons.

He is now a well-grown child, though not yet able to say more than a few words of Gaelic. His favourite amusement is to stand behind the door with a stick, waiting for any wandering pig or hen that may chance to come in, and then to dash out and pursue them. There are two young kittens in the kitchen also, which he ill-treats, without meaning to do them harm.

Whenever the old woman comes into my room with turf for the fire, he walks in solemnly behind her with a sod under each arm, deposits them on the back of the fire with great care, and then flies off round the corner with his long petticoats trailing behind him.

He has not yet received any official name on the island, as he has not left the fireside, but in the house they usually speak of him as 'Michaeleen beug' (i.e. 'little small-Michael').

Now and then he is slapped, but for the most part the old woman keeps him in order with stories of 'the long-toothed hag,' that lives in the Dun and eats children who are not good. He spends half his day eating cold potatoes and drinking very strong tea, yet seems in perfect health.

An Irish letter has come to me from Michael. I will translate it literally.

DEAR NOBLE PERSON,—I write this letter with joy and pride that you found the way to the house of my father the day you were on the steamship. I am thinking there will not be loneliness on you, for there will be the fine beautiful Gaelic League and you will be learning powerfully.

I am thinking there is no one in life walking with you now but your own self from morning till night, and great is the pity.

What way are my mother and my three brothers and my sisters, and do not forget white Michael, and the poor little child and the old grey woman, and Rory. I am getting a forgetfulness on all my friends and kindred.—I am your friend . . .

It is curious how he accuses himself of forgetfulness after asking for all his family by name. I suppose the first home-sickness is wearing away and he looks on his independent wellbeing as a treason towards his kindred.

One of his friends was in the kitchen when the letter was brought to me, and, by the old man's wish, he read it out loud as soon as I had finished it. When he came to the last sentence he hesitated for a moment, and then omitted it altogether.[1]

This young man had come up to bring me a copy of the 'Love Songs of Connaught,' which he possesses, and I persuaded him to read, or rather chant me some of them. When he had read a couple I found that the old woman knew many of them from her childhood, though her version was often not the same as what was in the book. She was rocking herself on a stool in the chimney corner beside a pot of indigo, in which she was dyeing wool, and several times when the young man finished a poem she took it up again and recited the verses with exquisite musical intonation, putting a wistfulness and passion into her voice that seemed to give it all the cadences that are sought in the profoundest poetry.

The lamp had burned low, and another terrible gale was howling and shrieking over the island. It seemed like a dream that I should be sitting here among these men and women listening to this rude and beautiful poetry that is filled with the oldest passions of the world.

The horses have been coming back for the last few days from their summer's grazing in Connemara. They are landed at the sandy beach where the cattle were shipped last year, and I went

[1] Synge says, in Notebook 17, that Martin's principal friend read the letter aloud 'but omitted with singular delicacy the sentence where Martin spoke of forgetting his own family. Then he folded up the letter and handed it back to me without comment. I have never seen a more beautiful and simple tact.' Synge stayed with the MacDonaghs on Inishmaan, and was helped in his learning of Irish by a son, Martin MacDonagh. Martin is called Michael in *The Aran Islands*.

down early this morning to watch their arrival through the waves. The hooker was anchored at some distance from the shore, but I could see a horse standing at the gunnel surrounded by men shouting and flipping at it with bits of rope. In a moment it jumped over into the sea, and some men, who were waiting for it in a curagh, caught it by the halter and towed it to within twenty yards of the surf. Then the curagh turned back to the hooker, and the horse was left to make its own way to the land.

As I was standing about a man came up to me and asked after the usual salutations:—

'Is there any war in the world at this time, noble person?'

I told him something of the excitement in the Transvaal, and then another horse came near the waves and I passed on and left him.

Afterwards I walked round the edge of the sea to the pier, where a quantity of turf has recently been brought in. It is usually left for some time stacked on the sandhills, and then carried up to the cottages in panniers slung on donkeys or any horses that are on the island.

They have been busy with it the last few weeks, and the track from the village to the pier has been filled with lines of red-petticoated boys driving their donkeys before them, or cantering down on their backs when the panniers are empty.

In some ways these men and women seem strangely far away from me. They have the same emotions that I have, and the animals have, yet I cannot talk to them when there is much to say, more than to the dog that whines beside me in a mountain fog.

There is hardly an hour I am with them that I do not feel the shock of some inconceivable idea, and then again the shock of some vague emotion that is familiar to them and to me. On some days I feel this island as a perfect home and resting place; on other days I feel that I am a waif among the people.[1] I can feel more with them than they can feel with me, and while I wander among them, they like me sometimes, and laugh at me sometimes, yet never know what I am doing.

[1] Synge reveals on typescript page 103 in Box-file G: 'In moments of loneliness I am drawn to the girls of the island, for in even remote sympathy with women there is an interchange of emotion that is independent of ideas.' And he adds in Notebook 17: 'In friendship a man approves of the conception that his friend forms of him and tries to become it . . . which is the reason why many friendships with women especially develop a man.'

In the evenings I sometimes meet with a girl who is not yet half through her 'teens, yet seems in some ways more consciously developed than any one else that I have met here. She has passed part of her life on the mainland, and the disillusion she found in Galway has coloured her imagination.

As we sit on stools on either side of the fire I hear her voice going backwards and forwards in the same sentence from the gaiety of a child to the plaintive intonation of an old race that is worn with sorrow. At one moment she is a simple peasant, at another she seems to be looking out at the world with a sense of prehistoric disillusion and to sum up in the expression of her grey-blue eyes the whole external despondency of the clouds and sea.

Our conversation is usually disjointed. One evening we talked of a town on the mainland.

'Ah, it's a queer place,' she said; 'I wouldn't choose to live in it. It's a queer place, and indeed I don't know the place that isn't.'

Another evening we talked of the people who live on the island or come to visit it.

'Father —— is gone,' she said; 'he was a kind man but a queer man. Priests is queer people, and I don't know who isn't.'

Then after a long pause she told me with seriousness, as if speaking of a thing that surprised herself, and should surprise me, that she was very fond of the boys.

In our talk, which is sometimes full of the innocent realism of childhood, she is always pathetically eager to say the right thing and be engaging.

One evening I found her trying to light a fire in the little side room of her cottage, where there is an ordinary fireplace. I went in to help her and showed her how to hold up a paper before the mouth of the chimney to make a draught, a method she had never seen. Then I told her of men who live alone in Paris and make their own fires that they may have no one to bother them. She was sitting in a heap on the floor staring into the turf, and as I finished she looked up with surprise.

'They're like me so,' she said; 'would any one have thought that!'

Below the sympathy we feel there is still a chasm between us.

'Musha,' she muttered as I was leaving her this evening, 'I think it's to hell you'll be going by and by.'

Occasionally I meet her also in a kitchen where young men go to play cards after dark and a few girls slip in to share the amusement. At such times her eyes shine in the light of the candles, and her cheeks flush with the first tumult of youth, till she hardly seems the same girl who sits every evening droning to herself over the turf.

A branch of the Gaelic League has been started here since my last visit, and every Sunday afternoon three little girls walk through the village ringing a shrill hand-bell, as a signal that the women's meeting is to be held,—here it would be useless to fix an hour, as the hours are not recognised.

Soon afterwards bands of girls—of all ages from five to twenty-five—begin to troop down to the schoolhouse in their reddest Sunday petticoats. It is remarkable that these young women are willing to spend their one afternoon of freedom in laborious studies of orthography for no reason but a vague reverence for the Gaelic. It is true that they owe this reverence, or most of it, to the influence of some recent visitors, yet the fact that they feel such an influence so keenly is itself of interest.

In the older generation that did not come under the influence of the recent language movement, I do not see any particular affection for Gaelic. Whenever they are able, they speak English to their children, to render them more capable of making their way in life. Even the young men sometimes say to me—

'There's very hard English on you, and I wish to God that I had the like of it.'

The women are the great conservative force in this matter of the language. They learn a little English in school and from their parents, but they rarely have occasion to speak with any one who is not a native of the islands, so their knowledge of the foreign tongue remains rudimentary. In my cottage I have never heard a word of English from the women except when they were speaking to the pigs or to the dogs, or when the girl was reading a letter in English. Women, however, with a more assertive temperament, who have had, apparently, the same opportunities, often attain a considerable fluency, as is the case with one, a relative of the old woman of the house, who often visits here.

In the boys' school, where I sometimes look in, the children surprise me by their knowledge of English, though they always speak in Irish among themselves. The school itself is a comfortless building in a terribly bleak position. In cold weather the children arrive in the morning with a sod of turf tied up with their books, a simple toll which keeps the fire well supplied, yet, I believe, a more modern method is soon to be introduced.[1]

I am in the north island again, looking out with a singular sensation to the cliffs across the sound. It is hard to believe that those hovels I can just see in the south are filled with people whose lives have the strange quality that is found in the oldest poetry and legend. Compared with them the falling off that has come with the increased prosperity of this island is full of discouragement. The charm which the people over there share with the birds and flowers has been replaced here by the anxiety of men who are eager for gain. The eyes and expression are different, though the faces are the same, and even the children here seem to have an indefinable modern quality that is absent from the men of Inishmaan.

My voyage from the middle island was wild. The morning was so stormy, that in ordinary circumstances I would not have attempted the passage, but as I had arranged to travel with a curagh that was coming over for the Parish Priest—who is to hold stations on Inishmaan—I did not like to draw back.

I went out in the morning and walked up to the cliffs as usual. Several men I fell in with shook their heads when I told them I was going away, and said they doubted if a curagh could cross the sound with the sea that was in it.

When I went back to the cottage I found the Curate had just come across from the south island, and had had a worse passage than any he had yet experienced.

The tide was to turn at two o'clock, and after that it was thought the sea would be calmer, as the wind and the waves would be running from the same point. We sat about in the kitchen all the

[1] Synge adds in Notebook 17: 'I feel more every day that it is criminal to deprive these people of their language and with it of the unwritten literature which is still as full and as distinguished as [that of] any European people. Already the boys are indifferent to these things, degraded by the dull courses of the national schools.' And on typescript page 107 in Box-file G he says: 'The books they are compelled to use are often absurd. In one of their spelling-books I found "advice" explained as "counsel"; a few of the boys may know what advice means but not many people on the island are likely to have heard of counsel.' These remarks are not really inconsistent with Synge's attacks on the Gaelic League. He was protesting against the League's pushing of a crude version of Irish upon the majority of Irish people whose native tongue was, by that time, English. Similarly he is here protesting against the imposition of crude English upon people whose native tongue is Irish.

morning, with men coming in every few minutes to give their opinion whether the passage should be attempted, and at what points the sea was likely to be at its worst.

At last it was decided we should go, and I started for the pier in a wild shower of rain with the wind howling in the walls. The schoolmaster and a priest who was to have gone with me came out as I was passing through the village and advised me not to make the passage; but my crew had gone on towards the sea, and I thought it better to go after them. The eldest son of the family was coming with me, and I considered that the old man, who knew the waves better than I did, would not send out his son if there was more than reasonable danger.

I found my crew waiting for me under a high wall below the village, and we went on together. The island had never seemed so desolate. Looking out over the black limestone through the driving rain to the gulf of struggling waves, an indescribable feeling of dejection came over me.

The old man gave me his view of the use of fear.

'A man who is not afraid of the sea will soon be drownded,' he said, 'for he will be going out on a day he shouldn't. But we do be afraid of the sea, and we do only be drownded now and again.'

A little crowd of neighbours had collected lower down to see me off, and as we crossed the sandhills we had to shout to each other to be heard above the wind.

The crew carried down the curagh and then stood under the lee of the pier tying on their hats with string and drawing on their oilskins.

They tested the braces of the oars, and the oar-pins, and everything in the curagh with a care I had not yet seen them give to anything, then my bag was lifted in, and we were ready. Besides the four men of the crew a man was going with us who wanted a passage to this island. As he was scrambling into the bow, an old man stood forward from the crowd.

'Don't take that man with you,' he said. 'Last week they were taking him to Clare and the whole of them were near drownded. Another day he went to Inisheer and they broke three ribs of the curagh, and they coming back. There is not the like of him for ill-luck in the three islands.'

'The divil choke your old gob,' said the man, 'you will be talking.'

We set off. It was a four-oared curagh, and I was given the last seat so as to leave the stern for the man who was steering with an oar, worked at right angles to the others by an extra thole-pin in the stern gunnel.

When we had gone about a hundred yards they ran up a bit of a sail in the bow and the pace became extraordinarily rapid.

The shower had passed over and the wind had fallen, but large, magnificently brilliant waves were rolling down on us at right angles to our course.

Every instant the steersman whirled us round with a sudden stroke of his oar, the prow reared up and then fell into the next furrow with a crash, throwing up masses of spray. As it did so, the stern in its turn was thrown up, and both the steersman, who let go his oar and clung with both hands to the gunnel, and myself, were lifted high up above the sea.

The wave passed, we regained our course and rowed violently for a few yards, when the same manœuvre had to be repeated. As we worked out into the sound we began to meet another class of waves, that could be seen for some distance towering above the rest.

When one of these came in sight, the first effort was to get beyond its reach. The steersman began crying out in Gaelic 'Siubhal, siubhal' ('Run, run'), and sometimes, when the mass was gliding towards us with horrible speed, his voice rose to a shriek. Then the rowers themselves took up the cry, and the curagh seemed to leap and quiver with the frantic terror of a beast till the wave passed behind it or fell with a crash beside the stern.

It was in this racing with the waves that our chief danger lay. If the wave could be avoided, it was better to do so, but if it overtook us while we were trying to escape, and caught us on the broadside, our destruction was certain. I could see the steersman quivering with the excitement of his task, for any error in his judgment would have swamped us.

We had one narrow escape. A wave appeared high above the rest, and there was the usual moment of intense exertion. It was of no use, and in an instant the wave seemed to be hurling itself upon us. With a yell of rage the steersman struggled with his oar to bring our prow to meet it. He had almost succeeded, when there was a crash and rush of water round us. I felt as if I had been struck upon the back with knotted ropes. White foam gurgled round my

A FOUR-OARED CURAGH

knees and eyes. The curagh reared up, swaying and trembling for a moment, and then fell safely into the furrow.

This was our worst moment, though more than once, when several waves came so closely together that we had no time to regain control of the canoe between them, we had some dangerous work. Our lives depended upon the skill and courage of the men, as the life of the rider or swimmer is often in his own hands, and the excitement of the struggle was too great to allow time for fear.

I enjoyed the passage. Down in this shallow trough of canvas, that bent and trembled with the motion of the men, I had a far more intimate feeling of the glory and power of the waves than I have ever known in a steamer.

Old Mourteen is keeping me company again, and I am now able to understand the greater part of his Irish.

He took me out to-day to show me the remains of some cloghauns, or beehive dwellings, that are left near the central ridge of the island. After I had looked at them we lay down in the corner of a little field, filled with the autumn sunshine and the odour of withering flowers, while he told me a long folk-tale which took more than an hour to narrate.

He is so blind that I can gaze at him without discourtesy, and after a while the expression of his face made me forget to listen, and I lay dreamily in the sunshine letting the antique formulas of the story blend with the suggestions from the prehistoric masonry I lay on. The glow of childish transport that came over him when he reached the nonsense ending—so common in these tales—recalled me to myself, and I listened attentively while he gabbled with delighted haste: 'They found the path and I found the puddle. They were drowned and I was found. If it's all one to me to-night, it wasn't all one to them the next night. Yet, if it wasn't itself, not a thing did they lose but an old back tooth'—or some such gibberish.

As I led him home through the paths he described to me—it is thus we get along—lifting him at times over the low walls he is too shaky to climb, he brought the conversation to the topic they are never weary of—my views on marriage.

He stopped as we reached the summit of the island, with the stretch of the Atlantic just visible behind him.

'Whisper, noble person,' he began, 'do you never be thinking on the young girls? The time I was a young man, the divil a one of them could I look on without wishing to marry her.'

'Ah, Mourteen,' I answered, 'it's a great wonder you'd be asking me. What at all do you think of me yourself?'

'Bedad, noble person, I'm thinking it's soon you'll be getting married. Listen to what I'm telling you: a man who is not married is no better than an old jackass. He goes into his sister's house, and into his brother's house; he eats a bit in this place and a bit in another place, but he has no home for himself; like an old jackass straying on the rocks.'

I have left Aran. The steamer had a more than usually heavy cargo, and it was after four o'clock when we sailed from Kilronan.

Again I saw the three low rocks sink down into the sea with a moment of inconceivable distress. It was a clear evening, and as we came out into the bay the sun stood like an aureole behind the cliffs of Inishmaan. A little later a brilliant glow came over the sky, throwing out the blue of the sea and of the hills of Connemara.

When it was quite dark, the cold became intense, and I wandered about the lonely vessel that seemed to be making her own way across the sea. I was the only passenger, and all the crew, except one boy who was steering, were huddled together in the warmth of the engine-room.

Three hours passed, and no one stirred. The slowness of the vessel and the lamentation of the cold sea about her sides became almost unendurable. Then the lights of Galway came in sight, and the crew appeared as we beat up slowly to the quay.

Once on shore I had some difficulty in finding any one to carry my baggage to the railway. When I found a man in the darkness and got my bag on his shoulders, he turned out to be drunk, and I had trouble to keep him from rolling from the wharf with all my possessions. He professed to be taking me by a short cut into the town, but when we were in the middle of a waste of broken buildings and skeletons of ships he threw my bag on the ground and sat down on it.

'It's real heavy she is, your honour,' he said; 'I'm thinking it's gold there will be in it.'

'Divil a hap'worth is there in it at all but books,' I answered him in Gaelic.

'Bedad, is mor an truaghé' ('It's a big pity'), he said; 'if it was gold was in it it's the thundering spree we'd have together this night in Galway.'

In about half an hour I got my luggage once more on his back, and we made our way into the city.

Later in the evening I went down towards the quay to look for Michael. As I turned into the narrow street where he lodges, some one seemed to be following me in the shadow, and when I stopped to find the number of his house I heard the 'Failte' (Welcome) of Inishmaan pronounced close to me.

It was Michael.

'I saw you in the street,' he said, 'but I was ashamed to speak to you in the middle of the people, so I followed you the way I'd see if you'd remember me.'

We turned back together and walked about the town till he had to go to his lodgings. He was still just the same, with all his old simplicity and shrewdness; but the work he has here does not agree with him, and he is not contented.

It was the eve of the Parnell celebration in Dublin, and the town was full of excursionists waiting for a train which was to start at midnight. When Michael left me I spent some time in an hotel, and then wandered down to the railway.

A wild crowd was on the platform, surging round the train in every stage of intoxication. It gave me a better instance than I had yet seen of the half-savage temperament of Connaught. The tension of human excitement seemed greater in this insignificant crowd than anything I have felt among enormous mobs in Rome or Paris.

There were a few people from the islands on the platform, and I got in along with them to a third-class carriage. One of the women of the party had her niece with her, a young girl from Connaught who was put beside me; at the other end of the carriage there were some old men who were talking in Irish, and a young man who had been a sailor.

When the train started there were wild cheers and cries on the platform, and in the train itself the noise was intense; men and women shrieking and singing and beating their sticks on the partitions. At several stations there was a rush to the bar, so the excitement increased as we proceeded.

At Ballinasloe there were some soldiers on the platform looking

'IT'S REAL HEAVY SHE IS, YOUR HONOUR,' HE SAID; 'I'M THINKING IT'S GOLD THERE WILL BE IN IT.'

for places. The sailor in our compartment had a dispute with one of them, and in an instant the door was flung open and the compartment was filled with reeling uniforms and sticks. Peace was made after a moment of uproar and the soldiers got out, but as they did so a pack of their women followers thrust their bare heads and arms into the doorway, cursing and blaspheming with extraordinary rage.

As the train moved away a moment later, these women set up a frantic lamentation. I looked out and caught a glimpse of the wildest heads and figures I have ever seen, shrieking and screaming and waving their naked arms in the light of the lanterns.

As the night went on girls began crying out in the carriage next us, and I could hear the words of obscene songs when the train stopped at a station.

In our own compartment the sailor would allow no one to sleep, and talked all night with sometimes a touch of wit or brutality, and always with a wonderful fluency with wild temperament behind it.

The old men in the corner, dressed in black coats that had something of the antiquity of heirlooms, talked all night among themselves in Gaelic. The young girl beside me lost her shyness after a while, and let me point out the features of the country that were beginning to appear through the dawn as we drew nearer Dublin. She was delighted with the shadows of the trees—trees are rare in Connaught—and with the canal, which was beginning to reflect the morning light. Every time I showed her some new shadow she cried out with naïve excitement—

'Oh, it's lovely, but I can't see it.'

This presence at my side contrasted curiously with the brutality that shook the barrier behind us. The whole spirit of the west of Ireland, with its strange wildness and reserve, seemed moving in this single train to pay a last homage to the dead statesman of the east.

PART III

A LETTER has come from Michael while I am in Paris. It is in English.[1]

My dear Friend,—I hope that you are in good health since I have heard from you before, its many a time I do think of you since and it was not forgetting you I was for the future.

I was at home in the beginning of March for a fortnight and was very bad with the Influence, but I took good care of myself.

I am getting good wages from the first of this year, and I am afraid I won't be able to stand with it, although it is not hard, I am working in a saw-mills and getting the money for the wood and keeping an account of it.

I am getting a letter and some news from home two or three times a week, and they are all well in health, and your friends in the island as well as if I mentioned them.

Did you see any of my friends in Dublin Mr. —— or any of those gentlemen or gentlewomen.

I think I soon try America but not until next year if I am alive.

I hope we might meet again in good and pleasant health.

It is now time to come to a conclusion, goodbye and not for ever, write soon.—I am your friend in Galway.

Write soon dear friend.

Another letter in a more rhetorical mood.

My dear Mr. S.,—I am for a long time trying to spare a little time for to write a few words to you.

Hoping that you are still considering good and pleasant health since I got a letter from you before.

[1] Synge edited these letters for publication. There was nothing private or remarkable in them, but with his usual scrupulous care for the feelings of the islanders he cut out anything that might lead to the slightest uneasiness. For example, he amended Martin MacDonagh's phrase 'I now see that your time is coming on for the future to come to Inishmaan' to 'I see now that your time is coming round to come to this place', and he left out these words by Martin: 'There was a great many strangers in our house this summer. . . . I must tell you that Sean my brother is married since the first of this month and he got a very good place and a nice woman. I am at home for about two months and I was very bad with a pain in my side and I spent for about a week in the hospital.'

I see now that your time is coming round to come to this place to learn your native language. There was a great Feis in this island two weeks ago, and there was a very large attendance from the South island, and not very many from the North.

Two cousins of my own have been in this house for three weeks or beyond it, but now they are gone, and there is a place for you if you wish to come, and you can write before you and we'll try and manage you as well as we can.

I am at home now for about two months, for the mill was burnt where I was at work. After that I was in Dublin, but I did not get my health in that city.—*Mise le mor mheas ort a chara.*

Soon after I received this letter I wrote to Michael to say that I was going back to them. This time I chose a day when the steamer went direct to the middle island, and as we came up between the two lines of curaghs that were waiting outside the slip, I saw Michael, dressed once more in his island clothes, rowing in one of them.

He made no sign of recognition, but as soon as they could get alongside he clambered on board and came straight up on the bridge to where I was.

'Bh-fuil tu go maith?' ('Are you well?') he said. 'Where is your bag?'

His curagh had got a bad place near the bow of the steamer, so I was slung down from a considerable height on top of some sacks of flour and my own bag, while the curagh swayed and battered itself against the side.

When we were clear I asked Michael if he had got my letter.

'Ah no,' he said, 'not a sight of it, but maybe it will come next week.'

Part of the slip had been washed away during the winter, so we had to land to the left of it, among the rocks, taking our turn with the other curaghs that were coming in.

As soon as I was on shore the men crowded round me to bid me welcome, asking me as they shook hands if I had travelled far in the winter, and seen many wonders, ending, as usual, with the inquiry if there was much war at present in the world.

It gave me a thrill of delight to hear their Gaelic blessings, and to see the steamer moving away, leaving me quite alone among them. The day was fine with a clear sky, and the sea was glittering beyond the limestone. Further off a light haze on the cliffs of the larger island, and on the Connaught hills, gave me the illusion that it was still summer.

A little boy was sent off to tell the old woman that I was coming, and we followed slowly talking, and carrying the baggage.

When I had exhausted my news they told me theirs. A power of strangers—four or five—a French priest among them, had been on the island in the summer; the potatoes were bad, but the rye had begun well, till a dry week came and then it had turned into oats.

'If you didn't know us so well,' said the man who was talking, 'you'd think it was a lie we were telling, but the sorrow a lie is in it. It grew straight and well till it was as high as your knee, then it turned into oats. Did ever you see the like of that in County Wicklow?'

In the cottage everything was as usual, but Michael's presence has brought back the old woman's humour and contentment. As I sat down on my stool and lit my pipe with the corner of a sod, I could have cried out with the feeling of festivity that this return procured me.

This year Michael is busy in the daytime, but at present there is a harvest moon, and we spend most of the evening wandering about the island, looking out over the bay where the shadows of the clouds throw strange patterns of gold and black. As we were returning through the village this evening a tumult of revelry broke out from one of the smaller cottages, and Michael said it was the young boys and girls who have sport at this time of the year. I would have liked to join them, but feared to embarrass their amusement. When we passed on again the groups of scattered cottages on each side of the way reminded me of places I have sometimes passed when travelling at night in France or Bavaria, places that seemed so enshrined in the blue silence of night one could not believe they would reawaken.

Afterwards we went up on the Dun, where Michael said he had never been before after nightfall, though he lives within a stone's-throw. The place gains unexpected grandeur in this light, standing out like a corona of prehistoric stone upon the summit of the island. We walked round the top of the wall for some time looking down on the faint yellow roofs, with the rocks glittering beyond them, and the silence of the bay. Though Michael is sensible of the beauty of the nature round him, he never speaks of it directly, and many of our evening walks are occupied with long Gaelic discourses about the movements of the stars and moon.

These people make no distinction between the natural and the supernatural.

This afternoon—it was Sunday, when there is usually some interesting talk among the islanders—it rained, so I went into the schoolmaster's kitchen, which is a good deal frequented by the more advanced among the people. I know so little of their ways of fishing and farming that I do not find it easy to keep up our talk without reaching matters where they cannot follow me, and since the novelty of my photographs has passed off I have some difficulty in giving them the entertainment they seem to expect from my company. To-day I showed them some simple gymnastic feats and conjurer's tricks, which gave them great amusement.

'Tell us now,' said an old woman when I had finished, 'didn't you learn those things from the witches that do be out in the country?'

In one of the tricks I seemed to join a piece of string which was cut by the people, and the illusion was so complete that I saw one man going off with it into the corner and pulling at the apparent joining till he sank red furrows round his hands.

Then he brought it back to me.

'Bedad,' he said, 'this is the greatest wonder ever I seen. The cord is a taste thinner where you joined it but as strong as ever it was.'

A few of the younger men looked doubtful, but the older people, who have watched the rye turning into oats, seemed to accept the magic frankly, and did not show any surprise that 'a duine uasal' (a noble person) should be able to do like the witches.

My intercourse with these people has made me realise that miracles must abound wherever the new conception of law is not understood. On these islands alone miracles enough happen every year to equip a divine emissary. Rye is turned into oats, storms are raised to keep evictors from the shore, cows that are isolated on lonely rocks bring forth calves, and other things of the same kind are common.

The wonder is a rare expected event, like the thunderstorm or the rainbow, except that it is a little rarer and a little more wonderful. Often, when I am walking and get into conversation with some of the people, and tell them that I have received a paper from Dublin, they ask me—

'And is there any great wonder in the world at this time?'

When I had finished my feats of dexterity, I was surprised to find that none of the islanders, even the youngest and most agile, could do what I did. As I pulled their limbs about in my effort to teach them, I felt that the ease and beauty of their movements has made me think them lighter than they really are. Seen in their curaghs between these cliffs and the Atlantic, they appear lithe and small, but if they were dressed as we are and seen in an ordinary room, many of them would seem heavily and powerfully made.

One man, however, the champion dancer of the island, got up after a while and displayed the salmon leap—lying flat on his face and then springing up, horizontally, high in the air—and some other feats of extraordinary agility, but he is not young and we could not get him to dance.

In the evening I had to repeat my tricks here in the kitchen, for the fame of them had spread over the island.

No doubt these feats will be remembered here for generations. The people have so few images for description that they seize on anything that is remarkable in their visitors and use it afterwards in their talk.

For the last few years when they are speaking of any one with fine rings they say: 'She had beautiful rings on her fingers like Lady ——,' a visitor to the island.

I have been down sitting on the pier till it was quite dark. I am only beginning to understand the nights of Inishmaan and the influence they have had in giving distinction to these men who do most of their work after nightfall.

I could hear nothing but a few curlews and other wild-fowl whistling and shrieking in the seaweed, and the low rustling of the waves. It was one of the dark sultry nights peculiar to September, with no light anywhere except the phosphorescence of the sea, and an occasional rift in the clouds that showed the stars behind them.

The sense of solitude was immense. I could not see or realise my own body, and I seemed to exist merely in my perception of the waves and of the crying birds, and of the smell of seaweed.

When I tried to come home I lost myself among the sandhills, and the night seemed to grow unutterably cold and dejected, as I groped among slimy masses of seaweed and wet crumbling walls.

After a while I heard a movement in the sand, and two grey shadows appeared beside me. They were two men who were going home from fishing. I spoke to them and knew their voices, and we went home together.

In the autumn season the threshing of the rye is one of the many tasks that fall to the men and boys. The sheaves are collected on a bare rock, and then each is beaten separately on a couple of stones placed on end one against the other. The land is so poor that a field hardly produces more grain than is needed for seed the following year, so the rye-growing is carried on merely for the straw, which is used for thatching.

The stooks are carried to and from the threshing field, piled on donkeys that one meets everywhere at this season, with their black, unbridled heads just visible beneath a pinnacle of golden straw.

While the threshing is going on sons and daughters keep turning up with one thing and another till there is a little crowd on the rocks, and any one who is passing stops for an hour or two to talk on his way to the sea, so that, like the kelp-burning in the summer-time, this work is full of sociability.

When the threshing is over the straw is taken up to the cottage and piled up in an outhouse, or more often in a corner of the kitchen, where it brings a new liveliness of colour.

A few days ago when I was visiting a cottage where there are the most beautiful children on the island, the eldest daughter, a girl of about fourteen, went and sat down on a heap of straw by the doorway. A ray of sunlight fell on her and on a portion of the rye, giving her figure and red dress with the straw under it a curious relief against the nets and oilskins, and forming a natural picture of exquisite harmony and colour.

In our own cottage the thatching—it is done every year—has just been carried out. The rope-twisting was done partly in the lane, partly in the kitchen when the weather was uncertain. Two men usually sit together at this work, one of them hammering the straw with a heavy block of wood, the other forming the rope,

THATCHING

the main body of which is twisted by a boy or girl with a bent stick specially formed for this employment.

In wet weather, when the work must be done indoors, the person who is twisting recedes gradually out of the door, across the lane, and sometimes across a field or two beyond it. A great length is needed to form the close network which is spread over the thatch, as each piece measures about fifty yards. When this work is in progress in half the cottages of the village, the road has a curious look, and one has to pick one's steps through a maze of twisting ropes that pass from the dark doorways on either side into the fields.

When four or five immense balls of rope have been completed, a thatching party is arranged, and before dawn some morning they come down to the house, and the work is taken in hand with such energy that it is usually ended within the day.

Like all work that is done in common on the island, the thatching is regarded as a sort of festival. From the moment a roof is taken in hand there is a whirl of laughter and talk till it is ended, and, as the man whose house is being covered is a host instead of an employer, he lays himself out to please the men who work with him.

The day our own house was thatched the large table was taken into the kitchen from my room, and high teas were given every few hours. Most of the people who came along the road turned down into the kitchen for a few minutes, and the talking was incessant. Once when I went into the window I heard Michael retailing my astronomical lectures from the apex of the gable, but usually their topics have to do with the affairs of the island.

It is likely that much of the intelligence and charm of these people is due to the absence of any division of labour, and to the correspondingly wide development of each individual, whose varied knowledge and skill necessitates a considerable activity of mind. Each man can speak two languages. He is a skilled fisherman, and can manage a curagh with extraordinary nerve and dexterity. He can farm simply, burn kelp, cut out pampooties, mend nets, build and thatch a house, and make a cradle or a coffin. His work changes with the seasons in a way that keeps him free from the dulness that comes to people who have always the same occupation. The danger of his life on the sea gives him the alertness of a primitive hunter, and the long nights he spends fishing in his curagh bring him some of the emotions that are thought peculiar to men who have lived with the arts.

As Michael is busy in the daytime, I have got a boy to come up and read Irish to me every afternoon. He is about fifteen, and is singularly intelligent, with a real sympathy for the language and the stories we read.

One evening when he had been reading to me for two hours, I asked him if he was tired.

'Tired?' he said, 'sure you wouldn't ever be tired reading!'

A few years ago this predisposition for intellectual things would have made him sit with old people and learn stories, but now boys like him turn to books and papers in Irish that are sent them from Dublin.

In most of the stories we read, where the English and Irish are printed side by side, I see him looking across to the English in passages that are a little obscure, though he is indignant if I say that he knows English better than Irish. Probably he knows the local Irish better than English, and printed English better than printed Irish, as the latter has frequent dialectic forms he does not know.

A few days ago, when he was reading a folk-tale from Douglas Hyde's *Beside the Fire*, something caught his eye in the translation.

'There's a mistake in the English,' he said, after a moment's hesitation; 'he's put "gold chair" instead of "golden chair".'

I pointed out that we speak of gold watches and gold pins.

'And why wouldn't we?' he said; 'but "golden chair" would be much nicer.'

It is curious to see how his rudimentary culture has given him the beginning of a critical spirit that occupies itself with the form of language as well as with ideas.

One day I alluded to my trick of joining string.

'You can't join a string, don't be saying it,' he said; 'I don't know what way you're after fooling us, but you didn't join that string, not a bit of you.'

Another day when he was with me the fire burned low and I held up a newspaper before it to make a draught. It did not answer very well, and though the boy said nothing I saw he thought me a fool.

The next day he ran up in great excitement.

'I'm after trying the paper over the fire,' he said, 'and it burned grand. Didn't I think, when I seen you doing it there was no good in it at all, but I put a paper over the master's (the schoolmaster's) fire and it flamed up. Then I pulled back the corner of the paper and I ran my head in, and believe me, there was a big cold wind blowing up the chimney that would sweep the head from you.'

We nearly quarrelled because he wanted me to take his photograph in his Sunday clothes from Galway, instead of his native homespuns that become him far better, though he does not like them as they seem to connect him with the primitive life of the island. With his keen temperament, he may go far if he can ever step out into the world.

He is constantly thinking.

One day he asked me if there was great wonder on their names out in the country.

I said there was no wonder on them at all.

'Well,' he said, 'there is great wonder on your name in the island, and I was thinking maybe there would be great wonder on our names out in the country.'

In a sense he is right. Though the names here are ordinary enough, they are used in a way that differs altogether from the modern system of surnames.

When a child begins to wander about the island, the neighbours speak of it by its Christian name, followed by the Christian name of its father. If this is not enough to identify it, the father's epithet—whether it is a nickname or the name of his own father—is added.

Sometimes when the father's name does not lend itself, the mother's Christian name is adopted as epithet for the children.

An old woman near this cottage is called 'Peggeen,' and her sons are 'Patch Pheggeen,' 'Seaghan Pheggeen,' etc.

Occasionally the surname is employed in its Irish form, but I have not heard them using the 'Mac' prefix when speaking Irish among themselves; perhaps the idea of a surname which it gives is too modern for them, perhaps they do use it at times that I have not noticed.

Sometimes a man is named from the colour of his hair. There is thus a Seaghan Ruadh (Red John), and his children are 'Mourteen Seaghan Ruadh,' etc.

Another man is known as 'an iasgaire' ('the fisher'), and his children are 'Maire an iasgaire' ('Mary daughter of the fisher'), and so on.

The schoolmaster tells me that when he reads out the roll in the morning the children repeat the local name all together in a whisper after each official name, and then the child answers. If he calls, for instance, 'Patrick O'Flaharty,' the children murmur, 'Patch Seaghan Dearg' or some such name, and the boy answers.

People who come to the island are treated in much the same way. A French Gaelic student was in the islands recently, and he is always spoken of as 'An Saggart Ruadh' ('the red priest') or as 'An Saggart Francach' ('the French priest'), but never by his name.

If an islander's name alone is enough to distinguish him it is used by itself, and I know one man who is spoken of as Eamonn. There may be other Edmunds on the island, but if so they have probably good nicknames or epithets of their own.

In other countries where the names are in a somewhat similar condition, as in modern Greece, the man's calling is usually one of the most common means of distinguishing him, but in this place, where all have the same calling, this means is not available.

Late this evening I saw a three-oared curagh with two old women in her besides the rowers, landing at the slip through a heavy roll. They were coming from Inishere, and they rowed up quickly enough till they were within a few yards of the surf-line, where they spun round and waited with the prow towards the sea, while wave after wave passed underneath them and broke on the remains of the slip. Five minutes passed; ten minutes; and still they waited with the oars just paddling in the water, and their heads turned over their shoulders.

I was beginning to think that they would have to give up and row round to the lee side of the island, when the curagh seemed suddenly to turn into a living thing. The prow was again towards the slip, leaping and hurling itself through the spray. Before it touched, the man in the bow wheeled round, two white legs came out over the prow like the flash of a sword, and before the next wave arrived he had dragged the curagh out of danger.

This sudden and united action in men without discipline shows well the education that the waves have given them. When the curagh was in safety the two old women were carried up through the surf and slippery seaweed on the backs of their sons.

In this broken weather a curagh cannot go out without danger, yet accidents are rare and seem to be nearly always caused by drink. Since I was here last year four men have been drowned on their way home from the large island. First a curagh belonging to the south island which put off with two men in her heavy with drink, came to shore here the next evening dry and uninjured, with the sail half set, and no one in her.

More recently a curagh from this island with three men, who were the worse for drink, was upset on its way home. The steamer was not far off, and saved two of the men, but could not reach the third.

Now a man has been washed ashore in Donegal with one pampooty on him, and a striped shirt with a purse in one of the pockets, and a box for tobacco.

For three days the people here have been trying to fix his identity. Some think it is the man from this island, others think that the man from the south answers the description more exactly. To-night as we were returning from the slip we met the mother of the man who was drowned from this island, still weeping and looking out over the sea. She stopped the people who had come over from the south island to ask them with a terrified whisper what is thought over there.

Later in the evening, when I was sitting in one of the cottages, the sister of the dead man came in through the rain with her infant, and there was a long talk about the rumours that had come in. She pieced together all she could remember about his clothes, and what his purse was like, and where he had got it, and the same of his tobacco box, and his stockings. In the end there seemed little doubt that it was her brother.

'Ah!' she said, 'it's Mike sure enough, and please God they'll give him a decent burial.'

Then she began to keen slowly to herself. She had loose yellow hair plastered round her head with the rain, and as she sat by the door suckling her infant, she seemed like a type of the women's life upon the islands.

For a while the people sat silent, and one could hear nothing but the lips of the infant, the rain hissing in the yard, and the breathing of four pigs that lay sleeping in one corner. Then one of the men began to talk about the new boats that have been sent to the south island, and the conversation went back to its usual round of topics.

The loss of one man seems a slight catastrophe to all except the immediate relatives. Often when an accident happens a father is lost with his two eldest sons, or in some other way all the active men of a household die together.

A few years ago three men of a family that used to make the wooden vessels—like tiny barrels—that are still used among the people, went to the big island together. They were drowned on their way home, and the art of making these little barrels died with them, at least on Inishmaan, though it still lingers in the north and south islands.

Another catastrophe that took place last winter gave a curious zest to the observance of holy days. It seems that it is not the custom for the men to go out fishing on the evening of a holy day, but one night last December some men, who wished to begin fishing early the next morning, rowed out to sleep in their hookers.

Towards morning a terrible storm rose, and several hookers with their crews on board were blown from their moorings and wrecked. The sea was so high that no attempt at rescue could be made, and the men were drowned.

'Ah!' said the man who told me the story, 'I'm thinking it will be a long time before men will go out again on a holy day. That storm was the only storm that reached into the harbour the whole winter, and I'm thinking there was something in it.'

To-day when I went down to the slip I found a pig-jobber from Kilronan with about twenty pigs that were to be shipped for the English market.

When the steamer was getting near, the whole drove was moved down on the slip and the curaghs were carried out close to the sea. Then each beast was caught in its turn and thrown on its side, while its legs were hitched together in a single knot, with a tag of rope remaining, by which it could be carried.

Probably the pain inflicted was not great, yet the animals shut their eyes and shrieked with almost human intonations, till the suggestion of the noise became so intense that the men and women who were merely looking on grew wild with excitement, and the pigs waiting their turn foamed at the mouth and tore each other with their teeth.

After a while there was a pause. The whole slip was covered with a mass of sobbing animals, with here and there a terrified woman crouching among the bodies, and patting some special favourite to keep it quiet while the curaghs were being launched.

Then the screaming began again while the pigs were carried out and laid in their places, with a waistcoat tied round their feet to keep them from damaging the canvas. They seemed to know where they were going, and looked up at me over the gunnel with an ignoble desperation that made me shudder to think that I had eaten of this whimpering flesh.[1] When the last curagh went out I was left on the slip with a band of women and children, and one old boar who sat looking out over the sea.

The women were over-excited, and when I tried to talk to them they crowded round me and began jeering and shrieking at me because I am not married. A dozen screamed at a time, and so rapidly that I could not understand all they were saying, yet I was able to make out that they were taking advantage of the absence of their husbands to give me the full volume of their contempt. Some little boys who were listening threw themselves down, writhing with laughter among the seaweed, and the young girls grew red with embarrassment and stared down into the surf.

For a moment I was in confusion. I tried to speak to them, but I could not make myself heard, so I sat down on the slip and drew out my wallet of photographs. In an instant I had the whole band clambering round me, in their ordinary mood.

When the curaghs came back—one of them towing a large kitchen table that stood itself up on the waves and then turned somersaults in an extraordinary manner—word went round that the ceannuighe (pedlar) was arriving.

He opened his wares on the slip as soon as he landed, and sold a quantity of cheap knives and jewellery to the girls and younger women. He spoke no Irish, and the bargaining gave immense amusement to the crowd that collected round him.

I was surprised to notice that several women who professed to know no English could make themselves understood without difficulty when it pleased them.

'The rings is too dear at you, sir,' said one girl using the Gaelic construction; 'let you put less money on them and all the girls will be buying.'

[1] In Notebook 17 Synge has this humorous dedication: 'To the little Irish pigs that have eaten filth all their lives to enable me to wander in Paris these leaves are dedicated with respect and sympathy.'

After the jewellery he displayed some cheap religious pictures—abominable oleographs—but I did not see many buyers.

I am told that most of the pedlars who come here are Germans or Poles, but I did not have occasion to speak with this man by himself.

I have come over for a few days to the south island, and, as usual, my voyage was not favourable.

The morning was fine, and seemed to promise one of the peculiarly hushed, pellucid days that occur sometimes before rain in early winter. From the first gleam of dawn the sky was covered with white cloud, and the tranquillity was so complete that every sound seemed to float away by itself across the silence of the bay. Lines of blue smoke were going up in spirals over the village, and further off heavy fragments of rain-cloud were lying on the horizon. We started early in the day, and, although the sea looked calm from a distance, we met a considerable roll coming from the south-west when we got out from the shore.

Near the middle of the sound the man who was rowing in the bow broke his oar-pin, and the proper management of the canoe became a matter of some difficulty. We had only a three-oared curagh, and if the sea had gone much higher we should have run a good deal of danger. Our progress was so slow that clouds came up with a rise in the wind before we reached the shore, and rain began to fall in large single drops. The black curagh working slowly through this world of grey, and the soft hissing of the rain gave me one of the moods in which we realise with immense distress the short moment we have left us to experience all the wonder and beauty of the world.

The approach to the south island is made at a fine sandy beach on the north-west. This interval in the rocks is of great service to the people, but the tract of wet sand with a few hideous fishermen's houses, lately built on it, looks singularly desolate in broken weather.

The tide was going out when we landed, so we merely stranded the curagh and went up to the little hotel. The cess-collector was at work in one of the rooms, and there were a number of men and boys waiting about, who stared at us while we stood at the door and talked to the proprietor.

When we had had our drink I went down to the sea with my

men, who were in a hurry to be off. Some time was spent in replacing the oar-pin, and then they set out, though the wind was still increasing. A good many fishermen came down to see the start, and long after the curagh was out of sight I stood and talked with them in Irish, as I was anxious to compare their language and temperament with what I knew of the other island.

The language seems to be identical, though some of these men speak rather more distinctly than any Irish speakers I have yet heard. In physical type, dress, and general character, however, there seems to be a considerable difference. The people of this island are more advanced than their neighbours, and the families here are gradually forming into different ranks, made up of the well-to-do, the struggling, and the quite poor and thriftless. These distinctions are present in the middle island also, but over there they have had no effect on the people, among whom there is still absolute equality.

A little later the steamer came in sight and lay to in the offing. While the curaghs were being put out I noticed in the crowd several men of the ragged, humorous type that was once thought to represent the real peasant of Ireland. Rain was now falling heavily, and as we looked out through the fog there was something nearly appalling in the shrieks of laughter kept up by one of these individuals, a man of extraordinary ugliness and wit.

At last he moved off towards the houses, wiping his eyes with the tail of his coat and moaning to himself 'Tá mé marbh,' ('I'm killed'), till some one stopped him and he began again pouring out a medley of rude puns and jokes that meant more than they said.

There is quaint humour, and sometimes wild humour, on the middle island, but never this half-sensual ecstasy of laughter. Perhaps a man must have a sense of intimate misery, not known there, before he can set himself to jeer and mock at the world. These strange men with receding foreheads, high cheek-bones, and ungovernable eyes seem to represent some old type found on these few acres at the extreme border of Europe, where it is only in wild jests and laughter that they can express their loneliness and desolation.

The mode of reciting ballads in this island is singularly harsh. I fell in with a curious man to-day beyond the east village, and we wandered out on the rocks towards the sea. A wintry shower came on while we were together, and we crouched down in the bracken, under a loose wall. When we had gone through the usual topics he asked me if I was fond of songs, and began singing to show what he could do.

The music was much like what I have heard before on the islands—a monotonous chant with pauses on the high and low notes to mark the rhythm; but the harsh nasal tone in which he sang was almost intolerable. His performance reminded me in general effect of a chant I once heard from a party of Orientals I was travelling with in a third-class carriage from Paris to Dieppe, but the islander ran his voice over a much wider range.

His pronunciation was lost in the rasping of his throat, and, though he shrieked into my ear to make sure that I understood him above the howling of the wind, I could only make out that it was an endless ballad telling the fortune of a young man who went to sea, and had many adventures. The English nautical terms were employed continually in describing his life on the ship, but the man seemed to feel that they were not in their place, and stopped short when one of them occurred to give me a poke with his finger and explain gib, topsail, and bowsprit, which were for me the most intelligible features of the poem. Again, when the scene changed to Dublin, 'glass of whisky,' 'public-house,' and such things were in English.

When the shower was over he showed me a curious cave hidden among the cliffs, a short distance from the sea. On our way he asked me the three questions I am met with on every side—whether I am a rich man, whether I am married, and whether I have ever seen a poorer place than these islands.

When he heard that I was not married he urged me to come back in the summer so that he might take me over in a curagh to the Spa in County Clare, where there is 'spree mor agus go leor ladies' ('a big spree and plenty of ladies').

Something about the man repelled me while I was with him, and though I was cordial and liberal he seemed to feel that I abhorred him. We arranged to meet again in the evening, but when I dragged myself with an inexplicable loathing to the place of meeting, there was no trace of him.

It is characteristic that this man, who is probably a drunkard and shebeener and certainly in penury, refused the chance of a shilling because he felt that I did not like him. He had a curiously mixed expression of hardness and melancholy. Probably his character has given him a bad reputation on the island, and he lives here with the restlessness of a man who has no sympathy with his companions.

I have come over again to Inishmaan, and this time I had fine weather for my passage. The air was full of luminous sunshine from the early morning, and it was almost a summer's day when I set sail at noon with Michael and two other men who had come over for me in a curagh.

The wind was in our favour, so the sail was put up and Michael sat in the stern to steer with an oar while I rowed with the others.

We had had a good dinner and drink and were wrought up by this sudden revival of summer to a dreamy voluptuous gaiety, that made us shout with exultation to hear our voices passing out across the blue twinkling of the sea.

Even after the people of the south island, these men of Inishmaan seemed to be moved by strange archaic sympathies with the world. Their mood accorded itself with wonderful fineness to the suggestions of the day, and their ancient Gaelic seemed so full of divine simplicity that I would have liked to turn the prow to the west and row with them for ever.

I told them I was going back to Paris in a few days to sell my books and my bed, and that then I was coming back to grow as strong and simple as they were among the islands of the west.

When our excitement sobered down, Michael told me that one of the priests had left his gun at our cottage and given me leave to use it till he returned to the island. There was another gun and a ferret in the house also, and he said that as soon as we got home he was going to take me out fowling on rabbits.

A little later in the day we set off, and I nearly laughed to see Michael's eagerness that I should turn out a good shot.

We put the ferret down in a crevice between two bare sheets of rock, and waited. In a few minutes we heard rushing paws underneath us, then a rabbit shot up straight into the air from the crevice at our feet and set off for a wall that was a few feet away. I threw up the gun and fired.

'Buail tu é,' screamed Michael at my elbow as he ran up the rock. I had killed it.

We shot seven or eight more in the next hour, and Michael was immensely pleased. If I had done badly I think I should have had to leave the islands. The people would have despised me. A 'duine uasal' who cannot shoot seems to these descendants of hunters a fallen type who is worse than an apostate.

The women of this island are before conventionality, and share some of the liberal features that are thought peculiar to the women of Paris and New York.[1]

Many of them are too contented and too sturdy to have more than a decorative interest, but there are others full of curious individuality.

This year I have got to know a wonderfully humorous girl, who has been spinning in the kitchen for the last few days with the old woman's spinning-wheel. The morning she began I heard her exquisite intonation almost before I awoke, brooding and cooing over every syllable she uttered.

I have heard something similar in the voices of German and Polish women, but I do not think men—at least European men—who are always further than women from the simple, animal emotions, or any speakers who use languages with weak gutturals, like French or English, can produce this inarticulate chant in their ordinary talk.

She plays continual tricks with her Gaelic in the way girls are fond of, piling up diminutives and repeating adjectives with a humorous scorn of syntax. While she is here the talk never stops in the kitchen. To-day she has been asking me many questions about Germany, for it seems one of her sisters married a German husband in America some years ago, who kept her in great comfort, with a fine 'capull glas' ('grey horse') to ride on, and this girl has decided to escape in the same way from the drudgery of the island.

This was my last evening on my stool in the chimney corner, and I had a long talk with some neighbours who came in to bid me prosperity, and lay about on the floor with their heads on low

[1] This links with Notebook 17: 'One woman also has interested me in a way that binds me more than ever to the islands. These women are before convention and share many things with the women of Paris or London who have freed themselves by a desperate personal effort from moral bondage of lady-like persons. Many women here are too sturdy and contented to have more than the decorative interest of wild deer, but I have found a couple that have been turned in on themselves by some circumstance of their lives and seem to sum up in the expressions of their blue grey eyes the whole external symphony of the sky and seas. They have wildness and humour and passion kept in continual subjection by the reverence for life and the sea that is inevitable in this place.'

stools and their feet stretched out to the embers of the turf. The old woman was at the other side of the fire, and the girl I have spoken of was standing at her spinning-wheel, talking and joking with every one. She says when I go away now I am to marry a rich wife with plenty of money, and if she dies on me I am to come back here and marry herself for my second wife.

I have never heard talk so simple and so attractive as the talk of these people. This evening they began disputing about their wives, and it appeared that the greatest merit they see in a woman is that she should be fruitful and bring them many children. As no money can be earned by children on the island this one attitude shows the immense difference between these people and the people of Paris.

The direct sexual instincts are not weak on the island, but they are so subordinated to the instincts of the family that they rarely lead to irregularity. The life here is still at an almost patriarchal stage, and the people are nearly as far from the romantic moods of love as they are from the impulsive life of the savage.

The wind was so high this morning that there was some doubt whether the steamer would arrive, and I spent half the day wandering about with Michael watching the horizon.

At last, when we had given her up, she came in sight far away to the north, where she had gone to have the wind with her where the sea was at its highest.

I got my baggage from the cottage and set off for the slip with Michael and the old man, turning into a cottage here and there to say good-bye.

In spite of the wind outside, the sea at the slip was as calm as a pool. The men who were standing about while the steamer was at the south island wondered for the last time whether I would be married when I came back to see them. Then we pulled out and took our place in the line. As the tide was running hard the steamer stopped a certain distance from the shore, and gave us a long race for good places at her side. In the struggle we did not come off well, so I had to clamber across two curaghs, twisting and fumbling with the roll, in order to get on board.

It seemed strange to see the curaghs full of well-known faces turning back to the slip without me, but the roll in the sound soon took off my attention. Some men were on board whom I had seen on the south island, and a good many Kilronan people on their way home from Galway, who told me that in one part of their passage in the morning they had come in for heavy seas.

As is usual on Saturday, the steamer had a large cargo of flour and porter to discharge at Kilronan, and, as it was nearly four o'clock before the tide could float her at the pier, I felt some doubt about our passage to Galway.

The wind increased as the afternoon went on, and when I came down in the twilight I found that the cargo was not yet all unladen, and that the captain feared to face the gale that was rising. It was some time before he came to a final decision, and we walked backwards and forwards from the village with heavy clouds flying overhead and the wind howling in the walls. At last he telegraphed to Galway to know if he was wanted the next day, and we went into a public-house to wait for the reply.

The kitchen was filled with men sitting closely on long forms ranged in lines at each side of the fire. A wild-looking but beautiful girl was kneeling on the hearth talking loudly to the men, and a few natives of Inishmaan were hanging about the door, miserably drunk. At the end of the kitchen the bar was arranged, with a sort of alcove beside it, where some older men were playing cards. Overhead there were the open rafters, filled with turf and tobacco smoke.

This is the haunt so much dreaded by the women of the other islands, where the men linger with their money till they go out at last with reeling steps and are lost in the sound. Without this background of empty curaghs, and bodies floating naked with the tide, there would be something almost absurd about the dissipation of this simple place where men sit, evening after evening, drinking bad whisky and porter, and talking with endless repetition of fishing, and kelp, and of the sorrows of purgatory.

When we had finished our whisky word came that the boat might remain.

With some difficulty I got my bags out of the steamer and carried them up through the crowd of women and donkeys that were still struggling on the quay in an inconceivable medley of flour-bags and cases of petroleum. When I reached the inn the old woman was in great good humour, and I spent some time talking by the kitchen fire. Then I groped my way back to the harbour, where, I was told, the old net-mender, who came to see me on my first visit to the islands, was spending the night as watchman.

PORTER

It was quite dark on the pier and a terrible gale was blowing. There was no one in the little office where I expected to find him, so I groped my way further on towards a figure I saw moving with a lantern.

It was the old man, and he remembered me at once when I hailed him and told him who I was. He spent some time arranging one of his lanterns, and then he took me back to his office—a mere shed of planks and corrugated iron, put up for the contractor of some work which is in progress on the pier.

When we reached the light I saw that his head was rolled up in an extraordinary collection of mufflers to keep him from the cold, and that his face was much older than when I saw him before, though still full of intelligence.

He began to tell how he had gone to see a relative of mine in Dublin when he first left the island as a cabin-boy, between forty and fifty years ago.

He told his story with the usual detail:—

We saw a man walking about on the quay in Dublin, and looking at us without saying a word. Then he came down to the yacht.

'Are you the men from Aran?' said he.

'We are,' said we.

'You're to come with me so,' said he.

'Why?' said we.

Then he told us it was Mr. Synge had sent him and we went with him. Mr. Synge brought us into his kitchen and gave the men a glass of whisky all round, and a half-glass to me because I was a boy—though at that time and to this day I can drink as much as two men and not be the worse of it. We were some time in the kitchen, then one of the men said we should be going. I said it would not be right to go without saying a word to Mr. Synge. Then the servant-girl went up and brought him down, and he gave us another glass of whisky, and he gave me a book in Irish because I was going to sea, and I was able to read in the Irish.

I owe it to Mr. Synge and that book that when I came back here, after not hearing a word of Irish for thirty years, I had as good Irish, or maybe better Irish, than any person on the island.

I could see all through his talk that the sense of superiority which his scholarship in this little-known language gave him above the ordinary seaman, had influenced his whole personality and been the central interest of his life.

On one voyage he had a fellow-sailor who often boasted that he had been at school and learned Greek, and this incident took place:—

One night we had a quarrel, and I asked him could he read a Greek book with all his talk of it.

'I can so,' said he.

'We'll see that,' said I.

Then I got the Irish book out of my chest, and I gave it into his hand.

'Read that to me,' said I, 'if you know Greek.'

He took it, and he looked at it this way, and that way, and not a bit of him could make it out. 'Bedad, I've forgotten my Greek,' said he.

'You're telling a lie,' said I.

'I'm not,' said he; 'it's the divil a bit I can read it.'

Then I took the book back into my hand, and said to him—

'It's the sorra a word of Greek you ever knew in your life, for there's not a word of Greek in that book, and not a bit of you knew.'

He told me another story of the only time he had heard Irish spoken during his voyages:—

One night I was in New York, walking in the streets with some other men, and we came upon two women quarrelling in Irish at the door of a public house.

'What's that jargon?' said one of the men.

'It's no jargon,' said I.

'What is it?' said he.

'It's Irish,' said I.

Then I went up to them, and you know, sir, there is no language like the Irish for soothing and quieting. The moment I spoke to them they stopped scratching and swearing and stood there as quiet as two lambs.

Then they asked me in Irish if I wouldn't come in and have a drink, and I said I couldn't leave my mates.

'Bring them too,' said they.

Then we all had a drop together.

While we were talking another man had slipped in and sat down in the corner with his pipe, and the rain had become so heavy we could hardly hear our voices over the noise on the iron roof.

The old man went on telling of his experiences at sea and the places he had been to.

'If I had my life over again,' he said, 'there's no other way I'd spend it. I went in and out everywhere and saw everything. I was never afraid to take my glass, though I was never drunk in my life, and I was a great player of cards though I never played for money.'

'There's no diversion at all in cards if you don't play for money,' said the man in the corner.

'There was no use in my playing for money,' said the old man, 'for I'd always lose, and what's the use in playing if you always lose?'

Then our conversation branched off to the Irish language and the books written in it.

He began to criticise Archbishop MacHale's version of *Moore's Irish Melodies* with great severity and acuteness, citing whole poems both in the English and Irish, and then giving versions that he had made himself.

'A translation is no translation,' he said, 'unless it will give you the music of a poem along with the words of it. In my translation you won't find a foot or a syllable that's not in the English, yet I've put down all his words mean, and nothing but it. Archbishop MacHale's work is a most miserable production.'

From the verses he cited his judgment seemed perfectly justified, and even if he was wrong, it is interesting to note that this poor sailor and night-watchman was ready to rise up and criticise an eminent dignitary and scholar on rather delicate points of versification and the finer distinctions between old words of Gaelic.

In spite of his singular intelligence and minute observation his reasoning was mediæval.

I asked him what he thought about the future of the language on these islands.

'It can never die out,' said he, 'because there's no family in the place can live without a bit of a field for potatoes, and they have only the Irish words for all that they do in the fields. They sail their new boats—their hookers—in English, but they sail a curagh oftener in Irish, and in the fields they have the Irish alone. It can never die out, and when the people begin to see it fallen very low, it will rise up again like the phœnix from its own ashes.'

'And the Gaelic League?' I asked him.

'The Gaelic League! Didn't they come down here with their organisers and their secretaries, and their meetings and their speechifyings, and start a branch of it, and teach a power of Irish for five weeks and a half!'[1]

'What do we want here with their teaching Irish?' said the man in the corner; 'haven't we Irish enough?'

'You have not,' said the old man; 'there's not a soul in Aran can count up to nine hundred and ninety-nine without using an English word but myself.'

It was getting late, and the rain had lessened for a moment, so I groped my way back to the inn through the intense darkness of a late autumn night.

[1] This was written, it should be remembered, some years ago. [J. M. S.]

PART IV

NO two journeys to these islands are alike. This morning I sailed with the steamer a little after five o'clock in a cold night air, with the stars shining on the bay. A number of Claddagh fishermen had been out all night fishing not far from the harbour, and without thinking, or perhaps caring to think, of the steamer, they had put out their nets in the channel where she was to pass. Just before we started the mate sounded the steam whistle repeatedly to give them warning, saying as he did so—

'If you were out now in the bay, gentlemen, you'd hear some fine prayers being said.'

When we had gone a little way we began to see the light from the turf fires carried by the fishermen flickering on the water, and to hear a faint noise of angry voices. Then the outline of a large fishing-boat came in sight through the darkness, with the forms of three men who stood on the deck shrieking and howling at us to alter our course. The captain feared to turn aside, as there are sandbanks near the channel, so the engines were stopped and we glided over the nets without doing them harm. As we passed close to the boat the crew could be seen plainly on the deck, one of them holding the bucket of red turf, and their abuse could be distinctly heard. It changed continually, from profuse Gaelic maledictions to the simpler curses they know in English. As they spoke they could be seen writhing and twisting themselves with passion against the light which was beginning to turn on the ripple of the sea. Soon afterwards another set of voices began in front of us, breaking out in strange contrast with the dwindling stars and the silence of the dawn.

Further on we passed many boats that let us go by without a word, as their nets were not in the channel. Then day came on rapidly with cold showers that turned golden in the first rays from the sun, filling the troughs of the sea with curious transparencies and light.

This year I have brought my fiddle with me so that I may have something new to keep up the interest of the people. I have played for them several tunes, but as far as I can judge they do not feel modern music, though they listen eagerly from curiosity. Irish airs like 'Eileen Aroon' please them better, but it is only when I play some jig like the 'Black Rogue'—which is known on the island—that they seem to respond to the full meaning of the notes. Last night I played for a large crowd, which had come together for another purpose from all parts of the island.

About six o'clock I was going into the school-master's house, and I heard a fierce wrangle going on between a man and a woman near the cottages to the west, that lie below the road. While I was listening to them several women came down to listen also from behind the wall, and told me that the people who were fighting were near relations who lived side by side and often quarrelled about trifles, though they were as good friends as ever the next day. The voices sounded so enraged that I thought mischief would come of it, but the women laughed at the idea. Then a lull came, and I said that they seemed to have finished at last.

'Finished!' said one of the women; 'sure they haven't rightly begun. It's only playing they are yet.'

It was just after sunset and the evening was bitterly cold, so I went into the house and left them.

An hour later the old man came down from my cottage to say that some of the lads and the 'fear lionta' ('the man of the nets'—a young man from Aranmor who is teaching net-mending to the boys) were up at the house, and had sent him down to tell me they would like to dance, if I would come up and play for them.

I went out at once, and as soon as I came into the air I heard the dispute going on still to the west more violently than ever. The news of it had gone about the island, and little bands of girls and boys were running along the lanes towards the scene of the quarrel as eagerly as if they were going to a race-course.

I stopped for a few minutes at the door of our cottage to listen to the volume of abuse that was rising across the stillness of the island. Then I went into the kitchen and began tuning the fiddle, as the boys were impatient for my music. At first I tried to play standing, but on the upward stroke my bow came in contact with the salt-fish and oilskins that hung from the rafters, so I settled myself at last on a table in the corner, where I was out of the way, and got one of the people to hold up my music before me, as I had no stand. I played a French melody first, to get myself used to the people and the qualities of the room, which has little resonance between the earth floor and the thatch overhead. Then I struck up the 'Black Rogue,' and in a moment a tall man bounded out from his stool under the chimney and began flying round the kitchen with peculiarly sure and graceful bravado.

The lightness of the pampooties seems to make the dancing on this island lighter and swifter than anything I have seen on the mainland, and the simplicity of the men enables them to throw a naïve extravagance into their steps that is impossible in places where the people are self-conscious.

The speed, however, was so violent that I had some difficulty in keeping up, as my fingers were not in practice, and I could not take off more than a small part of my attention to watch what was going on. When I finished I heard a commotion at the door, and the whole body of people who had gone down to watch the quarrel filed into the kitchen and arranged themselves around the walls, the women and girls, as is usual, forming themselves in one compact mass crouching on their heels near the door.

I struck up another dance—'Paddy get up'—and the 'fear lionta' and the first dancer went through it together, with additional rapidity and grace, as they were excited by the presence of the people who had come in. Then word went round that an old man, known as Little Roger, was outside, and they told me he was once the best dancer on the island.

For a long time he refused to come in, for he said he was too old to dance, but at last he was persuaded, and the people brought him in and gave him a stool opposite me. It was some time longer before he would take his turn, and when he did so, though he was met with great clapping of hands, he only danced for a few moments. He did not know the dances in my book, he said, and did not care to dance to music he was not familiar with. When the people pressed him again he looked across to me.

'John,' he said, in shaking English, 'have you got "Larry Grogan," for it is an agreeable air?'

I had not, so some of the young men danced again to the 'Black Rogue,' and then the party broke up. The altercation was still going on at the cottage below us, and the people were anxious to see what was coming of it.

About ten o'clock a young man came in and told us that the fight was over.

'They have been at it for four hours,' he said, 'and now they're tired. Indeed it is time they were, for you'd rather be listening to a man killing a pig than to the noise they were letting out of them.'

After the dancing and excitement we were too stirred up to be sleepy, so we sat for a long time round the embers of the turf, talking and smoking by the light of a candle.

From ordinary music we came to talk of the music of the fairies, and they told me this story, when I had told them some stories of my own:—

A man who lives in the other end of the village got his gun one day and went out to look for rabbits in a thicket near the small Dun. He saw a rabbit sitting up under a tree, and he lifted his gun to take aim at it, but just as he had it covered he heard a kind of music over his head, and he looked up into the sky. When he looked back for the rabbit, not a bit of it was to be seen.

He went on after that, and he heard the music again.

Then he looked over a wall, and he saw a rabbit sitting up by the wall with a sort of flute in its mouth, and it playing on it with its two fingers!

'What sort of rabbit was that?' said the old woman when they had finished. 'How could that be a right rabbit? I remember old Pat Dirane used to be telling us he was once out on the cliffs, and he saw a big rabbit sitting down in a hole under a flagstone. He called a man who was with him, and they put a hook on the end of a stick and ran it down into the hole. Then a voice called up to them—

' "Ah, Phaddrick, don't hurt me with the hook!" '

'Pat was a great rogue,' said the old man. 'Maybe you remember the bits of horns he had like handles on the end of his sticks? Well, one day there was a priest over and he said to Pat—

' "Is it the devil's horns you have on your sticks, Pat?"

' "I don't rightly know," said Pat, "but if it is, it's the devil's milk you've been drinking, since you've been able to drink, and the devil's flesh you've been eating and the devil's butter you've been putting on your bread, for I've seen the like of them horns on every old cow through the country." '

The weather has been rough, but early this afternoon the sea was calm enough for a hooker to come in with turf from Connemara,

THE HOOKER'S OWNER

though while she was at the pier the roll was so great that the men had to keep a watch on the waves and loosen the cable whenever a large one was coming in, so that she might ease up with the water.

There were only two men on board, and when she was empty they had some trouble in dragging in the cables, hoisting the sails, and getting out of the harbour before they could be blown on the rocks.

A heavy shower came on soon afterwards, and I lay down under a stack of turf with some people who were standing about, to wait for another hooker that was coming in with horses. They began talking and laughing about the dispute last night and the noise made at it.

'The worst fights do be made here over nothing,' said an old man next me. 'Did Mourteen or any of them on the big island ever tell you of the fight they had there threescore years ago when they were killing each other with knives out on the strand?'

'They never told me,' I said.

'Well,' said he, 'they were going down to cut weed, and a man was sharpening his knife on a stone before he went. A young boy came into the kitchen, and he said to the man—

' "What are you sharpening that knife for?"

' "To kill your father with," said the man, and they the best of friends all the time. The young boy went back to his house and told his father there was a man sharpening a knife to kill him.

' "Bedad," said the father, "if he has a knife I'll have one too."

'He sharpened his knife after that, and they went down to the strand. Then the two men began making fun about their knives, and from that they began raising their voices, and it wasn't long before there were ten men fighting with their knives, and they never stopped till there were five of them dead.

'They buried them the day after, and when they were coming home, what did they see but the boy who began the work playing about with the son of the other man, and their two fathers down in their graves.'

When he stopped, a gust of wind came and blew up a bundle of dry seaweed that was near us, right over our heads.

Another old man began to talk.

'That was a great wind,' he said, 'I remember one time there was a man in the south island who had a lot of wool up in shelter against the corner of a wall. He was after washing it, and drying it, and turning it, and he had it all nice and clean the way they could card it. Then a wind came down and the wool began blowing all over the wall. The man was throwing out his arms on it and trying to stop it, and another man saw him.

' "The devil mend your head!" says he, "the like of that wind is too strong for you."

' "If the devil himself is in it," said the other man, "I'll hold on to it while I can."

'Then whether it was because of the word or not I don't know, but the whole of the wool went up over his head and blew all over the island, yet, when his wife came to spin afterwards she had all they expected, as if that lot was not lost on them at all.'

'There was more than that in it,' said another man, 'for the night before a woman had a great sight out to the west in this island, and saw all the people that were dead a while back in this island and the south island, and they all talking with each other. There was a man over from the other island that night, and he heard the woman talking of what she had seen. The next day he went back to the south island, and I think he was alone in the curagh. As soon as he came near the other island he saw a man fishing from the cliffs, and this man called out to him—

' "Make haste now and go up and tell your mother to hide the poteen"—his mother used to sell poteen—"for I'm after seeing the biggest party of peelers and yeomanry passing by on the rocks was ever seen on the island." It was at that time the wool was taken with the other man above, under the hill, and no peelers in the island at all.'

A little after that the old men went away, and I was left with some young men between twenty and thirty, who talked to me of different things. One of them asked me if ever I was drunk, and another told me I would be right to marry a girl out of this island, for they were nice women in it, fine fat girls, who would be strong, and have plenty of children, and not be wasting my money on me.

When the horses were coming ashore a curagh that was far out after lobster-pots came hurrying in, and a man out of her ran up the sandhills to meet a little girl who was coming down with a bundle of Sunday clothes. He changed them on the sand and then went out to the hooker, and went off to Connemara to bring back his horses.

A young married woman I used often to talk with is dying of a fever—typhus I am told—and her husband and brothers have gone off in a curagh to get the doctor and the priest from the north island, though the sea is rough.[1]

I watched them from the Dun for a long time after they had started. Wind and rain were driving through the sound, and I could see no boats or people anywhere except this one black curagh splashing and struggling through the waves. When the wind fell a little I could hear people hammering below me to the east. The body of a young man who was drowned a few weeks ago came ashore this morning, and his friends have been busy all day making a coffin in the yard of the house where he lived.

After a while the curagh went out of sight into the mist, and I came down to the cottage shuddering with cold and misery.

The old woman was keening by the fire.

'I have been to the house where the young man is,' she said; 'but I couldn't go to the door with the air was coming out of it. They say his head isn't on him at all, and indeed it isn't any wonder and he three weeks in the sea. Isn't it great danger and sorrow is over every one on this island?'

I asked her if the curagh would soon be coming back with the priest.

'It will not be coming soon or at all to-night,' she said. 'The wind has gone up now, and there will come no curagh to this island for maybe two days or three. And wasn't it a cruel thing to see the haste was on them, and they in danger all the time to be drowned themselves?'

Then I asked her how the woman was doing.

'She's nearly lost,' said the old woman; 'she won't be alive at all to-morrow morning. They have no boards to make her a coffin, and they'll want to borrow the boards that a man below has had this two years to bury his mother, and she alive still. I heard them saying there are two more women with the fever, and a child that's not three. The Lord have mercy on us all!'

[1] The islands were just recovering from a typhus epidemic when Synge arrived. Again Notebook 17 is revealing: 'Norah, the girl who was spinning in this house last year, is very ill and some of the people say she is dying. A curagh went off this evening, faster than I thought possible, for the doctor and the priest, and I can see the sail now on the return journey through the rain that has begun to fall. I did not realize till tonight how fond I am of these people. . . . The thought of these young women dying with no doctor and no one who knows anything of illness made me unendurably wretched.' This last sentence comes from Box-file G, p. 171.

I went out again to look over the sea, but night had fallen and the hurricane was howling over the Dun. I walked down the lane and heard the keening in the house where the young man was. Further on I could see a stir about the door of the cottage that had been last struck by typhus. Then I turned back again in the teeth of the rain, and sat over the fire with the old man and woman talking of the sorrows of the people till it was late in the night.

This evening the old man told me a story he had heard long ago on the mainland:—

There was a young woman, he said, and she had a child. In a little time the woman died and they buried her the day after. That night another woman—a woman of the family—was sitting by the fire with the child on her lap, giving milk to it out of a cup. Then the woman they were after burying opened the door, and came into the house. She went over to the fire, and she took a stool and sat down before the other woman. Then she put out her hand and took the child on her lap, and gave it her breast. After that she put the child in the cradle and went over to the dresser and took milk and potatoes off it, and ate them. Then she went out. The other woman was frightened, and she told the man of the house when he came back, and two young men. They said they would be there the next night, and if she came back they would catch hold of her. She came the next night and gave the child her breast, and when she got up to go to the dresser, the man of the house caught hold of her, but he fell down on the floor. Then the two young men caught hold of her and they held her. She told them she was away with the fairies, and they could not keep her that night, though she was eating no food with the fairies, the way she might be able to come back to her child. Then she told them they would all be leaving that part of the country on the Oidhche Shamhna, and that there would be four or five hundred of them riding on horses, and herself would be on a grey horse, riding behind a young man. And she told them to go down to a bridge they would be crossing that night, and to wait at the head of it, and when she would be coming up she would slow the horse and they would be able to throw something on her and on the young man, and they would fall over on the ground and be saved.

She went away then, and on the Oidhche Shamhna the men went down and got her back. She had four children after that, and in the end she died.

It was not herself they buried at all the first time, but some old thing the fairies put in her place.

'There are people who say they don't believe in these things,' said the old woman, 'but there are strange things, let them say what they will. There was a woman went to bed at the lower village a while ago, and her child along with her. For a time they did not sleep, and then something came to the window, and they heard a voice and this is what it said—

' "It is time to sleep from this out."

'In the morning the child was dead, and indeed it is many get their death that way on the island.'

The young man has been buried, and his funeral was one of the strangest scenes I have met with. People could be seen going down to his house from early in the day, yet when I went there with the old man about the middle of the afternoon, the coffin was still lying in front of the door, with the men and women of the family standing round beating it, and keening over it, in a great crowd of people. A little later every one knelt down and a last prayer was said. Then the cousins of the dead man got ready two oars and some pieces of rope—the men of his own family seemed too broken with grief to know what they were doing—the coffin was tied up, and the procession began. The old women walked close behind the coffin, and I happened to take a place just after them, among the first of the men. The rough lane to the graveyard slopes away towards the east, and the crowd of women going down before me in their red dresses, cloaked with red petticoats, with the waistband that is held round the head just seen from behind, had a strange effect, to which the white coffin and the unity of colour gave a nearly cloistral quietness.

This time the graveyard was filled with withered grass and bracken instead of the early ferns that were to be seen everywhere at the other funeral I have spoken of, and the grief of the people was of a different kind, as they had come to bury a young man who had died in his first manhood, instead of an old woman of eighty. For this reason the keen lost a part of its formal nature, and was recited as the expression of intense personal grief by the young men and women of the man's own family.

When the coffin had been laid down, near the grave that was to be opened, two long switches were cut out from the brambles among the rocks, and the length and breadth of the coffin were marked on them. Then the men began their work, clearing off stones and thin layers of earth, and breaking up an old coffin that was in the place into which the new one had to be lowered. When a number of blackened boards and pieces of bone had been thrown up with the clay, a skull was lifted out, and placed upon a gravestone. Immediately the old woman, the mother of the dead man, took it up in her hands, and carried it away by herself. Then she sat down and put it in her lap—it was the skull of her own mother—and began keening and shrieking over it with the wildest lamentation.

As the pile of mouldering clay got higher beside the grave a heavy smell began to rise from it, and the men hurried with their work, measuring the hole repeatedly with the two rods of bramble. When it was nearly deep enough the old woman got up and came back to the coffin, and began to beat on it, holding the skull in her left hand. This last moment of grief was the most terrible of all. The young women were nearly lying among the stones, worn out with their passion of grief, yet raising themselves every few moments to beat with magnificent gestures on the boards of the coffin. The young men were worn out also, and their voices cracked continually in the wail of the keen.

When everything was ready the sheet was unpinned from the coffin, and it was lowered into its place. Then an old man took a wooden vessel with holy water in it, and a wisp of bracken, and the people crowded round him while he splashed the water over them. They seemed eager to get as much of it as possible, more than one old woman crying out with a humorous voice—

'Tabhair dham braon eile, a Mhourteen.' ('Give me another drop, Martin.')

When the grave was half filled in, I wandered round towards the north watching two seals that were chasing each other near the surf. I reached the Sandy Head as the light began to fail, and found some of the men I knew best fishing there with a sort of drag-net. It is a tedious process, and I sat for a long time on the sand watching the net being put out, and then drawn in again by eight men working together with a slow rhythmical movement.

As they talked to me and gave me a little poteen and a little bread when they thought I was hungry, I could not help feeling that I was talking with men who were under a judgment of death. I knew that every one of them would be drowned in the sea in a few years and battered naked on the rocks, or would die in his own cottage and be buried with another fearful scene in the graveyard I had come from.

When I got up this morning I found that the people had gone to Mass and latched the kitchen door from the outside, so that I could not open it to give myself light.

I sat for nearly an hour beside the fire with a curious feeling that I should be quite alone in this little cottage. I am so used to sitting here with the people that I have never felt the room before as a place where any man might live and work by himself. After a while as I waited, with just light enough from the chimney to let me see the rafters and the greyness of the walls, I became indescribably mournful, for I felt that this little corner on the face of the world, and the people who live in it, have a peace and dignity from which we are shut for ever.

While I was dreaming, the old woman came in in a great hurry and made tea for me and the young priest, who followed her a little later drenched with rain and spray.

The curate who has charge of the middle and south islands has a wearisome and dangerous task. He comes to this island or Inishere on Saturday night—whenever the sea is calm enough—and has Mass the first thing on Sunday morning. Then he goes down fasting and is rowed across to the other island and has Mass again, so that it is about midday when he gets a hurried breakfast before he sets off again for Aranmor, meeting often on both passages a rough and perilous sea.

A couple of Sundays ago I was lying outside the cottage in the sunshine smoking my pipe, when the curate, a man of the greatest kindliness and humour, came up, wet and worn out, to have his first meal. He looked at me for a moment and then shook his head.

'Tell me,' he said, 'did you read your Bible this morning?'

I answered that I had not done so.

'Well, begob, Mr. Synge,' he went on, 'if you ever go to Heaven, you'll have a great laugh at us.'

Although these people are kindly towards each other and to their children, they have no feeling for the sufferings of animals, and little sympathy for pain when the person who feels it is not in danger. I have sometimes seen a girl writhing and howling with toothache while her mother sat at the other side of the fireplace pointing at her and laughing at her as if amused by the sight.

A few days ago, when we had been talking of the death of President M'Kinley, I explained the American way of killing murderers, and a man asked me how long the man who killed the President would be dying.

'While you'd be snapping your fingers,' I said.

'Well,' said the man, 'they might as well hang him so, and not be bothering themselves with all them wires. A man who would kill a King or a President knows he has to die for it, and it 's only giving him the thing he bargained for if he dies easy. It would be right he should be three weeks dying, and there'd be fewer of those things done in the world.'

If two dogs fight at the slip when we are waiting for the steamer, the men are delighted and do all they can to keep up the fury of the battle.

They tie down donkey's heads to their hoofs to keep them from straying, in a way that must cause horrible pain, and sometimes when I go into a cottage I find all the women of the place down on their knees plucking the feathers from live ducks and geese.

When the people are in pain themselves they make no attempt to hide or control their feelings. An old man who was ill in the winter took me out the other day to show me how far down the road they could hear him yelling 'the time he had a pain in his head'.

There was a great storm this morning, and I went up on the cliff to sit in the shanty they have made there for men who watch for wrack. Soon afterwards a boy, who was out minding sheep, came up from the west, and we had a long talk.

He began by giving me the first connected account I have had of the accident that happened some time ago, when the young man was drowned on his way to the south island.

'Some men from the south island,' he said, 'came over and bought some horses on this island, and they put them in a hooker to take across. They wanted a curagh to go with them to tow the horses on to the strand, and a young man said he would go, and they could give him a rope and tow him behind the hooker. When they were out in the sound a wind came down on them, and the man in the curagh couldn't turn her to meet the waves, because the hooker was pulling her and she began filling up with water.

'When the men in the hooker saw it they began crying out one thing and another thing without knowing what to do. One man called out to the man who was holding the rope: "Let go the rope now, or you'll swamp her."

'And the man with the rope threw it out on the water, and the curagh half-filled already, and I think only one oar in her. A wave came into her then, and she went down before them, and the young man began swimming about; then they let fall the sails in the hooker the way they could pick him up. And when they had them down they were too far off, and they pulled the sails up again the way they could tack back to him. He was there in the water swimming round, and swimming round, and before they got up with him again he sank the third time, and they didn't see any more of him.'

I asked if any one had seen him on the island since he was dead.

'They have not,' he said, 'but there were queer things in it. Before he went out on the sea that day his dog came up and sat beside him on the rocks, and began crying. When the horses were coming down to the slip an old woman saw her son, that was drowned a while ago, riding on one of them. She didn't say what she was after seeing, and this man caught the horse, he caught his own horse first, and then he caught this one, and after that he went out and was drowned. Two days after I dreamed they found him on the Ceann gaine (the Sandy Head) and carried him up to the house on the plain, and took his pampooties off him and hung them up on a nail to dry. It was there they found him afterwards as you'll have heard them say.'

'Are you always afraid when you hear a dog crying?' I said.

'We don't like it,' he answered; 'you will often see them on the top of the rocks looking up into the heavens, and they crying. We don't like it at all, and we don't like a cock or hen to break anything in a house, for we know then some one will be going away. A while before the man who used to live in that cottage below died in the winter, the cock belonging to his wife began to fight with another cock. The two of them flew up on the dresser and knocked the glass of the lamp off it, and it fell on the floor and was broken. The woman caught her cock after that and killed it, but she could not kill the other cock, for it was belonging to the man who lived in the next house. Then himself got a sickness and died after that.'

I asked if he ever heard the fairy music on the island.

'I heard some of the boys talking in the school a while ago,' he said, 'and they were saying that their brothers and another man went out fishing a morning, two weeks ago, before the cock crew. When they were down near the Sandy Head they heard music near them, and it was the fairies were in it. I've heard of other things too. One time three men were out at night in a curagh, and they saw a big ship coming down on them. They were frightened at it, and they tried to get away, but it came on nearer them, till one of the men turned round and made the sign of the cross, and then they didn't see it any more.'

Then he went on in answer to another question:

'We do often see the people who do be away with them. There was a young man died a year ago, and he used to come to the window of the house where his brothers slept, and be talking to them in the night. He was married a while before that, and he used to be saying in the night he was sorry he had not promised the land to his son, and that it was to him it should go. Another time he was saying something about a mare, about her hoofs, or the shoes they should put on her. A little while ago Patch Ruadh saw him going down the road with broga arda (leather boots) on him and a new suit. Then two men saw him in another place.

'Do you see that straight wall of cliff?' he went on a few moments later, pointing to a place below us. 'It is there the fairies do be playing ball in the night, and you can see the marks of their heels when you come in the morning, and three stones they have to mark the line, and another big stone they hop the ball on. It's often the boys have put away the three stones, and they will always be back again in the morning, and a while since the man who owns the land took the big stone itself and rolled it down and threw it over the cliff, yet in the morning it was back in its place before him.'

I am in the south island again, and I have come upon some old men with a wonderful variety of stories and songs, the last, fairly often, both in English and Irish. I went round to the house of one of them to-day, with a native scholar who can write Irish, and we took down a certain number, and heard others. Here is one of the tales the old man told us at first before he had warmed to his subject. I did not take it down, but it ran in this way:—

There was a man of the name of Charley Lambert, and every horse he would ride in a race he would come in the first.

The people in the country were angry with him at last, and this law was made, that he should ride no more at races, and if he rode, any one who saw him would have the right to shoot him. After that there was a gentleman from that part of the country over in England, and he was talking one day with the people there, and he said that the horses of Ireland were the best horses. The English said it was the English horses were the best, and at last they said there should be a race, and the English horses would come over and race against the horses of Ireland, and the gentleman put all his money on that race.

Well, when he came back to Ireland he went to Charley Lambert, and asked him to ride on his horse. Charley said he would not ride, and told the gentleman the danger he'd be in. Then the gentleman told him the way he had put all his property on the horse, and at last Charley asked where the races were to be, and the hour and the day. The gentleman told him.

'Let you put a horse with a bridle and saddle on it every seven miles along the road from here to the racecourse on that day,' said Lambert, 'and I'll be in it.'

When the gentleman was gone, Charley stripped off his clothes and got into his bed. Then he sent for the doctor, and when he heard him coming he began throwing about his arms the way the doctor would think his pulse was up with the fever.

The doctor felt his pulse and told him to stay quiet till the next day, when he would see him again.

The next day it was the same thing, and so on till the day of the races. That morning Charley had his pulse beating so hard the doctor thought bad of him.

'I'm going to the races now, Charley,' said he, 'but I'll come in and see you again when I'll be coming back in the evening, and let you be very careful and quiet till you see me.'

As soon as he had gone Charley leapt up out of bed and got on his horse, and rode seven miles to where the first horse was waiting for him. Then he rode that horse seven miles, and another horse seven miles more, till he came to the racecourse.

He rode on the gentleman's horse, and he won the race.

There were great crowds looking on, and when they saw him coming in they said it was Charley Lambert, or the devil was in it, for there was no one else could bring in a horse the way he did, for the leg was after being knocked off of the horse and he came in all the same.

When the race was over, he got up on the horse was waiting for him, and away with him for seven miles. Then he rode the other horse seven miles, and his own horse seven miles, and when he got home he threw off his clothes and lay down on his bed.

After a while the doctor came back and said it was a great race they were after having.

The next day the people were saying it was Charley Lambert was the man who rode the horse. An inquiry was held, and the doctor swore that Charley was ill in his bed, and he had seen him before the race and after it, so the gentleman saved his fortune.

After that he told me another story of the same sort about a fairy rider, who met a gentleman that was after losing all his fortune but a shilling, and begged the shilling of him. The gentleman gave him the shilling, and the fairy rider—a little red man—rode a horse for him in a race, waving a red handkerchief to him as a signal when he was to double the stakes, and made him a rich man.

Then he gave us an extraordinary English doggerel rhyme which I took down, though it seems singularly incoherent when written out at length. These rhymes are repeated by the old men as a sort of chant, and when a line comes that is more than usually irregular they seem to take a real delight in forcing it into the mould of the recitative. All the time he was chanting the old man kept up a kind of snakelike movement in his body, which seemed to fit the chant and make it part of him.

The White Horse

*My horse he is white,
Though at first he was bay,
And he took great delight
In travelling by night
And by day.

*His travels were great
If I could but half of them tell,
He was rode in the garden by Adam,
The day that he fell.

*On Babylon plains
He ran with speed for the plate,
He was hunted next day
By Hannibal the great.

*After that he was hunted
In the chase of a fox,
When Nebuchadnezzar ate grass,
In the shape of an ox.

At the time of the Flood
He was rode by many a spark
And his courage was good
When Noah took him into the Ark.

He followed Moses who rode
Him through the red sea,
He then let him out and he sensibly
Galloped away.

*He was with king Pharaoh in Egypt
When fortune did smile,
And he rode him stately along
The gay banks of the Nile.

*He was with king Saul and all
His troubles went through,
He was with king David the day
That Goliath he slew.

And when he saw king David
Ahunted about by king Saul,
My horse took his leave
And bid farewell to them all.

He was with Juda when Juda
The Maccabeus the great
He rode on my horse
As the ancient historians relate.

He was with Cyrus whose name
Is in History found,
He rode on my horse at the taking
Of Babylon's town.

And the Jews remain in chains
And mercy implore
King Cyrus proclaimed again,
To have them restored.

He conducted them home
Straightways to Babylon's town
Where the King was restored once more
And solemnly crowned.

The poor captive Jews this news
Received with great joy.
My horse got the news
And pursues his journey to Troy.

*When (   ) came to Troy with joy,
My horse he was found,
He crossed over the walls and entered
The city I'm told.

On Africa plains my horse he conquered
That part of the gold globe,
And to try it again (he employed)
The patience of Job.

*I come on him again, in Spain,
And he in full bloom,
By the Hannibal the great he was rode,
And he crossing the Alps into Rome.

*The horse being tall
And the Alps very high,
His rider did fall
And Hannibal the great lost an eye.

My horse got no ease
Although his rider did fall,
He was mounted again by young Scipio
Who did him extol.

He was with Brian the Brave,
When Munster men he did command,
In thirty battles he drove
The wild Danes from the land.

And to tell you the truth
And the truth I like always to tell,
He was rode by St Ruth the day
That in Aughrim he fell.

But Sarsfield the brave
At the siege of Limerick's town
He rode on my horse, and crossed
Over the Channel I'm told.

At the battle of Clontarf,
He fought on Good Friday all day
And all that remained he drove them
Into the sea.

*He was with king James who sailed
To the Irish shore,
But at last he got lame,
When the Boyne's bloody battle was o'er.

*He was rode by the greatest of men
At famed Waterloo,
Brave Daniel O'Connell he sat
On his back it is true.

To shake off the yoke which Erin
Long patiently bore,
My horse he's fatigued
And he means to travel no more.

When banished from Erin
My horse was losing its way,
And by all its fatigues it 's no wonder
If now he was bay.

He's landed in Erin
In Kerry he does reside
His smith is at work for to fit him
With new shoes again.

*Brave Dan's on his back,
He's ready once more for the field.
He never will stop till the Tories,
He'll make them to yield.[1]

Grotesque as this long rhyme appears, it has, as I said, a sort of existence when it is crooned by the old man at his fireside, and it has great fame in the island. The old man himself is hoping that I will print it, for it would not be fair, he says, that it should die out of the world, and he is the only man here who knows it, and none of them have ever heard it on the mainland. He has a couple more examples of the same kind of doggerel, but I have not taken them down.

Both in English and in Irish the songs are full of words the people do not understand themselves, and when they come to say the words slowly their memory is usually uncertain.

All the morning I have been digging maidenhair ferns with a boy I met on the rocks, who was in great sorrow because his father died suddenly a week ago of a pain in his heart.

'We wouldn't have chosen to lose our father for all the gold there is in the world,' he said, 'and it's great loneliness and sorrow there is in the house now.'

Then he told me that a brother of his who is a stoker in the Navy had come home a little while before his father died, and that he had spent all his money in having a fine funeral, with plenty of drink at it, and tobacco.

'My brother has been a long way in the world,' he said, 'and seen great wonders. He does be telling us of the people that do

[1] This is the complete version of the poem. It is taken from Box-file G, pp. 185–90. Of the twenty-nine stanzas Synge printed only twelve and these are marked here by an asterisk.

come out to them from Italy, and Spain, and Portugal, and that it is a sort of Irish they do be talking—not English at all—though it is only a word here and there you'd understand.'

When we had dug out enough of roots from the deep crannies in the rocks where they are only to be found, I gave my companion a few pence, and sent him back to his cottage.

The old man who tells me the Irish poems is curiously pleased with the translations I have made from some of them.

He would never be tired, he says, listening while I would be reading them, and they are much finer things than his old bits of rhyme.

Here is one of them, as near the Irish as I am able to make it:—

Rucard Mor

I put the sorrow of destruction on the bad luck,
For it would be a pity ever to deny it,
It is to me it is stuck,
By loneliness my pain, my complaining.

It is the fairy-host
Put me a-wandering
And took from me my goods of the world.

At Mannistir na Ruaidthe
It is on me the shameless deed was done:
Finn Bheara and his fairy-host
Took my little horse on me from under the bag.

If they left me the skin
It would bring me tobacco for three months,
But they did not leave anything with me
But the old minister in its place.

Am not I to be pitied?
My bond and my note are on her,
And the price of her not yet paid,
My loneliness, my pain, my complaining.

The devil a hill or a glen, or highest fort
Ever was built in Ireland,
Is not searched on me for my mare,
And I am still at my complaining.

I got up in the morning,
I put a red spark in my pipe.
I went to the Cnoc-Maithe
To get satisfaction from them.

I spoke to them,
If it was in them to do a right thing,
To get me my little mare,
Or I would be changing my wits.

'Do you hear, Rucard Mor?
It is not here is your mare,
She is in Glenasmoil
With the fairy-men these three months.'

I ran on in my walking,
I followed the road straightly,
I was in Glenasmoil
Before the noon was ended.

I spoke to the fairy-man,
If it was in him to do a right thing,
To get me my little mare,
Or I would be changing my wits.

'Do you hear, Rucard Mor?
It is not here is your mare,
She is in Cnoc Bally Brishlawn
With the horseman of the music these three months.'

I ran off on my walking,
I followed the road straightly,
I was in Cnoc Bally Brishlawn
With the black fall of the night.

That is a place was a crowd
As it was seen by me,
All the weavers of the globe,
It is there you would have news of them.

I spoke to the horseman,
If it was in him to do a right thing,
To get me my little mare,
Or I would be changing my wits.

'Do you hear, Rucard Mor?
It is not here is your mare,
She is in Cnoc Cruachan,
In the back end of the palace.'

I ran off on my walking,
I followed the road straightly,
I made no rest or stop
Till I was in face of the palace.

That is the place was a crowd
As it appeared to me,
The men and women of the country,
And they all making merry.

Arthur Scoil (?) stood up
And began himself giving the lead,
It is joyful, light and active,
I would have danced the course with them.

They drew up on their feet
And they began to laugh,—
'Look at Rucard Mor,
And he looking for his little mare.'

I spoke to the man,
And he ugly and humpy,
Unless he would get me my mare
I would break a third of his bones.

'Do you hear, Rucard Mor?
It is not here is your mare,
She is in Alvin of Leinster,
On a halter with my mother.'

I ran off on my walking,
And I came to Alvin of Leinster.
I met the old woman—
On my word she was not pleasing.

I spoke to the old woman,
And she broke out in English:
'Get agone, you rascal,
I don't like your notions.'

'Do you hear, you old woman?
Keep away from me with your English,
But speak to me with the tongue
I hear from every person.'

'It is from me you will get word of her,
Only you come too late—
I made a hunting cap
For Conal Cath of her yesterday.'

I ran off on my walking,
Through roads that were cold and dirty,
I fell in with the fairy-man,
And he lying down on in the Ruaidthe.

'I pity a man without a cow,
I pity a man without a sheep,
But in the case of a man without a horse
It is hard for him to be long in the world.'

This morning, when I had been lying for a long time on a rock near the sea watching some hooded crows that were dropping shellfish on the rocks to break them, I saw one bird that had a large white object which it was dropping continually without any result. I got some stones and tried to drive it off when the thing had fallen, but several times the bird was too quick for me and made off with it before I could get down to him. At last, however, I dropped a stone almost on top of him and he flew away. I clambered down hastily, and found to my amazement a worn golf-ball! No doubt it had been brought out some way or other from the links in County Clare, which are not far off, and the bird had been trying half the morning to break it.

Further on I had a long talk with a young man who is inquisitive about modern life, and I explained to him an elaborate trick or corner on the Stock Exchange that I heard of lately. When I got him to understand it fully, he shouted with delight and amusement.

'Well,' he said when he was quiet again, 'isn't it a great wonder to think that those rich men are as big rogues as ourselves.'

The old story-teller has given me a long rhyme about a man who fought with an eagle. It is rather irregular and has some obscure passages, but I have translated it with the scholar.

Phelim and the Eagle

On my getting up in the morning
And I bothered, on a Sunday,
I put my brogues on me,
And I going to Tierny
In the Glen of the Dead People.
It is there the big eagle fell in with me,
He like a black stack of turf sitting up stately.

I called him a lout and a fool,
The son of a female and a fool,
Of the race of the Clan Cleopas, the biggest rogues in the land.
That and my seven curses
And never a good day to be on you,
Who stole my little cock from me that could crow the sweetest.

'Keep your wits right in you
And don't curse me too greatly,
By my strength and my oath
I never took rent of you,
I didn't grudge what you would have to spare
In the house of the burnt pigeons,
It is always useful you were to men of business.

'But get off home
And ask Nora
What name was on the young woman that scalded his head.
The feathers there were on his ribs
Are burnt on the hearth,
And they eat him and they taking and it wasn't much were thankful.'

'You are a liar, you stealer,
They did not eat him, and they're taking
Nor a taste of the sort without being thankful,
You took him yesterday
As Nora told me,
And the harvest quarter will not be spent till I take a tax of you.'

'Before I lost the Fianna
It was a fine boy I was,
It was not about thieving was my knowledge,
But always putting spells,
Playing games and matches with the strength of Gol Mac Morna,
And you are making me a rogue
At the end of my life.'

'There is a part of my father's books with me,
Keeping in the bottom of a box,
And when I read them the tears fall down from me.
But I found out in history
That you are a son of the Dearg Mor,
If it is fighting you want and you won't be thankful.'

The Eagle dressed his bravery
With his share of arms and his clothes,
He had the sword that was the sharpest
Could be got anywhere.
I and my scythe with me,
And nothing on but my shirt,
We went at each other early in the day.

We were as two giants
Ploughing in a valley in a glen of the mountains.
We did not know for the while which was the better man.
You could hear the shakes that were on our arms under each other,
From that till the sunset,
Till it was forced on him to give up.

I wrote a 'challenge boxail' to him
On the morning of the next day,
To come till we would fight without doubt at the dawn of day.
The second fist I drew on him
I struck him on the bone of his jaw,
He fell, and it is no lie there was a cloud in his head.

The Eagle stood up,
He took the end of my hand:—
'You are the finest man I ever saw in my life,
Go off home, my blessing will be on you for ever,
You have saved the fame of Eire for yourself till the Day of the Judgment.'

Ah! neighbours, did you hear
The goodness and power of Felim?
The biggest wild beast you could get,
The second fist he drew on it
He struck it on the jaw,
It fell, and it did not rise
Till the end of two days.

Well as I seem to know these people of the islands, there is hardly a day that I do not come upon some new primitive feature of their life.

Yesterday I went into a cottage where the woman was at work and very carelessly dressed. She waited for a while till I got into conversation with her husband, and then she slipped into the corner and put on a clean petticoat and a bright shawl round her neck. Then she came back and took her place at the fire.

This evening I was in another cottage till very late talking to the people. When the little boy—the only child of the house—got sleepy, the old grandmother took him on her lap and began singing to him. As soon as he was drowsy she worked his clothes off him by degrees, scratching him softly with her nails as she did so all over his body. Then she washed his feet with a little water out of a pot and put him into his bed.

When I was going home the wind was driving the sand into my face so that I could hardly find my way. I had to hold my hat over my mouth and nose, and my hand over my eyes while I groped along, with my feet feeling for rocks and holes in the sand.

I have been sitting all the morning with an old man who was making sugawn ropes for his house, and telling me stories while he worked. He was a pilot when he was young, and we had great talk at first about Germans, and Italians, and Russians, and the ways of seaport towns. Then he came round to talk of the middle island, and he told me this story which shows the curious jealousy that is between the islands:—

Long ago we used all to be pagans, and the saints used to be coming to teach us about God and the creation of the world. The people on the middle island were the last to keep a hold on the fire-worshipping, or whatever it was they had in those days, but in the long run a saint got in among them and they began listening to him, though they would often say in the evening they believed, and then say the morning after that, they did not believe. In the end the saint gained them over and they began building a church, and the saint had tools that were in use with them for working with the stones. When the church was half-way up the people held a kind of meeting one night among themselves, when the saint was asleep in his bed, to see if they did really believe and no mistake in it.

The leading man got up, and this is what he said: that they should go down and throw their tools over the cliff, for if there was such a man as God, and if the saint was as well known to Him as he said, then he would be as well able to bring up the tools out of the sea as they were to throw them in.

They went then and threw their tools over the cliff.

When the saint came down to the church in the morning the workmen were all sitting on the stones and no work doing.

'For what cause are you idle?' asked the saint.

'We have no tools,' said the men, and then they told him the story of what they had done.

He kneeled down and prayed God that the tools might come up out of the sea, and after that he prayed that no other people might ever be as great fools as the people on the middle island, and that God might preserve their dark minds of folly to them till the end of the world. And that is why no man out of that island can tell you a whole story without stammering, or bring any work to end without a fault in it.

I asked him if he had known old Pat Dirane on the middle island, and heard the fine stories he used to tell.

'No one knew him better than I did,' he said; 'for I do often be in that island making curaghs for the people. One day old Pat came down to me when I was after tarring a new curagh, and he asked me to put a little tar on the knees of his breeches the way the rain wouldn't come through on him.

'I took the brush in my hand, and I had him tarred down to his feet before he knew what I was at. "Turn round the other side now," I said, "and you'll be able to sit where you like." Then he felt the tar coming in hot against his skin and he began cursing my soul, and I was sorry for the trick I'd played on him.'

This old man was the same type as the genial, whimsical old

men one meets all through Ireland, and had none of the local characteristics that are so marked on Inishmaan.

When we were tired talking I showed some of my tricks and a little crowd collected. When they were gone another old man who had come up began telling us about the fairies. One night when he was coming home from the lighthouse he heard a man riding on the road behind him, and he stopped to wait for him, but nothing came. Then he heard as if there was a man trying to catch a horse on the rocks, and in a little time he went on. The noise behind him got bigger as he went along as if twenty horses, and then as if a hundred or a thousand, were galloping after him. When he came to the stile where he had to leave the road and got out over it, something hit against him and threw him down on the rock, and a gun he had in his hand fell into the field beyond him.

'I asked the priest we had at that time what was in it,' he said, 'and the priest told me it was the fallen angels; and I don't know but it was.'

'Another time,' he went on, 'I was coming down where there is a bit of a cliff and a little hole under it, and I heard a flute playing in the hole or beside it, and that was before the dawn began. Whatever any one says there are strange things. There was one night thirty years ago a man came down to get my wife to go up to his wife, for she was in childbed.

'He was something to do with the lighthouse or the coast-guards, one of them Protestants who don't believe in any of these things and do be making fun of us. Well, he asked me to go down and get a quart of spirits while my wife would be getting herself ready, and he said he would go down along with me if I was afraid.

'I said I was not afraid, and I went by myself.

'When I was coming back there was something on the path, and wasn't I a foolish fellow, I might have gone to one side or the other over the sand, but I went on straight till I was near it—till I was too near it—then I remembered that I had heard them saying none of those creatures can stand before you and you saying the *De Profundis*, so I began saying it, and the thing ran off over the sand and I got home.

'Some of the people used to say it was only an old jackass that was on the path before me, but I never heard tell of an old jackass would run away from a man and he saying the *De Profundis*.'

I told him the story of the fairy ship which had disappeared when the man made the sign of the cross, as I had heard it on the middle island.

'There do be strange things on the sea,' he said. 'One night I was down there where you can see that green point, and I saw a ship coming in and I wondered what it would be doing coming so close to the rocks. It came straight on towards the place I was in, and then I got frightened and I ran up to the houses, and when the captain saw me running he changed his course and went away.

'Sometimes I used to go out as a pilot at that time—I went a few times only. Well, one Sunday a man came down and said there was a big ship coming into the sound. I ran down with two men and we went out in a curagh; we went round the point where they said the ship was, and there was no ship in it. As it was a Sunday we had nothing to do, and it was a fine calm day, so we rowed out a long way looking for the ship, till I was further than I ever was before or after. When I wanted to turn back we saw a great flock of birds on the water and they all black, without a white bird through them. They had no fear of us at all, and the men with me wanted to go up to them, so we went further. When we were quite close they got up, so many that they blackened the sky, and they lit down again a hundred or maybe a hundred and twenty yards off. We went after them again, and one of the men wanted to kill one with a thole-pin, and the other man wanted to kill one with his rowing stick. I was afraid they would upset the curagh, but they would go after the birds.

'When we were quite close one man threw the pin and the other man hit at them with his rowing stick, and the two of them fell over in the curagh, and she turned on her side and only it was quite calm the lot of us were drowned.

'I think those black gulls and the ship were the same sort, and after that I never went out again as a pilot. It is often curaghs go out to ships and find there is no ship.

'A while ago a curagh went out to a ship from the big island, and there was no ship; and all the men in the curagh were drowned. A fine song was made about them after that, though I never heard it myself.

'Another day a curagh was out fishing from this island, and the men saw a hooker not far from them, and they rowed up to it to get a light for their pipes—at that time there were no matches—and when they got up to the big boat it was gone out of its place, and they were in great fear.'

Then he told me a story he had got from the mainland about a man who was driving one night through the country, and met a woman who came up to him and asked him to take her into his cart. He thought something was not right about her, and he went on. When he had gone a little way he looked back, and it was a pig was on the road and not a woman at all.

He thought he was a done man, but he went on. When he was going through a wood further on, two men came out to him, one from each side of the road, and they took hold of the bridle of the horse and led it on between them. They were old stale men with frieze clothes on them, and the old fashions. When they came out of the wood he found people as if there was a fair on the road, with the people buying and selling and they not living people at all. The old men took him through the crowd, and then they left him. When he got home and told the old people of the two old men and the ways and fashions they had about them, the old people told him it was his two grandfathers had taken care of him, for they had had a great love for him and he a lad growing up.

This evening we had a dance in the inn parlour, where a fire had been lighted and the tables had been pushed into the corners. There was no master of the ceremonies, and when I had played two or three jigs and other tunes on my fiddle, there was a pause, as I did not know how much of my music the people wanted, or who else could be got to sing or play. For a moment a deadlock seemed to be coming, but a young girl I knew fairly well saw my difficulty, and took the management of our festivities into her hands. At first she asked a coastguard's daughter to play a reel on the mouth organ, which she did at once with admirable spirit and rhythm. Then the little girl asked me to play again, telling me what I should choose, and went on in the same way managing the evening till she thought it was time to go home. Then she stood up, thanked me in Irish, and walked out of the door, without looking at anybody, but followed almost at once by the whole party.

When they had gone I sat for a while on a barrel in the public-house talking to some young men who were reading a paper in Irish. Then I had a long evening with the scholar and two story-tellers—both old men who had been pilots—taking down stories and poems. We were at work for nearly six hours, and the more matter we got the more the old men seemed to remember.

'I was to go out fishing to-night,' said the younger as he came in, 'but I promised you to come, and you're a civil man, so I wouldn't take five pounds to break my word to you. And now'—taking up his glass of whisky—'here's to your good health, and may you live till they make you a coffin out of a gooseberry bush, or till you die in childbed.'

They drank my health and our work began.

'Have you heard tell of the poet MacSweeny?' said the same man, sitting down near me.

'I have,' I said, 'in the town of Galway.'

'Well,' he said, 'I'll tell you his piece "The Big Wedding," for it's a fine piece and there aren't many that know it. There was a poor servant girl out in the country, and she got married to a poor servant boy. MacSweeny knew the two of them, and he was away at that time and it was a month before he came back. When he came back he went to see Peggy O'Hara—that was the name of the girl—and he asked her if they had had a great wedding. Peggy said it was only middling, but they hadn't forgotten him all the same, and she had a bottle of whisky for him in the cupboard. He sat down by the fire and began drinking the whisky. When he had a couple of glasses taken and was warm by the fire, he began making a song, and this was the song he made about the wedding of Peggy O'Hara.'

He had the poem in both English and Irish, but as it has been found elsewhere and attributed to another folk-poet, I need not give it.

We had another round of porter and whisky, and then the old man who had MacSweeny's wedding gave us a bit of a drinking song, which the scholar took down and I translated with him afterwards:—

'This is what the old woman says at the Beulleaca when she sees a man without knowledge—

'Were you ever at the house of the Still, did you ever get a drink from it? Neither wine nor beer is as sweet as it is, but it is well I was not burnt when I fell down after a drink of it by the fire of Mr. Sloper.

'I praise Owen O'Hernon over all the doctors of Ireland, it is he put drugs on the water, and it lying on the barley.

'If you gave but a drop of it to an old woman who does be walking the world with a stick, she would think for a week that it was a fine bed was made for her.'

After that I had to get out my fiddle and play some tunes for them while they finished their whisky. A new stock of porter was brought in this morning to the little public-house underneath my room, and I could hear in the intervals of our talk that a number of men had come in to treat some neighbours from the middle island, and were singing many songs, some of them in English of the kind I have given, but most of them in Irish.

A little later when the party broke up downstairs my old men got nervous about the fairies—they live some distance away—and set off across the sandhills.

The next day I left with the steamer.

PART THREE

IN WICKLOW, WEST KERRY AND CONNEMARA

IN WICKLOW[1]

AN AUTUMN NIGHT IN THE HILLS

A FEW years ago a pointer dog of my acquaintance was wounded by accident in a wild glen on the western slope of County Wicklow. He was left at the cottage of an under-keeper, or bailiff —the last cottage on the edge of two ranges of mountains that stretch on the north and west to the plain of Kildare—and a few weeks later I made my way there to bring him down to his master.

It was an afternoon of September, and some heavy rain of the night before had made the road which led up to the cottage through the middle of the glen as smooth as a fine beach, while the clearness of the air gave the granite that ran up on either side of the way a peculiar tinge that was nearly luminous against the shadow of the hills. Every cottage that I passed had a group of rowan trees beside it covered with scarlet berries that gave brilliant points of colour of curious effect.

Just as I came to the cottage the road turned across a swollen river which I had to cross on a range of slippery stones. Then, when I had gone a few yards further, I heard a bark of welcome, and the dog ran down to meet me. The noise he made brought two women to the door of the cottage, one a finely made girl, with an exquisitely open and graceful manner, the other a very old woman. A sudden shower had come up without any warning over the rim of the valley, so I went into the cottage and sat down on a

[1] Volume Four of the *Works* of 1910 consisted of 'In Wicklow', 'In West Kerry', 'In the Congested Districts', and 'Under Ether'. The volume in the 1911 Library edition was similar except that 'Under Ether' was omitted and the third section was re-named 'In Connemara'. Part Three of the present Oxford Synge *Prose* is based on the 1911 Library edition and contains all the above material, with certain additions to five essays and with two extra essays: 'An Autumn Night in the Hills', first published in April 1903 in *The Gael* (New York), and 'People and Places', made up (in accordance with Synge's practice) from various drafts and notebooks among the Synge material, particulars of which are given further on. The Stephens Typescript, page 1376, states: 'In compiling his material Synge's practice was to write down stories, phrases, unusual words and scraps of conversation. . . . He wrote his articles by collecting notes of kindred experiences into groups to which he could give titles. In doing this he did not interfere with the spontaneous quality of his first impressions, but combined recollections so as to make each article an artistic whole, internally balanced like a musical composition.'

sort of bench in the chimney-corner, at the end of a long low room with open rafters.

'You've come on a bad day,' said the old woman, 'for you won't see any of the lads or men about the place.'

'I suppose they went out to cut their oats,' I said, 'this morning while the weather was fine.'

'They did not,' she answered, 'but they're after going down to Aughrim for the body of Mary Kinsella, that is to be brought this night from the station. There will be a wake then at the last cottage you're after passing, where you saw all them trees with the red berries on them.'

She stopped for a moment while the girl gave me a drink of milk.

'I'm afraid it's a lot of trouble I'm giving you,' I said as I took it, 'and you busy, with no men in the place.'

'No trouble at all in the world,' said the girl, 'and if it was itself, wouldn't any one be glad of it in the lonesome place we're in?'

The old woman began talking again:

'You saw no sign or trace on the road of the people coming with the body?'

'No sign,' I said, 'and who was she at all?'

'She was a fine young woman with two children,' she went on, 'and a year and a half ago she went wrong in her head, and they had to send her away. And then up there in the Richmond asylum maybe they thought the sooner they were shut of her the better, for she died two days ago this morning, and now they're bringing her up to have a wake, and they'll bury her beyond at the churches, far as it is, for it's there are all the people of the two families.'

While we talked I had been examining a wound in the dog's side near the end of his lung.

'He'll do rightly now,' said the girl who had come in again and was putting tea-things on the table. 'He'll do rightly now. You wouldn't know he'd been hurted at all only for a kind of a cough he'll give now and again. Did they ever tell you the way he was hit?' she added, going down on her knees in the chimney-corner with some dry twigs in her hand and making a little fire on the flag-stone a few inches from the turf.

I told her I had heard nothing but the fact of his wound.

'Well,' she said, 'a great darkness and storm came down that night and they all out on the hill. The rivers rose, and they were there groping along by the turf track not minding the dogs. Then an old rabbit got up and run before them, and a man put up his gun and shot across it. When he fired that dog run out from behind a rock, and one grain of the shot cut the scruff off his nose, and another went in there where you were looking, at the butt of his ribs. He dropped down bleeding and howling, and they thought he was killed. The night was falling and they had no way they could carry him, so they made a kind of a shelter for him with sticks and turf, and they left him while they would be going for a sack.'

She stopped for a moment to knead some dough and put down a dozen hot cakes—cut out with the mouth of a tumbler—in a frying pan on the little fire she had made with the twigs. While she was doing so the old woman took up the talk.

'Ah,' she said, 'there do be queer things them nights out on the mountains and in the lakes among them. I was reared beyond in the valley where the mines used to be, in the valley of the Lough Nahanagan, and it's many a queer story I've heard of the spirit does be in that lake.'

'I have sometimes been there fishing till it was dark,' I said when she paused, 'and heard strange noises in the cliff.'

'There was an uncle of mine,' she continued, 'and he was there the same way as yourself, fishing with a big fly in the darkness of the night, and the spirit came down out of the clouds and rifted the waters asunder. He was afeared then and he run down to the houses trembling and shaking. There was another time,' she went on, 'a man came round to this county who was after swimming through the water of every lake in Ireland. He went up to swim in that lake, and a brother of my own went up along with him. The gentleman had heard tell of the spirit but not a bit would he believe in it. He went down on the bank, and he had a big black dog with him, and he took off his clothes.

' "For the love of God," said my brother, "put that dog in before you go in yourself, the way you'll see if he ever comes out of it." The gentleman said he would do that and they threw in a stick or a stone and the dog leapt in and swam out to it. Then he turned round again and he swam and he swam, and not a bit nearer did he come.

' "He's a long time swimming back," said the gentleman.

' "I'm thinking your honour'll have a grey beard before he

comes back," said my brother, and before the word was out of his mouth the dog went down out of their sight, and the inside out of him came up on the top of the water.'

By this time the cakes were ready and the girl put them on a plate for me at the table, and poured out a cup of tea from the tea-pot, putting the milk and sugar herself into my cup as is the custom with the cottage people of Wicklow. Then she put the tea-pot down in the embers of the turf and sat down in the place I had left.

'Well,' she said, 'I was telling you the story of that night. When they got back here they sent up two lads for the dog, with a sack to carry him on if he was alive and a spade to bury him if he was dead. When they came to the turf where they left him they saw him near twenty yards down the path. The crathur thought they were after leaving him there to die, and he got that lonesome he dragged himself along like a Christian till he got too weak with the bleeding. James, the big lad, walked up again him first with the spade in his hand. When he seen the spade he let a kind of a groan out of him.

'That dog's as wise as a child, and he knew right well it was to bury him they brought the spade. Then Mike went up and laid down the sack on the ground, and the minute he seen it he jumped up and tumbled in on it himself. Then they carried him down, and the crathur getting his death with the cold and the great rain was falling. When they brought him in here you'd have thought he was dead. We put up a settle bed before the fire, and we put him into it. The heat roused him a bit, and he stretched out his legs and gave two groans out of him like an old man. Mike thought he'd drink some milk so we heated a cup of it over the fire. When he put down his tongue into it he began to cough and bleed, then he turned himself over in the settle bed and looked up at me like an old man. I sat up with him that night and it raining and blowing. At four in the morning I gave him a sup more of the milk and he was able to drink it.

'The next day he was stronger, and we gave him a little new milk every now and again. We couldn't keep him near the fire. So we put him in the little room beyond by the door and an armful of hay in along with him. In the afternoon the boys were out on the mountain and the old woman was gone somewhere else, and I was chopping sticks in the lane. I heard a sort of a noise and there he was with his head out through the window looking out on me in the lane. I was afraid he was lonesome in there all by himself, so I put in one of our old dogs to keep him company. Then I stuffed an old hat into the window and I thought they'd be quiet together.

'But what did they do but begin to fight in there all in the dark as they were. I opened the door and out runs that lad before I could stop him. Not a bit would he go in again, so I had to leave him running about beside me. He's that loyal to me now you wouldn't believe it. When I go for the cow he comes along with me, and when I go to make up a bit of hay on the hill he'll come and make a sort of bed for himself under a haycock, and not a bit of him will look at Mike or the boys.'

'Ah,' said the old woman, as the girl got up to pour me out another cup from the tea-pot, 'it 's herself will be lonesome when that dog is gone, he's never out of her sight, and you'd do right to send her down a little dog all for herself.'

'You would so,' said the girl, 'but maybe he wouldn't be loyal to me, and I wouldn't give a thraneen for a dog as wasn't loyal.'

'Would you believe it,' said the old woman again, 'when the gentleman wrote down about that dog Mike went out to where she was in the haggard, and says, "They're after sending me the prescription for that dog," says he, "to put on his tombstone." And she went down quite simple, and told the boys below in the bog, and it wasn't till they began making game of her that she seen the way she'd been humbugged.'

'That 's the truth,' said the girl, 'I went down quite simple, and indeed it's a small wonder, that dog 's as fit for a decent burial as many that gets it.'

Meanwhile the shower had turned to a dense torrent of mountain rain, and although the evening was hardly coming on, it was so dark that the girl lighted a lamp and hung it at the corner of the chimney. The kitchen was longer than most that I have met with and had a skeleton staircase at the far end that looked vague and shadowy in the dim light. The old woman wore one of the old-fashioned caps with a white frill round the face, and entered with great fitness into the general scheme of the kitchen. I did not like leaving them to go into the raw night for a long walk on the mountains, and I sat down and talked to them for a long time, till the old woman thought I would be benighted.

'Go out now,' she said at last to the girl, 'go out now and see what water is coming over the fall above, for with this rain the water'll rise fast, and maybe he'll have to walk down to the bridge, a rough walk when the night is coming on.'

The girl came back in a moment.

'It's riz already,' she said. 'He'll want to go down to the bridge.' Then turning to me: 'If you'll come now I'll show you the way you have to go, and I'll wait below for the boys; it won't be long now till they come with the body of Mary Kinsella.'

We went out at once and she walked quickly before me through a maze of small fields and pieces of bog, where I would have soon lost the track if I had been alone.

The bridge, when we reached it, was a narrow wooden structure fastened up on iron bars which pierced large boulders in the bed of the river. An immense grey flood was struggling among the stones, looking dangerous and desolate in the half-light of the evening, while the wind was so great that the bridge wailed and quivered and whistled under our feet. A few paces further on we came to a cottage where the girl wished me a good journey and went in to wait for her brothers.

The daylight still lingered but the heavy rain and a thick white cloud that had come down made everything unreal and dismal to an extraordinary degree. I went up a road where on one side I could see the trunks of beech trees reaching up wet and motionless—with odd sighs and movements when a gust caught the valley—into a greyness overhead, where nothing could be distinguished. Between them there were masses of shadow, and masses of half-luminous fog with black branches across them. On the other side of the road flocks of sheep I could not see coughed and choked with sad guttural noises in the shelter of the hedge, or rushed away through a gap when they felt the dog was near them. Above everything my ears were haunted by the dead heavy swish of the rain. When I came near the first village I heard a loud noise and commotion. Many cars and gigs were collected at the door of the public-house, and the bar was filled with men who were drinking and making a noise. Everything was dark and confused yet on one car I was able to make out the shadow of a coffin, strapped in the rain, with the body of Mary Kinsella.

[PEOPLE AND PLACES][1]

CONTINUOUS wet weather in the early autumn is hurtful enough to the interests of the farmer, but in it Ireland becomes worthy in a wonderful way of the epithet given her by St. Columcille. It is not so much the few well known waterfalls like those of Deer Park and the Devil's Glen that one thinks of as giving the old saint his image but rather places like Glenmacnas and Glenmalure where after a stormy night's rain the whole valley is filled with a riot of waterfalls. Sometimes these sudden rainfalls are followed by a singularly beautiful morning and then each of these glens can be seen at its moment of most direct and wonderful colour [and] beauty. Glenmacnas, in particular, has a variety of streams and turns and vegetation. The moment Laragh is left behind several long curves of the river can be seen all leaping with a white exuberance in the sunshine. No English word seems to describe the swift gaiety of the water, but the musical 'brio' rises at once in one's mind. At one side of the river there is a thick oak wood—probably one of the survivals of old forest that are still found in this locality, and on the other between the river and the road a strip of bog which is covered at this season I am thinking of—the early autumn—with flowering dwarf furze-bushes, and flowering heath both set in masses of rushes and bog grasses of wonderful colour. Such patches of growth come out on these mornings after rain with extraordinary purity and richness of tint, and for the eye that is sensitive to colour there is nothing, I think, that is more beautiful.

All up the glen one can see as a background curving hills of bracken and mountain grass [with] wonderful lights and shadows from the clouds while at the very end of what one is able to see a blue mountain—blue with a luminous living blue like that of a precious stone—stands across the glen half covered up by a soft streamer of cloud. A little farther on one comes in sight of a river leaping over the left side of the glen and we are in Waterfall Land. This river—it is a mere rivulet running on naked rocks in

[1] From the beginning, Notebook 33 (probably written in 1907) is used. Synge here has a heading, 'The Waterfall Land'. It probably links with the epithet given by St. Columcille.

dry weather—comes from a peat covered table land between this glen and the next, and its water takes so much boggy substance with it that when it turns to foam the whiteness has a golden volume in the sunshine that is extraordinarily rich. At one place we can nearly see the line where it leaps into the valley.

Nearly opposite this faller there is another of a quite different nature. The right side of the glen in this place slopes up and ends with slightly overhanging rock that shows a blackened underside in ordinary weather. In flood time, however, thin sheets of water fall everywhere across it and form as they change endlessly in their shape a silvery lace-work of undreamable fineness against the black background of rock.

At one place the main river of the valley passes through a steep gulley with a pool—a devil's punch-bowl—and then it runs for a while through a flat alluvial space where it has shallow banks. Just here every flood covers nearly the whole surface of the valley and the road itself is ankle or even knee deep for nearly a quarter of a mile. Haycocks stand in a forlorn ring above their tanned reflections in a passing lake of blue. The cottages—this valley is rather thickly populated—are all placed on a high enough level to be beyond the reach of any ordinary flood but their soaked thatch gives a yellow counter note to the wet haycocks and the drowned oat-field that try to ripen in one or two places. The central waterfall when in full flood shows the golden tint I have already spoken of and [brings] wonderful life to an otherwise rather dead grey and green end of this exquisite glen.

As the road rises gradually along the side of the hill to pass out across the top of the waterfall one can look down on one's left on a little settlement of three or four cottages at the bottom of the glen where one can nearly always make out a boy shearing sheep or a tall girl with [bare] feet and something that looks like a sack for a petticoat and perhaps a weather-toned scarlet hat getting water from the river. . . .

Apart from the effects of the brilliant showery weather there is an eastwind haze peculiar to September that has wonderfully golden effects near sunset on the hills. The air on these times is quite still and the coming up and passing of such hue on the heather seems an important interesting event. All round in the valleys geese and cattle can be heard calling in the mist, and in the sky very often flocks of golden or green plover fly round and round [in an] infinity of crying. The sheep one sees against the light are transfigured by a golden halo that makes them appear like symbolical figures on stained glass. The foreground of flowering heather and dwarf furze gains new importance by the sharpness of the hill, and the skeletons of burnt furze that stick up here and there have a curious desolate symmetry. . . .

At the end of the Upper Lake at Glendalough one is quite shut off from the part that has been spoiled by civilization, and when one fishes there from dusk to midnight a feeling of isolation creeps over one that it would be hard to pass. A little wind is of use when one is fishing, but it is on perfectly still nights that the lake is most beautiful. The water catches and returns in a singular half-interpreting way the last light of the sky and the coloured depth and shadow of the cliffs. In some places a lip of white sand cuts off the real cliff from its double, but in other places the two are nearly unified. As the night comes on herons cry with a lonely desolate note that is echoed backwards and forwards among the hills, and stars begin to glitter in the sky and at one's feet in the water. One seems to be set on the side of a solitary cliff between two reaches of stars, yet in one's face [the] other cliff stands out with a purple density that is much more than darkness. . . .

[1]I have met an old [vagrant] who . . . believes he was a hundred years old last Michaelmas. . . . Though now alone . . . he has been married several times and reared children of whom he knows no more than a swallow knows of broods that have flown to the south. Like most tramps he has the humour of talk and ideas of a certain distinction . . . and this old marauder who [has] lived twice as long and perhaps ten times more fully than the men around him [is] aware of his distinction. . . . If you do not follow his sometimes mumbled phrases he will call a blight from heaven on your head, though your silver is only warming in his pouch.

Man is naturally a nomad . . . and all wanderers have finer intellectual and physical perceptions than men who are condemned to local habitations. The cycle, automobile and conducted tours are half-conscious efforts to replace the charm of the stage coach and of pilgrimages like Chaucer's. But the vagrant, I think, along with

[1] From here onwards parts of what are apparently random jottings (later worked up into the essay, 'The Vagrants of Wicklow') are used from Item 23, written in 1898.

perhaps the sailor, has preserved the dignity of motion with its whole sensation of strange colours in the clouds and of strange passages with voices that whisper in the dark and still stranger inns and lodgings, affections and lonely songs that rest for a whole life time with the perfume of spring evenings or the first autumnal smoulder of the leaves. . . .

[This] old man I have spoken of [wanders about] Wicklow. As he sleeps by Lough Bray and the nightjar burrs and snipe drum over his head and the grouse crow, and heather whispers round him, he hears in their voices the chant of singers in dark chambers of Japan and the clamour of tambourines and [the] flying limbs of dancers he knew in Algeria, and the rustle of golden fabrics of the east. As the trout splash in the dark water at his feet he forgets the purple moorland that is round him and hears waves that lap round a boat in some southern sea. He is not to be pitied.

His life has been a pageant not less grand than Loti's or George Borrow's and like all men of culture he has formed a strong concept of the interest of his own personal aspect. He is no leech-gatherer such as Wordsworth met upon the moors but is still full of scorn and humour and impatience. . . . There is something grandiose in a man who has forced all kingdoms of the earth to yield the tribute of his bread and who, at a hundred, begs on the wayside with the pride of an emperor. The slave and beggar are wiser than the man who works for recompense, for all our moments are divine and above all price though their sacrifice is paid with a measure of fine gold. Every industrious worker has sold his birthright for a mess of pottage, perhaps served him in chalices of gold. . . .

[1]These vagrants have no resemblance with the mendicants who show their sores near the churches of Italy, for mobility is a condition of the existence of a tramp in Ireland, and the greater number that one sees are vigorous women and men of fine physique. When they beg for money they do not make any pretext of infirmity, but ask simply. . . . These people commit crimes as rarely as any average class, and I have never seen a tramp who was drunk or unseemly. If they are treated with tact they are courteous and forbearing, and if anyone does not give them the recognition they think due to them in Wicklow, they are content to avenge them-

[1] From here onwards a passage from Box-file C, written in 1901, is used.

selves with a word of satire. I was in Arklow a few years ago with a man who had spent most of his life in tropical countries where he had acquired a certain brusqeness in dealing with the poor and a feeling for cold that made him carry many overcoats when travelling in his own country. As we were coming out of the station an old woman begged from him, and was refused a little sharply. She said nothing till he was arranging his coats on an outside car, then she edged towards him and called out in a shrill voice that could be heard all over the station, 'Are you sellin' coats?'... This freshness of wit which is equally sure in the women and the men and never loses a point that can be made for profit or revenge is a peculiarity of Irish tramps and distinguishes them, I think, from the rural beggars of other countries of Europe....

Horse races are nowhere more thoroughly appreciated than in County Wicklow, where the people seem to frequent them in a pure holiday spirit that is little inflamed by the fever of gambling. This primitive love of the sport is more apparent on the courses at some distance from Dublin, which are out of reach of the horsey riff-raff that cities always produce.

The races in Arklow, for example, are singularly unconventional, and no one can... watch them on the sand-hills in suitable weather, when the bay and the wooded glens in the background are covered with sunshine and the shadows of clouds, without thrilling to the tumult of humour that rises from the people.

A long course is indicated among the sand-hills by a few scattered flag posts, and at the portion nearest the town a rough paddock and grandstand—draped with green paper—are erected with about a hundred yards of the course roped off from the crowd.... Some half dozen fishermen, with green ribbons fastened to their jerseys or behind their hats, act as stewards at this place, and as they are usually drunk they reel about poking the public with a stick and repeating with endless and vain iteration, 'Keep outside the ropes.'

At either side a varied crowd collects and straggles round among the faded roulette tables, little groups of young men dancing horn-pipes to the music of a flute, and the numerous stalls which supply fruit, biscuits and cheap drinks. These stalls consist merely of a long cart covered by a crescent awning which rises from one end only, and gives them at a little distance a curious resemblance to the cars with sails which the Chinese employ. They are attended to by the semi-gipsy or tinker class, among [whom] women with curiously Mongolian features are not rare. All these are extraordinarily prolific, and at a few paces from each stall there is usually a pile of hay and sacking and harness that is literally crawling with half-naked children.

The wharfs of Arklow are within a stone's throw of the Race-course, and close to them are a number of roughly-cut trunks of trees where the mothers and babies of the fishermen and sailors of the place collect in multitudes, while the younger women who are more smartly dressed go down into the crowd. [On the other] side of the course high sandbanks go up which are utilized as another grandstand by the poorer families who wish to see the sport without mixing in the press of people. Here there are usually some groups where Irish is spoken, for some of the comparatively recent immigrants have revived Gaelic in this neighbourhood.

In the centre of the course there are a number of farmers from up the country riding about on heavy mares, sometimes bare-backed, sometimes with an old saddle tied on with rope, and often with a certain dignity of costume that is heightened by the old-fashioned rustic tall hat. A few old gigs and outside cars also camp on the sand just beyond the mass of the people who are on foot. These latter consist very largely of boys and girls who come by train, full of humour and enjoyment, but dressed modernly without any local distinction.

At length a few horses appear from the paddock and take a turn about the course to clear off the people, and the racing begins. . . .

[1]It is hard to go far anywhere in this country without meeting some person of real psychological or pictorial interest. The other day near Ballyduff I met one of the most delightful old women that I have yet fallen in with. She was coming along with a bottle of milk in one hand and a bundle of some sort in the other. When I got near she set down her bundle and looked at me with a little rogue-like smile.

'Have you any money?' she asked when I was opposite her. I told [her] I might find some about me.

'Well,' she said, 'I am very poor.' I told [her] I was poorer than she was because she had a bottle of milk and I had none. She pulled the cork out of her bottle and handed it to me.

[1] From here onwards Notebook 33 is used.

'Take a sup,' she said, 'maybe you're drouthy with walking in the sun.' She wore her hair, which was still a warm tint, in a great bush on her shoulders, and her little face had wrinkled up to a dimpled humorous pose, that is quite unique in this country. [One could no more] meet or talk to this old woman without smiling a little [than] one could look sternly at a rollicking, quizzical infant.

We were both too weary to talk for very long, and I was soon on my way again. At the next turn in the road near Laragh I came on a tinkers' camp in a fragment of a wood that grows at the apex of the meeting between the Annamoe river and the waters from Glendalough and Lough Nahanagan. Dusk was coming on rapidly yet no one seemed to be at the camp but two young children that I could see through a gate sitting up with the light of the fire full on their faces. They were singing a few bars of some droning song over and over again, that I could just hear above the noise of the two rivers and the waving of the black fir trees that stood above them.

People like these, like the old woman and these two beautiful children, are a precious possession for any country. They console us, one moment at least, for the manifold and beautiful life we have all missed who have been born in modern Europe. . . .

When night comes on after a day spent among these people one is faced again by questions no one can answer. All day in the sunshine in the glens where every leaf sparkles with peculiar lustre, and where air, foliage and water are filled with life, one has inevitable sympathy with vitality and with the people that unite in a rude way the old passions of the earth. Then twilight comes, and the mind is forced back to the so-called spiritual mood when we cry out with the saints. Often after these hot days I have spoken of a peculiar fog rises in the valleys of Wicklow so that the whole land seems to put [a] white virginal scarf about it to meet with the stars and night. Then through the mist lights come out in a few places from the cottages, and the [person] who knows their interiors . . . can [sense] the life of each separate group. How can one reconcile the often coarse liveliness of healthy men with the rapt mood that comes with the night? It is one of the endless antinomies. . . .

[1]I have come round Carrick and up a narrow road that leads back to Annamoe between two bare hills. Where it comes out

[1] From here onwards Notebook 24 (written probably in 1901) is used.

through a gap—at its highest point somewhat like the Wicklow Gap but much smaller—there is one lonely cottage and a row of larches that are bent and broken by the wind. Tonight the sun had set when I came up and this cottage stood against the blue hills that stretch round the valley behind Glendalough to Luggalaw and one luminous bar of cloud. No building could merge more perfectly in the country round it. Any decoration would have seemed misplaced against this timorous radiancy of colour but the low thatched roof and the stack of turf, with the bare-footed children that were running everywhere round them in the bogs gave the singular accent that is often absent in places where there is no trace of human life.

White mists were beginning to rise in the low marshy ground between these hills and the townland of Castle Kevin, and I could hear dogs barking through it and geese cackling on the bog. A lane runs round the valley to join the road to Laragh, and the few cottages along it were sending up blue lines of smoke. Quite near me an old man was driving sheep down from the hills through dense masses of purple heath.

What has given this vague but passionate anguish to the twilights of Ireland? At this season particularly when the first touch of autumn is felt in the evening air every cottage I pass by among the mountains, with an unyoked donkey cart lying [by] it and a hen going to roost on the three-legged pot beside the door, or perhaps a pool with rushes round it and a few children with the sadness of night coming upon them, makes me long that this twilight might be eternal and I pass these doors in endless pilgrimage. Yet they make me and, I believe, many or most people who feel these things, more dejected than any sight of misery.

At such moments one regrets every hour that one has lived outside Ireland and every night that one has passed in cities. Twilight and autumn are both full of the suggestion that we connect with death and the ending of earthly vigour, and perhaps in a country like Ireland this moment has an emphasis that is not known elsewhere. In another sense moments of supreme beauty and distinction make the impulses of the diurnal temperament jar against the impulses of the perpetual beauty which is hidden somewhere in the fountain from whence all life has come, and this jar leads us to the most profound and vain remorse anyone can experience. . . .

[1]I lay in the grass in a sort of dream with a near feeling of a number of scenes that I have been in. I saw the wet roads in Wicklow with sky and sunshine in the ruts, and corners of old woods, and the moving seaweeds that are round Aran; I saw Kerry with bright bays and many scattered people cutting patches of oats or driving their donkeys. Then I came back to the cottage with my throat dry thinking in what a little while I would be in my grave with the whole world lost to me.

In the laneway as I was turning in there were a number of tinkers yoking up for a journey. One of them took a nose bag from a pony he had been feeding and threw it to a man with a red mare across the road.

'There,' he said, 'put her nose into that.'

'I will surely,' said the man, 'what would I want putting her—— into it, I ask you in the name of God?'

[1] From here to the end a passage (probably written in 1908) in Box-file C is used.

THE VAGRANTS OF WICKLOW[1]

SOME features of County Wicklow, such as the position of the principal workhouses and holiday places on either side of the coach road from Arklow to Bray, have made this district a favourite with the vagrants of Ireland. A few of these people have been on the road for generations; but fairly often they seem to have merely drifted out from the ordinary people of the villages, and do not differ greatly from the class they come from. Their abundance has often been regretted; yet in one sense it is an interesting sign, for wherever the labourer of a country has preserved his vitality, and begets an occasional temperament of distinction, a certain number of vagrants are to be looked for. In the middle classes the gifted son of a family is always the poorest—usually a writer or artist with no sense for speculation—and in a family of peasants, where the average comfort is just over penury, the gifted son sinks also, and is soon a tramp on the roadside.

In this life, however, there are many privileges. The tramp in Ireland is little troubled by the laws, and lives in out-of-door conditions that keep him in good humour and fine bodily health. This is so apparent, in Wicklow at least, that these men rarely seek for charity on any plea of ill-health, but ask simply, when they beg: 'Would you help a poor fellow along the road?' or, 'Would you give me the price of a night's lodging, for I'm after walking a great way since the sun rose?'

The healthiness of this life, again, often causes these people to live to a great age, though it is not always easy to test the stories that are told of their longevity. One man, however, who died not long ago, claimed to have reached one hundred and two with a show of likelihood; for several old people remember his first appearance in a certain district as a man of middle age, about the year of the Famine, in 1847 or 1848. This man could hardly be classed with ordinary tramps, for he was married several times in different parts of the world, and reared children of whom he seemed to have forgotten, in his old age, even the names and sex. In his early life he spent thirty years at sea, where he sailed with someone he spoke

[1] Probably written in 1901–2; first published in Autumn 1906 in *The Shanachie* (Dublin).

of afterwards as 'Il mio capitane,' visiting India and Japan, and gaining odd words and intonations that gave colour to his language. When he was too old to wander in the world, he learned all the paths of Wicklow, and till the end of his life he could go the thirty miles from Dublin to the Seven Churches without, as he said, 'putting out his foot on a white road, or seeing any Christian but the hares and moon.' When he was over ninety he married an old woman of eighty-five. Before many days, however, they quarrelled so fiercely that he beat her with his stick, and came out again on the roads. In a few hours he was arrested at her complaint, and sentenced to a month in Kilmainham. He cared nothing for the plank-bed and uncomfortable diet; but he always gathered himself together, and cursed with extraordinary rage, as he told how they cut off the white hair which had grown down upon his shoulders. All his pride and his half-conscious feeling for the dignity of his age seemed to have set themselves on this long hair, which marked him out from the other people of this district; and I have often heard him saying to himself, as he sat beside me under a ditch: 'What use is an old man without his hair? A man has only his bloom like the trees; and what use is an old man without his white hair?'

Among the country people of the East of Ireland the tramps and tinkers who wander round from the West have a curious reputation for witchery and unnatural powers.

'There's great witchery in that country,' a man said to me once, on the side of a mountain to the east of Aughavanna, in Wicklow. 'There's great witchery in that country, and great knowledge of the fairies. I've had men lodging with me out of the West—men who would be walking the world looking for a bit of money—and every one of them would be talking of the wonders below in Connemara. I remember one time, a while after I was married, there was a tinker down there in the glen, and two women along with him. I brought him into my cottage to do a bit of a job, and my first child was there lying in the bed, and he covered up to his chin with the bed-clothes. When the tallest of the women came in, she looked around at him, and then she says—

' "That's a fine boy, God bless him,"

' "How do you know it's a boy," says my woman, "when it's only the head of him you see?"

' "I know rightly," says the tinker, "and it's the first too."

'Then my wife was going to slate me for bringing in people to bewitch her child, and I had to turn the lot of them out to finish the job in the lane.'

I asked him where most of the tinkers came from that are met with in Wicklow.

'They come from every part,' he said. 'They're gallous lads for walking round through the world. One time I seen fifty of them above on the road to Rathdangan, and they all match-making and marrying themselves for the year that was to come. One man would take such a woman, and say he was going such roads and places, stopping at this fair and another fair, till he'd meet them again at such a place, when the spring was coming on. Another, maybe, would swap the woman he had with one from another man, with as much talk as if you'd be selling a cow. It 's two hours I was there watching them from the bog underneath, where I was cutting turf, and the like of the crying and the kissing, and the singing and the shouting began when they went off this way and that way, you never heard in your life. Sometimes when a party would be gone a bit down over the hill, a girl would begin crying out and wanting to go back to her ma. Then the man would say: "Black hell to your soul, you've come with me now, and you'll go the whole way." I often seen tinkers before and since, but I never seen such a power of them as were in it that day.'

It need hardly be said that in all tramp life plaintive and tragic elements are common, even on the surface. Some are peculiar to Wicklow. In these hills the summer passes in a few weeks from a late spring, full of odour and colour, to an autumn that is premature and filled with the desolate splendour of decay; and it often happens that, in moments when one is most aware of this ceaseless fading of beauty, some incident of tramp life gives a local human intensity to the shadow of one's own mood.

One evening, on the high ground near the Avonbeg, I met a young tramp just as an extraordinary sunset had begun to fade, and a low white mist was rising from the bogs. He had a sort of table in his hands that he seemed to have made himself out of twisted rushes and a few branches of osier. His clothes were more than usually ragged, and I could see by his face that he was suffering from some terrible disease. When he was quite close, he held out the table.

'Would you give me a few pence for that thing?' he said. 'I'm

A WICKLOW VAGRANT

after working at it all day by the river, and for the love of God give me something now, the way I can get a drink and lodging for the night.'

I felt in my pockets, and could find nothing but a shilling piece.

'I wouldn't wish to give you so much,' I said, holding it out to him, 'but it is all I have, and I don't like to give you nothing at all, and the darkness coming on. Keep the table; it's no use to me, and you'll maybe sell it for something in the morning.'

The shilling was more than he expected, and his eyes flamed with joy.

'May the Almighty God preserve you and watch over you and reward you for this night,' he said, 'but you'll take the table; I wouldn't keep it at all, and you after stretching out your hand with a shilling to me, and the darkness coming on.'

He forced it into my hands so eagerly that I could not refuse it, and set off down the road with tottering steps. When he had gone a few yards, I called after him: 'There's your table; take it and God speed you.'

Then I put down his table on the ground, and set off as quickly as I was able. In a moment he came up with me again, holding the table in his hands, and slipped round in front of me so that I could not get away.

'You wouldn't refuse it,' he said, 'and I after working at it all day below by the river.'

He was shaking with excitement and the exertion of overtaking me; so I took his table and let him go on his way. A quarter of a mile further on I threw it over the ditch in a desolate place, where no one was likely to find it.

In addition to the more genuine vagrants a number of wandering men and women are to be met with in the northern parts of the county, who walk out for ferns and flowers in bands of from four or five to a dozen. They usually set out in the evening, and sleep in some ditch or shed, coming home the next night with what they have gathered. If their sales are successful, both men and women drink heavily; so that they are always on the edge of starvation, and are miserably dressed, the women sometimes wearing nothing but an old petticoat and shawl—a scantiness of clothing that is sometimes met with also among the road-women of Kerry.

These people are nearly always at war with the police, and are often harshly treated. Once after a holiday, as I was walking home through a village on the border of Wicklow, I came upon several policemen, with a crowd round them, trying to force a drunken flower-woman out of the village. She did not wish to go, and threw herself down, raging and kicking, on the ground. They let her lie there for a few minutes, and then she propped herself up against the wall, scolding and storming at every one, till she became so outrageous the police renewed their attack. One of them walked up to her and hit her a sharp blow on the jaw with the back of his hand. Then two more of them seized her by the shoulders and forced her along the road for a few yards, till her clothes began to tear off with the violence of the struggle, and they let her go once more.

She sprang up at once when they did so.

'Let this be the barrack's yard if you wish it,' she cried, tearing off the rags that still clung about her, 'Let this be the barrack's yard, and come on now, the lot of you.'

Then she rushed at them with extraordinary fury; but the police, to avoid scandal, withdrew into the town, and left her to be quieted by her friends.

Sometimes, it is fair to add, the police are generous and good-humoured. One evening, many years ago, when Whit Monday in Enniskerry was a very different thing from what it is now, I was looking out of a window in that village, watching the police, who had been brought in for the occasion, getting ready to start for Bray. As they were standing about, a young ballad-singer came along from the Dargle, and one of the policemen, who seemed to know him, asked him why a fine, stout lad the like of him wasn't earning his bread, instead of straying on the roads.

Immediately the young man drew up on the spot where he was, and began shouting a loud ballad at the top of his voice. The police tried to stop him; but he went on, getting faster and faster, till he ended, swinging his head from side to side, in a furious patter, of which I seem to remember—

Botheration
Take the nation,
Calculation,
In the stable,
Cain and Abel,
Tower of Babel,
And the Battle of Waterloo.

Then he pulled off his hat, dashed in among the police, and did not leave them till they had all given him the share of money he felt he had earned for his bread.

In all the circumstances of this tramp life there is a certain wildness that gives it romance and a peculiar value for those who look at life in Ireland with an eye that is aware of the arts also. In all the healthy movements of art, variations from the ordinary types of manhood are made interesting for the ordinary man, and in this way only the higher arts are universal. Beside this art, however, founded on the variations which are a condition and effect of all vigorous life, there is another art—sometimes confounded with it—founded on the freak of nature, in itself a mere sign of atavism or disease. This latter art, which is occupied with the antics of the freak, is of interest only to the variation from ordinary minds, and for this reason is never universal. To be quite plain, the tramp in real life, Hamlet and Faust in the arts, are variations; but the maniac in real life, and Des Esseintes and all his ugly crew in the arts, are freaks only.

THE OPPRESSION OF THE HILLS[1]

AMONG the cottages that are scattered through the hills of County Wicklow I have met with many people who show in a singular way the influence of a particular locality. These people live for the most part beside old roads and pathways where hardly one man passes in the day, and look out all the year on unbroken barriers of heath. At every season heavy rains fall for often a week at a time, till the thatch drips with water stained to a dull chestnut and the floor in the cottages seems to be going back to the condition of the bogs near it. Then the clouds break, and there is a night of terrific storm from the south-west—all the larches that survive in these places are bowed and twisted towards the point where the sun rises in June—when the winds come down through the narrow glens with the congested whirl and roar of a torrent, breaking at times for sudden moments of silence that keep up the tension of the mind. At such times the people crouch all night over a few sods of turf and the dogs howl in the lanes.

When the sun rises there is a morning of almost supernatural radiance, and even the oldest men and women come out into the air with the joy of children who have recovered from a fever. In the evening it is raining again. This peculiar climate, acting on a population that is already lonely and dwindling, has caused or increased a tendency to nervous depression among the people, and every degree of sadness, from that of the man who is merely mournful to that of the man who has spent half his life in the mad-house, is common among these hills.

Not long ago in a desolate glen in the south of the county I met two policemen driving an ass-cart with a coffin on it, and a little further on I stopped an old man and asked him what had happened.

'This night three weeks,' he said, 'there was a poor fellow below reaping in the glen, and in the evening he had two glasses of whisky with some other lads. Then some excitement took him, and he threw off his clothes and ran away into the hills. There was great rain that night, and I suppose the poor creature lost his way, and

[1] Written between 1898 and 1902. First published on 15 February 1905 in the *Manchester Guardian*.

was the whole night perishing in the rain and darkness. In the morning they found his naked foot-marks on some mud half a mile above the road, and again where you go up by a big stone. Then there was nothing known of him till last night, when they found his body on the mountain, and it near eaten by the crows.'

Then he went on to tell me how different the country had been when he was a young man.

'We had nothing to eat at that time,' he said, 'but milk and stirabout and potatoes, and there was a fine constitution you wouldn't meet this day at all. I remember when you'd see forty boys and girls below there on a Sunday evening, playing ball and diverting themselves; but now all this country is gone lonesome and bewildered, and there's no man knows what ails it.'

There are so few girls left in these neighbourhoods that one does not often meet with women that have grown up unmarried. I know one, however, who has lived by herself for fifteen years in a tiny hovel near a cross roads much frequented by tinkers and ordinary tramps. As she has no one belonging to her, she spends a good deal of her time wandering through the country, and I have met her in every direction, often many miles from her own glen. 'I do be so afeard of the tramps,' she said to me one evening. 'I live all alone, and what would I do at all if one of them lads was to come near me? When my poor mother was dying, "Now, Nanny," says she, "don't be living on here when I am dead," says she; "it'd be too lonesome." And now I wouldn't wish to go again' my mother, and she dead—dead or alive I wouldn't go again' my mother—but I'm after doing all I can, and I can't get away by any means.' As I was moving on she heard, or thought she heard, a sound of distant thunder.

'Ah, your honour,' she said, 'do you think it's thunder we'll be having? There's nothing I fear like the thunder. My heart isn't strong—I do feel it—and I have a lightness in my head, and often when I do be excited with the thunder I do be afeard I might die there alone in the cottage and no one know it. But I do hope that the Lord—bless His holy name!—has something in store for me. I've done all I can, and I don't like going again' my mother and she dead. And now good evening, your honour, and safe home.'[1]

[1] A version in Clip-binder 22 has this: 'This frail woman with prematurely white hair who had lived thus for fifteen years in her lonely cabin troubled by neurasthenia and

Intense nervousness is common also with much younger women. I remember one night hearing some one crying out and screaming in the house where I was staying. I went downstairs and found it was a girl who had been taken in from a village a few miles away to help the servants. That afternoon her two younger sisters had come to see her, and now she had been taken with a panic that they had been drowned going home through the bogs, and she was crying and wailing, and saying she must go to look for them. It was not thought fit for her to leave the house alone so late in the evening, so I went with her. As we passed down a steep hill of heather, where the nightjars were clapping their wings in the moonlight, she told me a long story of the way she had been frightened. Then we reached a solitary cottage on the edge of the bog, and as a light was still shining in the window, I knocked at the door and asked if they had seen or heard anything. When they understood our errand three half-dressed generations came out to jeer at us on the doorstep.

'Ah, Maggie,' said the old woman, 'you're a cute one. You're the girl likes a walk in the moonlight. Whist your talk of them big lumps of childer, and look at Martin Edward there, who 's not six, and he can go through the bog five times in an hour and not wet his feet.'

My companion was still unconvinced, so we went on. The rushes were shining in the moonlight, and one flake of mist was lying on the river. We looked into one bog-hole, and then into another, where a snipe rose and terrified us. We listened: a cow was chewing heavily in the shadow of a bush, two dogs were barking on the side of a hill, and there was a cart far away upon the road. Our teeth began to chatter with the cold of the bog air and the loneliness of the night. I could see that the actual presence of the bog had shown my companion the absurdity of her fears, and in a little while we went home.

The older people in County Wicklow, as in the rest of Ireland, still show a curious affection for the landed classes wherever they have lived for a generation or two upon their property. I remember an old woman, who told me, with tears streaming on her face, how much more lonely the country had become since the

hysteria and vague terrors . . . gives me a peculiar sense of pity. We hear every day of the horrors of overcrowding, yet these desolate dwellings on the hill with here an old widow dying far away from her friends and there a single woman with all the whims of overwrought virginity have perhaps a more utter, if higher sort of misery.'

'quality' had gone away, and gave me a long story of how she had seen her landlord shutting up his house and leaving his property, and of the way he had died afterwards, when the 'grievance' of it broke his heart. The younger people feel differently, and when I was passing this landlord's house, not long afterwards I found these lines written in pencil on the door-post:—

In the days of rack-renting
And land-grabbing so vile
A proud, heartless landlord
Lived here a great while.
When the League it was started,
And the land-grabbing cry,
To the cold North of Ireland
He had for to fly.

A year later the door-post had fallen to pieces, and the inscription with it.

ON THE ROAD[1]

ONE evening after heavy rains I set off to walk to a village at the other side of some hills, part of my way lying along a steep heathery track. The valleys that I passed through were filled with the strange splendour that comes after wet weather in Ireland, and on the tops of the mountains masses of fog were lying in white, even banks. Once or twice I went by a lonely cottage with a smell of earthy turf coming from the chimney, weeds or oats sprouting on the thatch, and a broken cart before the door, with many straggling hens going to roost on the shafts. Near these cottages little bands of half-naked children, filled with the excitement of evening, were running and screaming over the bogs, where the heather was purple already, giving me the strained feeling of regret one has so often in these places when there is rain in the air.

Further on, as I was going up a long hill, an old man with a white, pointed face and heavy beard pulled himself up out of the ditch and joined me. We spoke first about the broken weather, and then he began talking in a mournful voice of the famines and misfortunes that have been in Ireland.

'There have been three cruel plagues,' he said, 'out through the country since I was born in the West. First, there was the big wind in 1839, that tore away the grass and green things from the earth. Then there was the blight that came on the ninth of June in the year 1846. Up to then the potatoes were clean and good; but that morning a mist rose up out of the sea, and you could hear a voice talking near a mile off across the stillness of the earth. It was the same the next day, and the day after, and so on for three days or more; and then you could begin to see the tops of the stalks lying over as if the life was gone out of them. And that was the beginning of the great trouble and famine that destroyed Ireland. Then the people went on, I suppose, in their wickedness and their animosity of one against the other; and the Almighty God sent down the third plague, and that was the sickness called the choler. Then all the people left the town of Sligo—it's in Sligo I was

[1] Probably written at times after 1902. First published on 10 December 1908 in the *Manchester Guardian*.

reared—and you could walk through the streets at the noon of day and not see a person, and you could knock at one door and another door and find no one to answer you. The people were travelling out north and south and east, with the terror that was on them; and the country people were digging ditches across the roads and driving them back where they could, for they had a great dread of the disease.

'It was the law at that time that if there was sickness on any person in the town of Sligo you should notice it to the Governors, or you'd be put up in the gaol. Well, a man's wife took sick, and he went and noticed it. They came down then with bands of men they had, and took her away to the sick-house, and he heard nothing more till he heard she was dead, and was to be buried in the morning. At that time there was such fear and hurry and dread on every person, they were burying people they had no hope of, and they with life within them. My man was uneasy a while thinking on that, and then what did he do, but slip down in the darkness of the night and into the dead-house, where they were after putting his wife. There were beyond twoscore bodies, and he went feeling from one to the other. Then I suppose his wife heard him coming—she wasn't dead at all—and "Is that Michael?" says she. "It is then," says he; "and, oh, my poor woman, have you your last gasps in you still?" "I have, Michael," says she; "and they're after setting me out here with fifty bodies the way they'll put me down into my grave at the dawn of day." "Oh, my poor woman," says he; "have you the strength left in you to hold on my back?" "Oh, Micky," says she, "I have surely." He took her up then on his back, and he carried her out by lanes and tracks till he got to his house. Then he never let on a word about it, and at the end of three days she began to pick up, and in a month's time she came out and began walking about like yourself or me. And there were many people were afeard to speak to her, for they thought she was after coming back from the grave.'

Soon afterwards we passed into a little village, and he turned down a lane and left me. It was not long, however, till another old man that I could see a few paces ahead stopped and waited for me, as is the custom of the place.

'I've been down in Kilpeddar buying a scythe-stone,' he began, when I came up to him, 'and indeed Kilpeddar is a dear place, for it's threepence they charged me for it; but I suppose there must be a profit from every trade, and we must all live and let live.'

When we had talked a little more I asked him if he had been often in Dublin.

'I was living in Dublin near ten years,' he said; 'and indeed I don't know what way I lived that length in it, for there is no place with smells like the city of Dublin. One time I went up with my wife into those lanes where they sell old clothing, Hanover Lane and Plunket's Lane, and when my wife—she's dead now, God forgive her!—when my wife smelt the dirty air she put her apron up to her nose, and, "For the love of God," says she, "get me away out of this place." And now may I ask if it's from there you are yourself, for I think by your speaking it wasn't in these parts you were reared?'

I told him I was born in Dublin, but that I had travelled afterwards and been in Paris and Rome, and seen the Pope Leo XIII.

'And will you tell me,' he said, 'is it true that anyone at all can see the Pope?'

I described the festivals in the Vatican, and how I had seen the Pope carried through long halls on a sort of throne. 'Well, now,' he said, 'can you tell me who was the first Pope that sat upon that throne?'

I hesitated for a moment, and he went on:

'I'm only a poor, ignorant man, but I can tell you that myself if you don't know it, with all your travels. Saint Peter was the first Pope, and he was crucified with his head down, and since that time there have been Popes upon the throne of Rome.'

Then he began telling me about himself.

'I was twice a married man,' he said. 'My first wife died at her second child, and then I reared it up till it was as tall as myself—a girl it was—and she went off and got married and left me. After that I was married a second time to an aged woman, and she lived with me ten years, and then she died herself. There is nothing I can make now but tea, and tea is killing me; and I'm living alone, in a little hut beyond, where four baronies, four parishes, and four townlands meet.'

By this time we had reached the village inn, where I was lodging for the night; so I stood him a drink, and he went on to his cottage along a narrow pathway through the bogs.

THE PEOPLE OF THE GLENS[1]

HERE and there in County Wicklow there are a number of little known places—places with curiously melodious names, such as Aughavanna, Glenmalure, Annamoe, or Lough Nahanagan—where the people have retained a peculiar simplicity, and speak a language in some ways more Elizabethan than the English of Connaught, where Irish was used till a much later date. In these glens many women still wear old-fashioned bonnets, with a frill round the face, and the old men, when they are going to the fair, or to Mass, are often seen in curiously-cut frock-coats, tall hats, and breeches buckled at the knee. When they meet a wanderer on foot, these old people are glad to stop and talk to him for hours, telling him stories of the Rebellion, or of the fallen angels that ride across the hills, or alluding to the three shadowy countries that are never forgotten in Wicklow—America (their El Dorado), the Union and the Madhouse.

'I had a power of children,' an old man, who was born in Glenmalure, said to me once; 'I had a power of children, and they all went to California, with what I could give them, and bought a bit of a field. Then, when they put in the plough, it stuck fast on them. They looked in beneath it, and there was fine gold stretched within the earth. They're rich now and their daughters are riding on fine horses with new saddles on them, and elegant bits in their mouths, yet not a ha'porth did they ever send me, and may the devil ride with them to hell!'

Not long afterwards I met an old man wandering about a hill-side, where there was a fine view of Lough Dan, in extraordinary excitement and good spirits.

'I landed in Liverpool two days ago,' he said, when I had wished him the time of day; 'then I came to the city of Dublin this morning, and took the train to Bray, where you have the blue salt water on your left, and the beautiful valleys, with trees in them, on your right. From that I drove to this place on a jaunting-car to see some brothers and cousins I have living below. They're poor

[1] Stephens, in the private Stephens papers, says: 'The article is a collection of impressions of people seen at different times, perhaps years apart.' First published in Spring 1907 in *The Shanachie*.

people, Mister, honey, with bits of cabins, and mud floors under them, but they're as happy as if they were in heaven, and what more would a man want than that? In America and Australia, and on the Atlantic Ocean, you have all sorts, good people and bad people, and murderers and thieves, and pick-pockets; but in this place there isn't a being isn't as good and decent as yourself or me.'

I saw he was one of the old people one sometimes meets with who emigrated when the people were simpler than they are at present, and who often come back, after a lifetime in the States, as Irish as any old man who has never been twenty miles from the town of Wicklow. I asked him about his life abroad, when we had talked a little longer.

'I've been through perils enough to slay nations,' he said, 'and the people here think I should be rotten with gold, but they're better off the way they are. For five years I was a ship's smith, and never saw dry land, and I in all the danger and peril of the Atlantic Ocean. Then I was a veterinary surgeon, curing side-slip, splay-foot, spavin, splints, glanders, and the various ailments of the horse and ass. The lads in this place think you've nothing to do but to go across the sea and fill a bag with gold; but I tell you it is hard work, and in those countries the workhouses is full, and the prisons is full, and the crazyhouses is full, the same as in the city of Dublin.[1] Over beyond you have fine dwellings, and you have only to put out your hand from the window among roses and vines, and the red wine grape; but there is all sorts in it, and the people is better in this country, among the trees and valleys, and they resting on their floors of mud.'

In Wicklow, as in the rest of Ireland, the union, though it is a home of refuge for the tramps and tinkers, is looked on with supreme horror by the peasants. The madhouse, which they know better, is less dreaded.

One night I had to go down late in the evening from a mountain village to the town of Wicklow, and come back again into the hills. As soon as I came near Rathnew I passed many bands of girls and men making rather ruffianly flirtation on the pathway, and women who surged up to stare at me, as I passed in the middle of the road. The thick line of trees that are near Rathnew makes the

[1] In Box-file C is this: 'I said that I hoped he would warn the young men in Ireland and advise them to stay in their own country.'

way intensely dark, even on clear nights. and when one is riding quickly, the contrast, when one reaches the lights of Wicklow, is singularly abrupt. The town itself after nightfall is gloomy and squalid. Half-drunken men and women stand about, wrangling and disputing in the dull light from the windows, which is only strong enough to show the wretchedness of the figures which pass continually across them. I did my business quickly and turned back to the hills, passing for the first few miles the same noisy groups and couples on the roadway. After a while I stopped at a lonely public-house to get a drink and rest for a moment before I came to the hills. Six or seven men were talking drearily at one end of the room, and a woman I knew, who had been marketing in Wicklow, was resting nearer the door. When I had been given a glass of beer, I sat down on a barrel near her, and we began to talk.

'Ah, your honour,' she said, 'I hear you're going off in a short time to Dublin, or to France, and maybe we won't be in the place at all when you come back. There's no fences to the bit of farm I have, the way I'm destroyed running. The calves do be straying, and the geese do be straying, and the hens do be straying, and I'm destroyed running after them. We've no man in the place since himself died in the winter, and he ailing these five years, and there's no one to give us a hand drawing the hay or cutting the bit of oats we have above on the hill. My brother Michael has come back to his own place after being seven years in the Richmond Asylum; but what can you ask of him, and he with a long family of his own? And, indeed, it's a wonder he ever came back when it was a fine time he had in the asylum.'

She saw my movement of surprise, and went on:—

'There was a son of my own, as fine a lad as you'd see in the county—though I'm his mother that says it, and you'd never think it to look at me. Well, he was a keeper in a kind of private asylum, I think they call it, and when Michael was taken bad, he went to see him, and didn't he know the keepers that were in charge of him, and they promised to take the best of care of him, and, indeed, he was always a quiet man that would give no trouble. After the first three years he was free in the place, and he walking about like a gentleman, doing any light work he'd find agreeable. Then my son went to see him a second time, and "You'll never see Michael again," says he when he came back, "for he's too well off where he is." And, indeed, it was well for him, but now he's come home.' Then she got up to carry out some groceries she was buying to the ass-cart that was waiting outside.

'It's real sorry I do be when I see you going off,' she said, as she was turning away. 'I don't often speak to you, but it's company to see you passing up and down over the hill, and now may the Almighty God bless and preserve you, and see you safe home.'

A little later I was walking up the long hill which leads to the high ground from Laragh to Sugar Loaf. The solitude was intense. Towards the top of the hill I passed through a narrow gap with high rocks on one side of it and fir trees above them, and a handful of jagged sky filled with extraordinarily brilliant stars. In a few moments I passed out on the brow of the hill that runs behind the Devil's Glen, and smelt the fragrance of the bogs. I mounted again. There was not light enough to show the mountains round me, and the earth seemed to have dwindled away into a mere platform where an astrologer might watch. Among these emotions of the night one cannot wonder that the madhouse is so often named in Wicklow.

Many of the old people of the country, however, when they have no definite sorrow, are not mournful, and are full of curious whims and observations. One old woman who lived near Glen Macanass told me that she had seen her sons had no hope of making a livelihood in the place where they were born, so, in addition to their schooling, she engaged a master to come over the bogs every evening and teach them sums and spelling. One evening she came in behind them, when they were at work and stopped to listen.

'And what do you think my son was after doing?' she said; 'he'd made a sum of how many times a wheel on a cart would turn round between the bridge below and the Post Office in Dublin. Would you believe that? I went out without saying a word, and I got the old stocking, where I keep a bit of money, and I made out what I owed the master. Then I went in again, and "Master," says I, "Mick's learning enough for the likes of him. You can go now and safe home to you." And, God bless you, Avourneen, Mick got a fine job after on the railroad.'

Another day, when she was trying to flatter me, she said: 'Ah, God bless you, Avourneen, you've no pride. Didn't I hear you yesterday, and you talking to my pig below in the field as if it was your brother? And a nice clean pig it is, too, the crathur.' A year or two afterwards I met this old woman again. Her husband had died a few months before of the 'Influence,' and she was in pitiable distress, weeping and wailing while she talked to me. 'The poor old man is after dying on me,' she said, 'and he was great company. There's only one son left me now, and we do be killed working. Ah, Avourneen, the poor do have great stratagems to keep in their little cabins at all. And did you ever see the like of the place we live in? Isn't it the poorest, lonesomest, wildest, dreariest bit of a hill a person ever passed a life on?' When she stopped a moment, with the tears streaming on her face, I told a little about the poverty I had seen in Paris.

'God Almighty forgive me, Avourneen,' she went on, when I had finished, 'we don't know anything about it. We have our bit of turf, and our bit of sticks, and our bit to eat, and we have our health. Glory be to His Holy Name, not a one of the childer was ever a day ill, except one boy was hurted off a cart, and he never overed it. It's small right we have to complain at all.'

She died the following winter, and her son went to New York.

The old people who have direct tradition of the Rebellion, and a real interest in it, are growing less numerous daily, but one still meets with them here and there in the more remote districts.

One evening, at the beginning of harvest, as I was walking into a straggling village, far away in the mountains, in the southern half of the county, I overtook an old man walking in the same direction with an empty gallon can. I joined him; and when he had talked for a moment, he turned round and looked at me curiously.

'Begging your pardon, sir,' he said, 'I think you aren't Irish.' I told him he was mistaken.

'Well,' he went on, 'you don't speak the same as we do; so I was thinking maybe you were from another country.'

'I came back from France,' I said, 'two months ago, and maybe there's a trace of the language still upon my tongue.' He stopped and beamed with satisfaction.

'Ah,' he said, 'see that now. I knew there was something about you. I do be talking to all who do pass through this glen, telling them stories of the Rebellion, and the old histories of Ireland, and there's few can puzzle me, though I'm only a poor ignorant man.' He told me some of his adventures, and then he stopped again.

'Look at me now,' he said, 'and tell me what age you think I'd be.'

'You might be seventy,' I said.

'Ah,' he said, with a piteous whine in his voice, 'you wouldn't take me to be as old as that? No man ever thought me that age to this day.'

'Maybe you aren't far over sixty,' I said, fearing I had blundered; 'maybe you're sixty-four.' He beamed once more with delight, and hurried along the road.

'Go on, now,' he said, 'I'm eighty-two years, three months and five days. Would you believe that? I was baptized on the fourth of June, eighty-two years ago, and it's the truth I'm telling you.'

'Well, it's a great wonder,' I said, 'to think you're that age, when you're as strong as I am to this day.'

'I am not strong at all,' he went on, more despondingly, 'not strong the way I was. If I had two glasses of whisky I'd dance a hornpipe would dazzle your eyes; but the way I am at this minute you could knock me down with a rush. I have a noise in my head, so that you wouldn't hear the river at the side of it, and I can't sleep at nights. It's that weakens me. I do be lying in the darkness thinking of all that has happened in three-score years to the families of Wicklow—what this son did, and what that son did, and of all that went across the sea, and wishing black hell would seize them that never wrote three words to say were they alive or in good health. That's the profession I have now—to be thinking of all the people, and of the times that's gone. And, begging your pardon, might I ask your name?' I told him.

'There are two branches of the Synges in the County Wicklow,' he said, and then he went on to tell me fragments of folk-lore connected with my forefathers. How a lady used to ride through Roundwood 'on a curious beast' to visit an uncle of hers in Roundwood Park, and how she married one of the Synges and got her weight in gold—eight stone of gold—as her dowry: stories that referred to events which took place more than a hundred years ago.

When he had finished I told him how much I wondered at his knowledge of the country.

'There's not a family I don't know,' he said, 'from Baltinglass to the sea, and what they've done, and who they've married. You don't know me yet, but if you were a while in this place talking to

A MAN OF THE GLENS

myself, it's more pleasure and gratitude you'd have from my company than you'd have maybe from many a gentleman you'd meet riding or driving a car.'

⟨He told me of a disagreement he had had with a Member of Parliament about local history.

'One day I was near striking him on this stretch of the road. I was after telling him about two men were piked beyond that corner at the time of the Rebellion, and when I came to an end, "It's all lies you're telling," says he, "there's not a word of it true."

' "How's that," says I, "what in the name of God do you know of the histories of the world?"

' "It's all in my history book," says he, "and another way altogether."

' "Go home, then," says I, "and burn your history book, for it's all lies is in it, and you're the first man ever thought he knew the history of these places better than old Cavanagh—that's myself."

' "Well," says he, "I'm going home tomorrow, and I'll find out in the city of Dublin whether it's you is right or the book. Then when I come back in a twelve month—if we both have our health by the grace of God—I'll tell you about it."

'A year after he came back late in the evening to my little dwelling. I wasn't in at that time, but with the rage he had to see me he came down again at the dawn of day.

' "Ah, Cavanagh," says he, "you're the finest man for histories ever I seen. It's you were right and the book was wrong."

'Would you believe that?'⟩[1]

By this time we had reached a wayside public-house, where he was evidently going with his can, so, as I did not wish to part with him so soon, I asked him to come in and take something with me. When we went into the little bar-room, which was beautifully clean, I asked him what he would have. He turned to the publican:—

'Have you any good whisky at the present time?' he said.

'Not now; nor at any time,' said the publican; 'we only keep bad; but isn't it all the same for the likes of you that wouldn't know the difference?'

[1] The passage in angled brackets, from 'He told me' to ' "Would you believe that?" ', is in Synge's typescript in Box-file C, and was included in the original *Shanachie* article, but it was omitted from Volume Four of the *Works* of 1910.

After prolonged barging he got a glass of whisky, took off his hat before he tasted it, to say a prayer for my future, and then sat down with it on a bench in the corner.

I was served in turn, and we began to talk about horses and racing, as there had been races in Arklow a day or two before. I alluded to some races I had seen in France, and immediately the publican's wife, a young woman who had just come in, spoke of a visit she had made to the Grand Prix a few years before.

'Then you have been in France?' I asked her.

'For eleven years,' she replied.

'Alors vous parlez Français, Madame?'

'Mais oui, Monsieur,' she answered with pure intonation.

We had a little talk in French, and then the old man got his can filled with porter—the evening drink for a party of reapers who were working on the hill—bought a pennyworth of sweets, and went back down the road.

'That 's the greatest old rogue in the village,' said the publican, as soon as he was out of hearing; 'he 's always making up to all who pass through the place, and trying what he can get out of them. The other day a party told me to give him a bottle of XXX porter he was after asking for. I just gave him the dregs of an old barrel we had finished, and there he was, sucking in his lips, and saying it was the finest drink ever he tasted, and that it was rising to his head already, though he'd hardly a drop of it swallowed. Faith in the end I had to laugh to hear the talk he was making.'

A little later I wished them good evening and started again on my walk, as I had two mountains to cross.[1]

[1] In Box-file C, and in the *Shanachie* article, is this: 'The younger people of these glens are not so interesting as the old men and women, and though there are still many fine young men . . . who are extraordinarily gifted and agile, it too often happens, that the men under thirty are badly built, shy and despondent. Even among the old people, whose singular charm I have tried to interpret, . . . it is possible to find many individuals who are far from admirable either in body or mind. One would hardly stop to assert a fact so obvious if it had not become the fashion in Dublin, quite recently, to reject a fundamental doctrine of theology, and to exhalt the Irish peasant into a type of almost absolute virtue, frugal, self-sacrificing, valiant, and I know not what. There is some truth in this estimate, yet it is safer to hold with the theologians that, even west of the Shannon, the heart of man is not spotless, for though the Irish peasant has many beautiful virtues, it is idle to assert that he is totally unacquainted with the deadly sins, and many minor rogueries. He has however . . . a fine sense of humour and the greatest courtesy. When a benevolent visitor comes to his cottage, seeking a sort of holy family, the man of the house, his wife and all their infants, too courteous to disappoint him, play their parts with delight. When the amiable visitor, however, is out once more in the boreen, a storm of good-tempered irony breaks out behind him, that would suprrise him could he hear it. This irony I have met with many times . . . and I have always been overjoyed to hear it. It shows that, in spite of relief-works, Commissions and patronizing philanthropy—that sickly thing—the Irish peasant, in his own mind, is neither abject nor servile.'

AT A WICKLOW FAIR[1]

THE PLACE AND THE PEOPLE

A YEAR or two ago I wished to visit a fair in County Wicklow, and as the buying and selling in these fairs are got through very early in the morning I started soon after dawn to walk the ten or twelve miles that led to Aughrim, where the fair was to be held. When I came out into the air the cold was intense, though it was a morning of August, and the dew was so heavy that bushes and meadows of mountain grass seemed to have lost their greenness in silvery grey. In the glens I went through white mists were twisting and feathering themselves into extraordinary shapes, and showing blue hills behind them that looked singularly desolate and far away. At every turn I came on multitudes of rabbits feeding on the roadside, or on even shyer creatures—corncrakes, squirrels and snipe—close to villages where no one was awake.

Then the sun rose, and I could see lines of smoke beginning to go up from farmhouses under the hills, and sometimes a sleepy, half-dressed girl looked out of the door of a cottage when my feet echoed on the road. About six miles from Aughrim I began to fall in with droves of bullocks and sheep, in charge of two or three dogs and a herd, or with whole families of mountain people, driving nothing but a single donkey or kid. These people seemed to feel already the animation of the fair, and were talking eagerly and gaily among themselves. I did not hurry, and it was about nine o'clock when I made my way into the village, which was now thronged with cattle and sheep. On every side the usual half-humorous bargaining could be heard above the noise of the pigs and donkeys and lambs. One man would say: 'Are you going to not divide a shilling with me? Are you going to not do it? You're the biggest schemer ever walked down into Aughrim.'

A little further on a man said to a seller: 'You're asking too much for them lambs.' The seller answered: 'If I didn't ask it how would I ever get it? The lambs is good lambs, and if you buy them now you'll get home nice and easy in time to have your

[1] Stephens, in his private papers, says: 'A composite picture, written, probably, 1902–05.' First published on 9 May 1907 in the *Manchester Guardian*.

dinner in comfort, and if you don't buy them you'll be here the whole day sweating in the heat and dust, and maybe not please yourself in the end of all.'

Then they began looking at the lambs again, talking of the cleanness of their skin and the quality of the wool, and making many extravagant remarks in their praise or against them. As I turned away I heard the loud clap of one hand into another, which always marks the conclusion of a bargain.

A little further on I found a farmer I knew standing before a public-house, looking radiant with delight. 'It's a fine fair, Mister,' he said, 'and I'm after selling the lambs I had here a month ago and no one would look at them. Then I took them to Rathdrum and Wicklow, getting up at three in the morning, and driving them in the creel, and it all for nothing. But I'm shut of them now, and it's not too bad a price I've got either. I'm after driving the lambs outside the customs' (the boundary where the fair tolls are paid) 'and I'm waiting now for my money.' While we were talking, a cry of warning was raised: 'Mind yourselves below; there's a drift of sheep coming down the road.' Then a couple of men and dogs appeared, trying to drive a score of sheep that some one had purchased, out of the village, between the countless flocks that were standing already on either side of the way. This task is peculiarly difficult. Boys and men collect round the flock that is to be driven out, and try to force the animals down the narrow passage that is left in the middle of the road. It hardly ever happens, however, that they get through without carrying off a few of some one else's sheep, or losing some of their own, which have to be restored, or looked for afterwards.

The flock was driven by as well as could be managed, and a moment later an old man came up to us, and asked if we had seen a ewe passing from the west. 'A sheep is after passing,' said the farmer I was talking to, 'but it was not one of yours, for it was too wilful; it was a mountain sheep.' Sometimes animals are astray in this way for a considerable time—it is not unusual to meet a man the day after a fair wandering through the country, asking after a lost heifer, or ewe—but they are always well marked and are found in the end.

When I reached the green above the village I found the curious throng one always meets in these fairs, made up of wild mountain squatters, gentlemen farmers, jobbers and herds. At one corner of the green there was the usual camp of tinkers, where a swarm of

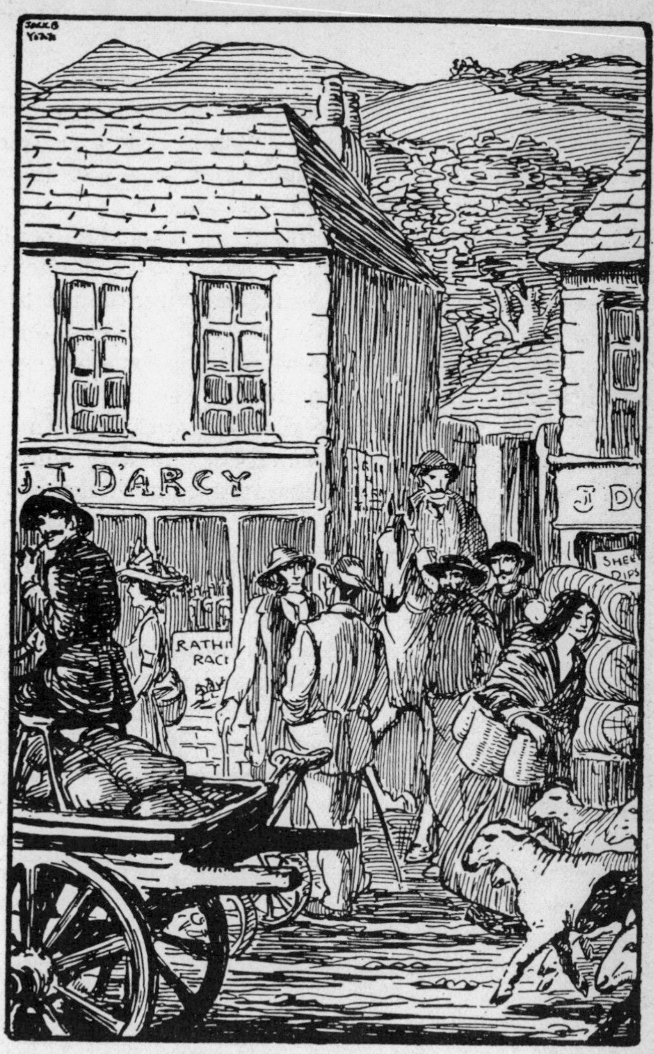

A WICKLOW FAIR

children had been left to play among the carts while the men and women wandered through the fair selling cans or donkeys. Many odd types of tramps and beggars had come together also, and were loitering about in the hope of getting some chance job, or of finding some one who would stand them a drink. Once or twice a stir was made by some unruly ram or bull, but in these smaller fairs there seldom is much real excitement till the evening, when the bad whisky that is too freely drunk begins to be felt.

When I had spoken to one or two men that I wished to see, I sat down near a bridge at the end of the green, between a tinker who was mending a can and a herd who was minding some sheep that had not been sold. The herd spoke to me with some pride of his skill in dipping sheep to keep them from the fly, and other matters connected with his work. 'Let you not be talking,' said the tinker, when he paused for a moment. 'You've been after sheep since you were that height' (holding his hand a little over the ground) 'and yet you're nowhere in the world beside the herds that do be reared beyond on the mountains. Those men are a wonder, for I'm told they can tell a lamb from their own ewes before it is marked, and that when they have five hundred sheep on the hills—five hundred is a big number—they don't need to count them or reckon them at all, but they just walk here and there where they are, and if one is gone away they'll miss it from the rest.'[1]

Then a woman came up and spoke to the tinker, and they went down the road together into the village. 'That man is a great villain,' said the herd, when he was out of hearing. 'One time he and his woman went up to a priest in the hills and asked him would he wed them for half a sovereign, I think it was. The priest said it was a poor price, but he'd wed them surely if they'd make him a tin can along with it. "I will, faith," said the tinker, "and I'll come back when it's done." They went off then, and in three weeks they came back, and they asked the priest a second time would he wed

[1] 'The herds who spend half their time walking through the mountains in dense clouds or mist are one of the most remarkable classes left in Ireland. To know these people in their own glens, to talk with them when it is raining and in the cold dawns and the twilights is a pleasure and privilege like few others. [There are] men who have a simplicity and sincerity that would cure any cynicism, and a fineness of form—in at least some of the men and women—with an expression of curious whimsical humour or despondency that never loses its interest. Beautiful as these Wicklow [glens] are in all seasons, when one has learned to know the people one does not love them as Wordsworth did for the sake of their home, but one feels a new glory given to the sunsets by the ragged figures they give light to.' This passage is in Synge's typescript in Box-file C but it was omitted from the published article.

them. "Have you the tin can?" said the priest. "We have not," said the tinker; "we had it made at the fall of night, but the ass gave it a kick this morning the way it isn't fit for you at all." "Go on now," says the priest. "It's a pair of rogues and schemers you are, and I won't wed you at all." They went off then, and they were never married to this day.'

As I went up again through the village a great sale of old clothing was going on from booths at each side of the road, and further on boots were set out for sale on boards laid across the tops of barrels, a very usual counter. In another place old women were selling quantities of damaged fruit, kippered herrings, and an extraordinary collection of old ropes and iron. In front of a public-house a ballad-singer was singing a song in the middle of a crowd of people. As far as I could hear it, the words ran like this:—

As we came down from Wicklow
With our bundle of switches;
As we came down from Wicklow,
Oh! what did we see?
As we came to the city
We saw maidens pretty,
And we called out to ask them to buy our heath-broom.
Heath-broom, freestone, black turf, gather them up.
Oh! gradh machree, Mavourneen,
Won't you buy our heath-broom?

When the season is over
Won't we be in clover,
With the gold in our pockets
We got from heath-broom.
It's home we will toddle,
And we'll get a naggin,
And we'll drink to the maidens that bought our heath-broom.
Heath-broom, freestone, black turf, gather them up.
Oh! gradh machree, Mavourneen,
Won't you buy our heath-broom?

Before he had finished a tinker arrived, too drunk to stand or walk, but leading a tall horse with his left hand, and inviting anyone who would deny that he was the best horseman in Wicklow to fight with him on the spot. Soon afterwards I started on my way home, driving most of the way with a farmer from the same neighbourhood.

A LANDLORD'S GARDEN IN COUNTY WICKLOW[1]

A STONE's throw from an old house where I spent several summers in County Wicklow, there was a garden that had been left to itself for fifteen or twenty years. Just inside the gate, as one entered, two paths led up through a couple of strawberry beds, half choked with leaves, where a few white and narrow strawberries were still hidden away. Further on was nearly half an acre of tall raspberry canes and thistles five feet high, growing together in a dense mass, where one could still pick raspberries enough to last a household for the season. Then, in a waste of hemlock, there were some half-dozen apple trees covered with lichen and moss, and against the northern walls a few dying plum trees hanging from their nails. Beyond them there was a dead pear tree, and just inside the gate, as one came back to it, a large fuchsia filled with empty nests. A few lines of box here and there showed where the flower-beds had been laid out, and when anyone who had the knowledge looked carefully among them many remnants could be found of beautiful and rare plants.

All round this garden there was a wall seven or eight feet high, in which one could see three or four tracks with well-worn holes, like the paths down a cliff in Kerry, where boys and tramps came over to steal and take away any apples or other fruits that were in season. Above the wall on the three windy sides there were rows of finely-grown lime trees, the place of meeting in the summer for ten thousand bees. Under the east wall there was the roof of a greenhouse, where one could sit, when it was wet or dry, and watch the birds and butterflies, many of which were not common. The seasons were always late in this place—it was high above the sea—and redpolls often used to nest not far off late in the summer; siskins did the same once or twice, and greenfinches, till the beginning of August, used to cackle endlessly in the lime trees.

Everyone is used in Ireland to the tragedy that is bound up with the lives of farmers and fishing people; but in this garden one seemed to feel the tragedy of the landlord class also, and of the in-

[1] Written some time after 1903. First published on 1 July 1907 in the *Manchester Guardian*.

numerable old families that are quickly dwindling away. These owners of the land are not much pitied at the present day, or much deserving of pity; and yet one cannot quite forget that they are the descendants of what was at one time, in the eighteenth century, a high-spirited and highly-cultivated aristocracy.[1] The broken greenhouses and mouse-eaten libraries, that were designed and collected by men who voted with Grattan, are perhaps as mournful in the end as the four mud walls that are so often left in Wicklow as the only remnants of a farmhouse. The desolation of this life is often of a peculiarly local kind, and if a playwright chose to go through the Irish country houses he would find material, it is likely, for many gloomy plays that would turn on the dying away of these old families, and on the lives of the one or two delicate girls that are left so often to represent a dozen hearty men who were alive a generation or two ago. Many of the descendants of these people have, of course, drifted into professional life in Dublin, or have gone abroad; yet, wherever they are, they do not equal their forefathers, and where men used to collect fine editions of *Don Quixote* and Molière, in Spanish and French, and luxuriantly bound copies of Juvenal and Persius and Cicero, nothing is read now but Longfellow and Hall Caine and Miss Corelli. Where good and roomy houses were built a hundred years ago, poor and tawdry houses are built now; and bad bookbinding, bad pictures, and bad decorations are thought well of, where rich bindings, beautiful miniatures and finely-carved chimney-pieces were once prized by the old Irish landlords.

To return to our garden. One year the apple crop was unusually plentiful, and every Sunday inroads were made upon it by some unknown persons. At last I decided to lie in wait at the dangerous hour—about twelve o'clock—when the boys of the neighbourhood were on their way home from Mass, and we were supposed to be busy with our devotions three miles away. A little before eleven I slipped out, accordingly, with a book, locked the door behind me, put the key in my pocket, and lay down under a bush. When I had been reading for some time, and had quite forgotten the thieves, I looked up at some little stir and saw a young man, in his Sunday clothes, walking up the path towards me. He stopped

[1] In Box-file C occurs this: 'Still, this class, with its many genuine qualities, had little patriotism, in the right sense, few ideas, and no seed for future life, so it has gone to the wall.'

when he saw me, and for a moment we gazed at each other with astonishment. At last, to make a move, I said it was a fine day. 'It is indeed, sir,' he answered with a smile, and then he turned round and ran for his life. I realized that he was a thief, and jumped up and ran after him, seeing, as I did so, a flock of small boys swarming up the walls of the garden. Meanwhile the young man ran round and round through the raspberry canes, over the strawberry beds and in and out among the apple trees. He knew that if he tried to get over the wall I should catch him, and that there was no other way out, as I had locked the gate. It was heavy running, and we both began to get weary. Then I caught my foot in a briar and fell. Immediately the young man rushed to the wall and began scrambling up it, but just as he was drawing his leg over the top I caught him by the heel. For a moment he struggled and kicked, then by sheer weight I brought him down at my feet, and an armful of masonry along with him. I caught him by the neck and tried to ask his name, but found we were too breathless to speak.

For I do not know how long we sat glaring at each other, and gasping painfully. Then by degrees I began to upbraid him in a whisper for coming over a person's wall to steal his apples, when he was such a fine well-dressed, grown-up young man. I could see that he was in mortal dread that I might have him up in the police courts, which I had no intention of doing, and when I finally asked him his name and address he invented a long story of how he lived six miles away, and had come over to this neighbourhood for Mass and to see a friend, and then how he had got a drought upon him, and thought an apple would put him in spirits for his walk home. Then he swore he would never come over the wall again if I would let him off, and that he would pray God to have mercy on me when my last hour was come. I felt sure his whole story was a tissue of lies, and I did not want him to have the crow of having taken me in. 'There is a woman belonging to the place,' I said, 'inside in the house helping the girl to cook the dinner. Walk in now with me, and we'll see if you're such a stranger as you'd have me think.' He looked infinitely troubled, but I took him by the neck and wrist and we set off for the gate. When we had gone a pace or two he stopped. 'I beg your pardon,' he said, 'my cap's after falling down on the over side of the wall. May I cross over and get it?' That was too much for me. 'Well, go on,' I said, 'and if ever I catch you again woe betide you.' I let him go then, and he rushed madly over the wall and disappeared. A few days later I discovered, not at all to my surprise, that he lived half a mile away, and was intimately related to a small boy who came to the house every morning to run messages and clean the boots. Yet it must not be thought that this young man was dishonest; I would have been quite ready the next day to trust him with a ten-pound note.

GLENCREE[1]

THIS morning the air is clear, and there is a trace of summer again. I am sitting in a nook beside the stream from the Upper Lake, close down among the heather and bracken and rushes. I have seen the people going up to Mass in the Reformatory and the valley seems empty of life.

I have gone on, mile after mile, of the road to Sally Gap, between brown dikes and chasms in the turf, with broken foot-bridges across them, or between sheets of sickly moss and bog-cotton that is unable to thrive. The road is caked with moss that breaks like pie-crust under my feet, and in corners where there is shelter there are sheep loitering, or a few straggling grouse. . . . The fog has come down in places; I am meeting multitudes of hares that run round me at a little distance—looking enormous in the mists—or sit up on their ends against the sky line to watch me going by. When I sit down for a moment the sense of loneliness has no equal. I can hear nothing but the slow running of water and the grouse crowing and chuckling underneath the band of cloud. Then the fog lifts and shows the white empty roads winding everywhere, with the added sense of desolation one gets passing an empty house on the side of a road.

When I turn back again the air has got stuffy and heavy and calm, with a cloud still down upon the glen; there is a dead heat in the air that is not natural so high up, and the silence is so great three or four wrens that are singing near the lake seem to fill the valley with sound. In most places I can see the straight ending of the cloud, but above the lake grey fingers are coming up and down, like a hand that is clasping and opening again. One longs for rain or wind or thunder. The very ewes and lambs have stopped bleating, and are slinking round among the stacks of turf.

I have come out again on the mountain road the third day of the fog. At first it was misty only, and then a cloud crept up the water gullies from the valley of the Liffey, and in a moment I am cut off

[1] Written in 1907. First published in Volume Four of the *Works* of 1910, which did not include the final paragraph. This has been added from Box-file C.

in a white silent cloud. The little turfy ridges on each side of the road have the look of glens to me, and every block of stone has the size of a house. The cobwebs on the furze are like a silvery net, and the silence is so great and queer, even weasels run squealing past me on the side of the road. . . . An east wind is rising. Once in every minute I see the little mounds in their natural shapes that have been mountains for a week. I see wet cottages on the other side of the glen that I had forgotten. Then, as I walk on, I see out over a cloud to the tops of real mountains standing up into the sky.

There is a dense white fog around the cottage, and we seem to be shut away from any habitation. All round behind the hills there is a moan and rumble of thunder coming nearer, at times with a fierce and sudden crash. The bracken has a nearly painful green in the strangeness of the light. Enormous sheep are passing in and out of the sky line.

There is a strange depression about the cottage to-night. The woman of the house is taken ill and has got into bed beside her mother-in-law, who is over ninety and is wandering in her mind. The man of the house has gone away ten miles for medicine, and I am left with the two children, who are playing silently about the door.

The larches in the haggard are dripping heavily with damp, and the hens and geese, bewildered with the noise and gloom, are cackling with uneasy dread. All one's senses are disturbed. As I walk backwards and forwards, a few yards above and below the door, the little stream I do not see seems to roar out of the cloud.

Every leaf and twig is heavy with drops, and a dog that has passed with a sad-eyed herd looked wet and draggled and afraid.

I remember lying in the heather one clear Sunday morning in the early autumn when the bracken had just turned. All the people of the district were at Mass in a chapel a few miles away, so the valleys were empty, and there was nothing to be heard but the buzzing of a few late bees and the autumn song of thrushes. The sky was covered with white radiant clouds, with soft outlines, broken in a few places by lines of blue sky of wonderful delicacy and clearness. In a little while I heard a step on a path beneath me, and a tramp came wandering round the bottom of the hill. There was a spring below where I was lying, and when he reached it he looked round to see if anyone was watching him. I was hidden by the ferns, so he knelt down beside the water, where there was a pool among the stones, pulled his shirt over his head, and began washing it in the spring. After a little he seemed satisfied, and began wringing the water out of it; then he put it on, dripping as it was, buttoned his old coat over it, and wandered on towards the village, picking blackberries from the hedge.

Before he was quite out of sight the first groups of people on their way home from the chapel began to appear on the paths round the hill, and I could hear the jolting of heavy outside cars. By his act of primitive cleanness this man seemed to have lifted himself also into the mood of the sky, and the indescribable half-plaintive atmosphere of the autumn Sundays of Wicklow. I could not pity him. The cottage men with their humour and simplicity and the grey farm-houses they live in have gained in a real sense—'Infinite riches in a little room', while the tramp has chosen a life of penury with a world for habitation.

IN WEST KERRY[1]

At Killarney a number of Irish speaking peasants crowded into the train, with their goods—the peasant is always reluctant to send his packages in the van—and an old man and woman speaking Irish only took their seats opposite me. When they looked at each other for the first time after the fuss of their entry they saw that they were acquaintances, and they had a long talk about their affairs and who was still living and who had died since they had met last. The old man had one son living with him still, but the old woman was alone in her little house since her man had found death. The old woman had few teeth and was greatly wizened and wrinkled and yet her eyes had so much sympathy and life and expression and her movements were so gracious that one could feel an extraordinary air of beauty hanging somewhere about her. The old man wore a fringe of beard under his chin, an imperial on his lip, and two long tufts of hair on the edges of his chin beneath the corners of his mouth, and for the rest was roughly shaved—a curious decoration that gave him a whimsical expression.[2]

At Tralee station—I was on my way to a village many miles beyond Dingle—I found a boy who carried my bag some way along the road to an open yard where the light railway starts for the west. There was a confused mass of peasants struggling on the platform, with all sort of baggage, which the people lifted into the train for themselves as well as they were able. The seats ran up either side of the cars, and the space between them was soon filled with sacks of flour, cases of porter, chairs rolled in straw, and other household goods. A drunken young man got in just before we started, and sang songs for a few coppers, telling us that he had spent all his money, and had nothing left to pay for his ticket. Then, when the carriage was closely packed, we moved slowly out of the station. At my side there was an old man who explained the Irish names of the places that we came to, and pointed out the Seven Pigs, a group of islands in the bay; Kerry Head, further off; and many distant mountains. Beyond him a dozen big women in

[1] First published in three successive numbers, Summer, Autumn, and Winter, 1907, of *The Shanachie*.

[2] This opening paragraph is from Notebook 45 and has not been published before.

shawls were crowded together; and just opposite me there was a young woman wearing a wedding ring, who was one of the peculiarly refined women of Kerry, with supreme charm in every movement and expression. The big woman talked to her about some elderly man who had been sick—her husband, it was likely—and some young man who had gone away to England, and was breaking his heart with loneliness.

'Ah, poor fellow!' she said; 'I suppose he will get used to it like another; and wouldn't he be worse off if he was beyond the seas in Saint Louis, or the towns of America?'

This woman seemed to unite the healthiness of the country people with the greatest sensitiveness, and whenever there was any little stir or joke in the carriage, her face and neck flushed with pleasure and amusement. As we went on there were superb sights—first on the north, towards Loop Head, and then when we reached the top of the ridge, to the south also, to Drung Hill, Macgillicuddy's Reeks, and other mountains of South Kerry. A little further on, nearly all the people got out at a small station; and the young woman I had admired, gathered up most of the household goods and got down also, lifting heavy boxes with the power of a man. Then two returned American girls got in, fine, stout-looking women, with distress in their expression, and we started again. Dingle Bay could now be seen through narrow valleys on our left, and had extraordinary beauty in the evening light. In the carriage next to ours a number of herds and jobbers were travelling, and for the last hour they kept up a furious altercation that seemed always on the verge of breaking into a dangerous quarrel, but no blows were given.

At the end of the line an old blue side-car was waiting to take me to the village where I was going. I was some time fastening on my goods, with the raggedy boy who was to drive me; and then we set off, passing through the usual streets of a Kerry town, with public-houses at the corners, till we left the town by a narrow quay with a few sailing boats and a small steamer with coal. Then we went over a bridge near a large water-mill, where a number of girls were standing about, with black shawls over their heads, and turned sharp to the right, against the face of the mountains. At first we went up hill for several miles, and got on slowly, though the boy jumped down once or twice and gathered a handful of switches to beat the tall mare he was driving. Just as the twilight was beginning to deepen we reached the top of the ridge and came out through a gap into sight of Smerwick Harbour, a wild bay with magnificent headlands beyond it, and a long stretch of the Atlantic. We drove on towards the west, sometimes very quickly, where the slope was gradual, and then slowly again when the road seemed to fall away under us, like the wall of a house. As the night fell the sea became like a piece of white silver on our right; and the mountains got black on our left, and heavy night smells began to come up out of the bogs. Once or twice I noticed a blue cloud over the edge of the road, and then I saw that we were nearly against the gables of a little village, where the houses were so closely packed together there was no light from any of them. It was now quite dark, and the boy got cautious in his driving, pulling the car almost into the ditch once or twice to avoid an enormous cavity where the middle of the road had settled down into the bogs. At last we came to another river and a public-house, and went up a hill, from which we could see the outline of a chapel; then the boy turned to me: 'Is it ten o'clock yet?' he said; 'for we're mostly now in the village.'

This morning, a Sunday, rain was threatening; but I went out west after my breakfast under Croagh Martin, in the direction of the Atlantic. At one of the first villages I came to I had a long talk with a man who was sitting on the ditch waiting till it was time for Mass. Before long we began talking about the Irish language.

'A few years ago,' he said, 'they were all for stopping it off; and when I was a boy they tied a gobban into my mouth for the whole afternoon because I was heard speaking Irish. Wasn't that great cruelty? And now when I hear the same busybodies coming around and telling us for the love of God to speak nothing but Irish, I've a good mind to tell them to go to hell. There was a priest out here a while since who was telling us to stay always where we are, and to speak nothing but Irish; but, I suppose, although the priests are learned men, and great scholars, they don't understand the life of the people the same as another man would. In this place the land is poor—you can see that for yourself—and the people have little else to live on; so that when there is a long family, one son will stay at home and keep on the farm, and the others will go away because they must go. Then when they once pass out of the Dingle station in Tralee they won't hear a word of Irish, or meet anyone who'd understand it; so what good, I ask you, is a man who hasn't got the English, and plenty of it?'

After I left him I went on towards Dunquin, and lay for a long time on the side of a magnificently wild road under Croagh Martin, where I could see the Blasket Islands and the end of Dunmore Head, the most westerly point of Europe. It was a grey day with a curious silence on the sea and sky and no sign of life anywhere, except the sail of one curagh—or niavogue, as they are called here—that was sailing in from the islands. Now and then a cart passed me filled with old people and children, who saluted me in Irish; then I turned back myself. I got on a long road running through a bog, with a smooth mountain on one side and the sea on the other, and Brandon in front of me, partly covered with clouds. As far as I could see there were little groups of people on their way to the chapel in Ballyferriter, the men in homespun and the women wearing blue cloaks, or, more often, black shawls twisted over their heads. This procession along the olive bogs, between the mountains and the sea, on this grey day of autumn seemed to wring me with the pang of emotion one meets everywhere in Ireland—an emotion that is partly local and patriotic, and partly a share of the desolation that is mixed everywhere with the supreme beauty of the world.

In the evening, when I was walking about the village, I fell in with a man who could read Gaelic, and was full of enthusiasm for the old language and of contempt for English.

'I can tell you,' he said, 'that the English I have is no more good to me than the cover of that pipe. Buyers come here from Dingle and Cork and Clare, and they have good Irish, and so has everyone we meet with, for there is no one can do business in this place who hasn't the language on his tongue.'

Then I asked him about the young men who go away to America.

'Many go away,' he said, 'who could stay if they wished to, for it is a fine place for fishing, and a man will get more money and better health for himself, and rear a better family, in this place than in many another. It's a good place to be in, and now, with the help of God, the little children will all learn to read and write in Irish, and that is a great thing, for how can people do any good, or make a song even, if they cannot write? You will be often three weeks making a song, and there will be times when you will think of good things to put into it that could never be beaten in the whole world; but if you cannot write them down you will forget them, maybe, by the next day, and then what good will be your song?'

After a while we went upstairs to a large room in the inn, where a number of young men and girls were dancing jigs and reels. These young people, although they are as Irish-speaking as the people of Connemara, are pushing forward in their ways of living and dress; so that this group of dancers could hardly have been known, by their appearance, from any Sunday party in Limerick or Cork. After a long four-hand reel, my friend, who was dressed in homespun, danced a jig to the whistling of a young man with great energy and spirit. Then he sat down beside me in the corner, and we talked about spring trawling and the price of nets. I told him about the ways of Aran and Connemara; and then he told me about the French trawlers who come to this neighbourhood in April and May.

'The Frenchmen from Fécamp,' he said, 'are Catholics and decent people; but those who come from Boulogne have no religion, and are little better than a wild beast would lep on you out of a wood. One night there was a drift of them below in the public-house, where there is a counter, as you've maybe seen, with a tin top on it. Well, they were talking together, and they had some little difference among themselves, and from that they went on raising their voices, till one of them out with his knife and drove it down through the tin into the wood! Wasn't that a dangerous fellow?'

Then he told me about their tobacco.

'The French do have two kinds of tobacco; one of them is called hay-tobacco, and if you give them a few eggs, or maybe nine little cabbage plants, they'll give you as much of it as would fill your hat. Then we get a pound of our own tobacco and mix the two of them together, and put them away in a pig's bladder—it's that way we keep our tobacco—and we have enough with that lot for the whole winter.'

This evening a circus was advertised in Dingle, for one night only; so I made my way there towards the end of the afternoon, although the weather was windy and threatening. I reached the town an hour too soon, so I spent some time watching the wild-looking fishermen and fisherwomen who stand about the quays. Then I wandered up and saw the evening train coming in with the usual number of gaily-dressed young women and half-drunken jobbers and merchants; and at last, about eight o'clock, I went to the circus field, just above the town, in a heavy splash of rain. The tent was set up in the middle of the field, and a little to the side of it a large crowd was struggling for tickets at one of the wheeled houses in which the acrobats live. I went round the tent in the hope of getting in by some easier means, and found a door in the canvas, where a man was calling out: 'Tickets, or money, this way,' and I passed in through a long winding passage. It was some time after the hour named for the show, but although the tent was almost filled there was no sign of the performers; so I stood back in a corner and watched the crowd coming in wet and dripping from the rain, which had turned to a downpour. The tent was lighted by a few flaring gas-jets round the central pole, with an opening above them, through which the rain shot down in straight whistling lines. The top of the tent was dripping and saturated, and the gas, shining sideways across, made it glitter in many places with the brilliancy of golden silk. When a sudden squall came with a rush from the narrow valleys behind the town, the whole structure billowed, and flapped and strained, till one waited every moment to see the canvas fall upon our heads. The people, who looked strangely black and swarthy in the uncertain light, were seated all round on three or four rows of raised wooden seats, and many who were late were still crushing forward, and standing in dense masses wherever there was room. At the entrance a rather riotous crowd began to surge in so quickly that there was danger of the place being rushed. Word was sent across the ring, and in a moment three or four of the women performers, with long streaming ulsters buttoned over their tights, ran out from behind the scenes and threw themselves into the crowd, forcing back the wild hillside people, fishwomen and drunken sailors, in an extraordinary tumult of swearing, wrestling and laughter. These women seemed to enjoy this part of their work, and shrieked with amusement when two or three of them fell on some enormous farmer or publican and nearly dragged him to the ground. Here and there among the people I could see a little party of squireens and their daughters, in the fashions of five years

THE CIRCUS

ago, trying, not always successfully, to reach the shilling seats. The crowd was now so thick I could see little more than the heads of the performers, who had at last come into the ring, and many of the shorter women who were near me must have seen nothing the whole evening, yet they showed no sign of impatience. The performance was begun by the usual dirty white horse, that was brought out and set to gallop round, with a gaudy horse-woman on his back who jumped through a hoop and did the ordinary feats, the horse's hoofs splashing and possing all the time in the green slush of the ring. An old door-mat was laid down near the entrance for the performers, and as they came out in turn they wiped the mud from their feet before they got up on their horses. A little later the clown came out, to the great delight of the people. He was followed by some gymnasts, and then the horse-people came out again in different dress and make-up, and went through their old turns once more. After that there was prolonged fooling between the clown and the chief horseman, who made many mediæval jokes, that reminded me of little circuses on the outer Boulevards of Paris, and at last the horseman sang a song which won great applause:—

Here's to the man who kisses his wife,
And kisses his wife alone;
For there's many a man kissed another man's wife
When he thought he kissed his own.

Here's to the man who rocks his child,
And rocks his child alone;
For there's many a man rocked another man's child
When he thought he rocked his own.

About ten o'clock there seemed to be a lull in the storm, so I went out into the open air with two young men who were going the road I had to travel. The rain had stopped for a moment, but a high wind was blowing as we made our way to a public-house to get a few biscuits and a glass of beer before we started. A sleepy barmaid, who was lolling behind the counter with a novel pricked up her ears when she heard us talking of our journey.

'Surely you are not going to Ballydavid,' she said, 'at such an hour of a night like this.'

We told her we were going to a place which was further away.

'Well,' she said, 'I wouldn't go to that place to-night if you had a coach-and-four to drive me in, and gave me twenty pounds into the bargain! How at all will you get on in the darkness when the roads will be running with water, and you'll be likely to slip down every place into some drain or ditch?'

When we went out and began to make our way down the steep hill through the town, the night seemed darker than ever after the glare of the bar. Before we had gone many yards a woman's voice called out sharply from under the wall: 'Mind the horse.' I looked up and saw the black outline of a horse's head right above me. It was not plain in such darkness how we should get to the end of our ten-mile journey; but one of the young men borrowed a lantern from a chandler in the bottom of the town, and we made our way over the bridge and up the hill, going slowly and painfully with just light enough, when we kept close together, to avoid the sloughs of water and piles of stones on the roadway. By the time we reached the top of the ridge and began to work down carefully towards Smerwick, the rain stopped, and we reached the village without any mishap.

I go out often in the mornings to the site of Sybil Ferriter's Castle, on a little headland reached by a narrow strip of rocks. As I lie there I can watch whole flights of cormorants and choughs and seagulls that fly about under the cliffs, and beyond them a number of niavogues that are nearly always fishing in Ferriter's Cove. Further on there are Sybil Head and three rocky points, the Three Sisters; then Smerwick Harbour and Brandon far away, usually covered with white airy clouds. Between these headlands and the village there is a strip of sandhill grown over with sea-holly, and a low beach where scores of red bullocks lie close to the sea, or wade in above their knees. Further on one passes peculiar horseshoe coves, with contorted lines of sandstone on one side and slaty blue rocks on the other, and necks of transparent sea of wonderful blueness between them.

I walked up this morning along the slope from the east to the top of Sybil Head, where one comes out suddenly on the brow of a cliff with a straight fall of many hundred feet into the sea. It is a place of indescribable grandeur, where one can see Carrantuohill and the Skelligs and Loop Head and the full sweep of the Atlantic, and, over all, the wonderfully tender and searching light that is seen only in Kerry. Looking down the drop of five or six hundred feet, the height is so great that the gannets flying close over the sea look like white butterflies, and the choughs like flies fluttering behind them. One wonders in these places why anyone is left in Dublin, or London, or Paris, when it would be better, one would think, to live in a tent or hut with this magnificent sea and sky, and to breathe this wonderful air, which is like wine in one's teeth.

Here and there on this headland there are little villages of ten or twenty houses, closely packed together without any order or roadway. Usually there are one or two curious beehive-like structures in these villages, used here, it is said, as pig-sties or store-houses. On my way down from Sybil Head I was joined by a tall young man, who told me he had been in the navy, but had bought himself out before his time was over.

'Twelve of us joined from this place,' he said, 'and I was the last of them that stayed in it, for it is a life that no one could put up with. It's not the work that would trouble you, but it's that they can't leave you alone, and that you must be ever and always fooling over something.'

He had been in South Africa during the war, and in Japan, and all over the world; but he was now dressed in homespuns, and had settled down here, he told me, for the rest of his life. Before we reached the village we met Maurice, the fisherman I have spoken of, and we sat down under a hedge to shelter from a shower. We began to talk of fevers and sicknesses and doctors—these little villages are often infested with typhus—and Maurice spoke about the traditional cures.

'There is a plant,' he said, 'which is the richest that is growing out of the ground, and in the old times the women used to be giving it to their children till they'd be growing up seven feet maybe in height. Then the priests and doctors began taking everything to themselves and destroyed the old knowledge, and that is a poor thing; for you know well it was the Holy Mother of God who cured her own Son with plants the like of that, and said after that no mother should be without a plant for ever to cure her child. Then she threw out the seeds of it over the whole world, so that it's growing every place from that day to this.'

I came out to-day, a holiday, to the Great Blasket Island with a schoolmaster and two young men from the village, who were coming for the afternoon only. The day was admirably clear, with a blue sea and sky, and the voyage in the long canoe—I had not been in one for two or three years—gave me indescribable enjoyment. We passed Dunmore Head, and then stood out nearly due west towards the Great Blasket itself, the height of the mountains round the bay and the sharpness of the rocks making the place singularly different from the sounds about Aran, where I had last travelled in a curagh.[1] As usual, three men were rowing—the man I have come to stay with,[2] his son, and a tall neighbour, all dressed in blue jerseys, homespun trousers and shirts, and talking in Irish only, though my host could speak good English when he chose to. As we came nearer the island, which seemed to rise like a mountain straight out of the sea, we could make out a crowd of people in their holiday clothes standing or sitting along the brow of the cliff watching our approach, and just beyond them a patch of cottages with roofs of tarred felt. A little later we doubled into a cove among the rocks, where I landed at a boat slip, and then scrambled up a steep zig-zag pathway to the head of the cliff, where the people crowded round us and shook hands with the men who had come with me.

This cottage where I am to stay is one of the highest of the group, and as we passed up to it through little paths among the cottages many white, wolfish-looking dogs came out and barked furiously. My host had gone on in front with my bag, and when I reached his threshold he came forward and shook hands with me again, with a finished speech of welcome. His eldest daughter, a young married woman of about twenty, who manages the house, shook hands with me also, and then, without asking if we were hungry, began making us tea in a metal tea-pot and frying rashers of bacon. She is a small, beautifully-formed woman, with brown hair and eyes—instead of the black hair and blue eyes that are usually found with this type in Ireland—and delicate feet and ankles that are not common in these parts, where the woman's work is so hard. Her sister, who lives in the house also, is a bonny girl of about eighteen, full of humour and spirits.

The schoolmaster made many jokes in English and Irish while the little hostess served our tea; and then the kitchen filled up with

[1] In a letter of 17 January 1907 to J. Hone, Synge says: '. . . the people of the Blaskets differ from the Donegal or Galway people and are in many ways peculiarly interesting.'

[2] He was known locally as the 'king', and his daughter, the hostess whom Synge admired, was known as the 'little queen'.

young men and women—the men dressed like ordinary fishermen, the women wearing print bodices and coloured skirts, that had none of the distinction of the dress of Aran—and a polka was danced, with curious solemnity, in a whirl of dust. When it was over it was time for my companions to go back to the mainland. As soon as we came out and began to go down to the sea, a large crowd, made up of nearly all the men and women and children of the island, came down also, closely packed round us. At the edge of the cliff the young men and the schoolmaster bade me goodbye and went down the zig-zag path, leaving me alone with the islanders on the ledge of the rock, where I had seen the people as we came in. I sat for a long time watching the sail of the canoe moving away to Dunquin, and talking to a young man who had spent some years in Ballyferriter, and had good English. The evening was peculiarly fine, and after a while, when the crowd had scattered, I passed up through the cottages, and walked through a boreen towards the north-west, between a few plots of potatoes and little fields of weeds that seemed to have gone out of cultivation not long ago. Beyond these I turned up a sharp, green hill, and came out suddenly on the broken edge of a cliff. The effect was wonderful. The Atlantic was right underneath; then I could see the sharp rocks of several uninhabited islands, a mile or two off, the Tearaught further away, and, on my left, the whole northern edge of this island curving round towards the west, with a steep, heathery face, a thousand feet high. The whole sight of wild islands and sea was as clear and cold and brilliant as what one sees in a dream, and alive with the singularly severe glory that is in the character of this place.

As I was wandering about I saw many of the young islanders, not far off, jumping and putting the weight—a heavy stone—or running races on the grass. Then four girls, walking arm-in-arm, came up and talked to me in Irish. Before long they began to laugh loudly at some signs I made to eke out my meaning, and by degrees the men wandered up also, till there was a crowd round us. The cold of the night was growing stronger, however, and we soon turned back to the village, and sat around the fire in the kitchen the rest of the evening.

At eleven o'clock the people got up as one man and went away, leaving me with the little hostess—the man of the house had gone to the mainland with the young men—her husband and sister. I told them I was sleepy, and ready to go to bed; so the little hostess lighted a candle, carried it into the room beyond the kitchen, and stuck it up on the end of the bed-post of one of the beds with a few drops of grease. Then she took off her apron, and fastened it up in the window as a blind, laid another apron on the wet earthen floor for me to stand on, and left me to myself. The room had two beds, running from wall to wall with a small space between them, a chair that the little hostess had brought in, an old hairbrush that was propping the window open, and no other article. When I had been in bed for some time, I heard the host's voice in the kitchen, and a moment or two later he came in with a candle in his hand, and made a long apology for having been away the whole of my first evening on the island, holding the candle while he talked very close to my face. I told him I had been well entertained by his family and neighbours, and had hardly missed him. He went away, and half an hour later opened the door again with the iron spoon which serves to lift the latch, and came in, in a suit of white homespuns, and said he must ask me to let him stretch out in the other bed, as there was no place else for him to lie. I told him that he was welcome, and he got into the other bed and lit his pipe. Then we had a long talk about this place and America and the younger generations.

'There has been no one drowned on this island,' he said, 'for forty years, and that is a great wonder, for it is a dangerous life. There was a man—the brother of the man you were talking to when the girls were dancing—was married to a widow had a public-house away to the west of Ballydavid, and he was out fishing for mackerel, and he got a great haul of them; then he filled his canoe too full, so that she was down to the edge of the water, and a wave broke into her when they were near the shore, and she went down under them. Two men got ashore, but the man from this island was drowned, for his oilskins went down about his feet, and he sank where he was.'

Then we talked about the chances of the mackerel season. 'If the season is good,' he said, 'we get on well; but it is not certain at all. We do pay £4 for a net, and sometimes the dogfish will get into it the first day and tear it into pieces as if you'd cut it with a knife. Sometimes the mackerel will die in the net, and then ten men would be hard set to pull them up into the canoe, so that if the wind rises on us we must cut loose, and let down the net into the bottom of the sea. When we get fish here in the night we go to Dunquin and sell them to buyers in the morning; and, believe me, it is a dangerous thing to cross that sound when you have too great a load taken into your canoe. When it is too bad to cross over we do salt the fish ourselves—we must salt them cleanly and put them in clean barrels—and then the first day it is calm buyers will be out after them from the town of Dingle.'

Afterwards he spoke of the people who go away to America, and the younger generations that are growing up now in Ireland.

'The young people is no use,' he said. 'I am not as good a man as my father was, and my son is growing up worse than I am.' Then he put up his pipe on the end of the bed-post. 'You'll be tired now,' he went on, 'so it's time we were sleeping; and, I humbly beg your pardon, might I ask your name?' I told him.

'Well, good night so,' he said, 'and may you have a good sleep your first night in this island.'

Then he put out the candle and we settled to sleep. In a few minutes I could hear that he was in his dreams, and just as my own ideas were begining to wander the house door opened, and the son of the place, a young man of about twenty, came in and walked into our room, close to my bed, with another candle in his hand. I lay with my eyes closed, and the young man did not seem pleased with my presence, though he looked at me with curiosity. When he was satisfied he went back to the kitchen, and took a drink of whisky and said his prayers; then, after loitering about for some time and playing with a little mongrel greyhound that seemed to adore him, he took off his clothes, clambered over his father, and stretched out on the inner side of the bed.

I awoke the next morning about six o'clock, and not long afterwards the host awoke also, and asked how I did. Then he wanted to know if I ever drank whisky; and when he heard that I did so, he began calling for one of his daughters at the top of his voice. In a few moments the younger girl came in, her eyes closing with sleep, and, at the host's bidding, got the whisky bottle, some water, and a green wine-glass out of the kitchen. She came first to my bedside and gave me a dram, then she did the same for her father and brother, handed us our pipes and tobacco, and went back to the kitchen.

There were to be sports at noon in Ballyferriter, and when we had talked for a while I asked the host if he would think well of my going over to see them. 'I would not,' he said; 'you'd do better to stay quiet in this place where you are; the men will be all drunk coming back, fighting and kicking in the canoes, and a man the like of you, who aren't used to us, would be frightened. Then, if you went, the people would be taking you into one public-house, and then into another, till you'd maybe get drunk yourself, and that wouldn't be a nice thing for a gentleman. Stay where you are in this island and you'll be safest so.'

When the son got up later and began going in and out of the kitchen, some of the neighbours, who had already come in, stared at me with curiosity as I lay in my bed; then I got up myself and went into the kitchen. The little hostess set about getting my breakfast, but before it was ready she partly rinsed the dough out of a pan where she had been kneading bread, poured some water into it, and put it on a chair near the door. Then she hunted about the edges of the rafters till she found a piece of soap, which she put on the back of a chair with a towel, and told me I might wash my face. I did so as well as I was able, in the middle of the people, and dried myself with the towel, which was the one used by the whole family.

The morning looked as if it would turn to rain and wind, so I took the advice I had been given and let the canoes go off without me to the sports. After a turn on the cliffs I came back to the house to write letters. The little hostess was washing up the breakfast things when I arrived with my papers and pens, but she made room for me at the table, and spread out an old newspaper for me to write on. A little later, when she had finished her washing, she came over to her usual place in the chimney corner, not far from where I was sitting, sat down on the floor, and took out her hair-pins and began combing her hair. As I finished each letter I had to say who it was to, and where the people lived; and then I had to tell her if they were married or single, how many children they had, and make a guess at how many pounds they spent in a year, and at the number of their servants. Just before I finished, the younger girl came back with three or four other young women, who were followed in a little while by a party of men.

I showed them some photographs of the Aran Islands and Wicklow, which they looked at with eagerness. The little hostess was especially taken with two or three that had babies or children in their foreground; and as she put her hands on my shoulders, and leaned over to look at them, with the confidence that is so usual in these places, I could see that she had her full share of the passion for children which is powerful in all women who are permanently and profoundly attractive. While I was telling her what I could about the children, I saw one of the men looking with peculiar amazement at an old photograph of myself that had been taken many years ago in an alley of the Luxembourg Gardens, where there were many statues in the background. 'Look at that,' he whispered in Irish to one of the girls, pointing to the statues; 'in those countries they do have naked people standing about in their skins.'

I explained that the figures were of marble only, and then the little hostess and all the girls examined them also. 'Oh! dear me,' said the little hostess, 'Is deas an rud do bheith ag siubhal ins an domhain mor' ('It's a fine thing to be travelling in the big world').

In the afternoon I went up and walked along the narrow central ridge of the island, till I came to the highest point, which is nearly three miles west of the village. The weather was gloomy and wild, and there was something nearly appalling in the loneliness of the place. I could look down on either side into a foggy edge of grey moving sea, and then further off I could see many distant mountains, or look out across the shadowy outline of Inishtooskert to the Tearaught rock. While I was sitting on the little mound which marks the summit of the island—a mound stripped and riddled by rabbits—a heavy bank of fog began to work up from the south, behind Valentia, on the other jaw of Dingle Bay. As soon as I saw it I hurried down from the pinnacle where I was, so that I might get away from the more dangerous locality before the cloud overtook me. In spite of my haste I had not gone half a mile when an edge of fog whisked and circled round me, and in a moment I could see nothing but a grey shroud of mist and a few yards of steep, slippery grass. Everything was distorted and magnified to an extraordinary degree; but I could hear the moan of the sea under me, and I knew my direction, so I worked along towards the village without trouble. In some places the island, on this southern side, is bitten into by sharp, narrow coves, and when the fog opened a little I could see across them, where gulls and choughs were picking about on the grass, looking as big as Kerry cattle or black mountain sheep. Before I reached the house the cloud had turned to a sharp shower of rain, and as I went in the water was dripping from my hat, 'Oh! dear me,' said the little hostess, when she saw me, 'Ta tu an-rhluc anois' ('You are very wet now'). She was alone in the house, breathing audibly, with a sort of simple self-importance, as she washed her jugs and teacups. While I was drinking my tea, a little later, some women came in with three or four little girls—the most beautiful children I have ever seen—who live in one of the nearest cottages. They tried to get the little girls to dance a reel together, but the smallest of them went and hid her head in the skirts of the little hostess. In the end two of the little girls danced with two of those who were grown up, to the lilting of one of them. The little hostess sat at the fire while they danced, plucking and drawing a cormorant for the men's dinner, and calling out to the girls when they lost the step of the dance.

In the evenings of Sundays and holidays the young men and girls go out to a rocky headland on the north-west, where there is a long, grassy slope, to dance and amuse themselves; and this evening I wandered out there with two men, telling them ghost stories in Irish as we went. When we turned over the edge of the hill we came on a number of young men lying on the short grass playing cards. We sat down near them, and before long a party of girls and young women came up also and sat down, twenty paces off, on the brink of the cliff, some of them wearing the fawn-coloured shawls that are so attractive and so much thought of in the south. It was just after sunset, and Inishtooskert was standing out with a smoky blue outline against the redness of the sky. At the foot of the cliff a wonderful silvery light was shining on the sea, which already, before the beginning of autumn, was eager and wintry and cold. The little group of blue-coated men lying on the grass, and the group of girls further off, had a singular effect in this solitude of rocks and sea; and in spite of their high spirits it gave me a sort of grief to feel the utter loneliness and desolation of the place that has given these people their finest qualities.

One of the young men had been thrown from a cart a few days before on his way home from Dingle, and his face was still raw and bleeding and horrible to look at; but the young girls seemed to find romance in his condition, and several of them went over and sat in a group round him, stroking his arms and face. When the card-playing was over I showed the young men a few tricks and feats, which they worked at themselves, to the great amusement of the girls, till they had accomplished them all. On our way back to the village the young girls ran wild in the twilight, flying and shrieking over the grass, or rushing up behind the young men and throwing them over, if they were able, by a sudden jerk or trip. The men in return caught them by one hand, and spun them round and round four or five times, and then let them go, when they whirled down the grassy slope for many yards, spinning like peg-tops, and only keeping their feet by the greatest efforts or good luck.

When we got to the village the people scattered for supper, and in our cottage the little hostess swept the floor and sprinkled it with some sand she had brought home in her apron. Then she filled a crock with drinking water, lit the lamp and sat down by the fire to comb her hair. Some time afterwards, when a number of young men had come in, as was usual, to spend the evening, some one said a niavogue was on its way home from the sports. We went out to the door, but it was too dark to see anything except the lights of a little steamer that was passing up the sound, almost beneath us, on its way to Limerick or Tralee. When it had gone by we could hear a furious drunken uproar coming up from a canoe that was somewhere out in the bay. It sounded as if the men were strangling or murdering each other, and it seemed almost miraculous that they should be able to manage their canoe. The people seemed to think they were in no special danger, and we went in again to the fire and talked about porter and whisky (I have never heard the men here talk for half an hour of anything without some allusion to drink), discussing how much a man could drink with comfort in a day, whether it is better to drink when a man is thirsty or at ordinary times, and what food gives the best liking for porter. Then they asked me how much porter I could drink myself, and I told them I could drink whisky, but that I had no taste for porter, and would only take a pint or two at odd times, when I was thirsty.

'The girls are laughing to hear you say that,' said an old man; 'but whisky is a lighter drink, and I'd sooner have it myself, and any old man would say the same.' A little later some young men came in, in their Sunday clothes, and told us the news of the sports.

This morning it was raining heavily, and the host got out some nets and set to work with his son and son-in-law, mending many holes that had been cut by dog-fish, as the mackerel season is soon to begin. While they were at work the kitchen emptied and filled continually with islanders passing in and out, and discussing the weather and the season. Then they started cutting each other's hair, the man who was being cut sitting with an oilskin round him on a little stool by the door, and some other men came in to sharpen their razors on the host's razor-strop, which seems to be the only one on the island. I had not shaved since I arrived, so the little hostess asked me after a while if I would like to shave myself before dinner. I told her I would, so she got me some water in the potato-dish and put it on a chair; then her sister got me a little piece of broken looking-glass and put it on a nail near the door, where there was some light. I set to work, and as I stood with my back to the people I could catch a score of eyes in the glass, watching me intently. 'That is a great improvement to you now,' said the host, when I had done; 'and whenever you want a beard, God bless you, you'll have a thick one surely.'

When I was coming down in the evening from the ridge of the island where I spend much of my time looking at the richness of the Atlantic on one side and the sad or shining greys of Dingle Bay on the other, I was joined by two young women and we walked back together. Just outside the village we met an old woman who stopped and laughed at us. 'Well, aren't you in good fortune this night, stranger,' she said, 'to be walking up and down in the company of women?'

'I am surely,' I answered; 'isn't that the best thing to be doing in the whole world?'

At our own door I saw the little hostess sweeping the floor, so I went down for a moment to the gable of the cottage, and looked out over the roofs of the little village to the sound, where the tide was running with extraordinary force. In a few minutes the little hostess came down and stood beside me—she thought I should not be left by myself when I had been driven away by the dust—and I asked her many questions about the names and relationships of the people that I am beginning to know.

Afterwards, when many of the people had come together in the kitchen, the men told me about their lobster-pots that are brought from Southampton, and cost half-a-crown each. 'In good weather,' said the man who was talking to me, 'they will often last for a quarter; but if storms come up on them they will sometimes break up in a week or two. Still and all, it is a good trade; and we do sell lobsters and crayfish every week in the season to a boat from England or a boat from France that does come in here, as you'll maybe see before you go.'

I told them I had often been in France, and one of the boys began counting up the numerals in French to show what he had learnt from their buyers. A little later, when the talk was beginning to flag, I turned to a young man near me—the best fiddler, I was told, on the islands—and asked him to play us a dance. He made excuses, and would not get his fiddle; but two of the girls slipped off and brought it. The young man tuned it and offered it to me, but I insisted that he should take it first. Then he played one or two tunes, without tone, but with good intonation and rhythm. When it was my turn I played a few tunes also; but the pitch was so low I could not do what I wanted, and I had not much success with the people, though the fiddler himself watched me with interest. 'That is great playing,' he said, when I had finished; 'and I never seen anyone the like of you for moving your hand and getting the sound out of it with the full drag of the bow.' Then he played a polka and four couples danced. The women, as usual, were in their naked feet, and whenever there was a figure for women only there was a curious hush and patter of bare feet, till the heavy pounding and shuffling of the men's boots broke in again. The whirl of music and dancing in this little kitchen stirred me with an extraordinary effect. The kindliness and merry-making of these islanders, who, one knows, are full of riot and severity and daring, has a quality and attractiveness that is absent altogether from the life of towns, and makes one think of the life that is shown in the ballads of Scotland.

After the dance the host, who had come in, sang a long English doggerel about a poor scholar who went to Maynooth and had great success in his studies, so that he was praised by the bishop. Then he went home for his holiday, and a young woman who had great riches asked him into her parlour and told him it was no fit life for a fine young man to be a priest, always saying Mass for poor people, and that he would have a right to give up his Latin and get married to herself. He refused her offers and went back to his college. When he was gone she went to the justice in great anger, and swore an oath against him that he had seduced her and left her with child. He was brought back for his trial, and he was in risk to be degraded and hanged, when a man rode up on a horse and said it was himself was the lover of the lady, and the father of her child.

Then they told me about an old man of eighty years, who is going to spend the winter alone on Inishvickillaun, an island six miles from this village. His son is making canoes and doing other carpenter's jobs on this island, and the other children have scattered also; but the old man refuses to leave the island he has spent his life on, so they have left him with a goat, and a bag of flour and stack of turf.

I have just been to the weaver's, looking at his loom and appliances. The host took me down to his cottage over the brow of the village, where some young men were finishing the skeleton of a canoe; and we found his family crowded round a low table on green stools with rope seats, finishing their dinner of potatoes. A little later the old weaver, who looks pale and sickly compared with the other islanders, took me into a sort of outhouse with a damp feeling in the air, where his loom was set up. He showed me how it was worked, and then brought out pieces of stuff that he had woven. At first I was puzzled by the fine brown colour of some of the material; but they explained it was from selected wools of the black or mottled sheep that are common here, and are so variegated that many tints of grey or brown can be had from their fleeces. The wool for the flannel is sometimes spun on this island; sometimes it is given to women in Dunquin, who spin it cheaply for so much a pound. Then it is woven, and finally the stuff is sent to a mill in Dingle to be cleaned and dressed before it is given to a tailor in Dingle to be made up for their own use. Such cloth is not cheap, but is of wonderful quality and strength. When I came out of the weaver's, a little sailing smack was anchored in the sound, and someone on board her was blowing a horn. They told me she was the French boat, and as I went back to my cottage I could see many canoes hurrying out to her with their cargoes of lobsters and crabs.

I have left the island again. I walked round the cliffs in the morning, and then packed my bag in my room, several girls putting their heads into the little window while I did so, to say it was a great pity I was not staying for another week or a fortnight. Then the men went off with my bag in a heavy shower, and I waited a minute or two while the little hostess buttered some bread for my lunch, and tied it up in a clean handkerchief of her own. Then I bid them good-bye, and set off down to the slip with three girls, who came with me to see that I did not go astray among the innumerable paths. It was still raining heavily, so I told them to put my cape, which they were carrying, over their heads. They did so with delight, and ran down the path before me, to the great amusement of the islanders. At the head of the cliff many people were standing about to bid me good-bye and wish me a good voyage.

The wind was in our favour, so the men took in their oars after rowing for about a quarter of a mile and lay down in the bottom of the canoe, while one man ran up the sail, and the host steered with an oar. At Dunquin the host hired me a dray, without springs, kissed my hand in farewell, and I was driven away.

When I got into the village [on the mainland] and sat down in the inn-parlour I missed to an extraordinary degree the faces that have been round me for these few weeks that seem so long. I do not feel the distress I felt sometimes when I left Aran but I have a despondency which is not preferable.

It is evening in these four white-washed inn walls with a lamp, a book and my papers, instead of the little queen and the old king and all their company. By this time they are wandering back from the head of the cliff and are gathering in the kitchen where the little queen has sanded the floor, and filled the water crock and pushed the nets into a corner. Yet I know even while I was there I was an interloper only, a refugee in a garden between four seas.

It is curious I have a jealousy for that Island—the whole island and its people—like the jealousy of men in love. The last days I was there a stranger—a middle-aged and simple-minded man from an inland district—[was staying there too,] and all the time I was making arrangements to come [away] I was urging him, I hardly know why, to come away also. At last I was successful and he came away in the canoe beside me, but without any particular plans. He made his own way to this village where he meant to stay a few days in the same inn, and I saw him in the afternoon. Then he disappeared. I made enquiries and I heard he had been seen late in the evening riding quickly towards Dunquin where one leaves for the Island. An inexplicable but fearful jealousy came over me; who was he that he should enjoy that life and quiet when I had left it? Who was he that he should sit in my place by the chimney and tell stories to the old men and boys? I was walking about my room in extravagant rage when I heard his step on the stairs, and he told me he had been out for a ride only.

What mystery of attraction is in that simple life.[1]

I have made my way round the foot of Dingle Bay and up the south coast to a cottage where I often lodge. As I was resting in a ditch some time in the afternoon, on a lonely mountain road, a little girl came along with a shawl over her head. She stopped in front of me and asked me where I was going, and then after a little talk: 'Well, man, let you come,' she said; 'I'm going your road as well as you.' I got up and we started. When I got tired of the hill I mounted, and she ran along beside me for several miles, till we fell in with some people cutting turf, and she stopped to talk to them.

Then for a while my road ran round an immense valley of magnificent rich turf bog, with mountains all round, and bowls where hidden lakes were lying bitten out of the cliffs.

As I was resting again on a bridge over the Behy where Diarmuid caught salmon with Grania, a man stopped to light his pipe and talk to me. 'There are three lakes above,' he said, 'Coomacarra, Coomaglaslaw and Coomasdhara; the whole of this place was in a great state in the bad times. Twenty years ago they sent down a 'mergency man to lodge above by the lake and serve processes on the people, but the people were off before him and lay abroad in the heather. Then in the course of a piece, a night came, with great rain out of the heavens, and my man said: "I'll get them this night in their own beds surely." Then he let call the peelers—they had peelers waiting to mind him—and down they came to the big stepping-stones they have above for crossing the first river coming out of the lakes. My man going in front to cross over, and the water was high up covering the stones. Then he gave two leps or three, and the peelers heard him give a great shriek

[1] This account (from 'When I got into the village', to 'that simple life') of Synge's feelings on leaving Great Blasket is in Notebook 40, but was omitted from the published article.

down in the flood. They went home after—what could they do? —and the 'mergency man was found in the sea stuck in a net.'

I was singularly pleased when I turned up the boreen at last to this cottage where I lodge, and looked down through a narrow gully to Dingle Bay. The people bade me welcome when I came in, the old woman kissing my hand.

There is no village near this cottage, yet many farms are scattered on the hills near it; and as the people are in some ways a leading family, many men and women look in to talk or tell stories, or to buy a few pennyworth of sugar or starch. Although the main road passes a few hundred yards to the west, this cottage is well known also to the race of local tramps who move from one family to another in some special neighbourhood or barony. This evening, when I came in, a little old man in a tall hat and long brown coat was sitting up on the settle beside the fire, and intending to spend, one could see, a night or more in the place.

I had a great deal to tell the people at first of my travels in different parts of the country, to the Blasket Islands—which they can see from here—Corkaguiney and Tralee; and they had news to tell me also of people who have married or died since I was here before, or gone away, or come back from America. Then I was told that the old man, Dermot (or Darby, as he is called in English), was the finest story-teller in Iveragh. Darby told his stories with fine expression and energy. Whenever there was a purely rhetorical question, such as 'Wasn't that a great wonder?' the people replied as if saying responses, 'It was indeed, Darby,' or whatever answer was required.[1] After a while he told us a long story in Irish, but spoke so rapidly and indistinctly—he had no teeth—that I could understand but few passages. When he had finished I asked him where he had heard the story.

'I heard it in the city of Portsmouth,' he said. 'I worked there fifteen years, and four years in Plymouth, and a long while in the hills of Wales; twenty-five years in all I was working at the other side; and there were many Irish in it, who would be telling stories in the evening, the same as we are doing here. I heard many good stories, but what can I do with them now and I an old lisping fellow, the way I can't give them out like a ballad?'

When he had talked a little more about his travels, and a bridge

[1] The two sentences from 'Darby told his stories' are taken from Notebook 44.

over the Severn, that he thought the greatest wonder of the world, I asked him if he remembered the famine.

'I do,' he said. 'I was living near Kenmare, and many 's the day I saw them burying the corpses in the ditch by the road. It was after that I went to England, for this country was ruined and destroyed. I heard there was work at that time in Plymouth; so I went to Dublin and took a boat that was going to England; but it was at a place called Liverpool they put me on shore, and then I had to walk to Plymouth, asking my way on the road. In that place I saw the soldiers after coming back from the Crimea, and they all broken and maimed.'

A little later, when he went out for a moment, the people told me he beats up and down between Killorglin and Ballinskelligs and the Inny river, and that he is a particular crabby kind of man, and will not take anything from the people but coppers and eggs.

'And he 's a wasteful old fellow with all,' said the woman of the house, 'though he 's eighty years old or beyond it, for whatever money he'll get one day selling his eggs to the coastguards, he'll spend it the next getting a drink when he 's thirsty, or keeping good boots on his feet.'

From that they began talking of misers, and telling stories about them.

'There was an old woman,' said one of the men, 'living beyond to the east, and she was thought to have a great store of money. She had one daughter only, and in the course of a piece a young lad got married to her, thinking he'd have her fortune. The woman died after—God be merciful to her!—and left the two of them as poor as they were before. Well, one night a man that knew them was passing to the fair of Puck, and he came in and asked would they give him a lodging for that night. They gave him what they had and welcome; and after his tea, when they were sitting over the fire—the way we are this night—the man asked them how they were so poor-looking, and if the old woman had left nothing behind her.

' "Not a farthing did she leave," said the daughter.

' "And did she give no word or warning or message in her last moments?" said the man.

' "She did not," said the daughter, "except only that I shouldn't comb out the hair of her poll and she dead."

' "And you heeded her?" said the man.

' "I did, surely," said the daughter.

' "Well," said the man, "to-morrow night when I'm gone let the two of you go down the Relic (the graveyard) and dig up her coffin and look in her hair and see what it is you'll find in it."

' "We'll do that," said the daughter, and with that they all stretched out for the night.

'The next evening they went down quietly with a shovel and they dug up the coffin, and combed through her hair, and there behind her poll they found her fortune, five hundred pounds, in good notes and gold.'

'There was an old fellow living on the little hill beyond the graveyard,' said Danny-boy, when the man had finished, 'and he had his fortune some place hid in his bed, and he was an old weak fellow, so that they were all watching him to see he wouldn't hide it away. One time there was no one in it but himself and a young girl, and the old fellow slipped out of his bed and went out of the door as far as a little bush and some stones. The young girl kept her eye on him, and she made sure he'd hidden something in the bush; so when he was back in his bed she called the people, and they all came and looked in the bushes, but not a thing could they find. The old man died after, and no one ever found his fortune to this day.'

'There were some young lads a while since,' said the old woman, 'and they went up of a Sunday and began searching through those bushes to see if they could find anything, but a kind of turkey-cock came up out of the stones and drove them away.'

'There was another old woman,' said the man of the house, 'who tried to take down her fortune into her stomach. She was near death, and she was all day stretched in her bed at the corner of the fire. One day when the girl was tinkering about, the old woman rose up and got ready a little skillet that was near the hob and put something into it and put it down by the fire, and the girl watching her all the time under her oxter, not letting on she had seen her at all. When the old woman lay down again the girl went over to put on more sods on the fire, and she got a look into the skillet, and what did she see but sixty sovereigns. She knew well what the old woman was striving to do, so she went out to the dairy and got a lump of fresh butter and put it down into the skillet, when the woman didn't see her do it at all. After a bit the old woman rose up and looked into the skillet, and when she saw the froth of the butter she thought it was the gold that was melted. She got back into her bed—a dark place, maybe—and she began sipping and sipping the butter till she had the whole of it swallowed. Then the girl made some trick to entice the skillet away from her, and she found the sixty sovereigns in the bottom and she kept them for herself.'

By this time it was late, and the old woman brought over a mug of milk and a piece of bread to Darby at the settle, and the people gathered at the table for their supper; so I went into the little room at the end of the cottage where I am given a bed.

When I came into the kitchen in the morning, old Darby was still asleep on the settle, with his coat and trousers over him, a red night-cap on his head, and his half-bred terrier, Jess, chained with a chain he carries with him to the leg of the settle.

'That's a poor way to lie on the bare board,' said the woman of the house, when she saw me looking at him; 'but when I filled a sack with straw for him last night he wouldn't have it at all.'

While she was boiling some eggs for my breakfast, Darby roused up from his sleep, pulled on his trousers and coat, slipped his feet into his boots and started off, when he had eaten a few mouthfuls, for another house where he is known, some five miles away.

Afterwards I went out on the cnuceen, a little hill between this cottage and the sea, to watch the people gathering carragheen moss, a trade which is much followed in this district during the spring tides of summer. I lay down on the edge of the cliff, where the heathery hill comes to an end and the steep rocks begin. About a mile to the west there was a long headland, 'Feakle Callaigh' ('The Witch's Tooth'), covered with mists, that blew over me from time to time with a swish of rain, followed by sunshine again. The mountains on the other side of the bay were covered, so I could see nothing but the strip of brilliant sea below me, thronged with girls and men up to their waists in the water, with a hamper in one hand and a stick in the other, gathering the moss, and talking and laughing loudly as they worked. The long frill of dark golden rocks covered with seaweed, with the asses and children slipping about on it, and the bars of silvery light breaking through on the further inlets of the bay, had the singularly brilliant liveliness one meets everywhere in Kerry. The scene last night of story-telling had an old-fashioned dignity and this outside pageant of curiously moving magnificence made me shudder to think of the seedy town life most of us are condemned to. I think especially of the commercial theatre with its stultifying vulgar character quite without one gleam of the light of the world.[1]

When the tide began to come in I went down one of the passes to the sea, and met many parties of girls and old men and women coming up with what they had gathered, most of them still wearing the clothes that had been in the sea, and were heavy and black with salt water. A little further on I met Danny-boy and we sat down to talk.

'Do you see that sandy head?' he said, pointing out to the east, 'that is called the Stooks of the Dead Women; for one time a boat came ashore there with twelve dead women on board her, big ladies with green dresses and gold rings, and fine jewelries, and a dead harper or fiddler along with them. Then there are graves again in the little hollow by the cnuceen, and what we call them is the Graves of the Sailors; for some sailors, Greeks or great strangers, were washed in there a hundred years ago, and it is there that they were buried.'

Then we began talking of the carragheen he had gathered and the spring-tides that would come again during the summer. I took out my diary to tell him the times of the moon, but he would hardly listen to me. When I stopped, he gave his ass a cut with his stick, 'Go on, now,' he said; 'I wouldn't believe those almanacks at all; they do not tell the truth about the moon.'

The greatest event in West Kerry is the horse-fair, known as Puck Fair, which is held in August. If one asks anyone, many miles east or west of Killorglin, when he reaped his oats or sold his pigs or heifers, he will tell you it was four or five weeks, or whatever it may be, before or after Puck. On the main roads, for many days past, I have been falling in with tramps and trick characters of all kinds, sometimes single and sometimes in parties of four or five, and as I am on the roads a great deal I have often met the same persons several days in succession—one day perhaps at Ballinskelligs, the next day at Feakle Callaigh, and the third in the outskirts of Killorglin.

Yesterday cavalcades of every sort were passing from the west with droves of horses, mares, jennets, foals and asses, with their owners going after them in flat or railed carts, or riding on ponies.

[1] These last two sentences are taken from Notebook 44.

The men of this house—they are going to buy a horse—went to the fair last night, and I followed at an early hour in the morning. As I came near Killorglin the road was much blocked by the latest sellers pushing eagerly forward, and early purchasers who were anxiously leading off their young horses before the roads became dangerous from the crush of drunken drivers and riders.

Just outside the town, near the first public-house, blind beggars were kneeling on the pathway, praying with almost Oriental volubility for the souls of anyone who would throw them a coin.

'May the Holy Immaculate Mother of Jesus Christ,' said one of them, 'intercede for you in the hour of need. Relieve a poor blind creature, and may Jesus Christ relieve yourselves in the hour of death. May He have mercy, I'm saying, on your brothers and fathers and sisters for evermore.'

Further on stalls were set out with cheap cakes and refreshments, and one could see that many houses had been arranged to supply the crowds who had come in. Then I came to the principal road that goes round the fair-green, where there was a great concourse of horses, trotting and walking and galloping; most of them were of the cheaper class of animal, and were selling, apparently to the people's satisfaction, at prices that reminded one of the time when fresh meat was sold for three pence a pound. At the further end of the green there were one or two rough shooting galleries, and a number of women—not very rigid, one could see—selling, or appearing to sell, all kinds of trifles: a set that come in, I am told, from towns not far away. At the end of the green I turned past the chapel, where a little crowd had just carried in a man who had been killed or badly wounded by a fall from a horse, and went down to the bridge of the river, and then back again into the main slope of the town. Here there were a number of people who had come in for amusement only, and were walking up and down, looking at each other—a crowd is as exciting as champagne to these lonely people, who live in long glens among the mountains—and meeting with cousins and friends. Then, in the three-cornered space in the middle of the town, I came on Puck himself, a magnificent he-goat (Irish puc), raised on a platform twenty feet high, and held by a chain from each horn, with his face down the road. He is kept in this position, with a few cabbages to feed on, for three days, so that he may preside over the pig-fair and the horse-fair and the day of winding up.

At the foot of this platform, where the crowd was thickest, a young ballad-singer was howling a ballad in honour of Puck, making one think of the early Greek festivals, since the time of which, it is possible, the goat has been exalted yearly in Killorglin.

The song was printed in on a green slip by itself. It ran:—

A New Song on the Great Puck Fair

BY JOHN PURCELL.

All young lovers that are fond of sporting, pay attention for a while,
I will sing you the praises of Puck Fair, and I'm sure it will make you smile;
Where the lads and lassies coming gaily to Killorglin can be seen,
To view the Puck upon the stage, as our hero dressed in green.

CHORUS

And hurra for the gallant Puck so gay,
For he is a splendid one:
Wind and rain don't touch his tail,
For his hair is thirty inches long.

Now it is on the square he's erected with all colours grand and gay;
There's not a fair throughout Ireland, but Puck Fair it takes the sway,
Where you see the gamblers in rotation, trick-o-the-loop and other games,
The ballad-singers and the wheel-of-fortune, and the shooting-gallery for to take aim.

CHORUS

Where is the tyrant dare oppose it?
Our old customs we will hold up still,
And I think we will have another—
That is, Home Rule and Purchase Bill.

Now, all young men that are not married, next Shrove can take a wife,
For before next Puck Fair we will have Home Rule, and then you will be settled down in life.
Now the same advice I give young girls for to get married and have pluck.
Let the landlords see that you defy them when coming to Fair of Puck.

Céad Míle Fáilte to the Fair of Puck.

When one makes the obvious elisions, the lines are not so irregular as they look, and are always sung to a measure; yet the whole, in spite of the assonance, rhymes, and the 'colours grand and gay' seems pitifully remote from any good spirit of ballad-making.

Across the square, a man and a woman, who had a baby tied on her back, were singing another ballad on the Russian and Japanese War, in the curious method of antiphony that is still heard in the back streets of Dublin. These are some of the verses:—

MAN

Now provisions are rising, 'tis sad for to state,
The flour, tea and sugar, tobacco and meat;
But, God help us! poor Irish, how must we stand the test

AMBO

If they only now stop the trade of commerce.

WOMAN

Now the Russians are powerful on sea and on land;
But the Japs they are active, they will them command,
Before this war is finished I have one word to say,

AMBO

There will be more shot and drowned than in the Crimea.

MAN

Now the Japs are victorious up to this time,
And thousands of Russians I hear they are dying.
Etc., etc.

And so it went on with the same alternation of the voices through seven or eight verses; and it was curious to feel how much was gained by this simple variation of the voices.

When I passed back to the fair-green, I met the men I am staying with, and went off with them under an archway, and into a back yard to look at a little two-year-old filly that they had bought and left for the moment in a loose box with three or four young horses. She was prettily and daintily shaped, but looked too light, I thought, for the work she will be expected to do. As we came out into the road, an old man was singing an outspoken ballad on women in the middle of the usual crowd. Just as we passed it came to a scandalous conclusion; and the women scattered in every direction, shrieking with laughter and holding shawls over their mouths.

At the corner we turned into a public-house, where there were men we knew, who had done their business also; and we went into the little alcove to sit down quietly for a moment. 'What will you take, sir,' said the man I lodge with, 'a glass of wine?'

I took beer and the others took porter, but we were only served after some little time, as the house was thronged with people.

The men were too much taken up with their bargains and losses to talk much of other matters; and before long we came out again, and the son of the house started homewards, leading the new filly by a little halter of rope.

Not long afterwards I started also. Outside Killorglin rain was coming up over the hills of Glen Car, so that there was a strained hush in the air, and a rich, aromatic smell coming from the bog myrtle or boggy shrub, that grows thickly in this place. The strings of horses and jennets scattered over the road did not keep away a strange feeling of loneliness that seems to hang over this brown plain of bog that stretches from Carrantuohill to Cuchulain's House.

Before I reached the cottage dense torrents of rain were closing down through the glens, and driving in white sheets between the little hills that are on each side of the way.

One morning in autumn I started in a local train for the first stage of my journey to Dublin, seeing the last of Macgillicuddy's Reeks, that were touched with snow in places, Dingle Bay and the islands beyond it. At a little station where I changed trains, I got into a carriage where there was a woman with her daughter, a girl of about twenty, who seemed uneasy and distressed. Soon afterwards, when a collector was looking at our tickets, I called out that mine was for Dublin, and as soon as he got out the woman came over to me.

'Are you going to Dublin?' she said.

I told her I was.

'Well,' she went on, 'here is my daughter going there too; and maybe you'd look after her, for I'm getting down at the next station. She is going up to a hospital for some little complaint in her ear, and she has never travelled before, so that she 's lonesome in her mind.'

I told her I would do what I could, and at the next station I was left alone with my charge, and one other passenger, a returned American girl, who was on her way to Mallow, to get the train for Queenstown. When her mother was lost sight of the young girl broke out into tears, and the returned American and myself had trouble to quiet her.

'Look at me,' said the American. 'I'm going off for ten years to America, all by myself, and I don't care a rap.'

When the girl got quiet again, the returned American talked to me about scenery and politics and the arts—she had been seen off by her sisters in bare feet, with shawls over their heads—and the life of women in America.

At several stations girls and boys thronged in to get places for Queenstown, leaving parties of old men and women wailing with anguish on the platform. At one place an old woman was seized with such a passion of regret, when she saw her daughters moving away from her for ever, that she made a wild rush after the train; and when I looked out for a moment I could see her writhing and struggling on the platform, with her hair over her face, and two men holding her by the arms.

Two young men had got into our compartment for a few stations only, and they looked on with the greatest satisfaction.

'Ah,' said one of them, 'we do have great sport every Friday and Saturday, seeing the old women howling in the stations.'

When we reached Dublin I left my charge for a moment to see after my baggage, and when I came back I found her sitting on a luggage barrow, with her package in her hand, crying with despair because several cabmen had refused to let her into their cabs, on the pretext that they dreaded infection.

I could see they were looking out for some rich tourist with his trunks, as a more lucrative fare; so I sent for the head porter, who had charge of the platform. When the porter arrived we chose a cab, and I saw my charge driven off to the hospital, sitting on the front seat, with her handkerchief to her eyes.

For the last few days—I am staying in the Kerry cottage I have spoken of already—the people have been talking of horse-races that were to be held on the sand, not far off, and this morning I set out to see them with the man and woman of the house and two of their neighbours. Our way led through a steep boreen for a quarter of a mile to the edge of the sea, and then along a pathway between the cliffs and a straight grassy hill. When we had gone some distance the old man pointed out a slope in front of us, where, he said, Diarmuid had done his tricks of rolling the barrel and jumping over his spear, and had killed many of his enemies. He told me the whole story, slightly familiarised in detail, but not very different from the version everyone knows. Then he told me about Oisin.

There used to be great gatherings of people and great dancings at one time on the stooks over the head of Inch, and one day the time there was a great crowd the people saw three strangers out beyond them on the sand as if it was a lady and her two servants walking with her. The people were saying some one would have a right to go and ask her would she dance along with them and after a while somebody asked her and she came up and joined them. Then she had to choose who it would be she would dance with and she chose Oisin. After the dance the two of them walked down the sand and the people were saying they had known each other before, and they watched them going till they came to the sea and then the two of them went down into it.

It was after three hundred years Oisin wanted to come back from the Tir-na-nOg. He was thinking it was only three years or maybe two years he was in the Tir-na-nOg, [but] his wife told him he would find none of the people were living in his time and none of the houses standing [and] not a thing in their places but docks and nettles and the like of that. Oisin said he would go, so she told him to put away the bay horse he had and to get on a white pony belonging to herself. Then she made him go through his exercises, lying out on his back on the white pony and turning up his feet in the air, to show that he wouldn't fall off it at all. When she saw he could do that she told him that he might go back to his country but wasn't ever to get down off the pony. He went away then and he found nothing in his own country but docks and nettles and the like of that. One time as he was riding along he saw two men trying to put up a bag of meal on a donkey's back but not able to do it. He tried to help them but wasn't [able to] with the weight of the sack so that there was shame of him and he took his foot from the stirrup and put it on the ground. Then the pony disappeared away from him and he turned into an old shaky man.[1]

A little further on he pointed across the sea to our left—just beyond the strand where the races were to be run—to a neck of sand where, he said, Oisin was called away to the Tir-na-nOg.

'The Tir-na-nOg itself,' he said, 'is below that sea, and a while since there were two men out in a boat in the night-time, and they got stuck outside some way or another. They went to sleep then, and when one of them wakened up he looked down into the sea, and he saw the Tir-na-nOg and people walking about, and side-cars driving in the squares.'

Then he began telling me stories of mermaids—a common subject in this neighbourhood.

'There was one time a man beyond of the name of Shee,' he said, 'and his master seen a mermaid on the sand beyond combing her hair, and he told Shee to get her, "I will," said Shee, "if you give me the best horse you have in your stable." "I'll do that," said the master. Then Shee got the horse, and when he saw the mermaid on the sand combing her hair, with her covering laid away from her, he galloped up, when she wasn't looking, and he picked up the covering and away he went with it. Then the waves rose up behind him and he galloped his best, and just as he was coming out at the top of the tide the ninth wave cut off his horse behind his back, and left himself and the half of his horse and the covering on the dry land. Then the mermaid came in after her covering, and the master got married to her, and she lived with him a long time, and had childen—three or four of them. Well, in the wind-up, the master built a fine new house, and when he was moving into it, and clearing the things out, he brought down an old hamper out of the loft and put it in the yard. The woman was going about, and she looked into the hamper, and she saw her covering hidden away in the bottom of it. She took it out then and put it upon her and went back into the sea, and her children used to be on the shore crying after her. I'm told from that day there isn't one of the Shees can go out in a boat on that bay and not be drowned.'

We were now near the sandhills, where a crowd was beginning to come together, and booths were being put up for the sale of

[1] This folk version of the Oisin story, beginning 'Then he told me about Oisin' (page 270) to 'old shaky man', is in Notebook 28, but was omitted from the published article.

apples and porter and cakes. A train had come in a little before at a station a mile or so away, and a number of the usual trick-characters, with their stock-in-trade, were hurrying down to the sea. The roulette man passed us first, unfolding his table and calling out at the top of his voice:

Come play me a game of timmun and tup,
The more you puts down the more you takes up.

'Take notice, gentlemen, I come here to spend a fortune, not to make one. Is there any sportsman in a hat or a cap, or a wig or a waistcoat, will play a go with me now? Take notice, gentlemen, the luck is on the green.'

The races had to be run between two tides while the sand was dry, so there was not much time to be lost, and before we reached the strand the horses had been brought together, ridden by young men in many variations of jockey dress. For the first race there was one genuine race-horse, very old and bony, and two or three young horses belonging to farmers in the neighbourhood. The start was made from the middle of the crowd at the near end of the strand, and the course led out along the edge of the sea to a post some distance away, back again to the starting-point, round a post, and out and back once more.

When the word was given the horses set off in a wild helter-skelter along the edge of the sea, with crowds cheering them on from the sandhills. As they got small in the distance it was not easy to see which horse was leading, but after a sort of check, as they turned the post, they began nearing again a few yards from the waves, with the old race-horse, heavily pressed, a good length ahead. The stewards made a sort of effort to clear the post that was to be circled, but without much success, as the people were wild with excitement. A moment later the old race-horse galloped into the crowd, twisted too suddenly, something cracked and jolted, and it limped out on three legs, gasping with pain. The next horse could not be stopped, and galloped out at the wrong end of the crowd for some little way before it could be brought back, so the last horses set off in front for the final lap.

The lame race-horse was now mobbed by onlookers and advisers, talking incoherently.

'Was it the fault of the jock?' said one man.

'It was not,' said another, 'for Michael (the owner) didn't

THE STRAND RACE

strike him, and if it had been his fault, wouldn't he have broken his bones?'

'He was striving to spare a young girl had run out in his way,' said another. 'It was for that he twisted him.'

'Little slut!' said a woman; 'what did she want beyond on the sand?'

Many remedies were suggested that did not sound reassuring, and in the end the horse was led off in a hopeless condition. A little later the race ended with an easy win for the wildest of the young horses. Afterwards I wandered up among the people, and looked at the sports. At one place a man, with his face heavily blackened, except one cheek and eye—an extraordinary effect—was standing shots of a wooden ball behind a board with a large hole in the middle, at three shots a penny. When I came past half an hour afterwards he had been hit in the mouth—by a girl some one told me—but seemed as cheerful as ever.

On the road, some little distance away, a party of girls and young men were dancing polkas to the music of a melodeon, in a cloud of dust. When I had looked on for a little while I met some girls I knew, and asked them how they were getting on.

'We're not getting on at all,' said one of them, 'for we've been at the races for two hours, and we've found no beaux to go along with us.'

When the horses had all run, a jennet race was held, and greatly delighted the people, as the jennets—there were a number of them—got scared by the cheering and ran wild in every direction. In the end it was not easy to say which was the winner, and a dispute began which nearly ended in blows. It was decided at last to run the race over again the following Sunday after Mass, and everyone was satisfied.

The day was magnificently bright, and the ten miles from Dingle Bay were wonderfully brilliant behind the masses of people, and the canvas booths, and the scores of upturned shafts. Towards evening I got tired taking or refusing the porter my friends pressed on me continually, so I wandered off from the racecourse along the path where Diarmuid had tricked the Fenians.

Later in the evening news had been coming in of the doings in the sandhills, after the porter had begun to take effect and the darkness had come on.

'There was great sport after you left,' a man said to me in the cottage this evening, 'They were all beating and cutting each other on the shore of the sea. Four men fought together in one place till the tide came up on them, and was like to drown them; but the priest waded out up to his middle and drove them asunder. Another man was left for dead on the road outside the lodges, and some gentleman found him and had him carried into his house, and got the doctor to put plasters on his head. Then there was a red-headed fellow had his finger bitten through, and the postman was destroyed for ever.'

'He should be,' said the man of the house, 'for Michael Patch broke the seat of his car into three halves on his head.'

'It was this was the cause of it all,' said Danny-boy: 'they brought in porter east and west from the two towns you know of, and the two porters didn't agree together, and it's for that the people went raging at the fall of night.'

I have been out to Bolus Head, one of the finest places I have met with. A little beyond Ballinskelligs the road turns up the side of a steep mountainy hill where one sees a brilliant stretch of sea, with many rocks and islands—Deenish, Scariff, the Hog's Head, and Dursey far away. As I was sitting on the edge of the road an old man came along and we began to talk. He had little English, but when I tried him in Irish we got on well, though he did not follow any Connaught forms I let slip by accident. We went on together, after a while, to an extraordinary straggling village along the edge of the hill. At one of the cottages he stopped and asked me to come in and take a drink and rest myself. I did not like to refuse him, we had got so friendly, so I followed him in, and sat down on a stool while his wife—a much younger woman—went into the bedroom and brought me a large mug of milk. As I was drinking it and talking to the couple, a sack that was beside the fire began to move slowly, and the head of a yellow, feverish-looking child came out from beneath it, and began looking at me with a heavy stare. I asked the woman what ailed it, and she told me it had sickened a night or two before with headache and pains all through it; but she had not had the doctor, and did not know what was the matter. I finished the milk without much enjoyment, and went on my way up Bolus Head and then back to this cottage, wondering all the time if I had the germs of typhus in my blood.

Last night when I got back to the cottage, I found that another 'travelling man' had arrived to stay for a day or two; but he was hard of hearing and a little simple in his head, so that we had not much talk. I went to bed soon after dark and slept till about two o'clock in the morning, when I was awakened by fearful screams in the kitchen. For a moment I did not know where I was; then I remembered the old man, and I jumped up and went to the door of my room. As I opened it I heard the door of the family room across the kitchen opening also, and the frightened whispers of the people. In a moment we could hear the old man, who was sleeping on the settle, pulling himself out of a nightmare, so we went back to our beds.

In the morning the woman told me his story:—

'He was living above on a little hillside,' she said, 'in a bit of a cabin, with his sister along with him. Then, after a while, she got ailing in her heart, and he got a bottle for her from the doctor, and he'd rise up every morning before the dawn to give her a sup of it. She got better then, till one night he got up and measured out the spoonful, or whatever it was, and went to give it to her, and he found her stretched out dead before him. Since that night he wakes up one time and another, and begins crying out for Maurya—that was his sister—and he half in his dreams. It was that you heard in the night, and indeed it would frighten any person to hear him screaming as if he was getting his death.'

When the little man came back after a while, they began asking him questions till he told his whole story, weeping pitiably. Then they got him to tell me about the other great event of his life also, in the rather childish Gaelic he uses.

He had once a little cur-dog, he said, and he knew nothing of the dog licence; then one day the peelers—the boys with the little caps—asked him into the barracks for a cup of tea. He went in cheerfully, and then they put him and his little dog into the lock-up till some one paid a shilling for him and got him out.

He has a stick he is proud of, bound with pieces of leather every few inches—like one I have seen with a beggar in Belmullet. Since the first night he has not had a nightmare again, and he lies most of the evening sleeping on the settle, and in the morning he goes round among the houses, getting his share of meal and potatoes.

I do not think a beggar is ever refused in Kerry. Sometimes, while we are talking or doing something in the kitchen, a man walks in without saying anything and stands just inside the door, with his bag on the floor beside him. In five or ten minutes, when the woman of the house has finished what she is doing, she goes up to him and asks: 'Is it meal or flour?' 'Flour,' says the man. She goes into the inner room, opens her sack, and comes back with two handfuls. He opens his bag and takes out a bundle carefully tied up in a cloth or handkerchief; he opens this again, and usually there is another cloth inside, into which the woman puts her flour. Then the cloths are carefully knotted together by the corners, put back in the bag, and the man mutters a 'God bless you,' and goes on his way.

The meal, flour and potatoes that are thus gathered up are always sold by the beggar, and the money is spent on porter or second-hand clothes, or very occasionally on food when he is in a neighbourhood that is not hospitable. The buyers are usually found among the coastguards' wives, or in the little public-houses on the roadside.

'Some of these men,' said the woman of the house, when I asked her about them, 'will take their flour nicely and tastily and cleanly, and others will throw it in any way, and you'd be sorry to eat it afterwards.'

The talk of these people is almost bewildering. I have come to this cottage again and again, and I often think I have heard all they have to say, and then some one makes a remark that leads to a whole new bundle of folk-tales, or stories of wonderful events that have happened in the barony in the last hundred years. To-night the people were unusually silent although several neighbours had come in, and to make conversation I said something about the bullfights in Spain that I had been reading of in the newspapers. Immediately they started off with stories of wicked or powerful bulls, and then they branched off to clever dogs and all the things they have done in West Kerry, and then to mad dogs and mad cattle and pigs—one incident after another, but always detailed and picturesque and interesting.

I have come back to the north of Dingle, leaving Tralee late in the afternoon. At the station there was a more than usually great crowd, as there had been a fair in the town and many people had come in to make their Saturday purchases. A number of messenger boys with parcels from the shops in the town were shouting for the owners, using many familiar names, Justin MacCarthy, Hannah Lynch and the like. I managed to get a seat on a sack of flour beside the owner, who had other packages scattered under our feet. When the train had started and the women and girls—the carriage was filled with them—had settled down into their places, I could see I caused great curiosity, as it was too late in the year for even an odd tourist, and on this line everyone is known by sight.

Before long I got into talk with the old man next me, and as soon as I did so the women and girls stopped their talk and leaned out to hear what we were saying.

He asked first if I belonged to Dingle, and I told him I did not.

'Well,' he said, 'you speak like a Kerry man, and you're dressed like a Kerry man, so you belong to Kerry surely.'

I told him I was born and bred in Dublin, and that I had travelled in many places in Ireland and beyond it.

'That's easy said,' he answered, 'but I'd take an oath you were never beyond Kerry to this day.'

Then he asked sharply:—'What do you do?'

I answered something about my wanderings in Europe, and suddenly he sat up, as if a new thought had come to him.

'Maybe you're a wealthy man?' he said.

I smiled complacently.

'And about thirty-five?'

I nodded.

'And not married?'

'No.'

'Well then,' he said, 'you're a damn lucky fellow to be travelling the world with no one to impede you.'

Then he went on to discuss the expenses of travelling.

'You'll likely be paying twenty pounds for this trip,' he said, 'with getting your lodging and buying your tickets, till you're back in the city of Dublin?'

I told him my expenses were not so heavy.

'Maybe you don't drink so,' said his wife, who was near us, 'and that way your living wouldn't be so costly at all.'

An interruption was made by a stop at a small station and the entrance of a ragged ballad-singer, who sang a long ballad about the sorrows of mothers who see all their children going away from them to America.

Further on, when the carriage was much emptier, a middle-aged man got in, and we began discussing the fishing season, Aran fishing, hookers, nobbies and mackerel. I could see, while we were talking, that he, in his turn, was examining me with curiosity. At last he seemed satisfied.

'Begob,' he said, 'I see what you are; you're a fish-dealer.'

It turned out that he was the skipper of a trawler, and we had a long talk, the two of us and a local man who was going to Dingle also.

'There was one time a Frenchman below,' said the skipper, 'who got married here and settled down and worked with the rest of us. One day we were outside in the trawler, and there was a French boat anchored a bit of a way off. "Come on," says Charley—that was his name—"and see can we get some brandy from that boat beyond." "How would we get brandy," says I, "when we've no fish, or meat, or cabbages or a thing at all to offer them?" He went down below then to see what he could get. At that time there were four men only working the trawler, and in the heavy season there were eight. Well, up he comes again and eight plates under his arm. "There are eight plates," says he, "and four will do us; so we'll take out the other four and make a swap with them for brandy." With that he set the eight plates on the deck and began walking up and down and looking on them.

' "The devil mend you," says I. "Will you take them up and come on, if you're coming?"

' "I will," says he, "surely. I'm choicing out the ones that have pictures on them, for it's that kind they do set store on." '

Afterwards we began talking of boats that had been upset during the winter, and lives that had been lost in the neighbourhood.

'A while since,' said the local man, 'there were three men out in a canoe, and the sea rose on them. They tried to come in under the cliff, but they couldn't come to land with the greatness of the waves that were breaking. There were two young men in the canoe, and another man was sixty, or near it. When the young men saw they couldn't bring in the canoe, they said they'd make a jump for the rocks and let her go without them, if she must go. Then they pulled in on the next wave, and when they were close in the two young men jumped on to a rock, but the old man was too stiff, and he was washed back again in the canoe. It came on dark after that, and all thought he was drowned, and they held his wake in Dunquin. At that time there used to be a steamer going in and out trading in Valentia and Dingle, and Cahirciveen, and when she came into Dingle two or three days after, there was my man on board her as hearty as a salmon. When he was washed back he got one of the oars, and kept her head to the wind; then the tide took him one bit and the wind took him another, and he wrought and he wrought till he was safe beyond in Valentia. Wasn't that a great wonder?' Then as he was ending his story we ran down into Dingle.

Often, when one comes back to a place that one's memory and imagination have been busy with, there is a feeling of smallness and disappointment, and it is a day or two before one can renew all one's enjoyment. This morning, however, when I went up the gap between Croagh Martin and then back to Slea Head, and saw Innishtooskert and Inishvickillaun and the Great Blasket Island itself, they seemed ten times more grey and wild and magnificent than anything I had kept in my memory. The cold sea and surf, and the feeling of winter in the clouds, and the blackness of the rocks, and the red fern everywhere, were a continual surprise and excitement.

Here and there on my way I met old men with tail-coats of frieze, that are becoming so uncommon. When I spoke to them in English they shook their heads and muttered something I could not hear; but when I tried Irish they made me long speeches about the weather and the clearness of the day.

In the evening, as I was coming home, I got a glimpse that seemed to have the whole character of Corkaguiney—a little line of low cottages with yellow roofs, and an elder tree without leaves beside them, standing out against a high mountain that seemed far away, yet was near enough to be dense and rich and wonderful in its colour.

Then I wandered round the wonderful forts of Fahan. The blueness of the sea and the hills from Carrantuohill to the Skelligs, the singular loneliness of the hillside I was on, with a few choughs and gulls in sight only, had a splendour that was almost a grief in the mind.

I turned into a little public-house this evening, where Maurice —the fisherman I have spoken of before—and some of his friends often sit when it is too wild for fishing. While we were talking a man came in, and joined rather busily in what was being said, though I could see he was not belonging to the place. He moved his position several times till he was quite close to me, then he whispered: 'Will you stand me a medium, mister? I'm hard set for money this while past.' When he had got his medium he began to give me his history. He was a journeyman tailor who had been a year or more in the place, and was beginning to pick up a little Irish to get along with. When he had gone we had a long talk about the making of canoes and the difference between those used in Connaught and Munster.

'They have been in this country,' said Maurice, 'for twenty or twenty-five years only, and before that we had boats; a canoe will cost twelve pounds, or maybe thirteen pounds, and there is one old man beyond who charges fifteen pounds. If it is well done a canoe will stand for eight years, and you can get a new skin on it when the first one is gone.'

I told him I thought canoes had been in Connemara since the beginning of the world.

'That may well be,' he went on, 'for there was a certain man going out as a pilot, up and down into Clare, and it was he made them first in this place. It is a trade few can learn, for it is all done within the head; you will have to sit down and think it out, and then make up when it is all ready in your mind.'

I described the fixed thole-pins that are used in Connaught—here they use two freely moving thole-pins, with the oar loose between them, and they jeered at the simplicity of the Connaught system. Then we got on the relative value of canoes and boats.

'They are not better than boats,' said Maurice, 'but they are more useful. Before you get a heavy boat swimming you will be up to your waist, and then you will be sitting the whole night like that; but a canoe will swim in a handful of water, so that you can get in dry and be dry and warm the whole night. Then there will be seven men in a big boat and seven shares of the fish; but in a canoe there will be three men only and three shares of the fish, though the nets are the same in the two.'

After a while a man sang a song, and then we began talking of tunes and playing the fiddle, and I told them how hard it was to get any sound out of one in a cottage with a floor of earth and a thatched roof over you.

'I can believe that,' said one of the men. 'There was a man a while since went into Tralee to buy a fiddle; and when he went into the shop an old fiddler followed him into it, thinking maybe he'd get the price of a pint. Well, the man was within choicing the fiddles, maybe forty of them, and the old fiddler whispered to him to take them out in the air, "for there's many a fiddle would sound well in here wouldn't be worth a curse outside," says he; so he was bringing them out and bringing them out till he found a good one among them.'

This evening, after a day of teeming rain, it cleared for an hour, and I went out while the sun was setting to a little cove where a high sea was running. As I was coming back the darkness began to close in except in the west, where there was a red light under the clouds. Against this light I could see patches of open wall and little fields of stooks, and a bit of laneway with an old man driving white cows before him. These seemed transfigured beyond any description.

Then I passed two men riding bare-backed towards the west, who spoke to me in Irish, and a little further on I came to the only village on my way. The ground rose towards it, and as I came near there was a grey bar of smoke from every cottage going up to the low clouds overhead, and standing out strangely against the blackness of the mountain behind the village.

Beyond the patch of wet cottages I had another stretch of lonely roadway, and a heron kept flapping in front of me, rising and lighting again with many lonely cries that made me glad to reach the little public-house near Smerwick.[1]

[1] In Box-file C on the back of the last page of typescript is a note in Synge's hand: 'Text of book on Wicklow and Kerry. If I am unable to revise further it may be printed with as many emendations as editor may think well. J. M. S.'

IN CONNEMARA[1]

FROM GALWAY TO GORUMNA

SOME of the worst portions of the Irish congested districts—of which so much that is contradictory has been spoken and written

[1] Originally published as a series of twelve articles in the *Manchester Guardian*, from 10 June 1905 to 26 July 1905. Yeats thought they were of inferior quality and said they should not be reprinted. However, a note was found, and still exists in Item 102, among Synge's papers, making it clear that he had considered reprinting them in a book and so they appeared in Volume Four of the *Works* of 1910. Yeats then withdrew his help and published separately as *J. M. Synge and the Ireland of His Time* the Introduction he had written for the 1910 edition. Synge's letter of 13 July 1905 to Stephen MacKenna further describes the assignment (Synge's letters to MacKenna have been published in *Irish Renaissance*, edited by Robin Skelton and David Clark (Dolmen Press, Dublin, 1966)):

> 'I've just come home from the *Guardian* business. Jack Yeats and myself had a great time and I sent off 3 articles a week for four weeks running. Would you believe that? But he, being a wiser man than I, made a better bargain, and though I had much the heavier job the dirty skunks paid him more than they paid me, and that's a thorn in my dignity! I got £25. 4*s*. 0*d*. which is more than I've ever had yet and still I'm swearing and damning.
>
> 'However we had a wonderful journey, and as we had a purse to pull on we pushed into out-of-the-way corners in Mayo and Galway that were more strange and marvellous than anything I've dreamed of. Unluckily my commission was to write on the "Distress" so I couldn't do anything like what I would have wished to do as an interpretation of the whole life. Besides of course we had not time in a month's trip to get to the bottom of things anywhere. As soon as I recover from this cold affair I'm off again to spend my £25. 4*s*. 0. on the same ground. There are sides of all that western life, the groggy-patriot-publican-general-shop-man who is married to the priest's half-sister and is second cousin once-removed of the dispensary doctor, that are horrible and awful. This is the type that is running the present United Irish League anti-grazier campaign, while they're swindling the people themselves in a dozen ways and then buying out their holdings and packing off whole families to America. The subject is too big to go into here, but at best it's beastly. All that side of the matter of course I left untouched in my stuff. I sometimes wish to God I hadn't a soul and then I could give myself up to putting those lads on the stage. God, wouldn't they hop! In a way it is all heartrending, in one place the people are starving but wonderfully attractive and charming, and in another place where things are going well, one has a rampant, double-chinned vulgarity I haven't seen the like of.'

Again, he says to MacKenna in a letter of 9 April 1907: 'I sometimes wish I had never left my garret in the rue d'Assas, . . . the scurrility and ignorance and treachery of some of the attacks upon me [because of *The Playboy*] have rather disgusted me with the middle-class Irish Catholic. As you know I have the wildest admiration for the Irish Peasants, and for Irish men of known or unknown genius—do you bow?—but between the two there's an ungodly ruck of fat-faced, sweaty-headed swine.' Observations such as these, with their awareness of the debilitating effects of commercialism, show that Yeats was quite wrong in saying that Synge was 'unfitted to think a political thought'. In fact, Synge shared with Yeats and Lady Gregory the 'dream of the noble and the beggar man', the admiration for the creative person of culture and for the creative peasant and a disdain for the man of money merely who manipulates the fruits of others' labours and contributes little him-

—lie along the further north coast of Galway Bay, and about the whole seaboard from Spiddal to Clifden. Some distance inland there is a line of railway; and in the bay itself a steamer passes in and out to the Aran Islands; but this particular district can only be visited thoroughly by driving or riding over some thirty or forty miles of desolate roadway. If one takes this route from Galway one has to go a little way only to reach places and people that are fully typical of Connemara. On each side of the road one sees small

self. A further instance of Synge's political insight is seen in the letter, of which there is a draft in Item 50, that he wrote to Maud Gonne resigning from her *Irlande Libre* organization, because he wished to work for the regeneration of Ireland in his own way, and he felt that he would never be able to do this if he got 'mixed up with a revolutionary and semi-military movement'.

His mother, who in some ways understood him, records his assurance that he was not a rebel since he thought Ireland would enjoy her own 'in years to come when socialistic ideas spread in England' and that things would 'change by degrees in the world' without fighting and there would be 'equality and no more grinding down of the poor' (Greene and Stephens, *J. M. Synge*, p. 63).

C. P. Scott of the *Manchester Guardian* thought highly of Synge's articles, and on several occasions asked him for more, particularly a series on 'Irish Types'. In a letter (now in Item 67) as late as 8 January 1909 Synge said:

'Dear Mr. Scott,

I was glad to get your letter of the — of December, and to hear that you were pleased with my article—the delay I had hardly noticed as I had been away for some time in Germany. I do not quite gather if you have used my article so far, and I would be glad to know if you [have] done so—or when you do—as I have a couple of articles on Kerry that I would like to send you when the other is out of the way. I am working at a new play at present but when that is off my hands I hope to do you the articles on the Types that we have been talking of for so long. It will depend a little however on my health which is not yet all that I could wish.'

In 1908, in Notebook 44, Synge had made these 'Notes for "Types" stuff': 'Major D. crowing like a cock in the small hours of the morning. Old —— in Annamoe coming in half an hour late to the end of his days because the hour of church was made an hour earlier. Wife dies and [he] marries nurse. At Annamoe church young man who carries on love affair with post cards. Pious father of a family who has a fixed idea that the servants habitually destroy his razors by cutting their corns. Family [who were] given to cures; once they were living on hot water and raw beef; the next time they were running about in their bare feet and living on strawberries and goat's milk.' And about the same time Synge gave Molly Allgood this outline of suggestions for an article on 'Irish Stage Land':

'Journey to Southern town (Wexford but you don't name it), the gathering in Harcourt St., the excitement of starting, the clear winter's morning as you pass down through Carrickmines, Bray and Greystones. The bewildered old woman who sells us apples in Wicklow. Then the company gets tired looking out of the windows and they sing songs (give Molly McGuish you gay old Turk) and any other quaint ones. You pass on and arrive in Wexford. Dinner. Visit the little theatre—describe Wexford Theatre entry etc. Rest and hurried tea before theatre. Describe dressing-room, the feeling of the audience, the striking matches in the gallery. Describe how you come out to go up the shaky stairs in the balcony and what you see there—the turmoil of packing after the show. Then take some other town and run all the other interesting experiences you have had, engine-driver, etc. into it. In this you can end by the late supper in Dundalk, the long wait for the train at three o'clock, the dancing in the dim light, the going out into the grey dawn, the sun rises as you get into the deserted station, you walk up and down; the train comes; you have glimpse of magnificent bright morning; you go to sleep and wake in Dublin.' Stephens Typescript, page 2121.

THE FERRYMAN OF DINISH ISLAND

square fields of oats, or potatoes, or pasture, divided by loose stone walls that are built up without mortar. Wherever there are a few cottages near the road one sees barefooted women hurrying backwards and forwards, with hampers of turf or grass slung over their backs, and generally a few children running after them, and if it is a market-day, as was the case on the day of which I am going to write, one overtakes long strings of country people driving home from Galway in low carts drawn by an ass or pony. As a rule one or two men sit in front of the cart driving and smoking, with a couple of women behind them stretched out at their ease among sacks of flour or young pigs, and nearly always talking continuously in Gaelic. These men are all dressed in homespuns of the grey natural wool, and the women in deep madder-dyed petticoats and bodices, with brown shawls over their heads. One's first feeling as one comes back among these people and takes a place, so to speak, in this noisy procession of fishermen, farmers, and women, where nearly everyone is interesting and attractive, is a dread of any reform that would tend to lessen their individuality rather than any very real hope of improving their well-being. One feels then, perhaps a little later, that it is part of the misfortune of Ireland that nearly all the characteristics which give colour and attractiveness to Irish life are bound up with a social condition that is near to penury, while in countries like Brittany the best external features of the local life—the rich embroidered dresses, for instance, or the carved furniture—are connected with a decent and comfortable social condition.

About twelve miles from Galway one reaches Spiddal, a village which lies on the borderland between the fairly prosperous districts near Galway and the barren country further to the west. Like most places of its kind, it has a double row of houses—some of them with two storeys—several public-houses with a large police barracks among them, and a little to one side a coastguard station, ending up at either side of the village with a chapel and a church. It was evening when we drove into Spiddal, and a little after sunset we walked on to a rather exposed quay, where a few weather-beaten hookers were moored with many ropes. As we came down none of the crews was to be seen, but threads of turf smoke rising from the open manhole of the forecastle showed that the men were probably on board. While we were looking down on them from the pier—the tide was far out—an old grey-haired man, with the inflamed eyes that are so common here from the continual itching of the turf-smoke, peered up through the man-hole and watched us with vague curiosity. A few moments later a young man came down from a field of black earth, where he had been digging a drain, and asked the old man, in Gaelic, to throw him a spark for his pipe. The latter disappeared for a moment, then came up again with a smouldering end of a turf sod in his hand, and threw it up on the pier, where the young man caught it with a quick downward grab without burning himself, blew it into a blaze, lit his pipe with it, and went back to his work. These people are so poor that many of them do not spend any money on matches. The spark of lighting turf is kept alive day and night on the hearth, and when a man goes out fishing or to work in the fields he usually carries a lighted sod with him and keeps it all day buried in ashes or any dry rubbish, so that he can use it when he needs it. On our way back to the village an old woman begged from us, speaking in English, as most of the people do to anyone who is not a native. We gave her a few halfpence, and as she was moving away with an ordinary 'God save you!' I said a blessing to her in Irish to show her that I knew her own language if she chose to use it. Immediately she turned back towards me and began her thanks again, this time with extraordinary profusion. 'That the blessing of God may be on you,' she said, 'on road and on ridgeway, on sea and on land, on flood and on mountain, in all the kingdoms of the world'—and so on, till I was too far off to hear what she was saying.

In a district like Spiddal one sees curious gradations of types, especially on Sundays and holidays, when everyone is dressed as their fancy leads them and as well as they can manage. As I watched the people coming from Mass the morning after we arrived this was curiously noticeable. The police and coastguards came first in their smartest uniforms; then the shopkeepers, dressed like the people of Dublin, but a little more grotesquely; then the more well-to-do country folk, dressed only in the local clothes I have spoken of, but the best and newest kind, while the wearers themselves looked well-fed and healthy, and a few of them, especially the girls, magnificently built; then, last of all, one saw the destitute in still the same clothes, but this time patched and threadbare and ragged, the women mostly barefooted, and both sexes pinched with hunger and the fear of it. The class that one would be most interested to see increase is that of the typical well-to-do people, but except in a few districts it is not numerous, and is always aspiring after the dress of the shop-people or tending to sink down again among the paupers.

Later in the day we drove on another long stage to the west. As before, the country we passed through was not depressing, though stony and barren as a quarry. At every crossroads we passed groups of young healthy-looking boys and men amusing themselves with hurley or pitching, and further back on little heights, a small field's breadth from the road, there were many groups of girls sitting out by the hour, near enough to the road to see everything that was passing, yet far enough away to keep their shyness undisturbed. Their red dresses looked peculiarly beautiful among the fresh green of the grass and opening bracken, with a strip of sea behind them, and, far away, the grey cliffs of Clare. A little further on, some ten miles from Spiddal, inlets of the sea begin to run in towards the mountains, and the road turns north to avoid them across an expanse of desolate bog far more dreary than the rocks of the coast. Here one sees a few wretched sheep nibbling in places among the turf, and occasionally a few ragged people walking rapidly by the roadside. Before we stopped for the night we had reached another bay coast-line, and were among stones again. Later in the evening we walked out round another small quay, with the usual little band of shabby hookers, and then along a road that rose in some places a few hundred feet above the sea; and as one looked down into the little fields that lay below it, they looked so small and rocky that the very thought of tillage in them seemed like the freak of an eccentric. Yet in this particular place tiny cottages, some of them without windows, swarmed by the roadside and in the 'boreens,' or laneways, at either side, many of them built on a single sweep of stone with the naked living rock for their floor. A number of people were to be seen everywhere about them, the men loitering by the roadside and the women hurrying among the fields, feeding an odd calf or lamb, or driving in a few ducks before the night. In one place a few boys were playing pitch with trousers buttons, and a little farther on half-a-score of young men were making donkeys jump backwards and forwards over a low wall. As we came back we met two men, who came and talked to us, one of them, by his hat and dress, plainly a man who had been away from Connemara. In a little while he told us that he had

NEAR CASTELLOE

THE POOREST PARISH

been in Gloucester and Bristol working on public works, but had wearied of it and come back to his country.

'Bristol,' he said, 'is the greatest town, I think, in all England, but the work in it is hard.'

I asked him about the fishing in the neighbourhood we were in. 'Ah,' he said, 'there's little fishing in it at all, for we have no good boats. There is no one asking for boats for this place, for the shop-keepers would rather have the people idle, so that they can get them for a shilling a day to go out in their old hookers and sell turf in Aran and on the coast of Clare.' Then we talked of Aran, and he told me of people I knew there who had died or got married since I had been on the islands, and then they went on their way.

BETWEEN THE BAYS OF CARRAROE

In rural Ireland very few parishes only are increasing in population, and those that are doing so are usually in districts of the greatest poverty. One of the most curious instances of this tendency is to be found in the parish of Carraroe, which is said to be, on the whole, the poorest parish in the country, although many worse cases of individual destitution can be found elsewhere. The most characteristic part of this district lies on a long promontory between Cashla Bay and Greatman's Bay. On both coast-lines one sees a good many small quays, with, perhaps, two hookers moored to them, and on the roads one passes an occasional flat space covered with small green fields of oats—with whole families on their knees weeding among them—or patches of potatoes; but for the rest one sees little but an endless series of low stony hills, with veins of grass. Here and there, however, one comes in sight of a fresh-water lake, with an island or two, covered with seagulls, and many cottages round the shore; some of them standing almost on the brink of the water, others a little higher up, fitted in among the rocks, and one or two standing out on the top of a ridge against the blue of the sky or of the Twelve Bens of Connaught.

At the edge of one of these lakes, near a school of lace or knitting—one of those that have been established by the Congested Districts Board—we met a man driving a mare and foal that had scrambled out of their enclosure, although the mare had her two off-legs chained together. As soon as he had got them back into one of the fields and built up the wall with loose stones, he came over to a stone beside us and began to talk about horses and the dying out of the ponies of Connemara. 'You will hardly get any real Connemara ponies now at all,' he said; 'and the kind of horses they send down to us to improve the breed are no use, for the horses we breed from them will not thrive or get their health on the little patches where we have to put them. This last while most of the people in this parish are giving up horses altogether. Those that have them sell their foals when they are about six months old for four pounds, or five maybe; but the better part of the people are working with an ass only, that can carry a few things on a straddle over her back.'

'If you've no horses,' I said, 'how do you get to Galway if you want to go to a fair or to market?'

'We go by the sea,' he said, 'in one of the hookers you've likely seen at the little quays while walking down by the road. You can sail to Galway if the wind is fair in four hours or less maybe; and the people here are all used to the sea, for no one can live in this place but by cutting turf in the mountains and sailing out to sell it in Clare or Aran, for you see yourselves there's no good in the land, that has little in it but bare rocks and stones. Two years ago there came a wet summer, and the people were worse off then than they are now maybe, with their bad potatoes and all; for they couldn't cut or dry a load of turf to sell across the bay, and there was many a woman hadn't a dry sod itself to put under her pot, and she shivering with cold and hunger.'

A little later, when we had talked of one or two other things, I asked him if many of the people who were living round in the scattered cottages we could see were often in real want of food. 'There are a few, maybe, have enough at all times,' he said, 'but the most are in want one time or another, when the potatoes are bad or few, and their whole store is eaten; and there are some who are near starving all times, like a widow woman beyond who has seven children with hardly a shirt on their skins, and they with nothing to eat but the milk from one cow, and a handful of meal they will get from one neighbour or another.'

'You're getting an old man,' I said, 'and do you remember if the place was as bad as it is now when you were a young man growing up?'

'It wasn't as bad, or a half as bad,' he said, 'for there were fewer people in it and more land to each, and the land itself was better at the time, for now it is drying up or something, and not giving its fruits and increase as it did.'

I asked him if they bought manures.

'We get a hundredweight for eight shillings now and again, but I think there's little good in it, for it's only a poor kind they send out to the like of us. Then there was another thing they had in the old times,' he continued, 'and that was the making of poteen (illicit whisky), for it was a great trade at that time, and you'd see the police down on their knees blowing the fire with their own

A MAN OF CARRAROE

breath to make a drink for themselves, and then going off with the butt of an old barrel, and that was one seizure, and an old bag with a handful of malt, and that was another seizure, and would satisfy the law; but now they must have the worm and the still and a prisoner, and there is little of it made in the country. At that time a man would get ten shillings for a gallon, and it was a good trade for poor people.'

As we were talking a woman passed driving two young pigs, and we began to speak of them.

'We buy the young pigs and rear them up,' he said, 'but this year they are scarce and dear. And indeed what good are they in bad years, for how can we go feeding a pig when we haven't enough, maybe, for ourselves? In good years, when you have potatoes and plenty, you can rear up two or three pigs and make a good bit on them; but other times, maybe, a poor man will give a pound for a young pig that won't thrive after, and then his pound will be gone, and he'll have no money for his rent.'

The old man himself was cheerful and seemingly fairly well-to-do; but in the end he seemed to be getting dejected as he spoke of one difficulty after another, so I asked him, to change the subject, if there was much dancing in the country. 'No,' he said, 'this while back you'll never see a piper coming this way at all, though in the old times it's many a piper would be moving around through those houses for a whole quarter together, playing his pipes and drinking poteen and the people dancing round him; but now there is no dancing or singing in this place at all, and most of the young people is growing up and going to America.'

I pointed to the lace-school near us, and asked him how the girls got on with the lace, and if they earned much money. 'I've heard tell,' he said, 'that in the four schools round about this place there is near six hundred pounds paid out in wages every year, and that is a good sum; but there isn't a young girl going to them that isn't saving up, and saving up till she'll have enough gathered to take her to America, and then away she will go, and why wouldn't she?'

Often the worst moments in the lives of these people are caused by the still frequent outbreaks of typhus fever, and before we parted I asked him if there was much fever in the particular district where we were.

'Just here,' he said, 'there isn't much of it at all, but there are places round about where you'll sometimes hear of a score and more stretched out waiting for their death; but I suppose it is the will of God. Then there is a sickness they call consumption that some will die of; but I suppose there is no place where people aren't getting their death one way or other, and the most in this place are enjoying good health, glory be to God! for it is a healthy place and there is a clean air blowing.'

Then, with a few of the usual blessings, he got up and left us, and we walked on through more of similar or still poorer country. It is remarkable that from Spiddal onward—that is, in the whole of the most poverty-stricken district in Ireland—no one begs, even in a roundabout way. It is the fashion, with many of the officials who are connected with relief works and such things, to compare the people of this district rather unfavourably with the people of the poor districts of Donegal; but in this respect at least Donegal is not the more admirable.

AMONG THE RELIEF WORKS

BEYOND Carraroe, the last promontory on the north coast of Galway Bay, one reaches a group of islands which form the lower angle of Connemara. These islands are little more than a long peninsula broken through by a number of small straits, over which, some twelve years ago, causeways and swing-bridges were constructed, so that one can now drive straight on through Annaghvaan, Lettermore, Gorumna, Lettermullan, and one or two smaller islands. When one approaches this district from the east a long detour is made to get round the inner point of Greatman's Bay, and then the road turns to the south-west till one reaches Annaghvaan, the first of the islands. This road is a remarkable one. Nearly every foot of it, as it now stands, has been built up in different years of famine by the people of the neighbourhood working on Government relief works, which are now once more in full swing; making improvements in some places, turning primitive tracts into roadways in others, and here and there building a new route to some desolate village.

We drove many miles, with Costello and Carraroe behind us, along a bog-road of curious formation built up on a turf embankment, with broad grassy sods at either side—perhaps to make a possible way for the barefooted people—then two spaces of rough broken stones where the wheel-ruts are usually worn, and in the centre a track of gritty earth for the horses. Then, at a turn of the road, we came in sight of a dozen or more men and women working hurriedly and doggedly improving a further portion of this road, with a ganger swaggering among them and directing their work. Some of the people were cutting out sods from grassy patches near the road, others were carrying down bags of earth in a slow, inert procession, a few were breaking stones, and three or four women were scraping out a sort of sandpit at a little distance. As we drove quickly by we could see that every man and woman was working with a sort of hang-dog dejection that would be enough to make any casual passer mistake them for a band of convicts.[1] The wages given on these works are usually a shilling

[1] In Notebook 36 Synge says: 'These are the relief works by which the situation is made satisfactory to the responsible classes whenever a crisis occurs. It gave me a strange feeling

RELIEF WORKS

INDIVIDUAL LOCAL LIFE

a day, and, as a rule, one person only, generally the head of the family, is taken from each house. Sometimes the best worker in a family is thus forced away from his ordinary work of farming, or fishing, or kelp-making for this wretched remuneration at a time when his private industry is most needed. If this system of relief has some things in its favour, it is far from satisfactory in other ways, and is not always economical. I have been told of a district not very far from here where there is a ganger, an overseer, an inspector, a paymaster, and an engineer superintending the work of two paupers only. This is possibly an exaggerated account of what is really taking place, yet it probably shows, not too inexactly, a state of things that is not rare in Ireland.

A mile or two further on we passed a similar band of workers, and then the road rose for a few feet and turned sharply on to a long causeway, with a swing-bridge in the centre, that led to the island of Annaghvaan. Just as we reached the bridge our driver jumped down and took his mare by the head. A moment later she began to take fright at the hollow noise of her own hoofs on the boards of the bridge and the blue rush of the tide which she could see through them, but the man coaxed her forward, and got her over without much difficulty. For the next mile or two there was a continual series of small islands and causeways and bridges that the mare grew accustomed to, and trotted gaily over, till we reached Lettermore, and drove for some distance through the usual small hills of stone. Then we came to the largest causeway of all, between Lettermore and Gorumna, where the proportion of the opening of the bridge to the length of the embankment is so small that the tide runs through with extraordinary force. On the outer side the water was banked up nearly a yard high against the buttress of the bridge, and on the other side there was a rushing, eddying torrent that recalled some mountain salmon-stream in flood, except that here, instead of the brown river-water, one saw the white and blue foam of the sea.

The remainder of our road to the lower western end of Gorumna led through hilly districts that became more and more white with stone, though one saw here and there a few brown masses of bog or an oblong lake with many islands and rocks. In

of pain, for there was not one of these people—usually chosen because they are the heads of families—who was not suffering like a soul in purgatory through the working-out of some badly calculated economic problem of distribution . . . it seemed a hopelessly futile expedient, with a sort of simplicity that I suppose recommends itself to the lawgiver.'

most places, if one looked round the hills a little distance from the road, one could see the yellow roofs and white gables of cottages scattered everywhere through this waste of rock; and on the ridge of every hill one could see the red dresses of women who were gathering turf or looking for their sheep or calves. Near the village where we stopped things are somewhat better, and a few fields of grass and potatoes were to be seen, and a certain number of small cattle grazing among the rocks. Here also one is close to the sea, and fishing and kelp-making are again possible. In the village there is a small private quay in connection with a shop where everything is sold, and not long after we arrived a hooker sailed in with a cargo of supplies from Galway. A number of women were standing about expecting her arrival, and soon afterwards several of them set off for different parts of the island with a bag of flour slung over an ass. One of these, a young girl of seventeen or eighteen, drove on with her load far into Lettermullan, the next island, on a road that we were walking also; and then sent the ass back to Gorumna in charge of a small boy, and took up the sack of flour, which weighed at least sixteen stone, on her back, and carried it more than a mile, through a narrow track, to her own home. This practice of allowing young girls to carry great weights frequently injures them severely, and is the cause of much danger and suffering in their after lives. They do not seem, however, to know anything of the risks they run, and their loads are borne gaily.

A little further on we came on another stretch of the relief works, where there were many elderly men and young girls working with the same curious aspect of shame and dejection. The work was just closing for the evening, and as we walked back to Gorumna an old man who had been working walked with us, and complained of his great poverty and the small wages he was given. 'A shilling a day,' he said, 'would hardly keep a man in tea and sugar and tobacco and a bit of bread to eat, and what good is it all when there is a family of five or six maybe, and often more?' Just as we reached the swing-bridge that led back to Gorumna another hooker sailed carefully in through the narrow rocky channel, with a crowd of men and women sitting along the gunwale. They edged in close to a flat rock near the bridge, and made her fast for a moment while the women jumped on shore; some of them carrying bottles, others with little children, and all dressed out in

CAUSEWAY TO GORUMNA

GATHERING SEAWEED FOR KELP

new red petticoats and shawls. They looked as they crowded up on the road as fine a body of peasant women as one could see anywhere, and were all talking and laughing eagerly among themselves. The old man told me in Irish that they had been at a pattern—a sort of semi-religious festival like the well-known festivals of Brittany—that had just been held some distance to the east on the Galway coast. It was reassuring to see that some, at least, of the island people are, in their own way, prosperous and happy. When the women were all landed the swing-bridge was pushed open, and the hooker was poled through to the bay on the north side of the islands. Then the men moored her and came up to a little public-house, where they spent the rest of the evening talking and drinking and telling stories in Irish.

KELP-BURNING

THE FERRYMAN OF DINISH ISLAND

WHEN wandering among lonely islands in the west of Ireland, like those of the Gorumna group, one seldom fails to meet with some old sailor or pilot who has seen something of the world, and it is often from a man of this kind that one learns most about the island or hill that he has come back to, in middle age or towards the end of his life. An old seafaring man who ferries chance comers to and from Dinish Island is a good example of this class. The island is separated from Furnace—the last of the group that is linked together by causeways and bridges—by a deep channel between two chains of rock. As we went to this channel across a strip of sandhill a wild-looking old man appeared at the other side, and began making signs to us and pushing off a heavy boat from the shore. Before he was half-way across we could hear him calling out to us in a state of almost incoherent excitement, and directing us to a ledge of rock where he could take us off. A moment later we scrambled into his boat upon a mass of seaweed that he had been collecting for kelp, and he poled us across, talking at random about how he had seen His Royal Highness the Duke of Edinburgh, and gone to America as interpreter for the emigrants in a bad season twenty-one years ago. As soon as we landed we walked across a bay of sand to a tiny schoolhouse close to the sea, and the old man turned back across the channel with a travelling tea merchant and a young girl who had come down to the shore. All the time they were going across we could hear him talking and vociferating at the top of his voice, and then, after a moment's silence, he came in sight again, on our side, running towards us over the sand. After he had been a little while with us, and got over the excitement caused by the sudden arrival of two strangers—we could judge how great it was by a line of children's heads who were peeping over the rocks and watching us with amazement—he began to talk clearly and simply. After a few of the remarks one hears from everyone about the loneliness of the place, he spoke about the school behind us.

'Isn't it a poor thing,' he said, 'to see a school lying closed up the like of that, and twenty or thirty scholars, maybe, running wild along the sea? I am very lonesome since that school was closed, for

THE DINISH FERRYMAN

there was a school-mistress used to come for a long while from Lettermullan, and I used to ferry her over the water, and maybe ten little children along with her. And then there was a school-mistress living here for a long while, and I used to ferry the children only; but now she has found herself a better place, and this three months there's no school in it at all.'

One could see when he was quiet that he differed a good deal, both in face and in his way of speaking, from the people of the islands, and when he paused I asked him if he had spent all his life among them, excepting the one voyage to America.

'I have not,' he said; 'but I've been many places, though I and my fathers have rented the sixth of this island for near two hundred years. My own father was a sailorman who came in here by chance and married a woman, and lived, a snug, decent man, with five cows or six, till he died at a hundred and three. And my mother's father, who had the place before him, died at a hundred and eight, and he wouldn't have died then, I'm thinking, only he fell down and broke his hip. They were strong, decent people at that time, and I was going to school—travelling out over the islands with my father ferrying me—till I was twenty years of age; and then I went to America and got to be a sailorman, and was in New York, and Baltimore, and New Orleans, and after that I was coasting till I knew every port and town of this country and Scotland and Wales.'

One of us asked him if he had stayed at sea till he came back to this island.

'I did not,' he said, 'for I went ashore once in South Wales, and I'm telling you Wales is a long country, for I travelled all a whole summer's day from that place till I reached Birkenhead at nine o'clock. And then I went to Manchester and to Newcastle-on-Tyne, and I worked there for two years. That's a rich country, dear gentlemen, and when a payman would come into the works on a Saturday you'd see the bit of board he had over his shoulder bending down with the weight of sovereigns he had for the men. And isn't it a queer thing to be sitting here now thinking on those times, and I after being near twenty years back on this bit of a rock that a dog wouldn't look at, where the pigs die and the spuds die, and even the judges and quality do come out and do lower our rents when they see the wild Atlantic driving in across the cursed stones.'

'And what is it brought you back,' I said, 'if you were doing well beyond in the world?'

'My two brothers went to America,' he said, 'and I had to come back because I was the eldest son, and I got married then, and I after holding out till I was forty. I have a young family now growing up, for I was snug for a while; and then bad times came, and I lost my wife, and the potatoes went bad, and three cows I had were taken in the night with some disease of the brain, and they swam out and were drowned in the sea. I got back their bodies in the morning, and took them down to a gentleman beyond who understands the diseases of animals, but he gave me nothing for them at all. So there I am now with no pigs, and no cows, and a young family running round with no mother to mind them; and what can you do with children that know nothing at all, and will often put down as much in the pot one day as would do three days, and do be wasting the meal, though you can't say a word against them, for it's young and ignorant they are? If it wasn't for them I'd be off this evening, and I'd earn my living easy on the sea, for I'm only fifty-seven years of age, and I have good health; but how can I leave my young children? And I don't know what way I'm going to go on living in this place that the Lord created last, I'm thinking, in the end of time; and it's often when I sit down and look around on it I do begin cursing and damning, and asking myself how poor people can go on executing their religion at all.'

For a while he said nothing, and we could see tears in his eyes; then I asked him how he was living now from one day to another.

'They're letting me out advanced meal and flour from the shop,' he said, 'and I'm to pay it back when I burn a ton of kelp in the summer. For two months I was working on the relief works at a shilling a day, but what good is that for a family? So I've stopped now to rake up weed for a ton, or maybe two tons, of kelp. When I left the works I got my boy put on in my place, but the ganger put him back; and then I got him on again, and the ganger put him back. Then I bought a bottle of ink and a pen and a bit of paper to write a letter and make my complaint, but I never wrote it to this day, for what good is it harming him more than another? Then I've a daughter in America has only been there nine months, and she's sent me three pounds already. I have another daughter, living above with her married sister, will be ready to go in autumn, and another little one will go when she's big enough. There is a man above has four daughters in America, and gets a pound a quarter from each one of them, and that is a great thing for a poor man. It's to America we'll all be going, and isn't it a fearful thing to think I'll be kept here another ten years, maybe, tending the children and striving to keep them alive, when I might be abroad in America living in decency and earning my bread?'

Afterwards he took us up to the highest point of the island, and showed us a fine view of the whole group and of the Atlantic beyond them, with a few fishing-boats in the distance, and many large boats nearer the rocks rowing heavily with loads of weed. When we got into the ferry again the channel had become too deep to pole, and the old man rowed with a couple of long sweeps from the bow.

'I go out alone in this boat,' he said, as he was rowing, 'across the bay to the northern land. There is no other man in the place would do it, but I'm a licensed pilot these twenty years, and a seafaring man.'

Then as we finally left him he called after us:

'It has been a great consolation to me, dear gentlemen, to be talking with your like, for one sees few people in this place, and so may God bless and reward you and see you safely to your homes.'

THE KELP MAKERS

SOME of those who have undertaken to reform the congested districts have shown an unfortunate tendency to give great attention to a few canonised industries, such as horse-breeding and fishing, or even bee-keeping, while they neglect local industries that have been practised with success for a great number of years. Thus, in the large volume issued a couple of years ago by the Department of Agriculture and Technical Instruction for Ireland, which claims to give a comprehensive account of the economic resources of the country, hardly a word has been said of the kelp industry, which is a matter of the greatest importance to the inhabitants of a very large district. The Congested Districts Board seems to have left it on one side also, and in the Galway neighbourhood, at least, no steps appear to have been taken to ensure the people a fair market for the kelp they produce, or to revise the present unsatisfactory system by which it is tested and paid for. In some places the whole buying trade falls into the hands of one man, who can then control the prices at his pleasure, while one hears on all sides of arbitrary decisions by which good kelp is rejected, and what the people consider an inferior article is paid for at a high figure. When the buying is thus carried on no appeal can be made from the decision of one individual, and I have sometimes seen a party of old men sitting nearly in tears on a ton of rejected kelp that had cost them weeks of hard work, while, for all one knew, it had very possibly been refused on account of some grudge or caprice of the buyer.

The village of Trawbaun, which lies on the coast opposite the Aran Islands, is a good instance of a kelp-making neighbourhood. We reached it through a narrow road, now in the hands of the relief workers, where we hurried past the usual melancholy line of old men breaking stones and younger men carrying bags of earth and sods. Soon afterwards the road fell away quickly towards the sea, through a village of many cottages huddled together, with bare walls of stone that had never been whitewashed, as often happens in places that are peculiarly poor. Passing through these, we came out on three or four acres of sandhill that brought us to a line of rocks with a narrow sandy cove between them just filling with the tide. All along the coast, a little above high-water mark, we could see a number of tall, reddish stacks of dried seaweed, some of which had probably been standing for weeks, while others were in various unfinished stages, or had only just been begun. A number of men and women and boys were hard at work in every direction, gathering fresh weed and spreading it out to dry on the rocks. In some places the weed is mostly gathered from the foreshore; but in this neighbourhood, at least in the early summer, it is pulled up from rocks under the sea at low water, by men working from a boat or curagh with a long pole furnished with a short crossbar nailed to the top, which they entangle in the weeds. Just as we came down, a curagh, lightly loaded by two boys, was coming in over a low bar into the cove I have spoken of, and both of them were slipping over the side every moment or two to push their canoe from behind. Several bare-legged girls, crooning merry songs in Gaelic, were passing backwards and forwards over the sand, carrying heavy loads of weed on their backs. Further out many other curaghs, more heavily laden, were coming slowly in, waiting for the tide; and some old men on the shore were calling out directions to their crews in the high-pitched tone that is so remarkable in this Connaught Irish. The whole scene, with the fresh smell of the sea and the blueness of the shallow waves, made a curious contrast with the dismal spectacle of the relief workers we had just passed, for here the people seemed as light-hearted as a party of schoolboys.

Further on we came to a rocky headland where some men were burning down their weed into kelp, a process that in this place is given nearly twelve hours. As we came up dense volumes of rich, creamy-coloured smoke were rising from a long pile of weed, in the centre of which we could see here and there a molten mass burning at an intense heat. Two men and a number of boys were attending to the fire, laying on fresh weed wherever the covering grew thin enough to receive it. A little to one side a baby, rolled up in a man's coat, was asleep beside a hamper, as on occasions like this the house is usually shut up and the whole family scatters for work of various kinds. The amount of weed needed to make a ton of kelp varies, I have been told, from three tons to five. The men of a family working busily on a favourable day can take a ton of the raw weed, and the kelp is sold at from three pounds fifteen shillings or a little less to five pounds a ton, so it is easy to see the importance of this trade. When all the weed intended for one furnace has been used the whole is covered up and left three or four days to cool; then it is broken up and taken off in boats or curaghs to a buyer. He takes a handful, tests it with certain chemicals, and fixes the price accordingly; but the people themselves have no means of knowing whether they are getting fair play, and although many buyers may be careful and conscientious, there is a very general feeling of dissatisfaction among the people with the way they are forced to carry on the trade. When the kelp has been finally disposed of it is shipped in schooners and sent away—for the most part, I believe, to Scotland, where it is used for the manufacture of iodine.

Complaints are often heard about the idleness of the natives of Connemara; yet at the present time one sees numbers of the people drying and arranging their weed until nightfall, and the bays where the weed is found are filled with boats at four or five o'clock in the morning, when the tide is favourable. The chances of a good kelp season depend, to some extent, on suitable weather for drying and burning the weed; yet on the whole this trade is probably less precarious than the fishing industry or any other source of income now open to the people of a large portion of these congested districts. In the present year the weather has been excellent, and there is every hope that a good quantity of kelp may be obtained. The matter is of peculiar importance this year, as for the last few months the shopkeepers have been practically keeping the people alive by giving out meal and flour on the security of the kelp harvest—one house alone, I am told, distributed fourteen tons during the last ten days—so that if the kelp should not turn out well, or the prices should be less than what is expected, whole districts will be placed in the greatest difficulty.

It is a remarkable feature of the domestic finance of this district that, although the people are so poor, they are used to dealing with fairly large sums of money. Thus four or five tons of kelp well sold may bring a family between twenty and thirty pounds, and their bills for flour (which is bought in bags of two hundredweight at a good deal over a pound a bag) must also be considerable. It is the same with their pig-farming, fishing, and other industries, and probably this familiarity with considerable sums causes a part, at least, of the sense of shame that is shown by those who are reduced to working on the roadside for the miserable pittance of a shilling a day.

THE BOAT BUILDERS

We left Gorumna in a hooker managed by two men, and sailed north to another district of the Galway coast. Soon after we started the wind fell, and we lay almost becalmed in a curious bay so filled with islands that one could hardly distinguish the channel that led to the open sea. For some time we drifted slowly between Dinish Island and Illaunearach, a stony mound inhabited by three families only. Then our pace became so slow that the boatmen got out a couple of long sweeps and began rowing heavily, with sweat streaming from them. The air was heavy with thunder, and on every side one saw the same smoky blue sea and sky, with grey islands and mountains beyond them, and in one place a ridge of yellow rocks touched by a single ray of sunlight. Two or three pookawns—lateen-rigged boats, said to be of Spanish origin—could be seen about a mile ahead of us sailing easily across our bows, where some opening in the islands made a draught from the east. In half an hour our own sails filled, and the boatmen stopped rowing and began to talk to us. One of them gave us many particulars about the prices of hookers and their nets, and the system adopted by the local boat-builders who work for the poorer fishermen of the neighbourhood.

'When a man wants a boat,' he said, 'he buys the timber from a man in Galway and gets it brought up here in a hooker. Then he gets a carpenter to come to his house and build it in some place convenient to the sea. The whole time the carpenter will be working at it the other man must support him, and give him whisky every day. Then he must stand around while he is working, holding boards and handing nails, and if he doesn't do it smart enough you'll hear the carpenter scolding him and making a row. A carpenter like that will be six weeks or two months, maybe, building a boat, and he will get two pounds for his work when he is done. The wood and everything you need for a fifteen-foot boat will cost four pounds, or beyond it, so a boat like that is a dear thing for a poor man.'

We asked him about the boats that had been made by the local boatwrights for the Congested Districts Board.

THE BOAT BUILDER

'There were some made in Lettermullan,' he said, 'and beyond in an island west of where you're going to-day there is an old man has been building boats for thirty years, and he could tell you all about them.'

Meanwhile we had been sailing quickly, and were near the north shore of the bay. The tide had gone so far out while we were becalmed that it was not possible to get in alongside the pier, so the men steered for a ledge of rock further out, where it was possible to land. As we were going in an anchor was dropped, and then when we were close to the rocks the men checked the boat by straining on the rope, and brought us in to the shore with a great deal of nicety.

Not long afterwards we made our way to see the old carpenter the boatman had told us of, and found him busy with two or three other men caulking the bottom of a boat that was propped up on one side. As we came towards them along the low island shore the scene reminded one curiously of some old picture of Noah building the Ark. The old man himself was rather remarkable in appearance, with strongly formed features, and an extraordinarily hairy chest showing through the open neck of his shirt. He told us that he had made several nobbies for the Board, and showed us an arrangement that had been supplied for steaming the heavy timber needed for boats of this class.

'At the present time,' he said, 'I am making our own boats again, and the fifteen-foot boats the people do use here have light timber, and we don't need to trouble steaming them at all. I get eight pounds for a boat when I buy the timber myself, and fit her all out ready for the sea. But I am working for poor men, and it is often three years before I will be paid the full price of a boat I'm after making.'

From where we stood we could see another island across a narrow sound, studded with the new cottages that are built in this neighbourhood by the Congested Districts Board.

'That island, like another you're after passing, has been bought by the Board,' said the old man, who saw us looking at them; 'and it is a great thing for the poor people to have their holdings arranged for them in one strip instead of the little scattered plots the people have in all this neighbourhood, where a man will often have to pass through the ground of maybe three men to get to a plot of his own.'

BOAT-BUILDING AT CARNA

This rearrangement of the holdings that is being carried out in most places where estates have been bought up by the Board, and resold to the tenants, is a matter of great importance that is fully appreciated by the people. Mere tenant purchase in districts like this may do some good for the moment by lowering rents and interesting the people in their land; yet in the end it is likely to prove disastrous, as it tends to perpetuate holdings that are not large enough to support their owners and are too scattered to be worked effectively. In the relatively few estates bought by the Board—up to March, 1904, their area amounted to two or three hundred thousand acres out of the three and a half million that are included in the congested districts—this is being set right, yet some of the improvements made at the same time are perhaps a less certain gain, and give the neighbourhoods where they have been made an uncomfortable look that is, I think, felt by the people. For instance, there is no pressing need to substitute iron roofs—in many ways open to objection—for the thatch that has been used for centuries, and is part of the constructive tradition of the people. In many districts the thatching is done in some idle season by the men of a household themselves, with the help of their friends, who are proud of their skill; and it is looked on as a sort of a festival where there is great talk and discussion, the loss of which is hardly made up for by the patch of ground which was needed to grow the straw, and is now free for other uses. In the same way, the improvements in the houses built by the Board are perhaps a little too sudden. It is far better, wherever possible, to improve the ordinary prosperity of the people till they begin to improve their houses themselves on their own lines, than to do too much in the way of building houses that have no interest for the people and disfigure the country. I remember one evening in another congested district—on the west coast of Kerry—listening to some peasants who discussed for hours the proportions of a new cottage that was to be built by one of them. They had never, of course, heard of proportion; but they had rules and opinions, in which they were deeply interested, as to how high a house should be if it was a certain length, with so many rafters, in order that it might look well. Traditions of this kind are destroyed for ever when too sweeping improvements are made in a district, and the loss is a great one. If any real improvement is to be made in many of these congested districts the rearrangement and sale of the holdings to the tenants, somewhat on the lines adopted by the Board, must be carried out on a large scale; but in doing so care should be taken to disorganise as little as possible the life and methods of the people. A little attention to the wells, and, where necessary, greater assistance in putting up sheds for the cattle and pigs that now live in the houses, would do a great deal to get rid of the epidemics of typhus and typhoid, and then the people should be left as free as possible to arrange their houses and way of life as it pleases them.

THE HOMES OF THE HARVESTMEN

THE general appearance of the North Mayo country[1] round Belmullet—another district of the greatest poverty—differs curiously from that of Connemara. In Mayo a waste of turf and bog takes the place of the waste of stones that is the chief feature of the coast of Galway. Consequently sods of turf are used for all sorts of work—building walls and ditches, and even the gables of cottages—instead of the loose pieces of granite or limestone that are ready to one's hand in the district we have left. Between every field one sees a thin bank of turf, worn away in some places by the weather, and covered in others with loose grass and royal flowering ferns. The rainfall of Belmullet is a heavy one, and in wet weather this absence of stone gives one an almost intolerable feeling of dampness and discomfort.

The last forty miles of our journey to Belmullet was made on the long car which leaves Ballina at four o'clock in the morning. It

[1] Synge had been in this part once before, in September 1904, and he wrote in Notebook 32:

'I came out here in the steamer that runs from Sligo to Belmullet. . . . Several times we stopped opposite long coves or openings in the rock, and curaghs came out for a load of salt or timber. The men and boys in them spoke Irish among themselves, and it seemed like hearing a quite familiar language to catch the Connaught turn and accent again after the two seasons when I heard Munster only. The curaghs were not quite the same cut as those in use in Aran, and several were shabby and battered to an extreme degree. . . . [Steaming on] outside Sligo Bay [we got] into the full swing and vigour of the Atlantic. There is no fuller life . . . than [the] endlessly incorruptible and virile brilliancy of these waves. Before one was long among them however we turned in south from the Stag Rocks into Broadstairs Bay. . . .

'About sunset I went out some distance on the Mullet and saw the evening coming down over Blacksod Bay filled with searching loveliness with low mists from the bogs and rose and purple colours on the sea. Here and there I passed a girl in the usual dress—a short red petticoat over bare feet and legs, a faded uncertain bodice and a white or blue rag swathing the head—who was looking after a few shadowy cattle or bringing them home from the bogs. . . .

'In Mayo one cannot forget that in spite of the beauty of the scenery the people in it are debased and nearly demoralized by bad housing and lodging and the endless misery of the rain. . . .

'For a passer through it is not easy to be just to the belated towns of Ireland. Belmullet in the evening is squalid and noisy, lonely and crowded at the same time and without appeal to the imagination. So at least one says for the moment. When one has passed six times up and down hearing a gramophone in one house, a fiddle in the next, then an accordion and a fragment of some traditional lullaby, with many crying babies, pigs and donkeys, and noisy girls and young men jostling in the darkness, the effect is not indistinct. All the light comes crossways from doors or windows of shops or in the North East [from] the flaring doorway of the forge so that the moving people are now dark outlines only then for an instant lit up from the east or west.'

was raining heavily as we set out, and the whole town was asleep; but during the first hour we met many harvestmen with scythe-handles and little bundles tied in red handkerchiefs, walking quickly into Ballina to embark for Liverpool or Glasgow. Then we passed Crossmolina, and were soon out on the bogs, where one drives for mile after mile, seeing an odd house only, scattered in a few places with long distances between them. We had been travelling all night from Connemara, and again and again we dozed off into a sort of dream, only to wake up with a start when the car gave a dangerous lurch, and see the same dreary waste with a few wet cattle straggling about the road, or the corner of a lake just seen beyond them through a break in the clouds. When we had driven about fifteen miles we changed horses at a village of three houses, where an old man without teeth brought out the new horses and harnessed them slowly, as if he was half in his sleep. Then we drove on again, stopping from time to time at some sort of post-office, where a woman or boy usually came out to take the bag of letters. At Bangor Erris four more passengers got up, and as the roads were heavy with the rain we settled into a slow jog-trot that made us almost despair of arriving at our destination. The people were now at work weeding potatoes in their few patches of tillage, and cutting turf in the bogs, and their draggled, colourless clothes—so unlike the homespuns of Connemara—added indescribably to the feeling of wretchedness one gets from the sight of these miserable cottages, many of them with an old hamper or the end of a barrel stuck in the roof for a chimney, and the desolation of the bogs.

Belmullet itself is curiously placed on an isthmus—recently pierced by a canal—that divides Broad Haven from Blacksod Bay. Beyond the isthmus there is a long peninsula some fourteen miles in length, running north and south, and separating these two bays from the Atlantic. As we were wandering through this headland in the late afternoon the rain began again, and we stopped to shelter under the gable of a cottage. After a moment or two a girl came out and brought us in out of the rain. At first we could hardly see anything with the darkness of the rain outside and the small window and door of the cottage, but after a moment or two we grew accustomed to it, and the light seemed adequate enough. The woman of the house was sitting opposite us at the corner of the fire, with two children near her, and just behind them a large wooden bed with a sort of red covering, and red curtains above it. Then there was the door, and a spinning-wheel, and at the end opposite the fire a couple of stalls for cattle and a place for a pig with an old brood sow in it, and one young one a few weeks old. At the edge of the fireplace a small door opened into an inner room, but in many of the cottages of this kind there is one apartment only. We talked, as usual, of the hardships of the people, which are worst in places like this, at some distance from the sea, where no help can be got from fishing or making kelp.

'All this land about here,' said the woman, who was sitting by the fire, 'is stripped bog'—that is, bog from which the turf has been cut—'and it is no use at all without all kinds of stuff and manure mixed through it. If you went down a little behind the house you'd see that there is nothing but stones left at the bottom, and you'd want great quantities of sand and seaweed and dung to make it soft and kind enough to grow a thing in it at all. The big farmers have all the good land snapped up, and there is nothing left but stones and bog for poor people like ourselves.'

The sow was snorting in the corner, and I said, after a moment, that it was probably with the pigs that they made the most of their money.

'In bad years,' she said, 'like the year we've had, when the potatoes are rotten and few, there is no use in our pigs, for we have nothing to give them. Last year we had a litter of pigs from that sow, and they were little good to us, for the people were afraid to buy at any price for fear they'd die upon their hands.'

One of us said something of the relief work we had seen in Connemara.

'We have the same thing here,' she said, 'and I have a young lad who is out working on them now, and he has a little horse beast along with him, so that he gets a week's pay for three days or four, and has a little moment over for our own work on the farm.'

I asked her if she had many head of cattle.

'I have not, indeed,' she said, 'nor any place to feed. There is some small people do put a couple of yearlings out on the grass you see below you running out to the sands; but where would I get money to buy one, or to pay the one pound eight, or near it, you do pay for every yearling you have upon the grass? A while since,' she went on, 'we weren't so bad as we are at this time, for we had a young lad who used to go to Scotland for the harvest, and be

A COTTAGE ON MULLET PENINSULA

OUTSIDE BELMULLET

sending us back a pound or two pounds maybe in the month, and bringing five or six or beyond it when he'd come home at the end of autumn; but he got a hurt and never overed it, so we have no one at this time can go from us at all.'

One of the girls had been carding wool for the spinning-wheel, so I asked her about the spinning and weaving.

'Most women spin their wool in this place,' she said, 'and the weaver weaves it afterwards for threepence a yard if it is a single weaving, and for sixpence a yard if it is double woven, as we do have it for the men. The women in this place have little time to be spinning, but the women back on the mountains do be mixing colours through their wool till you'd never ask to take your eyes from it. They do be throwing in a bit of stone colour, and a bit of red madder, and a bit of crimson, and a bit of stone colour again, and, believe me, it is nice stuffs they do make that you'd never ask to take your eyes from.'

The shower had now blown off, so we went out again and made our way down to a cove of the sea where a seal was diving at some distance from the shore, putting up its head every few minutes to look at us with a curiously human expression. Afterwards we went on to a jetty north of the town, where the Sligo boat had just come in. One of the men told us that they were taking over a hundred harvestmen to Sligo the next morning, where they would take a boat for Glasgow, and that many more would be going during the week. This migratory labour has many unsatisfactory features; yet in the present state of the country it may tend to check the longing for America that comes over those that spend the whole year on one miserable farm.

THE SMALLER PEASANT PROPRIETORS

THE car-drivers that take one round to isolated places in Ireland seem to be the cause of many of the misleading views that chance visitors take up about the country and the real temperament of the people. These men spend a great deal of their time driving a host of inspectors and officials connected with various Government Boards, who, although they often do excellent work, belong for the most part to classes that have a traditional misconception of the country people. It follows naturally enough that the carmen pick up the views of their patrons, and when they have done so they soon find apt instances from their own local knowledge that give a native popular air to opinions that are essentially foreign. That is not all. The car-driver is usually the only countryman with whom the official is kept in close personal contact; so that, while the stranger is bewildered, many distinguished authorities have been pleased and instructed by this version of their own convictions. It is fair to add that the carman is usually a small-town's man, so that he has a not unnatural grudge against the mountain squatter, for whom so much has apparently been done, while the towns are neglected, and also that the carman may be generally relied on when he is merely stating facts to anyone who is not a total stranger to the country.

We drove out recently with a man of this class, and as we left Belmullet he began to talk of an estate that has been sold to the tenants by the Congested Districts Board.

'Those people pay one or two pounds in the year,' he said, 'and for that they have a house, and a stripe of tilled land, and a stripe of rough land, and an outlet on the mountain for grazing cattle, and the rights of turbary, and yet they aren't satisfied; while I do pay five pounds for a little house with hardly enough land to grow two score of cabbages.'

He was an elderly man, and as we drove on through many gangs of relief workers he told us about the building of the Belmullet Workhouse in 1857, and I asked him what he remembered or had heard of the great famine ten years earlier.

'I have heard my father say,' he said, 'that he often seen the people dragging themselves along to the workhouse in Binghamstown, and some of them falling down and dying on the edge of the road. There were other places where he'd seen four or five corpses piled up on each other against a bit of a bank or the butt of a bridge, and when I began driving I was in great dread in the evenings when I'd be passing those places on the roads.'

It was a dark, windy day, and we went on through endless wastes of brown mountain and bog, meeting no one but an occasional woman driving an ass with meal or flour, or a few people drying turf and building it up into ricks on the roadside or near it. In the distance one could see white roads—often relief roads—twisting among the hills, with no one on them but a man here and there riding in with the mails from some forlorn village. In places we could see the white walls and gables of one of these villages against the face of a hill, and fairly frequently we passed a few tumbled-down cottages with plots of potatoes about them. After a while the carman stopped at a door to get a drink for his horse, and we went in for a moment or two to shelter from the wind. It was the poorest cottage we had seen. There was no chimney, and the smoke rose by the wall to a hole in the roof at the top of the gable. A boy of ten was sitting near the fire minding three babies, and at the other end of the room there was a cow with two calves and a few sickly-looking hens. The air was so filled with turf-smoke that we went out again in a moment into the open air. As we were standing about we heard the carman ask the boy why he was not at school.

'I'm spreading turf this day,' he said, 'and my brother is at school. To-morrow he'll stay at home, and it will be my turn to go.'

Then an old man came up and spoke of the harm the new potato crop is getting from the high wind, as indeed we had seen ourselves in several fields that we had passed, where whole lines of the tops were broken and withered.

'There was a storm like this three weeks ago,' he said, 'and I could hardly keep my old bonnet on me going round through the hills. This storm is as bad, or near it, and wherever there are loops and eddies in the wind you can see the tops all fluttered and destroyed, so that I'm thinking another windy day will leave us as badly off as we were last year.'

It seems that about here the damage of the sea-winds, where there is no shelter, does as much or more harm than the blight itself.

Still the blight is always a danger, and for several years past the people have been spraying their crops, with sufficiently good results to make them all anxious to try it. Even an old woman who could not afford to get one of the machines used for this purpose was seen out in her field a season or two ago with a bucketful of the solution, spraying her potatoes with an old broom—an instance which shows how eager the people are to adopt any improved methods that can be shown to be of real value. This took place in the neighbourhood of Aghoos—the place we were driving to—where an estate has been bought by the Congested Districts Board and resold to the tenants. The holdings are so small that the rents are usually about three pounds a year, though in some cases they are much less, and it is easily seen that the people must remain for a while at least as poor, or nearly as poor as they have been in the past. In barren places of this kind the enlarging of the holdings is a matter of the greatest difficulty, as good land is not to be had in the neighbourhood; and it is hard to induce even a few families to migrate to another place where holdings could be provided for them, while their absence would liberate part of the land in a district that is overcrowded. At present most of the holdings have, besides their tilled land, a stripe of rough bog-land, which is to be gradually reclaimed; but even when this is done the holdings will remain poor and small, and if a bad season comes the people may be again in need of relief. Still no one can deny the good that is done by making the tenants masters of their own ground and consolidating their holdings, and when the old fear of improvements, caused by the landlord system, is thoroughly forgotten, something may be done.

A great deal has been said of the curse of the absentee landlord; but in reality the small landlord, who lived on his property, and knew how much money every tenant possessed, was a far greater evil. The judicial rent system was not a great deal better, as when the term came to an end the careless tenant had his rent lowered, while the man who had improved his holding remained as he was—a fact which, of course, meant much more than the absolute value of the money lost. For one reason or another, the reduction of rents has come to be, in the tenants' view, the all-important matter; so that this system kept down the level of comfort, as every tenant was anxious to appear as poor as possible for fear of giving the landlord an advantage. These matters are well known; but at the present time the state of suspended land-purchase is tending to reproduce the same fear in a new form, and any tenants who have not bought out are naturally afraid to increase the price they may have to pay by improving their land. In this district, however, there is no fear of this kind, and a good many small grants have been given by the Board for rebuilding cottages and other improvements. A new cottage can be built by the occupier himself for a sum of about thirty pounds, of which the Board pays only a small part, while the cottages built by the Board on their own plan, with slated roofs on them, cost double, or more than double, as much. We went into one of the reslated cottages with concrete floors, and it was curious to see that, however awkward the building looked from the outside, in the kitchen itself the stain of the turf-smoke and the old pot-ovens and stools made the place seem natural and local. That at least was reassuring.

ERRIS

In the poorest districts of Connemara the people live, as I have already pointed out, by various industries, such as fishing, turf-cutting, and kelp-making, which are independent of their farms, and are so precarious that many families are only kept from pauperism by the money that is sent home to them by daughters or sisters who are now servant-girls in New York. Here in the congested districts of Mayo the land is still utterly insufficient—held at least in small plots, as it is now—as a means of life, and the people get the more considerable part of their funds by their work on the English or Scotch harvest, to which I have alluded before. A few days ago a special steamer went from Achill Island to Glasgow with five hundred of these labourers, most of them girls and young boys. From Glasgow they spread through the country in small bands and work together under a ganger, picking potatoes or weeding turnips, and sleeping for the most part in barns and outhouses. Their wages vary from a shilling a day to perhaps double as much in places where there is more demand for their work. The men go more often to the north of England, and usually work together, where it is possible, on small contracts for piecework arranged by one of themselves until the hay harvest begins, when they work by the day. In both cases they get fairly good wages, so that if they are careful and stay for some months they can bring back eight or nine pounds with them.

This morning people were passing through the town square of Belmullet—where our windows look out—towards the steamer, from two o'clock, in small bands of boys and girls, many of them carrying their boots under their arms and walking in bare feet, a fashion to which they are more used. Last night also, on our way back from a village that is largely inhabited by harvest people, we saw many similar bands hurrying in towards the town, as the steamer was to sail soon after dawn. This part of the coast is cut into by a great number of shallow tidal estuaries which are dry at low tide, while at full tide one sees many small roads that seem to run down aimlessly into the sea, till one notices, perhaps half a mile away, a similar road running down on the opposite headland. On our way, as the tide was out, we passed one of these sandy fords where there were a number of girls gathering cockles, and drove into Geesala, where we left our car and walked on to the villages of Dooyork, which lie on a sort of headland cut off on the south by another long estuary. It is in places like this, where there is no thoroughfare in any direction to bring strangers to the country, that one meets with the most individual local life. There are two villages of Dooyork, an upper and lower, and as soon as we got into the first every doorway was filled with women and children looking after us with astonishment. All the houses were quite untouched by improvements, and a few of them were broken-down hovels of the worst kind. On the road there were several women bringing in turf or seaweed on horses with large panniers slung over a straw straddle, on which usually a baby of two or three years old was riding with delight. At the end of the village we talked to a man who had been in America, and before that had often gone to England as a harvestman.

'Some of the men get a nice bit of money,' he said, 'but it is hard work. They begin at three in the morning, and they work on till ten at night. A man will sometimes get twelve shillings an acre for hoeing turnips, and a skilful man will do an acre or the better part of it in one day; but I'm telling you it is hard work, and before the day is done a man will be hard set to know if it's the soil or the turnips he's striking down on.'

I asked him where and how they lodged.

'Ah,' he said, 'don't ask me to speak to you of that, for the lodging is poor, surely.'

We went on then to the next village, a still more primitive and curious one. The houses were built close together, with passages between them, and low, square yards marked round with stones. At one corner we came on a group of dark brown asses with panniers, and women standing among them in red dresses, with white or coloured handkerchiefs over their heads; and the whole scene had a strangely foreign, almost Eastern, look, though in its own way it was peculiarly characteristic of Ireland. Afterwards we went back to Geesala, along the edge of the sea. This district has, unexpectedly enough, a strong branch of the Gaelic League, and small Irish plays are acted frequently in the winter, while there is also an Agricultural Co-operative Bank, which has done excellent work. These banks, on the Raiffeisen system, have been promoted in Ireland for the last nine or ten years by the Irish Agricultural Society, with aid from the Congested Districts Board, and in a small way they have done much good, and shown—to those who wished to question it—the business intelligence of the smallest tenant-farmers. The interest made by these local associations tends to check emigration, but in this district the distress of last year has had a bad effect. In the last few months a certain number of men have sold out the tenant-right of their holdings—usually to the local shopkeeper, to whom they are always in debt—and shipped themselves and their whole families to America with what remained of the money. This is probably the worst kind of emigration, and one fears the suffering of these families, who are suddenly moved to such different surroundings, must be great.

This district of the Erris Union, which we have now been through, is the poorest in the whole of Ireland, and during the last few months six or seven hundred people have been engaged on the relief works. Still, putting aside exceptionally bad years, there is certainly a tendency towards improvement. The steamer from Sligo, which has only been running for a few years, has done much good by bringing in flour and meal much more cheaply than could be done formerly. Typhus is less frequent than it used to be, probably because the houses and holdings are improving gradually, and we have heard it said that the work done in Aghoos by the fund raised by the *Manchester Guardian* some years ago was the beginning of this better state of things. The relief system, as it is now carried on, is an utterly degrading one, and many things will have to be done before the district is in anything like a satisfactory state. Yet the impression one gets of the whole life is not a gloomy one. Last night was St. John's Eve, and bonfires—a relic of Druidical rites—were lighted all over the country, the largest of all being placed in the town square of Belmullet, where a crowd of small boys shrieked and cheered and threw up firebrands for hours together. To-day, again, there was a large market in the square, where a number of country people, with their horses and donkeys, stood about bargaining for young pigs, heather brooms, homespun flannels, second-hand clothing, blacking-brushes, tinkers' goods and many other articles. Once when I looked out, the blacking-brush man and the card-trick man were getting up a fight in the corner of the square. A little later there was another stir, and I saw a Chinaman wandering about, followed by a wondering crowd. The sea in Erris, as in Connemara, and the continual arrival of islanders and boatmen from various directions, tend to keep up an interest and movement that is felt even far away in the villages among the hills.

THE INNER LANDS OF MAYO

THE VILLAGE SHOP

THERE is a curious change in the appearance of the country when one moves inland from the coast districts of Mayo to the congested portion of the inner edge of the country. In this place there are no longer the Erris tracts of bog or the tracts of stone of Connemara; but one sees everywhere low hills and small farms of poor land that is half turf-bog, already much cut away, and half narrow plots of grass or tillage. Here and there one meets with little villages, built on the old system, with cottages closely grouped together and filled with primitive people, the women mostly in bare feet, with white handkerchiefs over their heads. On the whole, however, one soon feels that this neighbourhood is far less destitute than those we have been in hitherto. Turning out of Swinford, soon after our arrival, we were met almost at once by a country funeral coming towards the town, with a large crowd, mostly of women, walking after it. The coffin was tied on one side of an outside car, and two old women, probably the chief mourners, were sitting on the other side. In the crowd itself we could see a few men leading horses or bicycles, and several young women who seemed by their dress to be returned Americans. When the funeral was out of sight we walked on for a few miles, and then turned into one of the wayside public-houses, at the same time general shop and bar, which are a peculiar feature of most of the country parts of Ireland. An old one-eyed man, with a sky-blue handkerchief round his neck, was standing at the counter making up his bill with the publican, and disputing loudly over it. Here, as in most of the congested districts, the shops are run on a vague system of credit that is not satisfactory, though one does not see at once what other method could be found to take its place. After the sale of whatever the summer season has produced—pigs, cattle, kelp, etc.—the bills are paid off, more or less fully, and all the ready money of a family is thus run away with. Then about Christmas time a new bill is begun, which runs on till the following autumn—or later in the harvesting districts—and quite small shopkeepers often put out relatively large sums in this way. The people keep no passbooks, so they have no check on the traders, and although direct fraud is probably rare it is likely that the prices charged are often exorbitant. What is worse, the shopkeeper in out-of-the-way places is usually the only buyer to be had for a number of home products, such as eggs, chickens, carragheen moss, and sometimes even kelp; so that he can control the prices both of what he buys and what he sells, while as a creditor he has an authority that makes bargaining impossible: another of the many complicated causes that keep the people near to pauperism! Meanwhile the old man's bill was made out, and the publican came to serve us. While he did so the old man spoke to us about the funeral, and I asked him about the returned Americans we had seen going after it.

'All the girls in this place,' he said, 'are going out to America when they are about seventeen years old. Then they work there for six years or more, till they do grow weary of that fixed kind of life, with the early rising and the working late, and then they do come home with a little stocking of fortune with them, and they do be tempting the boys with their chains and their rings, till they get a husband and settle down in this place. Such a lot of them is coming now there is hardly a marriage made in the place that the woman hasn't been in America.'

I asked a woman who had come in for a moment if she thought the girls kept their health in America.

'Many of them don't,' she said, 'working in factories with dirty air; and then you have likely seen that the girls in this place is big, stout people, and when they get over beyond they think they should be in the fashions, and they begin squeezing themselves in till you hear them gasping for breath, and that 's no healthy way to be living.'

When we offered the old man a drink a moment later, he asked for twopenny ale.

'This is the only place in Ireland,' he said, 'where you'll see people drinking ale, for it is from this place that the greatest multitudes go harvesting to England—it 's the only way they can live—and they bring the taste for ale back along with them. You'll see a power of them that come home at Michaelmas or Martinmas itself that will never do a hand's turn the rest of the year; but they will be sitting around in each other's houses playing cards through the night, and a barrel of ale set up among them.'

A VILLAGE SHOP

MARKET-DAY

I asked him if he could tell about how many went from Swinford and the country round in each year.

'Well,' he said, 'you'd never reckon them, but I've heard people to say that there are six thousand or near it. Trains full of them do be running every week to the city of Dublin for the Liverpool boat, and I'm telling you it's many are hard set to get a seat in them at all. Then if the weather is too good beyond and the hay is near saved of itself, there is some that get little to do; but if the Lord God sends showers and rain there is work and plenty, and a power of money to be made.'

While he was talking some men who were driving cattle from a fair came in and sat about in the shop, drinking neat glasses of whisky. They called for their drinks so rapidly that the publican called in a little barefooted girl in a green dress, who stood on a box beside a porter barrel rinsing glasses while he served the men. They all appeared to know the old man with one eye, and they talked to him about some job he had been doing on the relief works in this district. Then they made him tell a story for us of a morning when he had killed three wild ducks 'with one skelp of a little gun he had,' and the man who was sitting on a barrel at my side told me that the old man had been the best shot in the place till he got too fond of porter, and had had his gun and licence taken from him because he was shooting wild over the roads. Afterwards they began to make fun of him because his wife had run away from him and gone over the water, and he began to lose his temper. On our way back an old man who was driving an ass with heavy panniers of turf told us that all the turf of this district will be cut away in the next twenty years, and the people will be left without fuel. This is taking place in many parts of Ireland, and unless the Department of Agriculture, or the Congested Districts Board, can take steps to provide plantations for these districts there may be considerable suffering, as it is not likely that the people even then will be able to buy coal. Something has been done and a great deal has been said on the subject of growing timber in Ireland, but so far there has been little result. An attempt was made to establish an extensive plantation near Carna, in Connemara, first by the Irish Government in 1890, and then by the Congested Districts Board since 1902; but the work has been a complete failure. Efforts have been made on a smaller scale to encourage planting among the people, but I have not seen much good come from them. Some turf tracts in Ireland are still of great extent, but they are not inexhaustible, and even if turf has to be brought from them, in a few years, to cottagers great distances away, the cost of it will be a serious and additional hardship for the people of many poor localities.

THE SMALL TOWN

MANY of the smaller towns of the west and south of Ireland—the towns chiefly that are in or near the congested districts—have a peculiar character. If one goes into Swinford or Charlestown, for instance, one sees a large dirty street strewn in every direction with loose stones, paper, and straw, and edged on both sides by a long line of deserted-looking shops, with a few asses with panniers of turf standing about in front of them. These buildings are mostly two or three storeys high, with smooth slate roofs, and they show little trace of the older sort of construction that was common in Ireland, although there are often a few tiny and miserable cottages at the ends of the town that have been left standing from an older period. Nearly all towns of this class are merely trading centres kept up by the country people that live round them, and they usually stand where several main roads come together from large, out-of-the-way districts. In Swinford, which may be taken as a good example of these market towns, there are seven roads leading into the country, and it is likely that a fair was started here at first, and that the town as it is now grew up afterwards. Although there is at present a population of something over 1,300 people, and a considerable trade, the place is still too small to have much genuine life, and the streets look empty and miserable till a market-day arrives. Then, early in the morning, old men and women, with a few younger women of about thirty who have been in America, crowd into the town and range themselves with their asses and carts at both sides of the road, among the piles of goods which the shopkeepers spread out before their doors.

The life and peculiarities of the neighbourhood—the harvesting and the potato blight, for instance—are made curiously apparent by the selection of these articles. Over nearly every shop door we could see, as we wandered through the town, two scythe-blades fixed at right angles over the doorways, with the points and edges uppermost, and in the street below them there were numbers of hay-rakes standing in barrels, scythe-handles, scythe-blades bound in straw rope, reaping-hooks, scythe-stones, and other things of the kind. In a smith's forge at the end of the town we found a smith

A SMALL TOWN

fixing blades and hand-grips to scythe-blades for a crowd of men who stood round him with the blades and handles, which they had bought elsewhere, ready in their hands. In front of many shops also one could see old farmers bargaining eagerly for second-hand spraying machines, or buying supplies of the blue sulphate of copper that was displayed in open sacks all down the street. In other places large packing-cases were set up, with small trunks on top of them, and pasted over with advertisements of various Atlantic lines that are used by emigrants, and large pictures of the *Oceanic* and other vessels. Inside many of the shops and in the windows one could see an extraordinary collection of objects—saddles, fiddles, rosaries, rat-traps, the Shorter Catechism, castor-oil, rings, razors, rhyme-books, fashion plates, nit-killer, and fine-tooth combs. Other houses had the more usual articles of farm and household use, but nearly all of them, even drapers' establishments, with stays and ribbons in the windows, had a licensed bar at the end, where one could see a few old men or women drinking whisky or beer. In the streets themselves there was a pig-market going on at the upper end of the town near the court-house, and in another place a sale of barrels and churns, made apparently by a local cooper, and also of many-sided wooden bowls, pig-troughs, and the wooden bars and pegs that are used on donkeys' saddles to carry the panniers. Further down there were a number of new panniers set out, with long bundles of willow boughs set up beside them, and offered for sale by old women and children. As the day went on six or seven old-clothes brokers did a noisy trade from three large booths set up in the street. A few of the things sold were new, but most of them were more or less worn out, and the sale was carried on as a sort of auction, an old man holding up each article in turn and asking first, perhaps, two shillings for a greasy blouse, then cutting away the price to sixpence or even four-pence-halfpenny. Near the booths a number of strolling singers and acrobats were lounging about, and starting off now and then to sing or do contortions in some part of the town. A couple of these men began to give a performance near a booth where we were listening to the bargaining and the fantastic talk of the brokers. First one of them, in a yellow and green jersey, stood on his hands and did a few feats; then he went round with his hat and sold ballads, while the other man sang a song to a banjo about a girl:

. . . whose name it was, I don't know,
And she passed her life in a barber's shop
Making wigs out of sawdust and snow.

Not far away another man set up a stall, with tremendous shouting, to sell some little packets, and we could hear him calling out, 'There's envelopes, notepaper, a pair of boot-laces, and corn-cure for one penny. Take notice, gentlemen.'

All the time the braying of the asses that were standing about the town was incessant and extraordinarily noisy, as sometimes four or five of them took it up at the same time. Many of these asses were of a long-legged, gawky type, quite unusual in this country, and due, we were told, to a Spanish ass sent here by the Congested Districts Board to improve the breed. It is unfortunate that most attempts to improve the livestock of Ireland have been made by some off-hand introduction of a foreign type which often turns out little suited to the new conditions it is brought to, instead of by the slower and less exciting method of improving the different types by selection from the local breeds. We have heard a great deal in passing through Connemara of the harm that has been done by injudicious 'improving' of the ponies and horses, and while it is probable that some of the objections made to the new types may be due to local prejudice, it should not be forgotten that the small farmer is not a fool, and that he knows perfectly well when he has an animal that is suited to his needs.

Towards evening, when the market was beginning to break up, an outside car drove through the town, laden on one side with an immense American trunk belonging to a woman who had just come home after the usual period of six years that she had spent making her fortune. A man at a shop door who saw it passing began to talk about his own time in New York, and told us how often he had had to go down to Coney Island at night to 'recoup' himself after the heat of the day. It is not too much to say that one can hardly spend an hour in one of these Mayo crowds without being reminded in some way of the drain of people that has been and is still running from Ireland. It is, however, satisfactory to note that in this neighbourhood and west of it, on the Dillon estate, which has been bought out and sold to the tenants by the Congested Districts Board, there is a current of returning people that may do much good. A day or two ago we happened to ask for tea in a cottage which was occupied by a woman in a new American blouse, who had unmistakably come home recently from the States. Her cottage was perfectly clean and yet had lost none of the peculiar local character of these cottages. Almost the only difference that one could point to was a large photograph of the head of the Sistine Madonna, hanging over the fire in the little room where we sat, instead of the hideous German oleographs on religious subjects that are brought round by pedlars, and bought by most of the simpler Irish women for the sake of the subjects they represent.

POSSIBLE REMEDIES

It is not easy to improve the state of the people in the congested districts by any particular remedy or set of remedies. As we have seen, these people are dependent for their livelihood on various industries, such as fishing, kelp-making, turf-cutting, or harvesting in England; and yet the failure of a few small plots of potatoes brings them literally to a state of famine. Near Belmullet, during a day of storm, we saw the crop for next year in danger of utter ruin, and if the weather had not changed, by good luck, before much harm was done, the whole demoralizing and wretched business of the relief works would have had to be taken up again in a few months. It is obvious that the earnings of the people should be large enough to make them more or less independent of one particular crop, and yet, in reality, it is not easy to bring about such a state of things; for the moment a man earns a few extra pounds in a year he finds many good and bad ways of spending them, so that when a quarter of his income is cut away unexpectedly once in seven or eight years he is as badly off as before. To make the matter worse, the pig trade—which is often relied on to bring in the rent-money—is, as I have shown, dependent on the potatoes, so that a bad potato season means a dearth of food, as well as a business difficulty which may have many consequences. It is possible that by giving more attention to the supply of new seed potatoes and good manure—something in this direction is being done by the co-operative societies—the failure of the crop may be made less frequent. Yet there is little prospect of getting rid of the danger altogether, and as long as it continues the people will have many hardships.

The most one can do for the moment is to improve their condition and solvency in other ways, and for this purpose extended purchase on the lines adopted by the Congested Districts Board seems absolutely necessary. This will need more funds than the Board has now at its disposal, and probably some quicker mode of work. Perhaps in places where relief has to be given some force may have to be brought to bear on landlords who refuse to sell at fair terms. No amount of purchase in the poorer places will make the people prosperous—even if the holdings are considerably enlarged—yet there is no sort of doubt that in all the estates which the Board has arranged and sold to the tenants there has been a steady tendency towards improvement. A good deal may be done also by improved communications, either by railroad or by sea, to make life easier for the people. For instance, before the steamer was put on a few years ago between Sligo and Belmullet, the cost of bringing a ton of meal or flour by road from Ballina to Belmullet was one pound, and one can easily estimate the consequent dearness of food. That is perhaps an extreme case, yet there are still a good many places where things are almost as bad, and in these places the people suffer doubly, as they are usually in the hands of one or two small shopkeepers, who can dictate the price of eggs and other small articles which they bring in to sell. At present a steamer running between Westport and Belmullet, in addition to the Sligo boat, is badly needed, and would probably do a great deal of good more cheaply than the same service could be done by a line of railway. If the communications to the poorest districts could be once made fairly satisfactory it would be much easier for the Congested Districts Board, or some similar body, to encourage the local industries of the people and to enable them to get the full market value for what they produce.

The cottage industries that have been introduced or encouraged by the Board—lace-making, knitting, and the like—have done something; yet at best they are a small affair. In a few places the fishing industry has been most successfully developed, but in others it has practically failed, and led to a good deal of disappointment and wasted energy. In all these works it needs care and tact to induce the people to undertake new methods of work; but the talk sometimes heard of sloth and ignorance has not much foundation. The people have traditional views and instincts about agriculture and live stock, and they have a perfectly natural slowness to adopt the advice of an official expert who knows nothing of the peculiar conditions of their native place. The advice is often excellent, but there have been a sufficient number of failures in the work done by the Congested Districts Board, such as the attempt at forestry in Carna and the bad results got on certain of their example plots laid out to demonstrate the best methods of farming, to make the conservatism of the people a sign of, perhaps, valuable prudence. The Board and the Department of Agriculture and

Technical Education have done much excellent work, and it is not to be expected that improvements of this kind, which must be largely experimental, can be carried on without failures; yet one does not always pardon a sort of contempt for the local views of the people which seems rooted in nearly all the official workers one meets with through the country.

One of the chief problems that one has to deal with in Ireland is, of course, the emigration that I have mentioned so often. It is probably the most complicated of all Irish affairs, and in dealing with it it is important to remember that the whole moral and economic condition of Ireland has been brought into a diseased state by prolonged misgovernment and many misfortunes, so that at the present time normal remedies produce abnormal results. For instance, if it is observed in some neighbourhood that some girls are going to America because they have no work at home, and a lace school is started to help them, it too often happens that the girls merely use it as a means of earning money enough to pay for their passage and outfit, and the evil is apparently increased. Further, it should not be forgotten that emigrants are going out at the present time for quite opposite reasons. In the poorest districts of all they go reluctantly, because they are unable to keep themselves at home; but in places where there has been much improvement the younger and brighter men and girls get ambitions which they cannot satisfy in this country, and so they go also. Again, where there is no local life or amusements they go because they are dull, and when amusements and races are introduced they get the taste for amusements and go because they cannot get enough of them. They go as much from districts where the political life has been allowed to stagnate as from districts where there has been an excess of agitation that has ended only in disappointment. For the present the Gaelic League is probably doing more than any other movement to check this terrible evil, and yet one fears that when the people realize in five, or perhaps in ten, years that this hope of restoring a lost language is a vain one the last result will be a new kind of hopelessness and many crowded ships leaving Queenstown and Galway. Happily in some places there is a counter-current of people returning from America. Yet they are not very numerous, and one feels that the only real remedy for emigration is the restoration of some national life to the people. It is this conviction that makes most Irish politicians scorn all merely economic or

CHIEF PROBLEM

agricultural reforms, for if Home Rule would not of itself make a national life it would do more to make such a life possible than half a million creameries. With renewed life in the country many changes of the methods of government, and the holding of property, would inevitably take place, which would all tend to make life less difficult even in bad years and in the worst districts of Mayo and Connemara.

PART FOUR

ABOUT LITERATURE

VARIOUS NOTES[1]

(*a*) ALL theorizing is bad for the artist, because it makes him live in the intelligence instead of in the half sub-conscious faculties by which all real creation is performed. This is one reason why hostile criticism is harmful to an artist, because it forces him to construct systems and defend and explain his own work. . . .

Young and therefore fresh and living truths, views, what you will, have a certain diffidence or tenderness that makes it impossible to state them without the accompanying emotional or imaginative life in which they naturally arise. That is, they are stated in the arts; when they are dead only, the flesh is cleared away and the naked skeletons are shown by essayists and metaphysicians.

(*b*) [2]No one is less fond of theories and divisions in the arts than I am, and yet they cannot altogether be gone without. In these matters we need not expect to say anything very new but in applying for ourselves to our own life what is thought in different ways by many we [are] likely to hit on matters of some value. For a long time I have felt that Poetry roughly is of two kinds, the poetry of real life—the poetry of Burns and Shakespeare [and] Villon, and the poetry of a land of the fancy—the poetry of Spenser and Keats and Ronsard. That is obvious enough, but what is highest in poetry is always reached where the dreamer is leaning out to reality, or where the man of real life is lifted out of it, and in all the poets the greatest have both these elements, that is they are supremely engrossed with life, and yet with the wildness of their fancy they are always passing out of what is simple and plain. Such is the case with Dante and Chaucer and Goethe

[1] The sources of these various notes are as follows: (*a*), (*c*), (*d*), (*h*), (*i*), (*j*), written in 1908, Notebook 42; (*b*), written in 1908, Notebook 47; (*e*), probably written in 1898, Notebook 20; (*f*), Notebook 17; and (*g*), Notebook 15, probably written 1895–8. Notes (*a*), (*b*), (*c*), (*d*), (*h*), (*i*), and (*j*) were first published as 'Extracts from Note Books of J. M. Synge' in the Introduction (pp. ii–vi) to *Plays* by John M. Synge, Allen & Unwin, London, 1932.

[2] Punctuation and three words have been added to assist understanding. A version with four slight differences of interpretation of Synge's handwriting—'done' for 'gone', 'fairy' for 'fancy', 'Molay' for 'Malory', and 'became' for 'becomes'—is printed in the Oxford Synge *Poems*, pp. xiv–xv.

and Shakespeare. In Ireland Mr. Yeats, one of the poets of the fancy land, has interests in the world and for this reason his poetry has had a lifetime in itself,[1] but A.E., on the other hand, who is of the fancy land only, ended his career in poetry in his first volume.

It would be easy to carry this division a long way, to compare the romances of the Arthurian style with the modern realistic novel, Gottfried of Strasburg and Malory become real here and there . . . [suddenly] a real voice seems to speak out of their golden and burning words . . . and they are then extraordinarily powerful. So, on the other hand, it is only with Huysmans that the realistic becomes of interest.

(*c*) The shopman says that a work of art is not artistic if it is unwholesome, which is foolish; the fashionable critic says that it is absurd to say a work of art is unwholesome if it is good art, which

[1] Synge recorded few of his impressions of Yeats. Sometimes he was flippant: 'Yeats and I have been running the show [the Abbey]; Yeats looks after the stars, and I do the rest', and he tells MacKenna not to send 'MS. to Yeats and A.E. as what one likes the other hates' (letter to MacKenna, 23 February 1908); but he knows that basically he and Yeats are on the same side and after censuring someone for being too refined to share their enthusiasms or to join their movement and for admiring 'the drivel of George Moore', he ends, 'it is better to rave after the sun and moon as Yeats does than to be as sane as' [a pedant] (letter to MacKenna, June 1904). Believing that theorizing is bad for the artist, Synge did not presume to offer advice except to hint that MacKenna might be a bit more fastidious in his use of adjectives: 'your children are too often "little children", and their brothers "little brothers" —such adjectives are well enough in one sentence but they make one's stuff soft if too frequent' (letter to MacKenna, 23 February 1908). But when his help was earnestly sought by a young writer Synge supplied perceptive criticism. At a time when he was feeling very ill and striving to finish *Deirdre*, Synge wrote the following on 31 January 1909, only two days before he entered the Elpis Nursing Home, where he died on 24 March 1909:

'Dear Mr Nolan

'I am very unwell at the present time so I am unable to write to you as fully as I would wish about the poem you sent me the other day.

'I think there *is* something in it, and that you have certainly a capacity for verse-writing. It is likely that plenty of men who afterwards made themselves a place, of one kind or other in letters began with work not unlike yours —but also there are thousands who have begun with work like yours and got no further.

'You say something in your letter about abandoning the "ploughshare", and perhaps you will permit me to make a remark on it. I do *not* think it possible to be a fashionable doctor and a literary man at the same time, but I think it should be—and *is*—perfectly possible to combine some other study with that of letters, so that if a man finds, when he is thirty, that he cannot do anything worth doing in literature, he may have something else to do that is worth doing, instead of becoming a mere wreck and waster.

'I meant to criticise "Blumine" at length, but that is beyond me. It is unequal, as you say, and all, of course, very uncertain in its note. One moment you are Spenserian, then say Byronic, and then Wordsworthian. Some of your lines are not quite grammatically or verbally accurate and do not quite say what they ought—at least that was my impression when I read you. I don't think your story is a very good one in itself, or very well told—there is too much description and your characters are not alive enough. All these faults are *inevitable* in inexperienced work.

'When I am better again I will be always glad to give you any advice that I can.'

is foolish also. There are beautiful and interesting plants which are deadly, and others that are kindly. It is absurd to say a flower is not beautiful nor admire its beauty because it is deadly, but it is absurd also to deny its deadliness.

(*d*) Humour is the test of morals, as no vice is humorous. Bestial is in its very essence opposed to the idea of humour. . . . All decadence is opposed to true humour. The heartiness of real and frank laughter is a sign that cannot be mistaken that what we laugh [at] is not out of harmony with that instinct of sanity that we call so many names.

(*e*) Goethe's weakness [is] due to his having no national and intellectual mood to interpret. The individual mood is often trivial, perverse, fleeting, [but the] national mood [is] broad, serious, provisionally permanent. Three distinctions [are] to be sought: each work of art must have been possible to only one man at one period and in one place. Although only two suffice to give us art of the first importance such as much of the Gothic architecture, folk songs and airs, Dutch paintings, etc., the great artist, as Rembrandt or Shakespeare, adds his personal distinction to a great distinction of time and place.

The profound is always inimitable. This feeling that a work [of] art is unimportant when it could have been [produced by] anyone at any time is inherent in the nature of art and altogether healthy. Things have always a character and characters have always a mood. These moods are as perpetually new, as the sunsets. Profound insight finds the inner and essential mood of the things it treats of and hence gives us art that is absolutely distinct and inimitable—a thing never done before and never to be done again. Tennyson's complaint that all could grow the grain now that all possessed the seed is the proof, if one were needed, of his limitations. Pope also was easy to imitate.

(*f*) The aim of literature is to make the impossible seem inevitable or to make the inevitable seem impossible. . . .

Once men sought in art to make natural things beautiful. Now we seek to make beautiful things natural. Aran 3/11/99.

When the body dies the soul goes to Heaven or Hell. So our modern art is—must be—either divine or satanic. The psychological novel [is] still in its first stage, but our poetry is sophisticated. . . .

The supreme culture of German music and the adolescent stage of German literature show that each art has its own life independent of the life of the people. . . .

[The] American lack of literary sense [is] due to the absence in America of any mother tongue with a tradition for the whole population. . . . Has any bilingual person been great in style?

(*g*) Lyrics can be written by people who are immature, drama cannot. There is little great lyrical poetry. Dramatic literature is relatively more mature. Hence the intellectual maturity of most races is marked by a definite moment of dramatic creation. This is now felt in Ireland. Lyrical art is the art of national adolescence. Dramatic art is first of all a childish art—a reproduction of external experience—without form or philosophy; then after a lyrical interval we have it as mature drama dealing with the deeper truth of general life in a perfect form and with mature philosophy.

(*h*) The *artistic* value of any work of art is measured by its *uniqueness*. Its human value is given largely by its intensity and its richness, for if it is rich it is many-sided or universal, and, for this reason, sane—another word for wholesome—since all insanities are due to a one-sided excitement.

No personal originality is enough to make a rich work unique, unless it has also the characteristic of a particular [time] and locality and the life that is in it. For this reason all historical plays and novels and poems—except a very few that continue the tradition of a country—or like *Faust* and *Don Juan* renew some stock type—are relatively worthless. Every healthy mind is more interested in *Tit-Bits* than in *Idylls of the King*, or any of the other more or less artificial retellings of classical or saga stories. The most that one can claim for work of this kind—such as Keats's *Isabella*—when it is beautiful, is that [it] is made for a Utopia of art.

(*i*) All Utopian work is unsatisfying, first because it [is] weak and therefore vague and therefore wanting in uniqueness, and also because it is only the catastrophes of life that give substance and power to the tragedy and humour which are the two poles of art.

The religious art is a thing of the past only—a vain and foolish regret—and its place has been taken by our quite modern feeling for the beauty and mystery [of] nature, an emotion that has gradually risen up as religion in the dogmatic sense has gradually died. Our pilgrimages are not to Canterbury or Jerusalem, but to Killarney and Cumberland and the Alps. . . .

In my plays and topographical books I have tried to give humanity and this mysterious external world.

(*j*) Man has gradually grown up in this world that is about us, and I think that while Tolstoy is wrong in claiming that art should be intelligible to the peasant, he is right in seeking a criterion for the arts, and I think this is to be found in testing art by its compatibility with the outside world and the peasants or people who live near it. A book, I mean, that one feels ashamed to read in a cottage of Dingle Bay one may fairly call a book that is not healthy—or universal.

LA VIEILLE LITTÉRATURE IRLANDAISE[1]

LA littérature irlandaise se divise en deux parties: la littérature ancienne, écrite en celtique, et la littérature moderne, écrite en anglais par de jeunes écrivains qui ignorent à peu près complètement la langue originaire de leur pays. Ces deux littératures, bien qu'il existe entre elles des liens analogues à ceux qu'on retrouve (si la comparaison m'est permise) entre l'ancien et le nouveau testament, sont tellement différentes qu'il ne m'est pas possible de les traiter en même temps, et malgré l'intérêt, voire même la grande beauté, de quelques-uns de nos ouvrages modernes, c'est la vieille littérature et elle seule qui a une véritable importance européenne.

D'abord cette littérature est vaste. D'après O'Curry, l'un des premiers Irlandais qui ait étudié la question avec un réel sens critique, il existe dans les bibliothèques du collège de la Trinité de Dublin et de l'Académie d'Irlande assez de manuscrits pour exiger, dans le cas où l'on voudrait les publier, près de 60.000 pages in-quarto, imprimées en caractères serrés. Un autre écrivain, M. Douglas Hyde, très connu des folkloristes français, estime que pour imprimer tous les manuscrits qui sont actuellement dans les îles britanniques il faudrait 1.200 volumes in-octavo, ou même davantage.

C'est ce qui nous reste. Et les écrits perdus ? Dans un pays comme l'Irlande qui a souvent eu à souffrir des incursions des Danois, et qui finalement a été conquis par l'Angleterre après des luttes acharnées, l'on peut aisément se figurer qu'un grand nombre de manuscrits ont dû être détruits. Mais on n'est pas réduit aux suppositions. Ainsi dans l'histoire de Keating, qui écrivait au commencement du XVIIe siècle, on trouve des citations de plusieurs grands ouvrages qui n'existent plus et il faut se rappeler que dans l'ancienne Irlande chacun de ces gros livres constituait une petite bibliothèque. Duald MacFirbis, soixante ans plus tard, fit un catalogue de la littérature de son temps, et bien que le catalogue lui-même soit perdu, nous savons, par une phrase d'un autre ouvrage, qu'il fallait un grand livre pour faire une simple énumération des noms des auteurs et des titres de leurs ouvrages. Mais c'est

[1] An article in *L'Européen* of 15 March 1902.

surtout une liste dressée par O'Curry qui est intéressante à ce point de vue. Il a trouvé des allusions à plus de vingt recueils importants qui existaient avant l'an 1100. Or, comme on a écrit en irlandais jusqu'au XVIIe siècle, combien de pages précieuses ont dû disparaître sans laisser aucune trace!

Des manuscrits qui nous restent, les plus importants sont: le *Livre de la Vache brune*, le *livre de Leinster*, le *Livre Tacheté*, le *Livre Jaune de Lecain*, tous de grands recueils de littérature faits, on croit, à l'usage des princes ou des rois d'Irlande. On a souvent remarqué je ne sais quoi de charmant qui se dégage des seuls titres de ces livres séculaires.

Quand on se met à déchiffrer leurs pages vermoulues, on est étonné par la variété des matières. On y trouve de l'histoire, telles les *Annales des Quatre Maîtres*, des traités sur les lois primitives, dites les Lois des Bretons, puis des légendes épiques de toutes sortes, des narrations de bataille, des sièges, des aventures de terre et de mer, des banquets, des visions quasi-mystiques et des histoires d'amour dont la plupart sont tragiques. Ensuite on tombe sur des généalogies sans fin, entremêlées de traités topographiques qui cèdent la place, à leur tour, à des vies de saints, sans oublier une grande quantité de poésies, en vers compliqués, construits avec des assonances et des allitérations selon des règles extrêmement curieuses.

Tout cela a l'air tant soit peu chaotique, mais quand on se donne la peine de coordonner tous les fragments épiques — qui sont, en somme, la partie la plus intéressante de nos textes — on y trouve, plus ou moins complets, trois cycles qui se distinguent nettement entre eux. Le premier, le cycle mythologique proprement dit, contenant l'histoire des conflits primordiaux entre les hommes et les dieux, peut être considéré, à bien des égards, comme le plus important, quoique le plus obscur. Le deuxième s'occupe des héros Conchobar et Cuchulain — l'Achille de l'Irlande — et c'est ici surtout qu'on trouve des pages d'un grand intérêt littéraire. Plusieurs récits qui y appartiennent, tel que le *Sort des Fils d'Uisneach*, sont tous imprégnés de cette poésie particulièrement celtique qui réunit d'une façon inattendue une tendresse timide, un héroïsme rude et mâle et un amour infini pour les beautés de la nature. Le troisième cycle est consacré aux aventures de Finn et d'Ossian, le poète légendaire si connu en Europe grâce à l'imagination de MacPherson, l'instituteur écossais.

C'est à M. d'Arbois de Jubainville[1] que revient l'honneur d'avoir éclairé par de longs travaux toute cette mythologie irlandaise, et ses *cours de la littérature celtique* sont d'une valeur inestimable pour tous ceux qui voudraient se renseigner sur ce sujet. Cependant, les dures études initiales qui ont rendu ces textes à peu près compréhensibles sont dues surtout aux Allemands. Déjà, en 1853, Zeuss fit époque dans l'histoire des langues celtiques par la publication de sa *Grammatica celtica* et, depuis, Windisch et Zimmer l'ont suivi, faisant paraître de temps en temps des travaux philologiques d'une érudition admirable.

J'ai parlé plus haut de l'importance européenne de la littérature irlandaise et l'expression n'est pas exagérée. Dans nos légendes et dans les cycles dont je viens de parler, on trouve une mythologie qui forme avec la mythologie grecque de la première époque, un noyau de croyances les plus primitives que nous ayons des races indo-européennes. Telle, au moins, est la conclusion de M. Alfred Nutt, dans son essai sur l'idée du *Happy other world* dans la littérature irlandaise. Rien, par exemple, dans la littérature n'est aussi primitif que cette foi commune aux Grecs et Irlandais, foi en un autre monde où les morts continuent une vie semblable à l'existence terrestre sans espoir d'être récompensés pour leurs vertus ni appréhension d'être punis pour leurs méfaits. Dans cette étude de M. Alfred Nutt, étude qui fait suite à un ancien poème, le *Voyage de Bran*, traduit du vieil irlandais par M. Kunro Meyer, plusieurs questions relatives à la religion originaire des races indo-européennes, sont discutées avec soin, et le livre forme un chapitre extrêmement intéressant de la mythologie comparée.

Cette littérature est importante à un autre point de vue encore. La vie, les mœurs et les cultes qu'on y trouve dépeints ne sont autre chose que des phases de la civilisation de toutes les races celtiques de l'ouest de l'Europe au temps des Césars. Ainsi, en reconstituant le monde d'où sont sortis nos textes, on arrive à se former une idée assez nette des anciens Gaulois.

Enfin, pour conclure, je vais citer le poème panthéiste qui, d'après la légende, est le plus ancien poème de l'Irlande. Je me sers de la traduction de M. d'Arbois de Jubainville.

Je suis le vent qui souffle sur la mer,
Je suis la vague de l'océan,

[1] A leading Celtic scholar. Synge attended his lectures at the Sorbonne in 1898 and 1902. He was interested in the Irish cause and was a friend of Maud Gonne.

Je suis le bœuf aux sept combats;
Je suis le vautour sur le rocher;
Je suis une larme du soleil;
Je suis sanglier par la bravoure;
Je suis saumon dans l'eau;
Je suis lac dans la plaine;
Je suis parole de science;
Je suis le point de la lance qui livre les batailles;
Je suis le dieu qui crée ou forme dans la tête (de l'homme)
  le feu (de la pensée).
Qui est-ce qui jette la clarté dans l'assemblée sur la montagne?
  (Ici une glose ajoute: Qui éclaire chaque question sinon moi?)
Qui annonce les âges de la lune? (sinon moi).
Qui enseigne l'endroit où se couche le soleil? (sinon moi).

La date de ce poème et l'époque de la vie d'Amairgen, son auteur présumé, ne sont pas certaines, mais les vers sont assez remarquables en eux-mêmes.

THE POEMS OF GEOFFREY KEATING[1]

THE publication of the *Poems, Songs and Keenes of Geoffrey Keating* is an event of considerable interest in the history of Gaelic literature, for this volume is the first collected edition of the works of a Gaelic poet that has ever been given to the public. We have had anthologies of all kinds and, a few months ago, a book of original poems by Dr. Douglas Hyde, but till now no collected edition of the poems of any Gaelic writer. The existence of good native poetry was admitted, but till the new mood of intellectual patriotism arose in Ireland, there was no body of opinion from which students of the more literary aspect of Gaelic could gain the impulse that is needed for studies of this kind.

Geoffrey Keating, best known as the historian of pagan Ireland, was born in Co. Tipperary about the year 1570. After taking Orders in the Roman Catholic Church of his own country, he studied for several years at a theological college at Bordeaux, became a Doctor of Divinity, and returned to Ireland about 1610.

The second poem in this volume was written during his visit to France, and is a fair instance of the passionate yet fanciful poems written to Ireland from abroad by students and exiles, with a nostalgia so different from the *Heimweh* of Teutonic races. It begins thus:—

My blessing to you my writing,
To the pleasant noble island:
And it is pity I cannot see her hill-tops,
Though usual their red beacons.

A salutation to her nobles and to her clan meetings,
A particular salutation to her clerics,
A salutation to her weeping women,
A salutation to her learned men of poetry.

On his return to Ireland Keating seems to have gained some distinction as a preacher, but before long the rather outspoken morality of one of his sermons offended a lady who was said to be

[1] A review of *Danta Amhrain is Caointe, Sheathruin Ceitinn*, ed. Rev. J. C. MacErlean, S.J., in *The Speaker* of 8 December 1900.

too intimate with Sir George Carew, the president of Munster, and through her influence the Penal Laws were put in force against him. It is likely that it was this period of his life that gave the definitely sombre shade to his disposition that we find in most of his poetry. He was now a man of about forty, with all the scholarship of his century, a remarkable literary talent, and an extraordinary energy, and his physical and moral sufferings while he was thus hunted like a malefactor must have been intense. However, to his large and human, rather than strictly clerical, temperament, the adventure and incident of this episode may not have been without charm, and he seems to have wandered in disguise through the country, collecting materials for his history from the ancient manuscripts which were then scattered through Ireland.

There is a curious half-serious, half-humorous poem, written not improbably about this time, in which he repulses the love of a woman with characteristically direct language. I will give a couple of stanzas:—

Oh woman full of wiles,
Keep away from me thy hand,
I am not a man for these things,
Though thou art sick for my love.

Do not think me perverse,
Do not bend thy head,
Let our love be inactive
Forever, oh slender fairy.

After some time Carew ceased to have power in Munster, and Keating resumed his clerical duties; from which time little is known of him beyond what is found in his own writings.

The poems in this volume—great as is at times their literary interest—cannot be adequately judged without reference to their author, and Keating himself cannot be known without some reference to his elaborate prose works—*The History*, *The Three Shafts of Death*, a dissertation on human life and death somewhat resembling the *Imitation of Christ*, and *The Defence of the Mass*, a work of controversy. An early critic spoke of the history as '*insigne sed tamen insanum opus*', and the phrase is not wholly inappropriate, such is the medley it contains of Irish myth and of Biblical or classical history. Keating himself is not, of course, responsible for this mixture, as he merely transcribed and co-ordinated the stories which he found in the ancient manuscripts—a proceeding which gives his book a high antiquarian value, as most of his sources have since perished. Beyond this, however, the work has many personal traits of considerable interest, which show the shrewd observation, and naïve reasoning that are common to the learned men of his age and the peasants of our own. One might almost say that it is a history written in the spirit of the folktale. Thus when he is dealing with the story of Finntan, who is supposed to have lived in Ireland before the Flood, he says:—

> I do not understand how the historians found the accounts of the people who, they say, came to Ireland before the Flood unless it was the demons of the air—who were their fairy lovers the time that they were pagans—that gave the stories to them . . . for it cannot be said that it was the same Finntan who was living before the Flood that lived after it, for Scripture is against it in saying that no one of mankind escaped drowning except the eight who were in the ark only and it is evident that Finntan was not one of these.

There is another passage which deserves to be famous in which he compares the English writers of his day who dealt with Irish things to beetles that raise up their heads in the evening and fly out over lilies and roses till they find a heap of refuse in places where there are horses and cows and in this they make haste to bury themselves. All through the prose works we find the same large, open mind, rich in illustration both from nature and from his wide reading in the Fathers and in the Latin Classics. By keeping this view of the man before us when we turn to the poems we can correct the impression some of them are likely to give, that Keating, when mature, was the most mournful of men, seeing and brooding over nothing but the misery of Ireland. In his primary temperament he seems to have united a feeling for the humour of life that might have made him, in some circumstances, a disciple of Rabelais, with a piety worthy of St. Thomas à Kempis and it was nothing but the extraordinary desolation of his country that drew from him these poems, which are as stern and unrelieved as the patriotic poems of Leopardi.

The tone of his more serious work differs considerably from the tone of most of the Irish Gaelic poetry that has been printed hitherto. There is neither the note of the folk-poem nor the note of the clear nature-poetry, that sometimes broke through the bardic traditions of the early school. We find rather the expression of a half-mediaeval, half-modern temperament, writing verse when moved by some event in his own, or the national life, but remembering sometimes, when the pen was in his hand, that he was a priest and a scholar, and turning aside to drag in long Biblical allusions, or indulging in the abuse of adjectives that has been the curse of Irish literature. Apart, however, from this uncertainty of attitude, he has given expression to the agony of his country with a sustained personal dignity and a freedom from exaggeration that is thought rare with the Gaels.

AN IRISH HISTORIAN[1]

THIS volume is the fourth published by the Irish Texts Society, and in some ways the most important that they have brought out. It contains the text of the *Dionbhrollach* (breastplate or introduction) of Keating's history, with the first portion of the history itself, edited, with a translation, by Mr. David Comyn, who is already well known for his work in Gaelic literature. The members of the Irish Texts Society intend to publish the remainder of the history in several succeeding volumes, which will then form the first complete edition of this important work, and be of the greatest service to students of Irish literature and history. A considerable portion of Keating's text was edited and translated by Halliday, in 1811, but his work is now hard to procure, and students who have not access to a good library—that is a good number of Irish-speaking students—have had to put up with a chance volume of one of the translations, or with a small part of the history edited by P. W. Joyce, and the introduction, which was edited by Mr. Comyn himself a year or two ago, for the Gaelic League. The present edition will probably become the standard edition of Keating's history—by far his most considerable work—and both the editor and the Irish Texts Society are to be congratulated on their undertaking. The notes to the whole edition are to be published in a final volume, so that it is not yet possible to judge of this important section of the editor's work, but the text appears to have been very carefully edited, and the translation, if not always as pliant to the movement of Keating's language as could be wished, is faithfully and plainly written. It is to be regretted that Mr. Comyn has not given more attention to Keating's biography in his preface, where he brings together a few localities and dates without stating on what authority they are placed. He says, in passing, that a full biography of Keating is still a desideratum, but it may be doubted whether there are materials enough for such a work, and the preface to this edition would have been an excellent place to collect the facts that can be known. In another way the preface, or the tone of the preface, is perhaps open to

[1] A review of *Foras Feasa Ar Eirinn: The History of Ireland* by Geoffrey Keating, ed. David Comyn, in *The Speaker* of 6 September 1902.

criticism. Mr. Comyn, although he writes with caution, is too inclined to treat Keating as a serious historian—he seems to compare Keating's way of dealing with his materials with the way Dr. Liddell deals with early Roman history—instead of taking him frankly as a quaint, half-mediaeval writer with no notion of history in the modern sense of the word. In the later part of Keating's work—with which we are not dealing at present—he has to do with comparatively modern times, and his pages are sometimes of direct historical value, but the early part contained in this volume is chiefly useful for the information it gives about MSS., to which Keating had access, but which have since perished.

In another way, however, this work has historical interest of a high order. All through the introduction, and here and there in the history itself, there are passages which give wonderfully vivid glimpses of the way a learned Irishman at the beginning of the seventeenth century saw Ireland in her relation to England and Europe. Keating differs very considerably from other Irish writers of his time, and he can interpret for us, better than anyone else, a certain attitude of early Irish culture. Apart from his natural talent he owes a good deal to his foreign studies—he passed through a college at Bordeaux after taking Orders in his own country—which gave him a knowledge of the outside prosperity of the world with which to compare the things he saw in Ireland, while in a purely intellectual sense the intercourse he must have had with men who had been in touch with the first scholarship in Europe was of great use in correcting the narrowing influence of a simply Irish tradition. A comparison of the general expression of Keating's work with that of the annalists of his time recalls, in a curiously remote way, the difference that can be felt between the work of Irish writers of the present day who have spent part of their life in London or Paris, and the work of men who have not left Ireland. Keating's originality can be noticed in the freedom and plaintive dignity of his style as fully as in the comparative width of his views. In one place in the introduction he appeals to the reader to believe him rather than the English chroniclers, in this passage, which I translate a little differently from Mr. Comyn, in order to keep closer to Keating's tone:

> I am old, and a number of these people are young. I have seen and I understand the head-books of (Irish) history, and they have not seen them, and if they had seen them they would not have understood any-

thing. It was not for hatred or love of any tribe beyond another, nor at the order of anyone, nor in hope to get gain out of it, that I took in hand to write the history of Ireland, but because I thought it was not fitting that a country like Ireland for honour, and races as honourable as every race that inhabited it, should be swallowed up without any word or mention to be left about them.

This note can be felt in several other passages, one of which is perhaps worth quoting:

If it happens, indeed, that the land is praised by every historian who has written about Ireland, the people are dispraised by every new foreign historian who has written about them, and the thing that stirred me up to write this history of the Irish is the greatness of the pity I felt at the plain injustice that is done to them by these writers. If only, indeed, they had given their true report about the Irish, I do not know why they should not have been put in comparison with any race in Europe, in three things, as they are in bravery, in learning, and in being steadfast to the Catholic faith. . . .

These passages may be compared with Spenser's judgment that the Irish 'are now accounted the most barbarous nation in Christendom'. Keating's view is likely to have been quite as partial as Spenser's, yet the way he expresses it, and, indeed, this whole work, with its quaint learning and dignity, shows that one class at least in Ireland was far removed from barbarity. In another way the traditional knowledge of old or, at least, of middle Irish, which Keating shares with the Four Masters, Duald MacFirbis, and others, proves that an independent intellectual life existed in Ireland till that time, quite apart from the shifting political life that is seized by historians.

It is curious to follow the various ways in which Keating works out his defence. On one hand, he says that Ireland is a kingdom apart by herself, like a little world, which no foreigner can understand, and, on the other hand, he tries to keep Ireland in union with the general history of the world as it was then received. Thus he sets off some of his fanciful genealogies by quoting similar things from English history. 'Here follows', he says in one place, 'an example from a British author, where he gives the pedigree to Adam of a king who was over Britain, from which the reader will allow that it was possible for the Gaels to do the same thing.'

The best defence, however, is, he thinks, to be found in the records he quotes from, and if, as I have said, the personal note is a chief interest in this work, it must not be thought that the history itself is without a certain attractiveness. At the least it gives a general view of the legends in which the Irish, at an early date, mixed together a mass of native tradition, and the new biblical and classical history which had been brought to them from the continent. A good deal of this matter may be set at the side of the stories in Geoffrey of Monmouth where he traces the Trojan and Roman origin of the British, but there is also a large portion that deals with legends founded on a mythological basis.

In the succeeding volumes of the history, Mr. Comyn will have a less well known portion of the work to deal with, and their interest will be proportionately greater. It is to be hoped that the Irish Texts Society will be able to bring them out without much delay.

CELTIC MYTHOLOGY[1]

A USEFUL task has been done in bringing out an English version of this important work on Celtic mythology. The translation, due to Mr. Richard Irvine Best, has been carried out with so much care and taste that the reader who turns to it instead of to the original will lose nothing, or almost nothing, in so doing, while in the few pages of notes added to this edition he will find some interesting information brought together from other works on the subject. In a sense it is, perhaps, a little to be regretted that M. D'Arbois de Jubainville has chosen to put his work in the form of a discussion of the Irish myths, as they are found in the Book of Invasions (the *Leabhar Gabhala*, a twelfth-century account of the mythical colonisations of Ireland), for in following this plan he has had to begin with rather unattractive material, where the thread of Irish myth is much obscured by pseudo-classical or Biblical adaptations. A good deal, however, can be put forward in support of the plan he has adopted. 'We hope,' he says, in the introduction,

> that it will be considered in our favour that we have respected the ancient order in which Ireland has long since classified the fabulous tales that constitute the traditional form of her mythology. In substituting for this arrangement, consecrated by the ages, a newer and more methodical classification we should have broken to pieces in our hands the very picture we wished to hold up to view.

However that may be, the interest and value of the work are beyond dispute. Some of the views it gives, such as the estimate of early Celtic pantheism and its relation to the system of Scotus Erigena, have been questioned by other authorities, but as a general introduction to Irish mythology this work seems likely to take a place nearly as high as that of the *Grammatica Celtica* of Zeuss in the kindred subject of Celtic philology. M. D'Arbois de Jubainville has supplemented this volume by several others of great value, which, with his work in the *Revue Celtique*, have greatly helped to raise Old Irish studies to the place they now

[1] A review of *The Irish Mythological Cycle and Celtic Mythology*, by H. D'Arbois de Jubainville, translated from the French by R. I. Best, in *The Speaker* of 2 April 1904.

occupy. Probably to this day few persons among the general reading public are aware that philologists, especially continental philologists, are beginning to find Old Irish nearly, or quite, as important in the study of certain portions of Aryan grammar—Latin etymology, for instance—as Sanscrit itself; or to take a case nearer our present subject, that Irish mythology has been found to give, with the oldest mythology that can be gathered from the Homeric poems, the most archaic phase of Indo-European religion.

To illustrate the Greek kinship of these Irish legends, which is of a nature to interest many who are not mythologists, one instance may be given. In the early Irish myths a god is met with who is known as Lug the Long-handed, a name that is also found in Gaul in the first portion of the place-name Lugudunum, which has given us Lyon in modern French. This god Lug is a Celtic Hermes, and in one of the legends that relate to him he kills, with a stone, a certain god of night, Balor, just as Hermes kills the Argos. Here is the point of interest. Balor is also in some degree a counterpart of the Chimaera, and in his name we have the 'Belleros', which gives us 'Bellero-phontes' (the slayer of Belleros), or 'Bellero-phon', both Balor and Belleros being akin to the Greek verb *βάλλω* (to throw), as the Chimaera kills by throwing out a stream of fire, and Balor by an evil eye, which M. D'Arbois connects with the thunderbolt.

With relationships of this sort, some of which are perhaps open to criticism, but which are always suggestive, this volume is filled. There is, however, another connection in which, perhaps, Irish myths throw a still more interesting light on the history of European culture. The Lug just mentioned is sometimes associated with another god, the Dagda, whose name M. D'Arbois interprets as 'Good god', and thus connects him with the Latin divinity known as the Bona Dea. The Dagda owns a magic cauldron, which is spoken of on several occasions in common with the sword of Lug, and two other talismans. The cauldron, or one like it, is also found in the possession of Manannan mac Lir, an Irish sea god, and again, in Welsh romance, in the story of Branwen, daughter of Llyr, where it has the power of restoring the dead to life. It has been suggested, and it is far from impossible, that this cauldron is, or corresponds to, the early pagan germ from which sprang the legend, or a share of the legend, of the Holy Grail. Whether this is so or not, the Arthurian poetry proper—La Matière de Bretagne—had, to some extent at the least, a Celtic origin, and the study of these Irish myths with this connection in one's mind, is one of the most entrancing branches of scholarship. M. D'Arbois has dealt, for the most part, with anterior Greek or Indian relationships, but in his works we can get better, perhaps, than elsewhere a consecutive view of Irish mythology itself, with which one must grow familiar before it is possible to estimate its place in European archaeology. *The Irish Mythological Cycle* is in some ways his most important volume, and it may be said once more that this excellent translation is exceedingly welcome. The volume is printed and published in Dublin.

AN EPIC OF ULSTER[1]

THIS version of the epic tales relating to Cuchulain, the Irish mythical hero, should go far to make a new period in the intellectual life of Ireland. Henceforward the beauty and wonder of the old literature is likely to have an influence on the culture of all classes, and to give a new impulse to many lukewarm Irishmen who have been unsympathetic towards their country because they were ignorant of her real tradition. The beauty of this old literature has been known to Celtic scholars all over Europe for a considerable time, but the works in which they have dealt with it are addressed to scholars only, and are too learned, and too expensive for general use. A step in advance was made a few years ago by Miss Hull, who collected and published most of the translated stories of the Cuchulain Saga, but the arrangement of her book was not quite adequately carried out, and the translations themselves had no uniformity of style. Now, however, Lady Gregory has made a new selection of these stories, and, basing her work on the published texts and the translations made by scholars, she has put them into a wonderfully simple and powerful language that resembles a good deal the peasant dialect of the west of Ireland. Considerable praise is due to the way in which she has accomplished this rather delicate task, but it can hardly be claimed for her, as Mr. Yeats seems to do in his preface to this book, that she has 'discovered' the language she uses. Some time ago Dr. Douglas Hyde used a very similar language in his translations of the 'Love Songs of Connacht', and more recently Mr. Yeats himself has written some of his articles on folklore with this cadence in his mind, while a few other writers have been moving gradually towards it. The intellectual movement that has been taking place in Ireland for the last twenty years has been chiefly a movement towards a nearer appreciation of the country people, and their language, so that it is not too much to say that the translation of the old MSS. into this idiom is the result of an evolution rather than of a merely personal idea.

The peasant note alone, however, does not explain all the passages of this book. The peasants of the west of Ireland speak an

[1] A review of Lady Gregory's *Cuchulain of Muirthemne* in *The Speaker* of 7 June 1902.

almost Elizabethan dialect, and in the lyrical episodes it is often hard to say when Lady Gregory is thinking of the talk of the peasants and when she is thinking of some passage in the Old Testament. In several chapters, again, there are pages where battles and chariot-fights are described with a nearly Eastern prolixity, in a rich tone that has the cadence of the palace, and not the cadence of men who are poor. This union of notes, fugitive as it is, forms perhaps the most interesting feature of the language of the book. The Elizabethan vocabulary has a force and colour that make it the only form of English that is quite suitable for incidents of the epic kind, and in her intercourse with the peasants of the west Lady Gregory has learned to use this vocabulary in a new way, while she carries with her plaintive Gaelic constructions that make her language, in a true sense, a language of Ireland.

Apart from the actual translation, Lady Gregory has had a difficult task in the arrangement of these stories, many of which have come down to us in a rather bewildering state. The epic of Cuchulain began to take shape in pagan Ireland probably in the same way as the Homeric stories grew up in ancient Greece. The Irish tales, however, were never co-ordinated, for before the Gaels reached a period relatively modern enough to demand a single narrative from the separate stories of the cycle, the early civilisation of the country was altered by the coming of Christianity and of the Northern pirates. There is still a good deal of obscurity about the early history of this literature, but it is fairly certain that the chief Cuchulain stories took their present form from the seventh to the ninth century, although they have been preserved in scattered MSS. written several centuries later. The tales in these MSS. continually overlap, and are often contradictory, so that in order to construct a literary version arrangement of a somewhat elaborate kind was needful. On the whole, although it would be possible to criticise certain details in her work, Lady Gregory has done what was required with tact and success.

When we turn to the subject matter of these stories we find a new world of romance. Everywhere wildness and vigour are blended in a strange way with impetuous tenderness, and with the vague misgivings that are peculiar to primitive men. Most of the moods and actions that are met with are more archaic than anything in the Homeric poems, yet a few features, such as the imperiousness and freedom of the women, seem to imply an intellectual advance beyond the period of Ulysses. The chief women of the cycle, Maeve, Queen of Connaught, and Emer, wife of Cuchulain, and Etain, the daughter of Etar, King of the Riders of the Sidhe, are described in many passages of great clearness and beauty. The heroes who fight beside or for these women, Conchubar, and Fergus and Conall Caernach, are all large and living figures, that no one who cares for any ancient literature is likely to read of without delight.

The deeds of Cuchulain himself occupy, as may be supposed, a large portion of this book. In the first chapter we are told of his miraculous birth, and then the story goes on to the scene in his childhood where he kills a half magical watch-dog that had been let out on him by mistake, and takes the dog's place—whence his name, 'Cu', i.e. dog (Greek kuōn) of 'Culain' owner of the dog—till another can be procured. Afterwards we have many episodes of his life, and at the end we see him when he is mortally wounded, and betrayed by magic, strapping himself up against a pillar stone so erectly that fear comes down on his enemies and they camp round at a distance till they see a crow light on his shoulder.

The chapter that tells of the courting of Emer, who has the six gifts, the gifts of beauty, of voice, of needlework, of sweet speech, of wisdom, and of chastity, and becomes the wife of Cuchulain, is full of curious charm. Another episode, where Fand, the fairy woman, wins the hero from his wife, apart from the beauty of the composition, has a more scientific interest, as a recent writer, M. Pineau, has found in it the origin of an incident in the Nibelungenlied. The lamentation of Deirdre over the body of her husband and his two brothers, who have been killed by Conchubar that he may win her to be his own wife, is one of the finest passages in this book. It loses in quotation, yet a few stanzas must be given:

'That I would live after Naoise let no one think on the earth: I will not go on living after Ainnle and after Ardan. After them I myself will not live: three that would leap through the midst of battle; since my beloved is gone from me I will cry my fill over his grave.

'Oh, young man, digging the new grave, do not make the grave narrow: I will be along with them in the grave making lamentation and ochones!

'Many the hardship I met with along with the three heroes: I suffered want of house, want of fire, it is myself that used not to be troubled.

'Their new shields and their spears made a bed for me often. Oh, young man, put their three swords close over their grave. . . . What is country to me, or land, or lordship? What are swift horses? What are jewels and gold? Och, it is I will be lying to-night on the strand like the beautiful sons of Usnach.'

For readers who take more than literary interest in these stories a word of warning may be needed. Lady Gregory has omitted certain barbarous features, such as the descriptions of the fury of Cuchulain, and, in consequence, some of her versions have a much less archaic aspect than the original texts. Students of mythology will read this book with interest, yet for their severer studies they must still turn to the works of German scholars, and others, who translate without hesitation all that has come down to us in the MSS.

A TRANSLATION OF IRISH ROMANCE[1]

MOST of the early Irish romances are written in alternating fragments of prose and verse, like the old French tale of *Aucassin and Nicolette*, and for this and other reasons the translator of them has a task that is far from easy. The style of the verse portions is usually of a rather stiff elliptical kind, so that a plain literal version of them is somewhat unattractive. Prose versions, on the other hand, which can give the reader a sense that he is reading sometimes rather highly-pitched verse and sometimes simple prose, and are still natural and pleasing, can only be produced by writers of the greatest literary tact. In the present volume Mr. A. H. Leahy has adopted a plan which is perhaps more perilous still, and has translated all the verse portions of his text into English verse. For this he had, of course, many well-known examples, yet it may be doubted whether—putting aside a few paraphrases and imitations made by poets of genius—almost the whole mass of English verse translations, from the time of Pope down, is not a dreary and disheartening exhibition of useless ingenuity which has produced hardly anything of interest for those who care most for literature. A certain number of these verse translations, however, —Mr. Andrew Lang's translation of portions of *Aucassin and Nicolette* among them—have justified themselves, and writers have a perfect right to attempt this kind of work. In order to form an opinion of Mr. Leahy's verses one need not go far. In the opening of one of these romances, the very well known story of Deirdre and the sons of Usnach, a child cries out before it is born—a characteristically wild touch—and terrifies the men of Ulster. Cathbad, the Druid, is asked to explain the occurrence, and he answers in a piece of peculiar verse which Mr. Leahy translates thus:—

'Tis a maid who screamed wildly so lately,
Fair and curling shall locks round her flow,
And her eyes be blue-centred and stately
And her cheeks like the foxglove shall glow.

[1] A review of A. H. Leahy's *Heroic Romances of Ireland*, vol. i, in the *Manchester Guardian* of 28 December 1905.

For the tint of her skin we commend her,
  In its whiteness like snow newly shed;
And her teeth are all faultless in splendour,
  And her lips, like to coral, are red.
A fair woman is she, for whom heroes, that fight
In their chariots for Ulster, to death shall be dight.

That is seriously put forward in this elaborately edited volume as a translation from the Book of Leinster, a twelfth-century text, and yet it is hard to imagine a more deplorable misrepresentation of the spirit of these old verses. This kind of facile parody has been written very frequently by writers who have set out to translate Gaelic poetry, and their verse has shown to an extraordinary extent the provinciality which—at least till quite lately—has distinguished a good deal of Anglo-Irish taste. It is hardly too much to say that, while a great part of Gaelic poetry itself is filled with the most curious individuality and charm, there is probably no mass of tawdry commonplace jingle quite so worthless as the verse translations that have been made from it in Ireland during the last century. Occasionally a poem like Mangan's 'Dark Rosaleen', which was put forward as a translation, had an independent life and beauty, yet most of these verses were neither translations nor poetry. Those who know no Irish can get some idea of what Gaelic poetry has suffered in this kind of treatment by comparing the beautiful prose translations which Dr. Douglas Hyde wrote of the 'Love Songs of Connacht' with the verse translations—in themselves often pleasing enough—which he put in the same volume. When one is dealing with old texts, like those translated in the present volume, the matter is much worse. A stanza in 'The Courtship of Etain' is thus translated literally in the notes at the end of the book: 'If it should please thee in thy wise mind, place hand about my neck; a beginning of courtship, beautiful its colour, a man and a woman kissing each other.' In the text of the volume this is changed into:—

Is my neck and its beauty so pleasing?
  'Tis around it thine arms thou shalt place;
And 'tis known as a courtship's beginning
  When a man and a woman embrace.

A transfiguration which needs no comment! Sometimes, when Mr. Leahy keeps to a strictly trochaic or iambic movement, the effect is not so bad, but on the whole his verses are like those I have given, and as the stories often contain as much verse as prose the whole translation suffers.

In the prose portions the workmanship is very different, and Mr. Leahy shows so many of the qualities of an excellent translator—fearlessness, enthusiasm, and the scholar's conscience—that one reads every word with interest. In a few places he slips into phrases that are needlessly archaic, but on the whole his style is adequate and not without vigour. If he will translate the less known or unknown Irish romances into good prose many will thank him, and he will help to give a new life to these old romances, in which so much curious imagination has been long hidden away. In the present volume the stories chosen are among those that are already most widely known, and include 'Cuchulain's Sick Bed', 'The Courtship of Etain', the wonderful episode of the Tain bo Cuailnge, known as 'The Fight of the Ford' and some others. In the preface and special introductions several points of importance are discussed and there is a special note by Mr. Alfred Nutt which will be read with interest. The volume is well brought out.

IRISH HEROIC ROMANCE[1]

In this, the second volume of the Irish Romances translated by Mr. A. H. Leahy, he has adopted a method which differs considerably from that of the first volume, reviewed in these columns not long ago. The romances of the first volume were in prose and verse, and were translated into corresponding forms. The five stories now added, however, are in prose only, and we are given two translations, one in verse, and the other, on the opposite page, in literal and rugged prose. Mr. Leahy explains the reasons which led him to adopt this method. These tales, he says, 'appear suited for rapid prose recitations, which were apparently as much a feature in ancient as they are in modern Irish. Such pieces can hardly be reproduced in English prose so as to bring out their character; they are represented in English by the narrative ballad, and they have been rendered in this way.' This view of the matter will not be shared by everyone. In numberless villages in the west and south of Ireland there are now story-tellers who have a large store of folk-tales which they tell indifferently in English or Irish, and those of them who have fairly good English often give quite the same characteristics in both their versions. On the other hand, the English ballad forms used in the present work have a number of literary associations which, to say nothing of Mr. Leahy's rather crude versification, create a feeling that is by no means in harmony with the spirit of Irish story-telling. The note of the five stories now translated is, in some ways, nearer the note of the modern Irish folk-tale than to that of the more elaborate romances. They are all of the variety known as 'Tain' or 'Cattle Raid', and three of them at least have little interest that is not of a purely antiquarian kind. The 'Tain bo Fraich', however, has considerable value, and one fine passage filled with the peculiar delight in clear, natural colour which is so characteristic of Irish and Welsh romance. Find-abair, the daughter of the Queen of Connaught, sees a prince, who is her lover, swimming in a river with a branch of red rowan berries in his hand:

Exceedingly beautiful she thought it to see Fraech over the black pool;

[1] A review of A. H. Leahy's *Heroic Romances of Ireland,* vol. ii, in the *Manchester Guardian* of 6 March 1906.

the body of the great whiteness and the hair of great loveliness, the face of great beauty, the eye of great greyness, and he a soft youth without fault, without blemish . . . and the branch with the red berries between the throat and the white face.

The last tale in the volume, which tells how the great queen or goddess of war appeared to Cuchulain as a red-haired female satirist, and then, when he threw his spear at her, turned herself into a blackbird and told him how she would come against him in a great war that was soon to come, is a fine and characteristic fragment of archaic Irish fantasy. In reading it, as indeed in the other stories, one is tempted to wish that Mr. Leahy had taken more pains with his plain prose translations instead of producing these rhymed versions, which are in the scholar's way and are not likely to attract the general public.

IRISH FAIRY STORIES[1]

At the present time, when the tendencies of most Irish writers are towards sombreness of thought and language, it is not uninteresting to find in Mr. MacManus a survival of the older school that was founded, nearly a century ago, by Carleton and his successors. Like them Mr. MacManus writes with vigour, and with a real knowledge of the Irish peasantry, but does not reach a style of any particular interest when writing in his own person, or bring out the finer notes of the language spoken by the peasants. To give a specimen of his manner in this book one may quote almost anywhere:

> Nancy and Shamus were man and wife and lived all alone together for forty years; but at length a good-for-nothing streel of a fellow named Rory, who lived close by, thought what a fine thing it would be if Shamus would die, and he could marry Nancy and get the house, farm, and all the stock. So he up and said to Nancy:
>
> 'What a pity it is for such a fine-looking woman as you to be tethered with that ould complainin' good-for-nothing crony of a man that's as full of pains and aches as an egg's full of meat. . .' etc.

Such a style has a certain liveliness, yet when it is chosen by Irish writers, a great deal of what is most precious in the national life must be omitted from their work, or imperfectly expressed. On the other hand the rollicking note is present in the Irish character—present to an extent some writers of the day do not seem to be aware of—and it demands, if we choose to deal with it, a free rollicking style. In some of the dialogue of this book Mr. MacManus has caught the jovial note sharply and well, but the language of several of the stories has a familiarity that is not amusing, while it is without the intimate distinction good humorous writing requires.

This volume, it need hardly be said, is addressed to the general public rather than to folk-lorists. Three or four of the ten stories that are retold from the telling of the Donegal peasants are simple folk-tales, with no fairy or supernatural element whatever, and in the others, although wonders abound, there is little that has to do

[1] A review of Seumas MacManus's *Donegal Fairy Stories* in *The Speaker* of 21 June 1902.

with Irish fairy belief. Mr. MacManus is at his best in the directly humorous tales, such as 'Conal and Donal and Taig' which is excellently told. The supernatural stories have the wild imagination and variety that give charm to the invention of the Gael, but here the writer's method is less satisfactory.

Many of the incidents, such as that in which a dead man comes in a new shape to help a young adventurer who had released his dead body from the bailiffs, and again that of the well with blood and honey coming to the top of it, are found in other collections of Irish folk-tales. Others, such as that of the wine-cellar and the man who goes down every morning to drink wine, seem out of keeping with the details of Irish life which the story-tellers usually adhere to when they are not dealing with anything that is avowedly a wonder. 'Manis the Miller' and several of the other stories are to be found in different forms in other parts of Ireland; indeed, with endless variety of detail, the same themes seem to be present wherever the folk-tale has survived among the Gaels. On the whole, this book makes pleasant reading, and it is sure to delight children. It is well printed and brought out. The illustrations are numerous and are often fairly effective, yet the illustrator has not seen the Irish wonder world with a clear eye. It is to be feared that the old story-tellers, to whom the volume is gracefully dedicated, would be bewildered and perhaps scandalised, if they could be shown the shape given to some of the characters they helped to create.

LE MOUVEMENT INTELLECTUEL IRLANDAIS[1]

La tranquillité relative qui a régné ces dernières années en Irlande semble toucher à sa fin. Les agissements de *The United Irish League*, suivis de la proclamation récente de Lord Cadogan n'indiquent que trop clairement que nous sommes au seuil d'une nouvelle époque d'agitation politique. Maintenant si l'on veut se rendre compte, avant d'aborder cette nouvelle période, des progrès faits depuis la mort de Parnell, que trouve-t-on ? L'on sait que malgré l'utilité de *The Local Government Act* et de quelques autres mesures, des années se sont passées sans de grands événements parlementaires. L'habileté de MM. Redmond, Dillon et des plusieurs autres politiciens irlandais est indiscutable, mais un vrai chef populaire a fait défaut, et en Irlande rien ne se fait sans l'influence d'un personnage dominant. Cependant, dans un certain sens, cette période a été féconde — peut-être la plus féconde du siècle dernier — puis-qu'elle a vu naître, ou tout au moins s'épanouir, trois mouvements de la plus grande importance, *The Gaelic League*, association pour la préservation de la langue irlandaise, puis un mouvement pour le développement de l'agriculture et de l'élevage, et, finalement, une nouvelle activité intellectuelle qui est en train de nous créer une littérature.

Ces trois mouvements sont intimement liés; — il est rare de trouver quelqu'un qui s'occupe d'un seul d'entre eux sans s'intéresser en même temps aux autres — mais ici je vais parler du troisième, comme étant celui qui offre le plus d'intérêt général.

Quand, vers la fin du XVIIe siècle, la langue irlandaise cessa d'être employée comme langue littéraire, toutes les traditions intellectuelles du pays se perdirent. Dès ce moment ce furent plutôt les descendants des immigrés anglais qui firent de la littérature au lieu des descendants des races celtiques antérieures, et puisque ces écrivains ne possédaient ni une tradition, ni une langue à eux les plus doués d'entre eux passaient presque toujours en Angleterre, de sorte que leurs œuvres ne nous appartiennent pas. Parmi eux, on peut citer ces trois écrivains si remarquables dans la littérature anglaise, Burke, Goldsmith et Sterne.

[1] An article in *L'Européen* of 31 May 1902.

Cet état de choses dura longtemps, mais peu à peu, une connaissance croissante de la langue anglaise dans les classes populaires et une assimilation plus complète des gens d'extraction anglaise dotèrent le pays d'un nouveau terrain littéraire. En 1798, William Carlton naquit dans le comté de Tyrone, et, trente ans plus tard, il publia ses *Traits and Stories of the Irish Peasantry*, livre devenu célèbre, qui marque le commencement définitif de la littérature irlandaise moderne. Depuis ce moment, les écrivains irlandais ont été nombreux et féconds. On trouve des romanciers, des jeunes gens moitié littérateurs, moitié politiciens, qui abondèrent surtout vers l'année 1848, des poètes et quelques savants qui s'occupaient principalement des antiquités nationales. Néanmoins, il faut avouer que toute la littérature produite pendant les premiers trois quarts du siècle ne contient que peu de chose d'une réelle valeur. Le sentiment national a été trop ardent, trop conscient, si on peut le dire, chez la plupart de ces écrivains, de sorte que la prose dégénérait facilement chez eux en une rhétorique surchargée, tandis qu'en poésie on croyait avoir tout fait en chantant les anciennes gloires de l'Irlande. De plus, les littérateurs de cette époque écrivaient une langue qu'une grande partie du peuple autour d'eux n'était jamais arrivé à s'assimiler parfaitement. Il s'en suit que leur façon d'envisager la langue anglaise restait entièrement dépourvue de cette intimité spéciale qui, seule, peut donner naissance à de vraies œuvres de littérature.

Maintenant quand on passe à la génération actuelle, on trouve que ces défauts se sont amoindris, s'ils n'ont pas complètement disparu. Avec une culture un peu plus large le sentiment national a cessé d'être une obsession dominante, et, graduellement, la langue anglaise est devenue, dans la plus grande partie de l'Irlande, une véritable langue maternelle. C'est surtout dans l'œuvre de M. W. B. Yeats, écrivain de génie à la tête de la nouvelle école de la poésie irlandaise, qu'on voit la portée de cette amélioration. Chez lui, le sentiment national, tout en restant aussi profond que celui de ses prédécesseurs, se borne à donner un caractère distinctif à l'atmosphère dans laquelle s'épanouissent les créations délicates de son imagination. De l'autre côté, ses rythmes, composés avec une simplicité curieusement savante, font preuve d'une rare connaissance de la langue anglaise. Ce n'est pas en quelques lignes qu'on peut critiquer l'œuvre complète de M. Yeats qui, d'ailleurs, n'est pas inconnu à Paris, ayant collaboré à l'*Ermitage*, où M.

Dayray a parlé de lui il y a déjà longtemps, tandis que dans le *Mercure de France* son nom a été vu plus d'une fois. Je me borne donc à signaler ici l'étrange beauté de ses poèmes lyriques, sans pouvoir omettre, toutefois, les noms de deux livres, *The Secret Rose*, en prose, et *The Shadowy Waters*, petit drame en vers d'une distinction de langue et de sentiment des plus rares.

A part M. Yeats, nous avons un poète, M. George Russell, dont l'imagination extraordinaire n'arrive pas toujours à s'exprimer dans une forme pleinement satisfaisante. Dans les deux volumes qu'il a déjà publiés, on trouve quelques petits poèmes à peu près parfaits, à côté de beaucoup de pièces sans valeur.

Deux ou trois poètes moins importants ont fait paraître dernièrement des recueils assez intéressants, mais je les passe sous silence pour parler de *The Literary Theatre*, théâtre littéraire qui peut être considéré comme le point central du mouvement intellectuel. Les premières représentations eurent lieu au mois de mai 1899. On donna d'abord une pièce de M. Yeats, intitulée: *The Countess Cathleen*. On y voit la comtesse Cathleen, sorte de châtelaine, qui, au moment d'une disette en Irlande, vend son âme aux démons afin de venir en aide aux gens qui meurent de faim autour de son château. Cela semble bien innocent, mais à Dublin une partie du public est encore assez orthodoxe pour se trouver froissée devant une action pareille. Le clergé exprima une certaine désapprobation et, à chaque séance, on voyait des ivrognes scandalisés qui débitaient, du haut des galeries, des observations morales à l'adresse de M. Yeats et de ses confrères.

Cette pièce fut suivie d'un drame, *The Heather Field*, par M. Edward Martyn, disciple d'Ibsen, au moins par sa façon d'écrire. L'intrigue y est des plus simples. Un propriétaire irlandais demeurant dans sa propriété au milieu de ses fermiers, se trouve embarrassé par l'insuffisance de ses moyens. Rêveur idéaliste, au lieu de chercher des remèdes pratiques, il se figure qu'il peut arriver à convertir en des prairies fertiles le *Heather Field*, vaste bruyère non loin de sa maison, et réaliser, de la sorte, des bénéfices considérables. Bientôt des travaux sont entamés; on brûle les bruyères et on ensemence le terrain, tout en dépensant des sommes d'argent importantes. La femme du propriétaire, femme d'une nature dure et matérielle, se désole, prévoyant très nettement que c'est la ruine et non pas l'aisance qu'on va tirer du *Heather Field*. Enfin, à bout de patience, elle fait venir deux médecins pour constater l'aliénation mentale de son mari, afin de pouvoir prendre elle-même la direction de ses affaires. Cependant les médecins n'osent pas s'exprimer d'une façon définitive, et cet état de choses se prolonge jusqu'au printemps. Un jour, le petit garçon du propriétaire s'en va faire un tour à cheval dans le *Heather Field*. Vers midi il revient bruyant et joyeux. Ah! papa, s'écrie-t-il, c'est bien joli dans le *Heather Field*, la bruyère pousse partout. Et il en jette aux pieds de son père un grand bouquet qu'il vient de cueillir. Le père voyant ainsi tous ses rêves s'évanouir devient effectivement fou.

Dans cette courte analyse, on ne voit rien du drame. L'auteur a su faire de ce rêveur qui se console par de grands espoirs chimériques un personnage véritablement attirant. A côté de sa femme brutalement réaliste, il gagne toutes les sympathies. C'est du moins ce qui est arrivé quand on a joué cette pièce à Dublin. Ensuite, encouragé par un tel succès, on est allé donner une représentation du *Heather Field* à Londres, mais là, exception faite de quelques lettrés, personne n'a rien compris du sens intime de l'action. L'auditoire resta froid, et dans les journaux on trouva que c'était la femme qui avait raison, et que le mari n'était qu'*a dangerous impractical person*.

La deuxième année du *Literary Theatre* on donna des pièces de MM. Edward Martyn et George Moore avec un succès considérable, et au mois d'octobre de l'année passée les dernières représentations eurent lieu. On joua un drame, *Diarmuid and Grainne*, écrit en collaboration par MM. W. B. Yeats et George Moore et, ensuite, une petite pièce charmante, écrite en irlandais pour l'occasion par M. Douglas Hyde. Ce fut la première fois qu'on joua une pièce en irlandais sur une grande scène, et les places à bon marché du théâtre furent prises d'assaut par les enthousiastes de la *Gaelic League*. Malgré l'importance de cette association on sent presque toujours, dans les manifestations qu'elle organise (ainsi qu'il arrive si souvent dans tous les mouvements foncièrement populaires) le ridicule coudoyer des sentiments d'une profondeur insondable. Ainsi au commencement de la première représentation, on ne pouvait pas s'empêcher de sourire en voyant tout autour de la salle les belles Irlandaises de la *Gaelic League* qui baragouinaient dans un fort mauvais irlandais avec de jeunes commis tout pâles d'enthousiasme. Mais dans un entr'acte de *Diarmuid and Grainne* il arriva que, selon l'habitude de ce théâtre, les gens qui occupaient les galeries se mirent à chanter. Ce furent de vieilles chansons populaires. Jusqu'alors on n'avait jamais entendu ces mélodies chantées à l'unisson par beaucoup de voix avec les anciennes paroles irlandaises. L'auditoire tressaillit. Il y eut dans ces notes traînantes, d'une mélancolie que rien ne peut égaler, comme le râle d'une nation. On voyait une tête, puis une autre se pencher sur le programme. On pleurait.

Puis le rideau se leva, la pièce recommença au milieu d'une vive émotion. On venait de sentir flotter un instant dans la salle l'âme d'un peuple.

THE OLD AND NEW IN IRELAND[1]

TEN years ago, in the summer of 1892, an article on Literary Dublin, by Miss Barlow, author of *Bogland Studies* and some other charming work, appeared in a leading English weekly. After dealing with Professor Mahaffy, some other Irish writers, and the periodicals of Dublin, she summed up in these words: 'This bird's-eye view has revealed no brilliant prospect, and the causes of dimness considered, it is difficult to point out any quarter of the horizon as a probable source of rising light.'

No one who knows Ireland and Irish life will be likely to charge Miss Barlow with lack of insight, although when she wrote the literary movement which is now so apparent was beginning everywhere through the country. Ten years ago all, or nearly all, the writers who have since done well, W. B. Yeats, George Russell, Standish O'Grady, Edward Martyn, Lady Gregory, and Douglas Hyde were at work, but so obscurely that they were quite away from the eye of the general public. It is not

[1] An article in *The Academy and Literature* of 6 September 1902. In Notebook 30, there are drafts of this article. Synge did not publish all he drafted, and among the unprinted passages remaining in Notebook 30 are the following:

> 'Mr. W. B. Yeats is the first writer who has written in an Irish spirit with a full appreciation of English rhythms. . . . [he] has been attacked over and over by the Gaelic enthusiasts because he writes in English. The Gaelic enthusiasts when they write in Gaelic would certainly be attacked by Mr. Yeats, if he could read them. Most of us have a certain satisfaction when we read the productions of the Gaelic League that these writers use a language that is not intelligible outside their club-room doors. . . . The theory due to Mr. George Moore that Ireland must learn Irish in order to write a literature because the English language is too threadbare to serve the imagination is not quite tenable. . . . It is perhaps more difficult to write the English of [our] time than the English of Elizabethan writers, but their language in a sense could not express the things with which we are haunted . . . If a well is made foul no one can approach it, but the sea is indifferent to everything and in a certain [sense] the English language is like the sea which goes round the world as it does. . . . If Mr. Moore maintained that English literature had lost its vitality he could have made a much more plausible case, but it is absurd to say that in all the parts of the world where English is spoken, where people rage with it, and use it when they are filled with passion and love, that no body of men can ever rise up who will write the few score of plays or poems, or the few volumes on life and criticism that are all that is needed to make a chapter in literature. . . . If anyone will compare the wistful and delicate gaiety of a great part of the finer Irish jigs or the dancing of the peasants in the few localities where they are still quite unsophisticated with the Irish humours we are given by the Anglo-Irish writers of the last century he will feel how much there is in their country that has been pitifully interpreted. At the last representations of the Irish Literary Theatre a little drama by Dr. Douglas Hyde was acted in Irish and in this little drama there was a trace—a first rather tentative trace of the real Irish humour.'

easy to realise the change these years have made. In those days if an odd undergraduate of Trinity felt a vague longing to know more of Ireland and her past than he could learn from his teachers or companions, he had to wander on Aston's Quay and Bachelor's Walk, picking up ugly pamphlets with Grattan's Speeches in them, or Davis's Poems, or the true History of Ireland from before the Flood. If he wished to learn a little of the Irish language and went to the professor appointed to teach it in Trinity College, he found an amiable old clergyman who made him read a crabbed version of the New Testament, and seemed to know nothing, or at least to care nothing, about the old literature of Ireland, or the fine folk-tales and folk-poetry of Munster and Connaught. In the libraries he could find a few books on the antiquities of Ireland that had interest and scholarship, and with a few other volumes, such as W. Stokes' *Life of Petrie*, the antiquarian, he could make the beginning of an intellectual atmosphere for himself that gave life to Dublin. Most of the figures he called up were respectable students and scribes, but there were one or two men, like Clarence Mangan, who had the peculiar restlessness that goes everywhere with artistic life.

Those days had the incitement of the early spring in Ireland when there are wild evenings that are filled with uneasiness and hope, because they promise everything and give nothing but their promise. Now everything is changed. We have fine editions of books by W. B. Yeats and other Irish writers in all our bookshop windows. One evening we can read the *Shadowy Waters* and catch a tenuous sadness, such as we find in *Aglavaine et Selysette*, and the next evening we can go on to some new writer in the Irish language, and read some little work like *Faith and Famine*, by Father Dineen, where we have vigour and talent, using a form and psychology that recall the predecessors of *Titus Andronicus* or *Tamburlaine*.

This double way in which the new Irish spirit is showing itself has many points of interest. With the present generation the linguistic atmosphere of Ireland has become definitely English enough, for the first time, to allow work to be done in English that is perfectly Irish in its essence, yet has sureness and purity of form. A generation or two ago a few writers like Aubrey de Vere, who penetrated themselves with English thought and English traditions of literature, wrote of Ireland with a certain easiness and grace, but writers who lived close to the soul of their country were kept back by the uncertainty of her linguistic sense, and nearly always failed to reach the finer cadences of English.

Perhaps English critics when dealing with Irish men of talent have not always remembered this matter of language. The faults of early Anglo-Irish work are not due to this cause alone, yet it is accountable for many things, and no criticism can take us very far that does not make allowance for the phases of material. In this special case Ireland is not alone. The number of foreigners in America for whom English is a language they have either learned for themselves or picked up from parents who had learned it, tends more than anything else to cause the uncertainty of literary taste in that country. American artists and musicians are to be met with everywhere who have fine taste in their own art, yet who speak a crude jargon, and have comparatively little feeling for the intimate qualities of literature. Again, roughness of the spoken language—when it is not a primitive roughness—leads, or tends to lead, to burlesque writing, and with this in one's mind it is interesting to compare the school of Mark Twain with the crudely humorous 'typical Irishman', who was present everywhere in Irish writing till quite recently.

To return to Ireland. While the new blossom due, if these views are correct, to the final decay of Irish among the national classes of Leinster was beginning to open, the old roots in Munster and the West began also to put out a new growth. Some of this new Irish work has very considerable value, but what, one cannot but ask, will be its influence on the culture of Ireland? Will the Gaelic stifle the English once more, or will the English stifle the new hope of the Gaels?

The Gaelic League with the whole movement for language revival is so powerful that it is hard to think it will pass away without leaving a mark upon Ireland, yet its more definite hope seems quite certain to end in disappointment. No small island placed between two countries which speak the same language, like England and America, can hope to keep up a different tongue. English is likely to remain the language of Ireland, and no one, I think, need regret the likelihood. If Gaelic came back strongly from the West the feeling for English which the present generation has attained would be lost again, and in the best circumstances it is probable that Leinster and Ulster would take several centuries to assimilate Irish perfectly enough to make it a fit mode of expression for the finer emotions which now occupy literature. In the meantime, the opening culture of Ireland would be thrown back indefinitely, and there would, perhaps, be little gain to make up for this certain loss. Modern peasant Gaelic is full of rareness and beauty, but if it was sophisticated by journalists and translators—as it would certainly be sophisticated in the centuries I have spoken of—it would lose all its freshness, and then the limits, which now make its charm, would tend to prevent all further development. It is a different thing to defile a well and an inlet of the sea.

If, however, the Gaelic League can keep the cruder powers of the Irish mind occupied in a healthy and national way till the influence of Irish literature, written in English, is more definite in Irish life, the half-cultured classes may come over to the side of the others, and give an intellectual unity to the country of the highest value.

For the future of the Anglo-Irish writers everything is hopeful. The Irish reading public is still too limited to keep up an independent school of Irish men of letters, yet Irish writers are recognised, to some extent, as the best judges of Irish literary work, and it may be hoped that we have seen the last of careless writing addressed to an English public that was eager to be amused, and did not always take the trouble to distinguish in Irish books between what was futile and what had real originality and merit.

Religious questions, also, are beginning to put less restriction on Irish culture. Everywhere the Catholic population are becoming more alive to intellectual matters, and the harder forms of Protestantism are losing ground. There have been many fine scholars of this latter persuasion in Ireland, due to the influence of Trinity College, but as a class they have too often shown their kinship with the early reformers of whom Erasmus wrote: 'Evangelicos istos, cum multis aliis, tum hoc nomine praecipue odi, quod per eos ubique languent, fugent, jacent, intereunt bonae literae sine quibus quid est hominum vita?'

THE FAIR HILLS OF IRELAND[1]

WHEN this attractive and leisurely book made its appearance, a few days ago, its author, Mr. Stephen Gwynn, was standing as member of Parliament for Galway, and fighting, in the face of rotten eggs and decayed fish, what is said to have been the stormiest election that has taken place in Ireland for the last ten years. He is to be congratulated on the success of both his ventures. *The Fair Hills of Ireland*—the words are the refrain of a very well-known Irish song—is a guide-book, in the best sense of the words, addressed to travellers and friends of Ireland rather than to ordinary tourists. At the same time it is a sort of popular history, telling its story topographically instead of chronologically, and yet so effectively that one does not grumble at the confusion of the ages some are likely to fall into, as the author passes back and forward from the times of Cuchulain to those of O'Connell and from the rout of the Danes at Clontarf to the modern affairs of the new Irish creameries. Thus in one of the opening chapters we are brought to the Boyne valley and told about the wonderful pagan monuments at New Grange and Dowth, the early Christian antiquities at Monasterboice, the more advanced Norman buildings at Mellifont, and finally the doings of Sarsfield, William, and James at the Battle of the Boyne, the whole pleasantly united with a living description of the places as they are at present. The more legendary side of Irish history is treated of in the chapters on Tara, the famous home of the kings; on Armagh, with Emain Macha, a sort of Irish Troy, within a mile's walk; and on the town of Sligo, which lies under Benbulben, where Diarmuid ended his wanderings with Grannia. Kincora and Slemish bring us to the histories of Brian and St. Patrick respectively, and so the book proceeds. Throughout it is charmingly written—with an eye on the trout streams that Mr. Gwynn has so often dealt with before,—in an excellent patriotic spirit, kept in check by a scholarly urbanity which has been absent too frequently from patriotic writings in Ireland. The illustrations by Mr. Hugh Thomson add to the pleasantness of the book, which is likely to bring many minds into a more intelligent sympathy with Ireland, where, for good and for bad, the past is so living and the present so desirous to live.

[1] A review of Stephen Gwynn's *The Fair Hills of Ireland* in the *Manchester Guardian* of 16 November 1906.

THE WINGED DESTINY[1]

In *The Winged Destiny* Miss Fiona Macleod uses once more the rather ambitious style she has been building up in her more recent books. This style has met with a good deal of admiration, and, in many passages, it has, there is no doubt, an elaborate music that can only be attained by writers with a fine ear and a good command of the vocal elements of language. Yet unfortunately, while many of the sentences she delights in are so constructed that they can only be read slowly, their form and meaning do not satisfy when dwelt on. As one reads diligently forward one comes too often on sentences or phrases like these: 'The sea was a jubilation of blue and white, with green in the shaken tents of the loud-murmuring nomad host of billows. . . . A swirl of long-winged terns hung above a shoal of mackerel fry, screaming as they splashed continually into the moving dazzle. . . .'

And one ends with a feeling of uneasiness and distrust instead of the peculiarly intimate sympathy which work of this kind demands. With the matter one does not get on a great deal better. When we look into the depths of her heart for 'the patterns both of time and eternity', which one of her critics has found there, we come on passages like this: 'How futile all human longing, all passion of the heart, all travail of the spirit, beside this terrible reality of wind and vastness, of wind baying like a hound in a wilderness—a wilderness where the hound's voice would fall away at last, and the hound's shadow fade, and infinitude and eternity be beyond and above and behind and beneath.' Words which may have profound meaning, but which, it is to be feared, will appear to many as a terrible reality of wind and vastness. The first and better part of *The Winged Destiny* consists of studies and stories which deal with the more mystical side of Highland life, and are sometimes of considerable interest. All through them, however, there is rather too much reflection, that is made up of a sort of esoteric platitude, and rather too much description, that is so nearly over-written that one grows afraid of it, as one grows afraid of a singer who is working on the limit of his compass. Besides these stories there is a collection

[1] A review of Fiona Macleod's *The Winged Destiny* in *The Academy and Literature* of 12 November 1904.

of essays on various writers of the Irish movement and similar subjects. Some of these essays are judicious and sympathetic, and quietly written, but they have no very particular merit as contributions to criticism, and they do not show a very great surety of taste. In the whole book one sympathises most, perhaps, with the keen feeling apparent in it—beneath the details of which one cannot approve—for the islands of Scotland, other out-of-the-way places, and those who live in them.

GOOD PICTURES IN DUBLIN[1]

The New Municipal Gallery

ON Monday the 20th of January the new Municipal Gallery of Modern Art in Dublin was opened by the Lord Mayor at a ceremony attended by the representatives of all classes and parties in Ireland. This new gallery contains a collection of pictures that would attract attention in any town in Europe, but its establishment in Dublin in the first few years of the new century is particularly noteworthy. A hundred years ago an epoch of Irish culture—the culture of Ireland before the Union—was breaking up, and now many have pleasure in seeing a new intellectual life, of which this gallery is one of the results, gaining ground daily. In many ways this newer life seems peculiarly remote from the life of Dublin in the eighteenth century, yet there is a certain link between them which may become more apparent in the next few years.

Until recently the political affairs of Ireland were directed, to a large extent, by leaders, like Parnell, from the Protestant and landlord classes, but now after the experience of a century the more native portion of the people have reached a stage in which they have little trouble in finding political leaders among themselves. In the arts, however, it is different. Although the Irish popular classes have sympathy with what is expressed in the arts they are necessarily unfamiliar with artistic matters, so that for many years to come artistic movements in Ireland will be the work of individuals whose enthusiasm or skill can be felt by the less-trained instincts of the people. These individuals, a few here and there like the political leaders of the nineteenth century, will be drawn from the classes that have still some trace or tradition of the older culture and yet for various reasons have lost all hold on direct political life. The history of the founding of this new gallery and the work done for it by Mr. Hugh Lane and a few others since 1902 is a good instance of these new courses in Irish affairs.

The pictures of this collection are now hung in 17, Harcourt-street, one of the finest of the older Dublin houses, formerly the town house of Lord Clonmel, and the fine ceilings, chimney-

[1] An article in the *Manchester Guardian* of 24 January 1908.

pieces, and staircases add to the pleasure of one's imagination by their own value and the associations that are connected with them. The pictures themselves have for the most part extraordinary merit. Many of them are from the Forbes and Durand Ruel collections, and Mr. Lane himself has handed over his collection of pictures and drawings of British schools. In one room we have the work of Irish artists, in another English painting, and, finally, two large rooms of French and Continental schools, as fine a collection of its kind, perhaps, as can be found outside Paris. Many students, one believes, will be drawn to Dublin to look at Manet's 'Le Concert aux Tuilleries', or his fine and characteristic portrait of Mlle. Eva Gonzales, or at 'The Present' of Alfred Stevens, or at the large decorative picture of the beheading of John the Baptist by Puvis de Chavannes. The collection of Corot's work is the most representative to be found in any public gallery in these islands, and there are also fine examples of the other great landscape painters of his time. In a very different line, some eight pictures by Mancini have extraordinary power. On the staircase there is an interesting series of portraits of contemporary Irish men and women, painted by Mr. J. B. Yeats, R.H.A., Mr. William Orpen, A.R.H.A., and one or two others.

This gallery will impress everyone who visits it, but for those who live in Dublin it is peculiarly valuable. Perhaps no one but Dublin men who have lived abroad also can quite realise the strange thrill it gave me to turn in from Harcourt-street—where I passed by to school long ago—and to find myself among Monets, and Manets and Renoirs, things I connect so directly with the life of Paris. The morning of my first visit was brilliantly sunny, and this magnificent house, with the clear light in the windows, brought back, I do not know how, the whole feeling I have had so often in the Louvre and a few other galleries abroad, but which does not come to one in the rather stiff picture galleries one is used to in England and Ireland. This Dublin gallery, one is tempted to hope, will have a living atmosphere, and become, like the Louvre and the Luxembourg, a sort of home for one's mind. A new building has been promised by the Corporation of Dublin, but for the time being at least things are well as they are, and I have always felt that pictures are more easily enjoyed when hung in places built for the uses of life, whether palaces or houses, than in formal picture galleries that are built for the purpose.

When one thinks that this collection will now be open to all Dublin people, and that the young men of talent, the writers as well as the painters, will be able to make themselves familiar with all these independent and vigorous works, it is hard to say how much is owed to Mr. Hugh Lane, Alderman Kelly, the Corporation of Dublin, and the artists and others who have carried through this undertaking with such complete success.

A CELTIC THEATRE[1]

WITHIN the last few years several attempts have been made to establish a modern theatre of real merit and vitality. While the most recent of these, the Irish Literary Theatre, was being organised in Dublin, a somewhat similar movement was in progress among the Breton-speaking peasantry of Low or Western Brittany. There is not at first sight much resemblance between these two movements. One is an attempt to replace the worthless plays now familiar to the public by artistic work, the other a survival of the sincere, if sometimes grotesque, religious drama of the Middle Ages; yet they are both produced by the Celtic imagination, and give expression to a limited but puissant nationality. . . . [A modern version in Breton of a mystery play] seems in many ways rough, crude writing—fit to draw peals of laughter from the professional litterateur—yet it has a certain early vigour which recalls the first pre-Elizabethan dramas. Whatever one may think of this composition, it seems to have been most effective in the hands of the peasant actors who form the real interest of the movement. It is strange that the Celtic races should have evolved about the same time a unique body of actors in Brittany, and a few poets in Ireland who are producing works that seem incomplete when played with the accent and tradition of the London stage. Unfortunately the players act in Breton, and our poets write in English.

[1] From an article in *The Freeman's Journal* of 22 March 1900. The rest of the article consists of a summary of Anatole Le Braz's account of the arrangements for the presentation of a play in Brittany.

ANATOLE LE BRAZ[1]

SON of a village schoolmaster, Anatole Le Braz grew up among the scenes he writes of, and it is here, perhaps, one may best mark the difference between him and those who are interested in the Celtic movement in Ireland. He passed his childhood in close contact with the Breton peasantry, speaking chiefly in their language, sharing their simple Christianity; and now, undisturbed by any political or social creed, he sees with a vague and unpractical disquiet the waning of much that he intimately loves. In Ireland it is different. The same survivals of the old have not for us the charms of lingering regret, but rather the incitement of a thing that is rare and beautiful, and still apart from our habitual domain. If an Irishman of modern culture dwells for a while in Inishmaan, or Inisheer, or, perhaps, anywhere among the mountains of Connaught, he will not find there any trace of an external at-homeness, but will rather yield himself up to the entrancing newness of the old. Here, again, lies one great interest of this movement of the Celtic races, for whenever the two streams of humanity—the old and the new—flow for but a moment side by side, blending old attachments with new indomitable joys, this moment grows rich with a pregnant luxuriance undreamed of hitherto, and from moments such as these depend the purer movements of mankind. All who really achieve come seeking in quiet places a sphere for half-tangible fulfilment, and therefore it is that each nation is privileged before others that bears within her own bosom a lofty and prophetic aspiration. The day of fulfilment may be unhopefully postponed, but when its dawn reddens at length the bars of her prison, she will rise unsoiled, if grey-haired, from her sleep of secular enchantment, and her chains, not of diamond, falling in twain, will pass out to the palace of her dream.

[1] From an article in the *Daily Express* (Dublin) of 28 January 1899. The rest of the article is little more than quotation from Le Braz.

[THREE FRENCH WRITERS][1]

IN Huysmans we have a man sick with monotony trying to escape by any vice or sanctity from the sameness of Parisian life, and in Pierre Loti a man who is tormented by the wonder of the world . . . till at last his one preoccupation becomes a terrified search for some sign of the persistence of the person. Like most wanderers, he fears death more than others, because he has seen many shadowy or splendid places where he has had no time to live, and has lived in other places long enough to feel in breaking from them a share of the desolation which is completed in death. . . . In reading [them] one cannot escape a feeling of unreality, a feeling that one is outside what is vital in the growth of European thought, and that an appeal is being made to young men without health, and to women without occupation, rather than to those who count, singly or collectively, in contemporary intellectual life. In work like this neither the sensibility of Pierre Loti nor the fantastic erudition of Huysmans can quite make up for the lack of a mind definitely trained to measure the newer thoughts which come together near the real activities of life, for, usually, such minds, and such minds alone, are influenced by the wider sympathies which reinforce and justify the more serious claims of literature. . . .

It is interesting to note that the most exquisite prose style attained perhaps by any recent French writer has been used and acquired by Anatole France in the treatment of a plain local mood. The half-cynical optimism which he has shown so admirably in the books dealing with Monsieur Bergeret, and elsewhere, is simply the frank philosophy of large classes among the French, who are kept healthy by an ironical attitude towards their own distress. No one, it is possible, will consider this humorous optimism, even when completed, as Anatole France completes it, by socialistic ideals, as a high form of practical philosophy, but some may ask where at the present time we can find a better one that is fearless and perfectly healthy. . . . [In fact,] to[2] find work

[1] From an article on 'Loti and Huysmans' in *The Speaker* of 18 April 1903, and from an unpublished article on Anatole France, 'A Tale of Comedians'. The rest of these two articles consists of outlines of the actions of novels by these three writers.

[2] The draft of 'A Tale of Comedians' (in Item 110) is used from here to the end.

which interprets the real life of France, and is fully appreciated there, one must turn to . . . Anatole France. . . . In his best work, while remaining true to the distinctive tradition of French writing—the tradition which has given us Frère Jean, Tartuffe, and Pangloss—he has contrived to express with curious exactness the irony and the rather fatalistic gaiety which now form the essential mood of the French people. . . .

[He has a] mastery of the Paris dialect . . . and [is able] to give it a delicacy which is absent from the work of men like Flaubert and Balzac who, with all their talent, had not this supremely fine sense for the shades of spoken language. . . .

It is interesting to notice how many of the more important writers of the last quarter of a century have used dialogue for their medium, and thus kept up a direct relation with the spoken language, and the life of those who speak it. How much more effective, for instance, has been the varied treatment of dialogue by Maeterlinck, Oscar Wilde, Anatole France, Ibsen and others, from any elaborate prose produced during the same period. With Flaubert and Pater elaborate prose reached a climax after which only two developments were possible: one has given us Huysmans and Mallarmé who make pitiful efforts to gain new effects by literary devices, the other gives us a simple dialogue such as is seen in Anatole France, and some other writers whose nearness to him I have just noticed.

When one has done praising and enjoying the work of Anatole France one has to remember that his is exquisite satirical work with the limitations and drawbacks that belong to satire, and that if it is looked at in any other way it will show many features from which a less favourable judgement must be drawn. In making a final estimate, however, of Anatole France himself it should not be forgotten that with him as with Voltaire, to whom he owes much, a practical effort to bring justice and peace into the world, exists beside the negative mood shown in his works. This practical effort has brought him into many places where men of letters are not very often seen, and those who heard him speak in public at the time of the Affaire Dreyfus, and who remember the grave power of his words, will not be likely to find in him—as some critics have found—a shallow sophist without sincerity or depth.

[A NOTE ON BOUCICAULT AND IRISH DRAMA][1]

SOME recent performances of *The Shaughraun* at the Queen's Theatre in Dublin have enabled local playgoers to make an

[1] This was published in the 'Literary Notes' section, page 630, of *The Academy and Literature* of 11 June 1904. It is unsigned, but Maurice Bourgeois in *John Millington Synge and the Irish Theatre* (Constable, London, 1913), p. 262, identifies it on the authority of F. J. Fay as being by Synge. Bourgeois adds that the three subsequent paragraphs in this 'Literary Notes' section are presumably also by Synge. This is a reasonable assumption, and accordingly the paragraphs are printed here.

'The Irish Texts Society promise a long talked of Irish–English Dictionary in a few weeks. It will be edited by the Rev. P. S. Dinneen, and is likely to be exceedingly useful to students of Irish, who hitherto have had no very satisfactory dictionary to work with. It is curious to note that some of the earliest Irish dictionaries were brought out in Paris, where an English–Irish dictionary was printed in 1732, and an Irish–English dictionary in 1768, which latter was published by Dr. John O'Bryan, titular bishop of Cloyne, "with a view", as he says in his preface, "not only to preserve for the natives of Ireland, but also to recommend to the notice of those in other countries, a language which is asserted by very learned foreigners to be the most ancient and best preserved dialect of the old Celtic tongue of the Gauls and Celtiberians." A naively expressed wish which, in one way or other, has been amply fulfilled in the work of modern scholars! More lately the dictionaries most used have been a large work by O'Reilly, which is not all that could be wished, and a useful volume published in 1849 by Thomas de Vere Coneys, then professor of Irish at Trinity College, Dublin. This work was better in several ways than anything that had preceded it, but it is characteristic of last-century Irish scholarship in T.C.D. that it was compiled "as a manual for students of the Irish Bible", so that its vocabulary was more or less restricted to words found in Scripture. Great care has been taken to make the work now promised as complete as possible, so that there is little doubt it will be more successful than anything of the kind we have had till now. Father Dinneen is already well known to Gaelic readers as the author of a little play and some other original work, and as the editor of several volumes of poetry.'

'In the O'Growney Memorial Volume, compiled by Miss Agnes O'Farrelly, M.A., the story is told of a remarkable priest and scholar, Eugene O'Growney, who did more probably than any one else to bring about the present movement in Ireland for the restoration of the Gaelic language. In thinking of him one is often reminded of another Irish enthusiast of fine character, Father Mathew, the apostle of temperance; and one cannot help wondering whether the work of the recent enthusiast will have a more lasting effect than that of the other, which is now little more than a memory.'

'Mr. Frank Hugh O'Donnell is the author of a pamphlet dealing with various aspects of The Stage Irishman of Pseudo-Celtic Drama, asking—and riotously endeavouring to answer—such questions as "Is the Irish Literary Theatre Irish?" "Does it represent Irish tradition and legend?" and "Is it mainly a sort of Ibsen-cum-Maeterlinck-ism on Liffey?" Such a discussion should prove stimulating and if carried on without rancour and in a helpful spirit should also prove useful. A young literary movement is never the worse for adverse and candid criticism. It should never be forgotten that half the troubles of England in Ireland have arisen from ignorance of the Irish character, ignorance founded on the biased views of British and Irish historians and on the absurd caricatures which infest the majority of plays and novels dealing with Irish folk and affairs. Lever, Lover, Boucicault and "Punch" have achieved much in the way of making the Irish character a sealed book to Englishmen.'

interesting comparison between the methods of the early Irish melodrama and those of the Irish National Theatre Society. It is unfortunate for Dion Boucicault's fame that the absurdity of his plots and pathos has gradually driven people of taste away from his plays, so that at the present time few are perhaps aware what good acting comedy some of his work contains. The characters of Conn the Shaughraun, and in a less degree those of Mrs. O'Kelly and Moya as they were played the other day by members of Mr. Kennedy Miller's company, had a breadth of naive humour that is now rare on the stage. Mr. James O'Brien especially, in the part of Conn, put a genial richness into his voice that it would be useless to expect from the less guttural vocal capacity of French or English comedians, and in listening to him one felt how much the modern stage has lost in substituting impersonal wit for personal humour. It is fortunate for the Irish National Theatre Society that it has preserved—in plays like *The Pot of Broth*—a great deal of what was best in the traditional comedy of the Irish stage, and still has contrived by its care and taste to put an end to the reaction against the careless Irish humour of which everyone has had too much. The effects of this reaction, it should be added, are still perceptible in Dublin, and the Irish National Theatre Society is sometimes accused of degrading Ireland's vision of herself by throwing a shadow of the typical stage Irishman upon her mirror.

CAN WE GO BACK INTO OUR MOTHER'S WOMB?

A Letter to the Gaelic League

By *A Hedge Schoolmaster*[1]

MUCH of the writing that has appeared recently in the papers takes it for granted that Irish is gaining the day in Ireland and that this country will soon speak Gaelic. No supposition is more false. The Gaelic League is founded on a doctrine that is made up of ignorance, fraud and hypocrisy. Irish as a living language is dying out year by year—the day the last old man or woman who can speak Irish only dies in Connacht or Munster—a day that is coming near—will mark a station in the Irish decline which will be final a few years later. As long as these old people who speak Irish only are in the cabins the children speak Irish to them—a child will learn as many languages as it has need of in its daily life—but when they die the supreme good sense of childhood will not cumber itself with two languages where one is enough. It will play, quarrel, say its prayers and make jokes of good and evil, make love when it's old enough, write if it has wit enough, in this language which is its mother tongue. This result is what could be expected beforehand and it is what is taking place in Ireland in every Irish-speaking district

I believe in Ireland. I believe the nation that has made a place in history by seventeen centuries of manhood, a nation that has begotten Grattan and Emmet and Parnell will not be brought to complete insanity in these last days by what is senile and slobbering in the doctrine of the Gaelic League. There was never till this time a movement in Ireland that was gushing, cowardly and maudlin, yet now we are passing England in the hysteria of old

[1] Written in 1907 after the *Playboy* row, but not published until now in its entirety. A slightly shorter version appeared in the Greene and Stephens biography, pp. 262–3. A version in Synge's handwriting is in Notebook 49. A typed and apparently later version, omitting the first paragraph of the version in Notebook 49, is in Item 52. In the complete version here printed, the first paragraph is taken from Notebook 49 and the rest from Item 52. The last three lines, from 'and yet he'll give the pity' to 'face of her own sons', are lightly scored out in Item 52.

women's talk. A hundred years ago Irishmen could face a dark existence in Kilmainham Jail, or lurch on the halter before a grinning mob, but now they fear any gleam of truth. How are the mighty fallen! Was there ever a sight so piteous as an old and respectable people setting up the ideals of Fee-Gee because, with their eyes glued on John Bull's navel, they dare not be Europeans for fear the huckster across the street might call them English.

This delirium will not last always. It will not be long—we will make it our first hope—till some young man with blood in his veins, logic in his wits and courage in his heart, will sweep over the backside of the world to the uttermost limbo this credo of mouthing gibberish. (I speak here not of the old and magnificent language of our manuscripts, or of the two or three dialects still spoken, though with many barbarisms, in the west and south, but of the incoherent twaddle that is passed off as Irish by the Gaelic League.) This young man will teach Ireland again that she is part of Europe, and teach Irishmen that they have wits to think, imaginations to work miracles, and souls to possess with sanity. He will teach them that there is more in heaven and earth than the weekly bellow of the Brazen Bull-calf and all his sweaty gobs, or the snivelling booklets that are going through Ireland like the scab on sheep, and yet he'll give the pity that is due to the poor stammerers who mean so well though they are stripping the nakedness of Ireland in the face of her own sons.

Synge was by nature well equipped for the roads. Though his health was often bad he had beating under his ribs a brave heart that carried him over rough tracks. He gathered about him very little gear, and cared nothing for comfort except perhaps that of a good turf fire. He was, though young in years, 'an old dog for a hard road and not a young pup for a tow-path'.

Now that he is gone there is nothing sad in my memory of him, except that he is gone.[1]

Dublin, 8 July JACK B. YEATS

[1] There is a version not quite identical with this, under the title 'With Synge in Connemara', by Jack B. Yeats, in W. B. Yeats's *J. M. Synge and the Ireland of his Time*, Cuala Press, Dundrum, 1911.

INDEX

J. M. Synge died in 1909 and *The Works of John M. Synge* was published in four volumes by Maunsel & Co., Dublin, in 1910. Since then the canon of his work has remained largely unaltered. Nevertheless, much unpublished material exists, for the most part of great interest and significance for the understanding of Synge's methods of work and development. This material, including notebooks, poems, early drafts of the plays, and fragments of poetic drama, has now been thoroughly explored in order to create this definitive edition which not only collects together all that is of significance in his printed and in his unprinted work, but also, by a careful use of worksheets and early drafts, indicates much of the process of creation which occurred before the production of the printed page. The *Collected Works* is in four volumes, under the general editorship of Professor Robin Skelton, of the University of Victoria, British Columbia, who began the series with his edition of the poems and translations.

This second volume, edited by the late Dr. Alan Price, of The Queen's University, Belfast, author of *Synge and Anglo-Irish Drama*, assembles all Synge's prose writings of any merit or interest. Over half of it consists of a reprint of *The Aran Islands* and *In Wicklow, West Kerry and Connemara,* checked and supplemented where necessary by collation with Synge's own manuscripts and proofs. About a quarter consists of articles and reviews not previously collected, and the rest, including most of Part One, was never published before. Thus the prose of Synge can here be seen as a whole and should lead to a deeper understanding of both the writer and the Anglo-Irish literary revival. Thirty-five drawings by Jack B. Yeats are included.

The plays, edited by Professor Ann Saddlemyer, of Victoria College, University of Toronto, are published in two volumes.

Originally published by Oxford University Press, and now published by arrangement with them, the volumes of the *Collected Works* are also available in hardcover bindings.

Cover design by James Gillison.
Cover picture: J. M. Synge in Connemara, a drawing by Jack B. Yeats, reproduced by courtesy of the Berg Collection of The New York Public Library, Astor, Lenox & Tilden Foundations, and of Michael B. Yeats and Anne Yeats.

Colin Smythe Ltd., Gerrards Cross, Buckinghamshire
0–86140–135–2 Hbk and 0–86140–059–3 Pbk

The Catholic University of America Press, Washington, D.C.
0–8132–0565–4 Hbk and 0–8132–0564–6 Pbk